Those who can, teach

Those who can, teach

2nd edition

Kevin Ryan
University of Chicago

James M. Cooper
University of Houston

Houghton Mifflin Company
Boston   Atlanta   Dallas
Geneva, Illinois   Hopewell, New Jersey
Palo Alto   London

Library of Congress Catalog Card Number: 74-15588

ISBN: 0-395-18622-6

Contents

v

Acknowledgments

Whenever any of us put pen to paper, we are indebted to many people. However, in the writing of this book we were especially conscious of the help given by the following people: Robert H. Anderson for his excellent critical readings and suggestions; Myra Sadker, whose help in gathering data was invaluable; Ernie Lundquist for sharing with us the secrets of the Cosmic Apple and for running out for coffee and sandwiches; Joseph Blatt and Roberta Osler for their work on the annotated list of audiovisual materials; Marge Coffing for her editorial assistance on the first drafts; William Geulcher for his aid in developing the case materials in Chapter Four; Marion Crowley, Rhoda Stockwell, and Kathy Carey for their assistance in typing the several drafts of this book; and our colleagues and students for their many good ideas and continuing support. Very special acknowledgment is due to our wives, Marilyn and Sue, for the substantial intellectual and psychological contributions they made to this book.

Preface

This is a book of questions. In fact, it was written in the first place to answer the question, "What are the things people beginning their formal study of education should do?" We think the answer is questions—questions that are keys to the central issues and problems of education—and we have organized the book around such questions. We must warn you, though: the questions look deceptively simple, like an innocent packet of fishhooks. We have embellished these question-hooks with lures and baited them with dainty morsels. And, like good fishermen, all we want you to do is swallow them. We believe that, once that happens, the hooks will stick in your vitals and our work will be done. Putting aside this discomfiting metaphor, we hope that these questions provide direction and focus to your study well beyond the time you spend with this book. For those of you who are contemplating careers in teaching, we believe that pursuing answers to these questions will help you clarify your career goals.

In writing this book, we put aside many cherished rules of textbook writing. "Authors should be distant and remote"; we have tried not to be. "The authors' bias should be suppressed or at least well-hidden"; our biases are all too evident. "Textbooks should be deadly serious, especially about such a sacred matter as education"; we genuinely enjoyed writing our book and hope we can provide an occasional smile. "Textbooks should be free of distracting materials"; ours is filled with distractions, as a flip through the pages will prove. "Textbooks should be uncontroversial and safe"; we would be disappointed if ours did not provoke controversy. "Textbooks should treat the reader as a passive recipient of their wisdom"; we have written a book for active, responsive readers. "Textbooks are written for the authors' professional colleagues"; this book was written for students. "Textbooks should cover everything, at least once-over-lightly"; we have sacrificed comprehensive treatment in order to highlight what we consider most critical in education today.

Perhaps our most serious departure from the rules is that, when discussing the schools and the teaching profession, we occasionally lack the appropriate reverent tone. The reason is simple. We don't have the appropriate reverence. While we are truly proud of many of the accomplishments of our schools and of the dedication of so many teachers, we are nevertheless convinced that schools can and should be much more effective. We need a curriculum not for the past but for the future. We need better trained, more skillful teachers. We need teachers with a clearer grasp of why and how they are developing the human potential of their students. We can do much better.

This is a second edition of *Those Who Can, Teach.* We originally wrote this book because we couldn't find the kind of textbook our students and the students of many of our colleagues needed and wanted. We wrote it in the particular manner we did because it felt more honest to write it this way and because it was certainly more fun. Since the publication of the original edition we have received a good deal of comment and feedback from students and faculty members who have used the book. Many people wrote us letters and thousands returned the "Invitation to Respond" form that appears in this edition on page 403. Incidentally, we believe we're the first ones to have used a feedback form in a textbook. Since the original edition of *Those Who Can, Teach,* the use of feedback forms has become something of a mini-fad. We found the feedback from our readers immensely helpful in this revision. We hope that you, too, will share your reactions and insights about the book with us. Also, if there are news clippings, jokes, quotes, or pictures that you think should be included in the next edition, please send them to us. At the very least, please use the "Invitation to Respond" form.

In this second edition, *Those Who Can, Teach* has been changed in a number of ways. At the time we wrote the first edition, it seemed as if the society and the schools were falling apart. Since then, many schools have responded to the crisis in education and many more are valiantly groping with new approaches. We aren't quite as negatively critical of the schools in this edition. Also, we have reorganized the book, trying to respond more directly to prospective teachers' felt needs. Said another way, we're trying to start the book with the reader's prime interests rather than our own.

Further, we've done a good deal of addition and subtraction in this edition. Fresh material, reflecting new developments in education such as moral education, career education, year-round schools, the educational employment situation, and bilingual education, has been added. Some marginal or outdated materials have been dropped. Many of the pictures and illustrations are also new.

A final word about the title. George Bernard Shaw, the great English playwright with the razor tongue, had many unpleasant things to say about schools and education, but one of his cruelest remarks was reserved for teachers: "He who can, does. He who cannot, teaches." The world has taken a lot of turns since Shaw wrote that line. Education is no longer a luxury of the leisure class. The teacher can no longer be a silly, foppish pedant. Teaching is a much more demanding and crucial occupation than it ever was before. Developing man's human potential is serious work. Now those who can, teach.

Kevin Ryan
University of Chicago

James M. Cooper
University of Houston

Teachers

1   Why teach?

In this first chapter we hope to engage you in serious investigation of the various motives for becoming a teacher and, in particular, of your own motivations. We will also discuss the problems inherent in such decision making and some useful tools for making these decisions. Various career opportunities in education are presented along with an analysis of current employment opportunities in the field. Finally, five cases that illustrate different motivations for teaching are narrated and then analyzed.

Chapter contents	
	Pitfalls in choosing to teach
	Overfamiliarity
	Personal miscalculations
	Being a captive of experience
	The casual choice
	Sources of useful experience
	Real encounters
	Vicarious experiences
	Guidance
	Reflection
	Are there going to be job openings in education?
	There's more to education than teaching
	Career opportunities in education
	Motives for teaching
	Case studies in motivation to teach

If you teach, it is very likely that by the end of your second year of teaching you will have had both of the following experiences:

1   You will be at a party, or some other social gathering, and be asked what you do. One of the guests will express interest in the fact that you are a teacher and will ask you questions about how you like teaching. Shortly, the person will tell you that he (or she) has always wanted to be a teacher and regrets the day he (or she) became a stockbroker/housewife/bookkeeper/salesman/airline stewardess/disc jockey. He (or she) may give it all up and become a teacher yet.

or

2   You will get to know an experienced teacher who confides in you that she deeply regrets having become a teacher. In college she felt rather sure that she was cut out for teaching, and she actually enjoyed it in the beginning. But gradually she became bored with the whole thing — bratty kids, pushy administrators, the same old faces in the teachers' lounge, the instant-expert parents and the boring curriculum. Now she feels trapped in teaching and can't see any satisfying way to get out.

The purpose of this chapter is to keep you from becoming "the other person" in either of these two scenes. It is to help you make a good decision about what to do with your life, particularly if you are undecided about becoming a teacher.

Centuries ago, Francis Bacon told us that "knowledge is power." Much earlier still, Socrates recognized the special power of self-knowledge when he urged, "Know thyself." An understanding of one's motives in something as important as a career choice can help prevent faulty decision making. A superficial motivation to teach can, and frequently does, lead to failure and disappointment. For instance, you may admire and want to emulate a former teacher. And you may, out of respect for this person, decide to teach without ever analyzing whether or not you have the capacity or drive. Or you may think it is admirable to like and help children. But, in the process of actually working with, say, sixth-graders, you may discover that you can't stand sixth-graders, or that you're not even particularly interested in children.

Clarifying your motives helps you identify your strengths as a prospective teacher as well as cope with your shortcomings.[1] Someone whose desire to teach grows out of a passion for art history has to know how to guard against hostility toward students who don't share his love of art. More than a few frustrated teachers have been heard to mutter, "Those ungrateful little monsters aren't worthy of Shakespeare" (or French infinitives, or Victorian poetry, or the niceties of quadratic equations). In any event, we have written this chapter—and, indeed, the entire book—in the hope that you will use it to gain a greater understanding of how you and a career in education might fit together.

Pitfalls in choosing to teach

The most common difficulty facing someone trying to decide on a career is not having enough data. The young person who decides to be a business executive or a physical therapist or an interior decorator usually does so without a deep understanding of what his future occupation entails. Rarely do prospective workers know the daily demands of the job or the kinds and degree of expertise needed. Nor do they know enough about the satisfactions they may derive from performing well in a particular career. As a result, a career choice is frequently a response to fragmentary information or to a highly romanticized view of an occupation. The choice of a teaching career, however, usually involves a somewhat different set of problems. One of the pitfalls, in fact, is *over*familiarity.

Overfamiliarity

A college student contemplating a career in teaching usually has far too much data at his disposal; in other words, he has been overexposed to teachers and schools. A major portion of his life since he was five or six has been spent in schools and around teachers. Schools, he thinks, can hold no more surprises for him. Becoming a teacher seems to him like marrying the girl next door. (Anyone who *is* married to the girl next door could alert him to some of the surprises he is in for!)

[1] We are violating a time-honored textbook convention by switching voices. We find that in writing this book we sometimes speak to the reader in the third person, such as "the reader will note" or "one might

Most of the 200,000 or so new teachers who enter American schools each year receive a rude awakening. Although the routines — homeroom, clubs, bells, books, and ball games — are all familiar to the new teacher, there is much about life in school he doesn't fully appreciate. Most new teachers, for example, have had relatively pleasant experiences as students. If they had not succeeded in school, they probably would not be in a position to become teachers. As a result, new teachers are frequently astounded by how difficult learning is for some children and by how unhappy many children are in school. Many students are difficult to reach and apparently unconcerned about learning. Beginning teachers are surprised at the amount of administrative and clerical work that goes with the job. And they often have been unaware that good teaching takes so much time-consuming preparation. Another shock for many is the amount of energy, both physical and emotional, that teaching requires. Somehow these facets of teaching rarely get communicated to the audience of students. We will examine this topic in more detail in a later chapter.

It may be erroneous or misleading to say that the problem is overfamiliarity. Too much data is usually not a problem in itself. Applying prior information to the solution of a problem is the sticky part. What each of us knows about teaching needs to be evaluated for accuracy and supplanted, if necessary, by new information and, especially, new perspectives.

Personal miscalculations

Knowledge about teaching and schools is only half the prerequisite to a sound career choice, and probably not the most important half. Knowing your own capabilities and limitations is the other half.

- Do you really like children?
  What age groups do you enjoy most?
- Do you consider a particular age group especially stimulating and compatible?
- Do you really enjoy helping people learn new skills and gain new knowledge?
- How do you know this?
- Can you take satisfaction from work which frequently offers few tangible results?
- Would you enjoy working with children with special learning problems?
- How would you describe your energy level?
- Do you have stamina?
- Are you comfortable dealing with and having to manage twenty-five or thirty people at once?
- Can you live satisfactorily on the salary currently earned by teachers?

argue." At other times we use the more intimate second person, as in "you may not agree" or "we would like you to . . ." We are inconsistent in this matter because our mood is inconsistent. We wish to speak more directly to the reader at some times than others. We also find that we use "you" when we feel more urgency about an issue.

It is also conventional to refer to the teacher as "he." Since teaching is an occupation with large numbers of both men and women, we have chosen to refer to the teacher sometimes as "she" and sometimes as "he."

- Do you have status hang-ups which could get in your way?
- Are you confident that you can teach different ethnic groups and social classes?
- With which would you be most and least successful?
- How do you know this?

These are only a few of the questions you should be asking about yourself.

Being a captive of experience

In recent years the country has become increasingly concerned about the schools that serve the urban poor. Report after report has chronicled the ineffectiveness and waste that characterize so many large city schools. Large numbers of idealistic young people responded to the plight of the urban schools by seeking teaching positions in them. Although they did so for the very best reasons, many failed miserably. Their backgrounds and educational experiences had left them not only unprepared for the encounter but, in fact, served as stumbling blocks. These young teachers wanted their pupils to be like the children they had known in their own suburban or rural schools. They went into urban schools with the idea of totally replacing the culture of the children with the culture they brought with them from white America. This story is sad for both the children and the teachers. It goes without saying that we are all deeply influenced by our past experience. Occasionally, however, we need to transcend our own personal experience to avoid becoming its slave. Personal experience can exert too strong an influence on our career choice. For example, some people choose teaching because their own school years were pleasant and carefree, and they hope by becoming teachers to recapture past happiness. The opposite also occurs. In the same way that some people are said to become psychiatrists in an attempt to solve their own problems, people who have had particularly troubling or frustrating experiences in school may become teachers in an unconscious quest to resolve their early problems. By "returning to the scene," they are seeking an opportunity to work out unresolved conflicts. We must, therefore, draw on our experience, but must use it in a thoughtful, balanced way.

We should add that being a captive of one's experience can have the opposite effect. Many potentially creative and inspiring teachers reject careers in education because of the drabness of their own school experience. They see in teaching very little opportunity to express their imagination and creativity and so never seriously consider it as a career. This is particularly disappointing as education is beginning to change and there is a greater opportunity than ever for dynamic, creative teachers.

The casual choice

Many people make the decision to teach in a careless, unreflective manner. Compared to professions like architecture or medicine, which require long and arduous training periods, the "entrance dues" for teaching are relatively low. Candidates for teaching certificates are subjected to relatively little pressure or competition. Most do not have to make the heavy sacrifices of time or effort that might prompt them to think long and hard about whether they really want to teach. The majority, in fact, can get teaching certificates while pursuing a bachelor's degree. As a result, the decision to become a teacher is frequently casual and unexamined. Although this state of affairs is not necessarily harmful, it can contribute to disastrous mistakes.

Sources of useful experience

There is no single foolproof method of making an intelligent career choice. Individuals learn in such diverse ways, and they differ so much in what they already know and need to learn, that we can only suggest sketchy guidelines. We recognize four categories of experience that are potentially fruitful in the quest for an answer to "Should I teach?"

Real encounters

Anyone who plans to be a teacher should test himself against "the real world" often and in as many situations as possible. "The real world" for a prospective teacher is real people—children or adolescents who are seeking some kind of help. Many teaching candidates avoid real contacts with the young until they begin student teaching, only to find the young considerably different from the romantic images they had been manufacturing. "Those nasty little fifth-graders are so disgustingly . . . human!" as one shocked student teacher put it. Frequently, too, teaching candidates limit their encounters to normal elementary and secondary school students. They never consider teaching mentally retarded children or the physically handicapped or the imprisoned, or even becoming a specialist such as a reading teacher. They have exposed themselves to only one segment of the real world.

Increasingly, school districts are employing students as teacher aides and assistant teachers, both during the regular school year and in summer school. And a good number of teacher education programs have cooperative arrangements with schools that allow college students opportunities to play a variety of roles within the school, often as part of their coursework in education. Even some high schools now encourage their students to work with younger children as part of their educational experience. Schools, however, do not define the limits of the "real world." There is much to be said for nonschool contact with children, such as camp counseling, playground work, after-school recreation projects, working in orphanages and settlement houses, and youth-related church work. Other possibilities are coaching a team or sponsoring a club. The opportunities are many. The important thing, however, is to get your feet wet—to get the feel of working with children in a helping relationship.

Vicarious experiences

Not all learning has to take place in "the school of hard knocks." In fact, civilization itself requires that we be able to capitalize on the experience of others. Artists and other talented people can make the experience of others accessible to us for enjoyment, edification, or both. One result of the widespread interest in the schools over the last few years is that accounts and dramatizations of school-

© 1970 United Features Syndicate, Inc.

Last day

The last bell rang.
The building filled with shouts and cheers
And emptied soon. Yet one still sat.
He looked at me, and I could see in that thin face
An awful realization no other child had known:
The year was gone.

I knew, but I was older. I could bear
The lost and sickish feeling of farewell
From simple familiarity with it.
I went back to where he sat;
I said there would be other years.
I said that I would write him letters in the summer.
Somehow he knew, this child who had never had a letter in his life,
That warm words are always somehow cold on paper,
And never take the place of being close.

Slowly he gathered up his books.
Walking toward the door, he looked around the room.
What did he see? What had this been to him?
I knew, and yet I could not know.
It was the end
Of a year.

Reese Danley Kilgo, *Phi Delta Kappan* 51, no. 475 (May 1970): Reprinted by permission of the author and publisher.

related experiences are becoming increasingly available. There are great fictional classics about teachers and schools such as *Goodbye, Mr. Chips* by James Hilton and *The Corn is Green* by Emlyn Williams, and more recent novels like Bel Kaufman's *Up the Down Staircase* and Evan Hunter's *Blackboard Jungle*. Within the last few years we have also seen a spate of realistic accounts by teachers of their own experiences, including *The Way It Spozed To Be* and *How to Survive in Your Native Land* by James Herndon, *36 Children* by Herbert Kohl, *Death at an Early Age* by Jonathan Kozol, *The Lives of Children* by George Dennison, and *Hassling* by Sylvia Williams. You may prefer these books to fiction because they present children, schools, and teachers as they are in the raw, instead of transforming reality for a heightened effect.

Films and television are another source of vicarious experience. Although there have always been great films about teachers and teaching in the schools, such as *In the Early World* and *Near Home,* it has been only recently that there has been so much box-office attention paid to school life. Some of the popular films are *Conrack, The Prime of Miss Jean Brodie, Rachel! Rachel!, To Sir, With Love, Up the Down Staircase,* and *The Paper Chase.*[2] Television dealt with school life most notably in "Room 222" and "Lucas Tanner."

[2] Especially recommended for those who want to become classroom tyrants.

Why teach?

These vicarious experiences can be a valuable source of learning and testing for prospective teachers, particularly if they approach the experience somewhat more critically than does the ordinary viewer or reader. We need to remember that books, films, and television portray school life as a much more intense and heightened set of human encounters than the normal teacher faces. Also, the media school seems to have a much higher concentration of attractive sex symbols than does the normal school. Then, too, the flux and flow of life in a real school is just not visible. The drama of teaching is quiet, long-term, and terribly real.

Guidance

Another aid is the advice and counsel of those who know you; besides parents and friends (who may be too close to you to be objective), there are former teachers, career placement counselors, people you have worked for, and education professors. The latter group, your professors of education, will have the added perspective of familiarity with the demands of teaching. Some cautions should be exercised here, however. First of all, choose people who know you fully rather than those who have just seen you at your better moments. Second, do not expect an IBM printout of hard data with a firm decision at the end. If you get a few glimpses of insight from the person whose advice you are seeking, be satisfied. Third, be cautious, since many of us are compulsive advice-givers. Frequently people generalize on the basis of too little knowledge, and they are often just plain wrong. Receive advice openly, but follow it cautiously.[3]

[3] Although our good friend Ernie Lundquist has tried to claim credit for this thought, we believe that Shakespeare's Polonius beat him to it.

As we said earlier, decision making about a career in teaching is difficult because we are overfamiliar with schools. Even making use of all the data-gathering methods mentioned above does not in itself ensure good decision making. The most important aspect of the real school encounters, guidance, and vicarious experiences we collect is that they provide us with data for reflection. By "reflection" we simply mean the process of sitting down and trying to understand fully our experience and its implications for us. We are often so busy experiencing things, or getting ready to experience them, that we fail to reflect on what we have done in a manner that would assure getting the most from it.

We cannot stress this point about reflection enough. It goes to the very heart of the reasons why we are writing this book. Both of us are convinced that many people make very sloppy decisions about becoming teachers. They have not asked fundamental questions about themselves and about schools. This is precisely the reason why we have organized this book around a series of questions, such as "Why teach?" and "What is a school?" It is also the reason why we periodically ask you to stop and reflect on a particular question. Occasionally, we ask you to commit yourself in writing since doing so can be helpful in clarifying exactly what you mean. We have also included case studies, anecdotal material, and actual accounts by teachers. We hope that you will regard them as vicarious experience to stimulate your own reflection. In effect, we are much less interested in telling you something than in presenting you with some tough questions. Although the questions, like "What makes a teacher a teacher?" may sound simple, their answers are frequently quite complex—if they are answerable at all. It is our hope that you will use these questions not only to guide your career choice, but to reflect on the whole phenomenon of teaching and learning.

Discovering whether or not one wants to, and is suited to, teach is an important part of career decison making. Also, it is the major focus of this chapter. There is, however, another part that depends upon the external world: will there be jobs in education? It is to this question that we will now move briefly.

Are there going to be job openings in education?

In the 1960s, the United States went through a rare social experience. We became inundated with adolescents and young adults. The number of young people between the ages of fourteen and twenty-four increased during the decade of the sixties by a staggering 52 percent. This great bulge in the youth population put a tremendous strain on the social agencies serving this group. Welfare and recreational agencies, police departments (fourteen to twenty-four are the high crime years), and schools were all hit with this largely unexpected number of young customers. For education, it meant a grave teacher shortage throughout much of the decade. People became used to the idea of a high demand for teachers. Apparently, few noticed 1) that a high percentage of the students in this sixties population bulge was graduating from college and becoming teachers, and 2) that the number of school-age children to be taught (and, thus, the number of career opportunities) was leveling off. The result was that in the early 1970s the teacher shortage was suddenly replaced by a teacher surplus. We went from famine to feast in the space of a few short years.

Why teach?

Demography or the science of life statistics is a relatively new field, and in the recent past educators have not applied the findings of demographers very well. We have tended to underestimate the relevance of global words like "shortage" and "surplus" to our field, particularly in regard to future projections of population. Although the surplus of teachers is being given a good deal of publicity at present, it seems the worst of the surplus is behind us. Two things are happening. First, the number of college students going into teacher preparation has fallen dramatically during the early seventies. Probably as a direct response to the publicity about the very real job shortage in teaching and the general uncertainty within the educational employment market, a large number of young people chose other careers. Second, and directly related, is the matter of the supply of teachers. According to the research division of the National Education Association, the supply of new teachers ready to take up positions in the public schools will fall by one-third between the school years 1972–73 and 1976–77. In the school year 1972–73, there were 243,200 newly certified teachers ready to assume new teaching positions. Five years later the projection is that the number of beginning teachers will be down to 164,550.

While these figures should be encouraging to those who have been concerned about the possibility of employment in the public schools, it does not mean that the surplus is over and that we are heading back to a shortage situation. Even in 1976, we will be preparing and certifying three people for every two teaching positions. This figure, in turn, is softened by the fact that traditionally 25 to 30 percent of the newly prepared and certified fail to seek employment as teachers.[4] It does appear, though, that after an extreme surplus of teachers in 1973–74, the situation is correcting itself.

A warning

We have not had much experience in applying data on trends in population and teacher education enrollment to the educational job market. The information about employment prospects that you pick up here and elsewhere should be evaluated carefully and with some suspicion. For one thing, the educational job market changes rather rapidly. There is a great deal of movement in and out of the teaching profession, and this, of course, affects the availability of jobs. Also, these figures are affected by the economy. For instance, when times are good, there is more money for schools. The ratio of teachers to pupils goes down, creating more openings. When times are economically poor, the opposite is true. And teachers tend to hold onto their jobs more. The teachers' professional organizations have insisted for some time that what we have is an undersupply of money rather than an oversupply of teachers. They argue that there would be no surplus of teachers if we would reduce class size and get a lower pupil-teacher ratio.

Another factor to consider is that a teacher is not a teacher is not a teacher. Teachers are prepared for different specialties (special education, primary grade, all level art, high-school social studies) and the job market in each one of these sub-fields is different and changes frequently. It is silly, therefore, to make decisions on whether or not to become a special education teacher because you have heard that there is, in general, a surplus of teachers. Even throughout the worst of the teacher surplus there were some sub-fields with serious shortages.

[4] We will deal further with this surprising and troubling issue in Chapter Four, "How People Become Teachers."

Another factor that influences the job market is location. Some communities are rich in teachers, while others are paupers. University towns normally have a great surplus of teachers. On the other hand, rural America is having difficulty attracting and holding teachers. Apparently, large numbers of new teachers want to be in or near the cities, "where the action is" . . . or is supposed to be.

The young person considering a career in education should try to get the most up-to-the-minute data possible on the teacher supply and demand picture. He should carefully consider it before making a choice about a career in education and in particular about a particular sub-field within education. This is especially true for people who are unable to wait for openings in their area of teaching interest.[5] Sources of data to begin your search are your school's career counseling office, the National Education Association, the Office of Education of the U.S. Department of Health, Education, and Welfare and the U.S. Department of Labor.

A final note

One of the side benefits of the teacher surplus has been that schools have been able to be more selective. Instead of having to take whomever came along, schools have had the rare opportunity to choose the better prepared teachers among those available. The fact that "not just anyone (or any college graduate) can become a teacher" will improve the teaching profession and its public image.

Another consideration is that there has never been a surplus of good teachers. No matter what the job market at a particular moment, education has never been in a position to stringently apply high standards and ensure that children consistently encounter highly skilled and dedicated professionals. In other words, if you are good, there will be a place for you.

And, lastly, America is becoming an educational society. We are realizing that, as individuals and as a people, the achievement of our goals is dependent on achieving high levels of education. This means we are committed to more and better education, to lifelong learning in and out of schools. Almost fifty years ago, President Calvin Coolidge said, "The business of America is business." Today and into the future, "the business of America is education."

Teaching is where the action is.

There's more to education than teaching

Our tendency throughout this book is to write as if education offered only a single career pattern—elementary or secondary teaching. Although convenient for the authors, this is misleading. There is great diversity within the career labeled "teaching," from nursery school to graduate school and from remedial reading to astrophysics. Also, there are countless careers in education other than teaching. Some of these occupations, such as school librarian, are closely related to schools and children, while others, like project officer for the U.S. Office of Education, are physically quite remote from children.

[5] Because the employment picture does change so rapidly, particularly in the sub-fields, we have chosen not to report any figures here. We urge you, however, to seek this information from current sources.

In the same vein, we don't mean to give the impression that there is one, and only one, appropriate career in education for any given person. On the contrary, education is a field that offers many opportunities to move from one type of work to another. A common progression is from classroom teaching to a vice-principalship or principalship. Besides becoming department or grade-level chairmen, many experienced teachers choose to become guidance counselors. Still others go into teacher education or a related field like educational publishing.

We are outlining below, for three reasons, the careers available in education. First, most people think of education as a field composed of teachers and principals, and we frankly want to expand public awareness of the wealth of careers in education. Second, we want to point out, to students who find they are not interested in teaching, the variety of non-classroom jobs available in education. Third, we want to illustrate the variety of opportunities open to people once they have embarked on a career in education. What follows, then, is a list of some of the positions available in education.

Career opportunities in education

Rapid change is characteristic of modern existence. More people, more problems, more technological advances, and more of everything are causing the rate of change to accelerate geometrically. The repercussions have been pronounced in almost all careers, but especially so in the professions. Until recently, though, education has been very slow to change. Many of us were taught in the same manner as were our parents, because traditional ideas and approaches seemed perfectly adequate. Those quiet days seem to be over, though; the pace of change is catching up with the schools. Social philosophers and future-watchers are anticipating massive changes in the ways children learn, teachers teach, and schools operate. New shifting patterns, revised decisions about what should be learned in schools, instruction by computers and other new media, learning drugs, manipulation of the genetic code—all will have an explosive impact on education in the decades ahead.

Education has been characterized as a "growth industry." While it may be reassuring to know that there will continue to be important, attractive careers in education, right now your career choice is what matters most. Your personal happiness will depend in large measure upon the decision you make. We see a direct relationship between the number of unsuited and unsatisfied people in education and the casualness that all too often characterizes career choices in education. We urge you, then, to use the resources available to you—your experience, the counsel of others, the data available from agencies, and, most important, your own thoughtful reflections—in planning your future.

Pre-elementary, elementary, and high-school education (public and private)
  Paraprofessional (assistant teacher, educational technician, teacher aide)
  Teacher
    Nursery school and preschool, kindergarten, elementary, junior and senior high school
  Supervisor (most supervisory positions are combined with teaching responsibilities)

Grade-level chairman, department chairman, critic teacher, master teacher
Consultant
  Curriculum, teaching process, specialized areas, affective education
Guidance
  Academic counseling, personal counseling, career guidance, college placement
Administration
  Assistant or vice-principal, principal, special project director, associate superintendent (business, maintenance, personnel, curriculum), superintendent
School specialist
  Librarian, school psychologist, nurse, dietician, coach, research director, attendance officer

Junior college, college and university education
Teacher
  Teaching assistant; instructor; lecturer; assistant, associate, and full professor
Department chairman
Administration
  Dean (of the faculty, of students, of instruction, etc.), vice president, provost, president
Special services
  Registrar, career guidance and placement, admissions officer; research director, librarian, health service personnel

Government
  State department of education (curriculum, instruction, certification, research, etc.)
Federal agencies
  Office of Education (Washington, D.C. and regional offices), research and development centers, regional laboratories, overseas schools sponsored by the State and Defense Departments for dependents, UNESCO and other international education agencies

Foundations
  Executive
  Program officer and staff
  Researcher or writer

Business
Communications industry
  TV or radio reporter, newspaper educational reporter, freelance or magazine writer on education, writer for professional journals (i.e., *English Journal,* or *Today's Schools*)
Publishing
  Textbook editor or writer, curriculum materials developer, salesman of educational materials
Private consulting firms providing specialized expertise to schools, i.e., computers, new technology, inservice training, research services

Training and education departments in large businesses or corporations, responding to personal growth or work-related competencies of employees[6]

Private training or educational firms, providing services not available in public schools, such as advanced reading skills, more effective child-raising techniques, and others[7]

Professional organizations

National Education Association and American Federation of Teachers
Executive and staff positions, researcher or writer, field worker
Specialized teacher associations, i.e., National Association of Mathematics Teachers, National Association of Secondary School Principals
Educational fraternities, i.e., Phi Delta Kappa and Pi Lambda Theta

Motives for teaching

We would like you to take a moment to write down what you feel are your motives for wanting to be a teacher. If you are unsure whether or not you want to be a teacher (this probably applies to the majority of readers), list your motives both for and against becoming a teacher. A space is provided below. You may not wish to use it, but we suggest that you write down your list in some permanent place. Although the purpose of this list is to help you think about yourself and analyze your career choice, you may wish to save it for future reference.

There is a reason why we referred to your motives, in the plural. Most of us have mixed motives, some altruistic and some selfish, about most of the things that are important to us. Our motives often conflict and occasionally they are incompatible. In any event, one motive is rarely sufficient to explain a choice as complex as the career in which we plan to spend our lives.

_____

_____

_____

_____

_____

_____

_____

_____

_____

[6] It is our belief that the last quarter of the twentieth century will see a major growth in this sector of the educational community.

[7] See footnote 6.

If you did not stop reading to think about the question or commit yourself to writing an answer—well, you're probably like a majority of readers. What kept you from doing so? The answer to this question may tell you a good deal about yourself as a learner and about the educational system of which you are a product. Have you been trained to devour pages without really confronting the issues conveyed by the words? Have you been conditioned to think that the answers of other people—experts, authors, teachers—are more important or more "right" than yours? Are you the product of an educational system that claims it wants you to think independently but functions by forcing answers on you and requiring you to spit them back? Probably you are. If so, it is our hope that this will be a different kind of book and a different type of reading-questioning-thinking experience for you. We want it to be unlike so much else we read: things we pick up, spend time with and put down again without having been moved or changed in any way. Being teachers ourselves, we want this book to have an impact on you and to help you make a good decision about whether or not to be a teacher. We want you to be seeking answers to the questions that can lead you to be a good teacher. For these reasons, you need to read this book in a different way. Encounter it. Participate in it. Fight with it. Laugh with it. Laugh at it. Improve it by adding yourself to it. You will be asked and nudged to do things that are not in keeping with your natural style of learning. Doing them, however, may help you identify more clearly how you learn best and give you a sense of the various ways one can learn and can know something.

We're asking you to invest something of yourself in this book. That old tired cliche, "you get out of it what you put into it," applies here. So, again, if you didn't think about and write down an answer to "What is a school?" go back and have a try at it.

There must be a nearly infinite number of answers to the question, "What are my motives for wanting to become a teacher?" Here are a few examples you might check against your own list:

- I really like the idea of having control over and influence on 30 (or 150) kids every day.
- Teachers are my favorite people, and I want to stay among them.
- I can't think of anything else to do with my major.
- Teaching seems to be a fairly safe, low-risk occupation with a lot of attractive benefits.
- The instruction I had in school was just incredibly bad, and I want to correct that situation.
- I don't know what I want to do. So I'll teach for a while until I make up my mind.
- My parents would really be pleased if I were a teacher.
- I just love children—especially the scruffy, unattractive ones everyone else ignores.
- I would rather be a big fish in a little pond than a little fish in that great big world out there.
- One of my students might become a famous painter, or the president of a major corporation or who knows what. It would be nice to strongly influence just one significant life.
- I've never wanted to do anything else. As far back as I can remember, I've always wanted to teach.

Why teach?

Dialogue

Jim   *I'm having a little trouble with this list.*

Kevin   *What's the matter? Can't you find your motive on it?*

Jim   *Seriously, it could be confusing to the reader. For instance this one: "the desire to work out one's own problems." This seems much more likely to be an unconscious motive than the others do.*

Kevin   *I agree, but some of the other motives can be hidden, too, like the desire for respect and prestige. On the other hand, some people go into teaching to relieve the anxiety and discomfort they feel about particular social wrongs. They are consciously seeking to work out something that is a problem to them.*

Jim   *All right, but I'm troubled about another thing. The way we've separated out these motives and the way we've written the cases make it appear that individuals are driven by a single motive. Life just isn't that way. As we said earlier, we are driven by many motives, some of which may contradict each other.*

Kevin   *You're right. The way we've done it makes a very complex phenomenon seem too simple. But if we tried to portray the full range of human motivations in each case, we'd have five novels instead of five brief case studies. But you bring up a good point, and I hope the reader is forewarned.*

Jim   *One final point. This reads like THE list. We don't mean to give this impression, do we?*

Kevin   *Oh, no, we've left out all sorts of motives. For instance, some men who go into teaching because they want to coach a state championship athletic team; some girls who become teachers because they want an occupational "insurance policy" in case something happens to their husbands or their marriages; people who use teaching as a second job so they can support themselves in what they really want to do, like writing; and people who espouse a particular religious doctrine or economic system and are seeking converts. No, this list doesn't scratch the surface. We're just trying to get people to begin thinking about why they want to teach.*

- I really want to become a principal (or a coach, or a guidance counselor, or a college professor, or an educational researcher) and this seems to be the way one has to start.
- Education seems like it's going to be the action field of the future and I want to be part of it.
- I am happiest when I'm explaining something and helping people to grow.
- I don't like business and its grubby dog-eat-dog world, and teaching seems like a more humanistic option.
- I don't like what is happening to our society and teaching seems to be a way to improve things.

Case studies in motivation to teach

The rest of this chapter is composed of five case studies that illustrate some common motives for going into teaching. Each case study is followed by a set of questions and a comment by the authors. The cases are intended as examples of how particular abstract motives take shape in the lives of teachers. We offer these case studies to you as vicarious experiences to use in testing your own motivations. You may also want to discuss the cases and the accompanying questions with other people. The shared experience of reading the cases and responding to the questions should aid in probing and understanding your own motivations. And, finally, the cases and accompanying comments raise important issues about the nature of teaching.

The five motives we have chosen are:

1 the desire to work out one's own problems
2 the desire to aid in the renewal of society
3 the desire for respect and prestige
4 the desire to help children prepare for life
5 the desire to teach a particular subject

Case Number One
The desire to work out one's own problems

Jean was a new teacher in a Chicago high school whose student population was fairly evenly mixed between black and white. As a white teacher, Jean worried a lot about her ability to "relate to" black children. On one visit from her college supervisor, she told him that she was pleased with the way things were going. The supervisor asked what particular aspects of the class pleased her, and she replied that she had achieved a good relationship with her black students. The supervisor asked how she had accomplished this, and Jean answered that she had spent a great deal of time talking with them as a group and that, under her sponsorship, the students had formed a Black Student Union and an activist committee. She felt that her black students were "really getting their thing

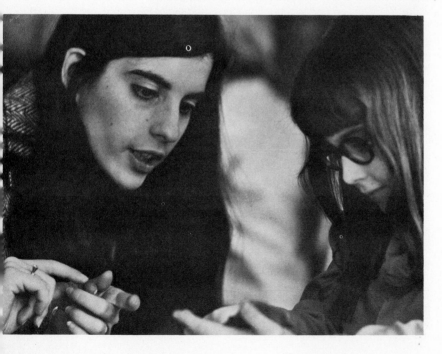

together!" The supervisor, a youngish man with a great deal of experience in urban situations, was not as pleased with her well-being and apparent success as Jean was.

"Jean," he said, facing her, "what do you really want to do here? Is it your goal to organize the black students into a power coalition? Is that what you feel you're getting paid to do?"

"Well," she replied, "these kids just have to get organized. The only answer to the social oppression they've been living under is to organize and begin making their weight felt as a group."

"That may or may not be true," said the supervisor, "but that's not the point at issue. You have a mixed class of children, and you're here to help them acquire some understanding of each other along with skills, knowledge and outlooks that will help them survive and excel in society. But you wanted the black students to like you, so you identified with their feelings of separateness and their prejudices about whites. And, if you will, you have created two factions in your class and you treat each differently."

"*I* didn't do that!" Jean contested hotly. "Society did."

"No, Jean, you did," said the supervisor. "Instead of encouraging your students to confront and understand their prejudices, and creating an atmosphere that would allow them to emerge as individuals capable of solving their own human problems, you encouraged them to value their prejudices and to think that they were right to maintain those prejudices. As a white teacher teaching blacks and whites, you have a tremendous opportunity to help the black understand the white. You say you understand these kids, and that's important, but it's equally important that they understand you and other people like you. Is it your goal for black students to come to you whenever they have a problem with the whites and have you solve it for them? What happens when you are no longer around and those kids run into that problem? Do you think they're going to love you and respect you for not teaching them how to work with whites? Not on your life. They're going to hate you for using them and failing to teach them what they need to know to get along."

"I honestly feel that I owe them something," Jean said. "And I just can't work it out that easily. What are you telling me to do? To ignore their problems and go back to 'business as usual' with the workbooks and all that?"

"You *do* owe them something, but *'them'* means all of those kids. You've got a rare opportunity here to help both the black kids and the white kids learn how to master themselves and to handle their prejudices so that they can settle the problems of living together without being dependent on you and the other white liberals for help. You can get these kids to confront their fears, bring them out in the open, and deal honestly and rationally with them in class. You can deal with it through the subject matter, through composition, through general class discussion. These kids may discover that they are much more alike than different, regardless of their color."

"I really don't think it will work," said Jean. "The black kids are angry and they've heard too much discussion and too much bull to take more of it from a white teacher."

"Look," the supervisor replied, "I taught psychology in a junior college about eight years ago before coming to the University. I had white kids from Cicero and back of the stockyards who weren't exactly thrilled at having a black teacher. But I knew that this class was okay when in the middle of a unit on perception and prejudice, one of those white kids said that he had thrown a stone at Martin Luther King on his march into Cicero, and that he was amazed at his own ignorance in doing such a thing. Then a black got up and said that he had attacked white people on the street for no good reason, and he too was amazed at his own prejudice. Here was a bunch of kids who were learning to see people as people. It can be done if the teacher has a clear sense of how his subject matter can help people understand themselves.

"When a student in the class began talking about 'whitey' or 'niggers,' as they did in the early meetings, we'd ask the class to stop and consider their feelings in view of the reading we'd done on fears and aggression. In that way each member of the class was forced to come face to face with his own doubts and fears. I'm a teacher, Jean, and I tried to use my subject matter and my objectivity to help people see themselves as they are. The more they understood themselves, the more they understood others in the class as people. That's why they could admit their failings in front of a whole class of people like themselves. I really feel, Jean, that teaching English gives you a good opportunity to do some of the same things. There seems to be one lesson that you have yet to learn about teaching, and that is . . . "

"Yes?"

"That teaching is a relationship to be ended, not to be continued."

"I don't understand what you mean by that," Jean said, with a puzzled look. "Would you explain?"

"Sure," said the supervisor. "A mature teacher prepares his students for independence, not dependence. He tries to get them to the point where they are able to fend for themselves. And I guess that's what I'm questioning about your relationship with your students. Are you really doing that for them?"

"I don't know," said Jean, softly. "I honestly don't know."

Questions

1   How would you characterize the personal problems Jean seems to be working out in her teaching?
2   Have you had experience with teachers who seemed to be working out personal problems in their classes? What kinds of problems? What was the effect on the class?

3 Have you ever known personal problems to be used effectively in a classroom? If not, can you imagine circumstances in which they might be made use of effectively?
4 How do you evaluate the advice Jean received from her supervisor?
5 If you had been Jean's supervisor, what would you have advised her?
6 What are some of the implications of the supervisor's statement that a "mature teacher prepares his students for independence, not dependence"? What are some ways that elementary- and secondary-school teachers can stimulate independence?
7 Did the supervisor think that organizing a union of black students would have a bad effect on the school?
8 Was the supervisor simply telling Jean to teach the subject matter in which she had been trained? What instructional technique did Jean's supervisor use in dealing with the problems of his students?

Comment

Insecurity is endemic to the beginning teacher. She wants assurance. As a result, some teachers seek to be popular with their students. There is a difference, however, between popularity and a genuine helping relationship. Popularity may make a real helping relationship impossible. In a sense, this is what Jean did with her black students. She achieved quick popularity by organizing their political aspirations, and that was why, as her supervisor pointed out, she thought she understood their needs. But she had really given the students not what they needed but only what she thought they needed. Had Jean better understood what she herself *needed*, as well as what she wanted, then her relationship with the students would have been more mature. Jean's experience illustrates the importance of examining one's own motives before attempting to motivate others. Perhaps if Jean had examined her own motives a bit more deeply, she would have realized that she had to overcome fear of rejection by her black students before she could teach effectively. The very fact that Jean spent much of her time worrying about relating to black students, rather than relating to Roger, Mark, Frances, and Lucy Ann as persons, tells us that she had not grasped the importance of teaching at a personal level; she had, in truth, not yet acknowledged the individuality of her black students.

One characteristic of a mature person is the ability to work out one's own problems in an objective way. If Jean could have realized that her own fears of rejection and of confronting explosive feelings were detrimental to her, she would have seen that the purpose of mature teaching is to help children discover that they can face and handle their own fears. The supervisor tried to show her that she was forcing students to need her support rather than making them independent of her. He was trying to tell her that her popularity may have been gained at the cost of her integrity as a teacher.

Case number two
The desire to aid in the renewal of society
Fred was in his late thirties. His disposition was so pleasant, and a smile came so readily to his face, that one of his fellow teachers in the large metropolitan

high school referred to him as "everybody's father." Fred was remarkable for his ability to remain relaxed when everyone else was tense, and he frequently broke up emotionally charged situations with an appropriate quip or question.

Each year Fred asked to teach the slow freshman history class and, of course, his request was always granted, for the slow or "basic" classes were regarded by the other teachers as "punishment." Year after year, Fred happily worked with children nobody else really wanted.

Fred's freshman history class was one of the most active in the whole school; he took his students beyond the walls of the school on expeditions to day court, the police station and jail, through industrial plants in the area—and he even snuck in a baseball game one day. Yet his classes were not characterized by fun and games. The students worked very hard on long and involved homework assignments, intricate discussions of problems, and searching tests.

At one point in a particular academic year, Fred invited another teacher to give a talk to his class on shipbuilding in the eighteenth century. The talk went well, and after the session the other teacher, Mr. Dixon, commented to Fred that the temper of the discussion following his talk had been very different from what he had anticipated; the questions were thoughtful and displayed observation of detail that the guest speaker had not expected from a "bunch of basics."

Fred greeted Mr. Dixon's remarks with a chuckle. "You know, Earl," he said, "they really amaze me too sometimes. Most of these kids really have behavior problems, not intellectual ones. If you looked at their case histories, you'd find that the majority of them were 'dropped through the ranks'!"

"What do you mean?" asked Mr. Dixon.

"I mean that they were in regular classes a good bit of their scholastic lives. But, when they became problems in class, their teachers decided that the cause of their poor behavior was that the work was too hard for them. So, the majority of children in this class really represent the rebels, the nonconformists, the 'antisocials'! They're the kids about whom teachers say, 'I don't care if they learn any history at all as long as they become good citizens.'"

"Yes, but you must admit that very few of them will go to college. Most basics just drop out," said Mr. Dixon.

"Maybe you're missing my point," said Fred. "I guess I'm saying that a person can't be a 'good citizen' unless he is a contributing member of society, and that he should contribute something that he thinks is worth contributing. If he can't get the basic tools that make a person productive, how can he be a good citizen? It's a lot more than getting a job or making a decent living. If that were the case, we could put these kids through an industrial arts program and that would be the end of it. No, in some ways, I feel that these kids are much more capable than the kids we send to the university."

"In what sense?"

"In the sense that they are the least accepting of society as it exists now," replied Fred. "If you talked to some of them for an hour or so, you'd find that they really feel the school is hypocritical in many ways, and they aren't afraid to point out the hypocrisies. They'll tell you, for instance, that there are two sets of rules in the school, two sets of discipline procedures, two sets of privileges, and all the rest."

"But I hear the same thing from my 'honors' classes, " protested Mr. Dixon. "Those kids know about the double system too. They often tell me that an honor student here can get away with anything from cutting class to smoking in the john. The 'double system' isn't any secret in this school."

"You've got me wrong again, Earl. I know about that, but that wasn't what I was talking about. What these kids are saying is not that we expect too much of them, but too little. For instance, if a kid dropped from an A to a C in your honors history course, what would happen to him?"

"He'd probably go in and see the counselor—by request."

Fred replied, "That's right. When he does poorly, people get concerned. They try to help him take a look at what's wrong. If one of these kids goes from a C to an F, though, everyone says, 'Well, what more do you expect? He's only a basic and doesn't have the ability to sustain a C.' And they get all the inexperienced teachers and martinets in the school. Oh, they know that if they become real problems, they'll get counseling and possibly even better teaching. But that isn't their complaint. They know that the system isn't out to punish them. It just doesn't care enough about them to want to punish them. They know that the system would rather they just go away and not bother anyone. That's the double standard in this school—those that are cared about and those that aren't: that's what these kids will tell you. It's not injustice, it's no justice at all."

"Is this why you request basic classes every year?" asked Mr. Dixon.

"That's part of it," said Fred. "But it's not the whole reason. I'm not quite that altruistic. No, I see in these kids something that frightens me. They have capability, but if it isn't developed it can become capability for hate, a hate based on fear. They're a mark for anyone who comes along with a good strong 'hate' message; I know it and it frightens me. They can rant and 'bitch,' but they have to be taught to analyze critically, to think through problems and to care about other people. In my mind, that is what a good citizen does. He has a developed capability for understanding, and that is what I am trying to do—develop that capability. I think these kids need that capability developed even more than the kids in the honors classes do, because that attention the honors children get in the course of their day here will pull them through. Plenty of people challenge them, listen to them, and chastise them when they need it. But with these kids it's a different story."

"You know," said Mr. Dixon, "you're not just talking about the basic classes. I think the same thing is generally true of average classes. It seems that a kid who's really bright gets a lot of attention, and so does the kid who is really slow, but it's that kid in the middle . . ."

"You're right," said Fred. "The kids in this class are the bottom of that middle group in terms of the concern they arouse from the system. And they know it. Yet, as you saw today, they are capable. We owe them a decent set of expectations. I've maintained high expectations from the kids. I would prefer to slightly over-match them intellectually than undermatch them, because no development is possible when you're being undermatched constantly."

"You know," said Mr. Dixon, "you make a pretty strong argument for your way of teaching, but someone could use the same argument to justify a very academic college-prep course which would really be irrelevant for those kids."

"Only if his aim was to teach a very academic college-prep course. The course is a means to an end, in my mind, not an end in itself. My course is somewhat scholarly and academic, but it's not a waste of time for the kids. When we study the court system, for instance, we confront the problem of giving each man his due. We talk about the difficulties of guaranteeing the individual his rights and the group its rights. I like to feel, Earl, that the goal of schooling is not more schooling, but rather an ability to push back against the society in a constructive way."

"Fred," Mr. Dixon said, "I'd like you to come to my class in American history and make the same points with them that you've made with me. You seem to be talking about several problems that have come up in our class. I just wonder how you'd fare with those kids. They have some very strong opinions of their own."

"I'll take my chances any time after next week, Earl. We're going down to the legislative session at the Capitol next week."

Questions

1. How is Fred's commitment to social renewal specifically manifested in his classroom teaching?
2. According to Fred, what is the criterion for assignment to basic classes in his school? Was this true of your high school?
3. What is the double standard of which Earl Dixon spoke, and how do you explain it? What is the double standard of which Fred spoke, and how do you explain it? Did either of these double standards exist in your school?
4. In what sense are Fred's basic students more capable than the college-prep students? In what sense are they a more dangerous element in society? Do you agree with Fred's analysis here?
5. In what ways is Fred different from most of the teachers you have known? How are his expectations for his students different?
6. What does Fred see as the role of academic disciplines in education? If you had to, how would you argue against his position?

John Dewey (1859–1952)

John Dewey, the father of progressivism, is widely considered the single most influential figure in the history of American educational thought.

No prodigy as a child, Dewey attended public schools and the University of Vermont. As a graduate student in philosophy at Johns Hopkins University, he met and was deeply influenced by William James, the philosophical pragmatist. Dewey recognized the implications for education of James' argument that ideas are valuable only insofar as they help to solve human problems. Calling his own philosophy *instrumentalism,* to emphasize the principle that ideas are instruments, Dewey argued that philosophy and education are identical, both involving the practical, experimental attempt to improve the human condition.

The public school curriculum in the nineteenth century was scholarly and classical, designed to improve the mind by filling it with large doses of approved culture. Dewey denounced this curriculum as the invention of a parasitical leisure class, totally unsuited to the demands of industrialized society. He claimed that the schools were divorced from life, and that they failed to teach children how to *use* knowledge. The schools, he said, should teach children not what to think but how to think through "continuous reconstruction of experience." In *Democracy and Education,* published in 1916, Dewey pointed out that Americans were being called upon to make crucial political decisions unprecedented in history, and that the schools offered no preparation for the responsibility of citizenship in a democracy. Dewey called for concentrated study of democratic processes as they are manifested in the units of political organization with which the child is familiar—the school, the local community, and the state government—in ascending order of complexity. But his most radical suggestion was that students be given the power to make decisions affecting life in the school in a democratic way. Participation in life, rather than preparation for it, he considered the watchword of an effective education.

In 1893 Dewey established an elementary school at the University of Chicago which was experimental in two senses: in its use of experiment and inquiry as the method by which the children learned, and in its role as a laboratory for the transformation of the schools. The activities and occupations of adult life served as the core of the curriculum and the model teaching method. Children began by studying and imitating simple domestic and industrial tasks; in subsequent years they studied the historical development of industry, invention, group living, and nature. This curriculum was in keeping with Dewey's argument, espoused in *The School and Society,* that we must "make each one of our schools an embryonic community life, active with types of occupations that reflect the life of the larger society and permeated with the spirit of art, history, and science." Dewey also believed it to be the absence of cooperative intellectual relations among teachers that caused young children's learning to be directed by a single teacher and older children's learning to be compartmentalized.

From the late 1920s to the early 1940s—the era of progressive education—a massive attempt was made to implement Dewey's ideas, but the rigid manner in which they were interpreted led to remarkable extravagances in some progressive schools. Some considered it useless to teach geography because maps changed so rapidly. Some would encourage a student who, when his teacher asked why he was not studying for an exam, replied that he wanted to come to it fresh! The role of subject matter was gradually played down in progressive schools; the method and process were regarded as more important. The rationale was that it was more important to produce a "good citizen" than a person who was "educated" in the classical sense. Dewey fought vehemently against these corruptions of his views well into his nineties.

Throughout his long life, Dewey was a social activist, marching for women's right to vote, heading a commission to investigate the assassination of Trotsky, organizing a protest against the dismissal of a colleague at the City College of New York, and the like. Though he had enormous influence on the schools and on American intellectual life, his advocacy of a socialist economy and welfare state caused him to be characterized by some as an archfoe of the American way of life. In recent years, Dewey has once again been championed by educational critics and practitioners who consider his ideas a blueprint for more relevant and humanistic schooling, even in our own times.

Comment

John Dewey, the American teacher and philosopher, called attention to our need to educate the young in the entire range of skills necessary for citizenship in a complex technological society. Many of Dewey's ideas were misapplied or corrupted. What Fred was reacting against is a case in point. In Fred's school as in many others, Dewey's concept of citizenship has been completely perverted.

During the thirties many schools adopted the policy of awarding a grade for citizenship. This grade was originally intended as a measure of the student's ability to use the processes of democracy in a profitable, efficient way. However, as the democratic processes Dewey had introduced to the classroom degenerated into empty forms, the citizenship grade became more and more a judgment of conduct. As long as the student "played the game" of democracy in the classroom, displaying a compliant attitude and voting for class officers who were officers in name only, he was given a high grade in citizenship. Citizenship became a code word among teachers. A teacher who was given a class of "low achievers" or "discipline problems" was sometimes told, "Don't worry about the academics with these children. Just make them 'good citizens.'" This meant that the teacher would not be expected to teach the students anything, for they were not capable of learning, but that he had better keep them docile and out of everyone else's way. Parents were told that their son wasn't a very good student but that he was "an excellent citizen." This meant that though he didn't learn anything, he did everything that students were supposed to do without question.

The use of the word "citizenship" as synonymous with "docile conduct" was a travesty of Dewey's intention. He envisioned training for citizenship as a process of working out in class actual problems that arise in a democracy. Dewey valued informed dissent, and wanted children to develop the intellectual wherewithal to make reasonable decisions based on the disciplined study of alternatives. He would have considered the use of a citizenship grade as a conduct mark an absolute travesty of the system he had designed, for good citizens were not docile sheep who could be "conned" with impunity. They were men and women who could make the tough decisions that democracy needs in order to function as a system. He realized that the schools were an appropriate place to teach students about the nature of such decisions and to give them "low risk" but real practice in decision making in a context where mistakes were not "for keeps."

The long-term effect of the misinterpretation of Dewey was to discredit citizenship as an appropriate goal for schooling. Citizenship became too closely associated with conformity and "following orders." Yet, in the case of Fred, we see a person consciously attempting to develop educated citizens. Fred's convictions are very close to Dewey's idea of citizenship in many ways. His visits to courthouses, legislative sessions, and factories, and the classroom study of major social problems, are very much in keeping with what Dewey had in mind when he spoke of "educating for freedom."

Case number three
The desire for respect and prestige

Miss Karen Woodbury had been teaching for two years, in a Seattle elementary school where she had a reputation for being prim and aloof. Because she was young, Karen felt it necessary to hold herself somewhat apart from her students in order to gain the respect she thought a teacher should be accorded. But lately some of her students were becoming bothersome—to be more accurate, they were rude and impudent. Karen was finding it increasingly difficult to control her sixth-grade class. In fact, she occasionally found herself having to shout to compete with the roar of the classroom. These incidents were not frequent, but she admitted to herself that they were increasing as her frustration mounted.

One day Karen went to a fellow teacher hoping to find out what impression she made on students and why she was getting such mixed signals from them. Some unknown boys from down the hall at times yelled out, "Hey, Teach!" or "Hey, Babe!" to her considerable embarrassment. They had even started hanging around her classroom before school in the morning, and she didn't know how to handle them. Then there was the day the principal had called her attention to complaints from the book room that dictionaries used in her room were defaced by four-letter words. That was even more upsetting, since she thought she had conveyed her distaste for improper language. When swear words were muttered in class she tried to show that she was not going to make an issue over utterances she wished she hadn't heard.

After describing these occurrences to Joyce, who was in her fourth year of teaching, Karen added, "My teachers were respected. In fact, one reason I went into teaching was that I admired one of my teachers very much. Why do I have trouble getting students to respect me? Other teachers aren't having the same problems, are they? What do you think I should do?"

After a pause, Joyce replied, "Karen, you're young and attractive, which might explain some of the four-letter words. Part of this is just body chemistry. These kids want attention and affection from their teacher. And sometimes they react oddly to a young teacher. Kids will do things like writing or saying dirty words to shock an innocent teacher and therefore get attention, or at least to get attention directed at their handiwork and maybe some recognition from their friends."

"But what should I do?" Karen interrupted.

"I'm no expert," came the reply, "but try dealing with dirty words in a direct, unembarrassed way. Let them know where you stand and that you demand respect, but keep your cool. If you find yourself losing control of them, try to go back to dealing with each one as an individual. Give the annoying ones attention, too—don't just ignore them because they don't behave the way you think a student should."

"What can I do about the kids I don't even know?" Karen asked.

"Well, those kids who call you 'Teach' aren't committing a crime. They're probably just trying to make you talk to them so they can find out what you're like. Tell them your name and get to know theirs. Once they stop being anonymous, they won't seem a threat to you either. . . . But, if you want my opinion there is a more important problem. The kids in your *own* classes probably don't know you, Karen. You don't seem to be involved with them in a personal way at all."

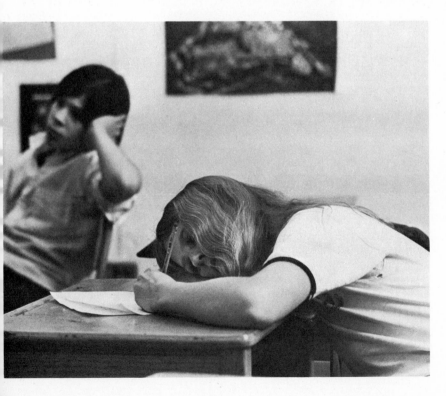

Why teach?

"I try to be friendly, but a teacher has to maintain distance, too."

"Karen, I don't want to sound harsh, but are you sure you aren't just marking time? Isn't teaching a haven for you while you wait to get married?"

Karen reddened a little and protested, "I can't help wanting to get married and have a family of my own someday."

"Kids have a way of knowing if teaching is just a job for you. They don't know you as a member of their community, just as an adult who comes to school each day and leaves again. Any young teacher gets tested by students who are really trying to find out how deeply you're committed to them. For these kids the teacher has to be willing to grapple with their problems or they'll consider her a distant stranger unable to touch them. . . . Do you like being in the classroom with them, Karen?"

"Well, I thought I did, until these incidents made me wonder what was going wrong," she replied a little heatedly.

"Karen, you're an interesting person. In the teacher's lounge you talk about the women's movement, election reform, and other things that matter to you, but in your teacher role you project a less interesting personality. Maybe you have some idealized view of a prim teacher who follows the syllabus and keeps herself aloof. The kids deserve some of your mirth and charm, too, not just the modest reserve of your image of the 'teacher'."

"Do I really do that?" came the shocked question.

"I'm only guessing," said Joyce, "but I suspect your students would respect you more if they sensed you really cared about them. Decide for yourself the extent of your commitment to this career. Ask yourself if you took this job to be detached and reflective or if you're prepared to get your feet wet, to get involved with the kids' interests and problems—which may not seem so trivial after a while. Those thirty kids in your class demand that you interact with them. Teaching is more than transfer of knowledge—it's a commitment to being involved with their lives. Students admire the teacher who is open about her own natural interests and instincts, and open to theirs. They're as preoccupied with mating, ideas, and activities as you are. But you haven't let them see your real self alive and stimulated by the world around you. Try letting them see the real you and see what happens. . . . Wow, I didn't mean to make a speech. That will teach you to ask advice!"

"Thanks, Joyce," said Karen with a genuine smile, "this has been hard to hear but I'll see what I can do."

Questions

1 Do you agree with Joyce's analysis of the problem and her advice to Karen? If not, how would you analyze the problem and what advice would you offer?

2 Do you feel that being a teacher insures respect and prestige? What is the difference between respect for a role and respect for an individual?

3 Joyce accused Karen of using teaching as a haven while she waited to get married. What do you think about young women doing this? What do you think of young men who use teaching as a stepping-stone to school administration?

4 How could her desire for respect and prestige be used to strengthen Karen's effectiveness as a teacher?

5 Other than those suggested in the case, what are some ways in which the desire for prestige and respect can inhibit effectiveness?

6 As motives, how would you distinguish between prestige and respect?

7 Do you feel that the desire for prestige and respect is satisfied equally for men and women teachers?

8 What did Joyce mean when she said, "Your students don't know you as a member of their community."

Comment

Of all the professions and so-called "middle class" occupations, teaching probably has the least prestige. Yet the individual teacher often commands a great deal of respect. Almost everyone, during the course of his life, has felt the influence of a teacher in making a watershed decision. Often a businessman, receiving a service award, will thank "dear old Mrs. Swanson," the fifth-grade teacher who made him sit down and master grammar, thereby proving to himself that he could indeed succeed at things that at first seemed difficult to him. If you asked that man to diagram a complex sentence or define a dangling participle, his answer would probably be little better than guesswork. For what he learned from "dear old Mrs. Swanson" was perhaps not so much grammar as a certain respect for the language. She may have been a person who believed in what she taught and did her best to communicate the richness her study and experience had added to her own life. In doing so, she earned for herself the kind of respect that only teachers can merit—a grudging respect that is by no means earned by everyone who occupies a classroom. And teachers themselves usually know who among their colleagues is a real teacher and who is simply doing a job. While the desire for prestige and respect are motivating factors for many teachers, others associate teaching with a genteel uninvolved life, strict routine, and prescribed methods: the proper old schoolmarm who never uttered a "damn" or questioned the views or decisions of a male superior. Today a person who embodies the "Genteel Ideal" of the teacher would do well to get into some nice related career like Educational Paleontology.

In Western history the teacher has traditionally been regarded as a more or less passive person, philanthropically untempted by power or fortune, and interested in solving problems through reflection rather than action. The teacher has traditionally been a person who loved knowledge for its own sake, and pursued it in that spirit. The same tradition, however, has contributed to the passive image of the teacher reflected in the popular refrain, "Those who can't do, teach." The teacher, with his short workday and long vacations, is expected to spend much of his leisure time preparing himself to teach by reading and studying. It may be that this expectation—the image of the teacher as scholar—motivates some people to enter teaching. Society seems to consider it a necessity for certain people to remove themselves sufficiently from the struggle of life so as to maintain a dispassionate view of it, and society is willing to sustain them (at not too high a level) and even reward them (but with praise rather than things). For many young people who reject the values of corporate life, teaching seems a good alternative. Like Chaucer's scholar in *The Canterbury Tales,* they prefer being "poor but honest" to being rich but corrupt. They may believe that their rejection of affluence and power allows them to maintain an innocence and incorruptibility that free them from the guilts of living, as if powerlessness were an atonement or penance for the collective guilt of society. The walls of the classroom may seem to keep out the world, so that contemplation and reflection can reign and one can view it with detachment. This attitude, considered as a motive for entering teaching, has positive and negative aspects.

On the positive side, the classroom has the potential to be a reflective haven where things proceed according to an orderly pattern and children learn to think rationally. Routines, ground rules, and control of self probably do, in some fashion, pervade most constructive teaching-learning experiences. A teacher whose classroom is built on respect, self-control, restraint, and rational problem solving will develop many commendable qualities in her students (provided that these phenomena are reciprocal, i.e., that the teacher respects the student and has good self-control herself). Students in her class will come to feel that the world can be an orderly place where people can develop by giving and taking in an orderly way.

On the negative side, however, are the specters of irrelevance and of tyranny by an adult among children. The classroom is not hermetically sealed from the outside world; the skills and values developed there are not an end in themselves but simply a means to an end outside the classroom. Scholarship is not the end of scholarship, for the student is not compelled to live the life or accept the values of the teacher. He has a right to demand that the skills of the classroom be transferable to his present or future life. Therefore, the teacher who thinks of the classroom as his little refuge from the world, where scholarship, rationality, and peace prevail, is thinking not of a school but of a medieval monastery where monks spent their lives copying and illuminating the works of others.

Years ago, Edgar Allen Poe wrote a popular short story called "The Masque of the Red Death" about a group of nobles who thought they could avoid the plagues raging across the countryside by gathering behind high castle walls and indulging in merriment with no thought of what lay beyond the castle moat. But, Poe's story tells us, they could not sustain their abandon. The striking clock and red shadows gave witness to a presence that could not be ignored. The Red Death was already among them, and no amount of carousing could hold him off past the stroke of midnight. This situation parallels the notion of a classroom as a haven from life's problems and stresses; the specter of life is already inside the door when the children enter. They bring it with them. The best the teacher can do is to show the child that life is not frightening to her, that she can consider it rationally and even with pleasure, preparing herself for it even as she prepares the children.

The individual considering a career in teaching should realize that, unlike sore feet, which come with the job, prestige and respect don't. You will not find anything but the most surface respect and prestige as a beginning teacher. Although there is potential for considerable respect and prestige, they must be earned.

Case number four
The desire to help children prepare for life

Jerry joined a Florida high-school teaching staff after graduating from college with a fine academic record, and the intensity with which he took on students' problems soon won him the respect of the rest of the faculty. He made himself constantly available to students, both during and after school. Students from many different classes brought their most personal problems to him, and Jerry often would spend his evenings at home discussing personal crises in the lives of his students. His office and his home were always open to the students, and it wasn't long before he was constantly busy with such problems.

In the late winter of his first year, some students in Jerry's sophomore English class asked to be transferred. Jerry had sensed that something was wrong from the apparent hostility of some of his students, but when he heard that students wanted to transfer out, he was deeply hurt.

After a few days of brooding, Jerry approached one of the senior teachers and related his problem. The older teacher told Jerry that he would "check around," and during the next week he stopped some of Jerry's students to find out what was going on. Then he reported back to Jerry.

"Jerry, a fairly consistent picture is beginning to emerge."

"Fire away. And remember, I'm a big boy, so don't feel you have to be kind."

"Don't worry. Tact isn't my long suit. First, the good news—a lot of those sophomores love you. They think you're the best teacher they ever had."

"And?"

"There seems to be an equally large number in that class who are really put out with you."

"I know that, but why?"

"They claim that all they do in your class is waste time. As one kid told me, 'All we do in here is discuss stupid stuff like drugs, pollution, boy-girl relationships, and civil rights.' Another said, 'It ain't English. It's sumpin' else!'"

"Is that all of it?"

"No. There seems to be a deeper problem. A lot of your kids feel like second-class citizens in your class."

"What's that mean?"

"They claim that you've got a very close relationship with about half the members of the class, that you see them after class and they feel free to call you up. The complainers feel that they are frozen out. They feel that in terms of your affection there's a definite in-group and out-group."

"Well I guess there is, but it really isn't my fault."

"That's your view, but not theirs. They feel excluded and they think that success in your class is no longer determined impartially or on the ability to handle English assignments. They feel the insiders have a distinct advantage. From my sampling it seems that the in-group, the ones who are involved in the discussions, are the naturally verbal ones; the others, who probably need the verbal training, sense they aren't getting any and that you don't really care about them as much."

"I can't believe I'm hearing this! You mean to say those kids want to diagram sentences and all that old-fashioned bit? Those kids have *really* missed the whole point!"

"Listen, Jerry, I've heard both sides. If you want my opinion it's you who's missed the boat."

"What do you mean?"

"You've got to make a decision. Either you set yourself up as a therapist-counselor and assume an entirely new role or you start becoming an English teacher and help all your students gain understanding of their lives and problems through literary and composition experiences. What do you want to be, Jerry? A counselor or an English teacher?"

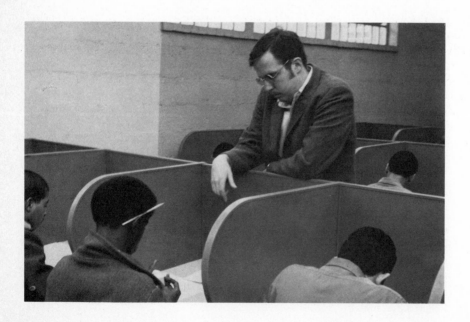

1　If Jerry had come to you for advice, what advice would you have given him? And why?

2　How do Jerry and the older teacher differ in their views on helping children prepare themselves for life? Which of the two would you side with?

3　Do you feel that Jerry's disgruntled students were fair to him? If you were a parent of one of those students, how would you feel?

4　If you agree with the statement, "Human problems are more important than subject matter," what was wrong with Jerry's approach?

5　If teachers are to help children prepare themselves for life, who decides what kind of life they should prepare for? you? other teachers? parents? the government?

6　What are some of the problems involved in teaching a "more relevant" curriculum?

Comment

One of Jerry's problems was that, while he probably saw clearly what kinds of behavior should be encouraged in particular students, he lost sight of the goals of the class as a group. In ministering to the individual problems of certain pupils, he neglected the needs of others. He forgot that students in his class were under pressure to achieve, and that they expected these needs to be met in Jerry's class. Perhaps Jerry, to whom high achievement came easily, had a tendency to play down the importance of academic successes, even though they formed the foundation of his own lifestyle and career. The children, however, could not afford to play his game. When he lost sight of the need to pursue certain predetermined goals, such as learning to write well, Jerry became increasingly blind to the reasons why he was teaching English and to the students' expectations of him as their English teacher.

Most primary teachers are aware that their students need to *do,* as well as to talk and listen, but, as pupils advance to the upper grades, verbal skills are increasingly emphasized, often at the expense of action. Secondary teachers sometimes lose sight of the relationship between performance and learning; Jerry, with the best intentions, frustrated his students by neglecting to define goals in his class. The class lost its sense of performance and accomplishment. Jerry was no longer a teacher, but was becoming a counselor, a therapist or, at worst, a babysitter.

In the same way that we investigate our own motives to answer the question, "Why teach?", children demand to know, "Why learn?" In one way or another, they ask teachers this question every day. When the child asks the teacher, "Why are we doing this?" he is really asking, "So what??" "So what if I can't define causes of the Civil War?" "So what if I can't recognize a lyric poem?" The child needs to understand the function that underlies the form. He wants to know what this task or information does for him as a person attempting to solve his own life problems. About the best the teacher can do is to tell the child, as candidly as possible, what these particular tasks have meant to him in his own life. Perhaps they have enabled the teacher to think of himself as an educated man, or to explain reality to himself more effectively. If the tasks the teacher assigns have had no real meaning in his own life, perhaps he had better not teach them; if he is obligated to do so, he would do well to ask someone to whom these learning exercises "make sense" to "teach" him about their value.

As knowledge proliferates and there is more and more to learn, people are beginning to feel overwhelmed. Learning any particular segment of knowledge may appear rather arbitrary. As a result, students are more frequently asking "So what?" about what is taught in schools. These questions will not go away. No matter how tired we become of the word "relevant," it will remain a pivotal idea for teachers for many years.

For a little exercise in relevance testing, open a textbook in your major subject to one of the chapter openings. Read the first two pages or so of the chapter and then ask yourself, "So what?" If you can come up with two or three defenses of its relevance, approach one of your friends in another field of study and try to explain to him why it is vitally important that he be familiar with the content of these two pages.[8] You may find yourself feeling like a used-car salesman attempting to sell an old wreck to a minister. If your friend remains unconvinced, it may not necessarily mean that the information in the book is worthless; it may have implications you are unaware of. But try it and see, remembering that students in your future classes who ask you "So what?" have less vested interests in education than does your friend. The issue here is quite clear: if you can't answer when you're asked "So what?" you may spend your career trying to force people to do what they really don't want to do. If you do develop a rationale for what you teach, you'll spend your time helping people do things that you and they value and like to do.

Case number five
The desire to teach a particular subject
Sarah was a veteran of thirty-three years in a fifth-grade classroom. She had spent the last fifteen years in a moderately large Pittsburgh elementary school. This particular year had not been pleasant for her, though, because of a young male teacher who had been added to the staff and who was also a fifth-grade teacher. The language-composition program had for a good many years been considered by the other teachers in the school as Sarah's private domain, but the young teacher, Mr. Walker, had shown signs of what Sarah termed "uncooperation." When she received a note from the principal asking her to drop by, she knew that it had something to do with Mr. Walker.

When Sarah walked into the principal's office, she did not feel particularly uncomfortable; she had been there a thousand times before, and the principal, Mr. Paul, was an old hand at the game. As he said, they had "soldiered" together for more years than either wanted to remember.

After a cordial exchange of amenities, Mr. Paul got right down to business. "Sarah," he said, "you know why I asked you here. It's this business with Mr. Walker. I can't help hearing the static between you two, and knowing you so well, I thought that, well, maybe we could see what the problem was."

---

[8] It is unfair and therefore not allowable to use our book in this test.

"David," Sarah began, "you know me, probably as well as anyone around here knows me. I've spent a good deal of time putting together that language-composition program, and it's a good one. You know that I want only the very best for the children, and that I consider in detail each of the offerings that we bring into the comp program."

"Yes, I know that's true."

"Well," Sarah continued, "this young man comes into the school and just plain refuses to use the program that I spent so long developing with the other people on the staff."

"Doesn't he use it at all?" asked Mr. Paul.

"Not for the important things. One of the areas I've always really stressed has been outlining and notetaking. When I suggested — rather pleasantly, I may add — that he work on these skills with the children, he said that he preferred not to use the guide with the book. He said he would rather teach these skills through the science program. Then do you know what he said when I asked him why?"

"What?"

"He said that our method for teaching outlining taught the children to organize other people's thinking, but not their own. He said that he considered it better for the children to learn to organize their own thinking by observing phenomena and then deciding upon the appropriate logic for schematizing, whatever that means. I pointed out to him the importance of organizing other people's thinking as a prerequisite to organizing their own, so that they could take a sensible set of notes on the reading or the lesson. He said that life experiences weren't that way, that they didn't come neatly organized for us. All these years, I've tried to show children something about how great minds work, and I've produced kids that could think with the best, David."

"Yes, Sarah," said Mr. Paul. "But it seems to me that his point is valid. Now look. You're a real teacher. You've been at the game long enough to see some real changes in the way people live, and in how people think. Children today are thinking differently, and I guess in some ways better, than they did when you and I were in grammar school, and we've never particularly thought that the way we learned was the best anyway. Now, why does this guy scare you so much? He's only another young teacher, and you've seen 'em come and go for a long time."

"David, I don't know. I'm not sure," responded Sarah. "It's just that he seems so sure he's right. He seems so well-prepared, so creative, and he seems to be telling me that I've been wrong all of these years in the way I've tried to send children out of my class. I was very good in college, David — Phi Beta Kappa from Cornell, and in English, too."

"I know you, Sarah, and you're certainly as well qualified for this job as anyone I've seen. Yet here's a guy who's trying to bring in a skill that we really haven't developed before. I don't think that outlining is a formal skill; I think it's a functional skill, a life skill as opposed to a literary exercise, and I know that you agree with me. Now, as an administrator, I would like to see both ends of this skill spectrum be taught. We have two people admirably qualified to do a job for these kids. My question to you is why you two have to work at cross-purposes? Perhaps I miss the nuances of the situation, but I feel that you could learn a great deal from each other."

"Do you want me to make him the director of literature and composition for fifth grade?" Sarah asked testily.

"Did I say that, Sarah? You were teaching children before he could button his own pants. I'm not so sold on youth that I think we should all genuflect to it. No, that's not at all what I want. Do you know what I really want?"

"No," Sarah answered. "What do you want me to do?"

"I just want you to say to yourself, and mean it, that this guy is a good teacher and that he could be one of the very fine ones; that's all I want you to do, because once you recognize that, I know you're enough of a pro to figure out how to take advantage of his ability and how to bring him along."

After a long pause, Sarah sighed deeply and replied, "Perhaps you're right, David. I guess I've been feeling threatened . . . and unnecessarily. I don't have to apologize for my career. He's not asking me to, either, is he?"

"No, he's not. As a matter of fact, he requested transfer here from Bradley so he could work with you in the language program. It says so right in his file."

"Why didn't you tell me that? I had a right to know."

"Maybe I should have told you, Sarah, but there's only one empire-builder around here, and that's me. All you need is a few disciples and the other teachers wouldn't see a dollar of the budget. No thanks."

"Dave," said Sarah, as she arranged her purse on her arm, "you've just reconfirmed my prejudices. You've got to be some sort of a sneaky devil to be a good principal."

Questions

1 What was there about Sarah's personality and about her motive for teaching that led her into conflict with Mr. Walker?
2 From the information available, how would you characterize Mr. Walker's motivation to teach?

3 How would you respond to the judgment that the principal, David Paul, manipulates his teachers?
4 In what ways can the decision to teach a particular subject or grade level reflect an individual's personality and character?

Comment

Teaching style is directly related to the personality of the teacher. Sarah and Mr. Walker chose different approaches to the teaching of English because of their differing personalities and values. Sarah had taught for many years and was more tradition-minded. She organized the curriculum around a formal approach to the structure of learning. Students were explicitly instructed in notetaking and outlining, rather than acquiring those skills in the process of organizing their own ideas. Sarah's Great Ideas approach reflected her respect for learning what others have accomplished, while Mr. Walker thought it more important to allow children to develop their own personalities through more independent and individual instruction. The disagreement between the two, though it had other ramifications, reflected the conflict between traditional and experimental approaches.

Understanding why a person prefers one pattern of reality to another provides an excellent key to personality. Two people watch the same event; one sees a problem being solved while the other sees a problem being created. Sarah viewed Mr. Walker as a problem because of the method he used to teach children; the principal thought Walker was an asset for children.

Once Sarah saw that there was more than one approach to a single problem, she began to fear it less. If she had been dissatisfied with the language program, or felt reservations about her own ability to handle it, the problem would have been seriously magnified. This case illustrates how people reveal themselves by the problems to which they are drawn.

If you ever watch passengers on a train or bus attack the daily newspaper, you will get some real, if incomplete, insights into the values of the different readers. The man in the dark grey is likely to turn to the business section first to check the stock quotations. Another will begin by studying the hands set out in the daily bridge lesson. A college student with books on the seat beside him might turn directly to the second page, where world news is reported and interpreted in depth. A high school girl may turn directly to Ann Landers. Each of these people has identified himself with a problem area which can serve as a very rough index to his personality, motives, and behavior patterns.

A college student's choice of major is a more reliable guide to personality than are his newspaper reading habits. In choosing a study program, a person is selecting an "arena" or environment whose problems, methods, and materials are tailored to his abilities and his interests. Some fields are highly logical and exacting. Others demand less methodology and logic, but more human emotion, involvement, and even physical labor. Every prospective teacher owes it to himself to understand the requirements of teaching, and the kinds of commitment it requires, for these are the factors that determine the rewards and challenges of the job. Society is generally miserly in its formal rewards for a job well done, and this is no less true in teaching. For this reason, it is particularly important to choose a subject matter and grade level that are rewarding in themselves to the young teacher. Commitment to the goals and methodology of a particular subject or level, and enjoyment of the problems it poses, are among the major rewards of teaching.

In choosing one subject matter field over another, a person is deciding to highlight one aspect of his life over another. To choose to become a teacher, and to teach a particular program, can mean that the person is attempting to illustrate those things in his own life which he feels must be worked out or solved, or, perhaps, those things which are worth solving and which he is competent to solve.

Discussion questions

1 Can you draw any conclusions about the relationship between your personal experience and your expectations of teaching? At what ages were you happiest and unhappiest in school? (Compare your answers with those of your friends. Did many of you like or dislike the same grade? If so, how do you explain this?) What subjects did you like best? What grade or subject do you imagine yourself teaching? With what kinds of educational experiences are you totally unfamiliar?

2 What are you doing right now in an effort to answer the question, "Should I teach?" What could you do? What will you do? What "real world" opportunities are available to you?

3 Reflect on the list of careers in education on pp. 14–16. If you were to graduate today, what position would you choose? What position might you eventually aim for? Are there any positions listed that you have never considered before but might be interested in? What effect might an oversupply of teachers have on your decision?

4 What is the present and projected teacher supply in the field that currently interests you most? in the geographic area?

5 Can you see the influence of John Dewey, or of the corrupted versions of Dewey's ideas, in your own education? How relevant do you think his ideas are today?

6 Which of the case studies do you identify with most strongly? least strongly? Do you disagree with our interpretation of any of the cases? In what way?

7 What are some other possible motivations to teach which we haven't mentioned?

For further reading

- Allen, George N. *Undercover Teacher.* New York: Doubleday, 1960. "Inside story" by a reporter who disguised himself as a teacher in a Brooklyn junior high school. Somewhat sensational, but an interesting glimpse of the teaching profession.
- Ashton-Warner, Sylvia. *Teacher.* New York: Simon & Schuster, 1963. An autobiographical account of Ms. Warner's years teaching Maori children in New Zealand. The book is rich in detail and a clear statement of her approach to education.
- Braithwaite, Edward R. *To Sir, With Love.* Englewood Cliffs, N. J.: Prentice-Hall, 1960. A British Guianan living in London becomes a teacher in a British secondary school. The book describes his trials and eventual success teaching lower class London teenagers.

- Brembeck, Cole F. *The Discovery of Teaching*. Englewood Cliffs, N. J.: Prentice-Hall, 1962. The book is composed of actual case situations centering on students and teachers.
- Burrup, Percy E. *The Teacher and the Public School System*. New York: Harper & Row, 1967. An analysis of the structure, functioning, and offerings of educational institutions, the nature of teaching and teachers and weaknesses needing correction in teaching and teacher education.
- Chase, Virginia. *The End of the Week*. New York: Macmillan, 1953. An account of the lives of thirteen elementary-school students both in and out of school. A touching and insightful view.
- Fuchs, Estelle. *Teachers Talk: Views from Inside City Schools*. Garden City, New York: Doubleday, 1969. A collection of teachers' statements about themselves, schools, and learning during their initial four months of teaching in an urban setting. The author analyzes these statements, explicating the underlying assumptions of the teachers and suggesting alternative actions.
- Hentoff, Nat. *Our Children Are Dying*. New York: Viking Press, 1966. An account of a New York City principal, Elliot Shapiro, as he deals with the massive problems of educating children in New York City slums. The author, a skilled journalist and commentator, depicts the frustrations and hopes of a dedicated educator making his daily rounds.
- Herndon, James. *The Way It Spozed to Be*. New York: Simon and Schuster, 1967. A highly personal account of the author's first year of teaching poor black children in an urban setting. Few authors have as deep a sense of the complexity of the human condition and the process of schooling.
- Herndon, James. *How to Survive in Your Native Land*. New York: Simon and Schuster, 1971. This book is a collection of essays of reflections and anecdotes. Different from his first book *The Way It Spozed to Be,* this book reflects the author's eight years of teaching experience in a middle class suburb. The book is peppered with wit and wisdom and advice on how to succeed.
- Hersey, John. *The Child Buyer*. New York: Alfred A. Knopf, 1960. A biting satire of American values and of the school as an extension of those values. The author is a major American novelist.
- Hilton, James. *Goodbye, Mr. Chips*. Boston: Little, Brown, 1934. A short and sentimental novel depicting the life of a British schoolmaster from youth to old age.
- Hunter, Evan. *Blackboard Jungle*. Cambridge, Mass.: Bentley, 1971 (reprint of 1954 edition). A very popular novel about a new teacher's uphill struggle in an urban high school. Although quite absorbing, somewhat stereotypic and excessively violent.
- Kaufman, Bel. *Up the Down Staircase*. Englewood Cliffs, N. J.: Prentice-Hall, 1964. An easy-to-read, humorous and poignant semi-fictionalized account of a beginning teacher's experience in a New York City high school. A thoroughly enjoyable book.
- Kozol, Jonathan. *Death at an Early Age*. Boston: Houghton Mifflin, 1967. A first-year teacher's account of life in a Boston ghetto school. Tyrannization of the children, cynicism, condescension, racism, and anti-intellectualism are dominant themes in Kozol's account. The book has become a rallying point for critics and educational reformers.
- Ladd, Edward T., and Sayres, William C., eds. *Social Aspects of Education: A Casebook*. Englewood Cliffs, N.J.: Prentice-Hall, 1962. Approximately twenty detailed cases of actual school experiences involving racial segregation, discipline, school organization, and curriculum reform. Each case is followed by an insightful analysis.

- Morris, Van Cleve, *et al. Becoming an Educator.* Boston: Houghton Mifflin, 1963. Several major figures in American education discuss a key area, a grey level, or a foundation field of education. A valuable book for those contemplating teaching.
- Moustakas, Clark E. *The Alive and Growing Teacher.* New York: Philosophical Library, 1959. A group of teachers and principals discuss an array of personal and professional problems and activities. The author concludes with an analysis of the teacher.
- Rasey, Marie Y. *It Takes Time.* New York: Harper & Row, 1953. A novel that focuses on a young woman's choice to become an elementary-school teacher. Much valuable description of various teaching methods.
- Ryan, Kevin, ed. *Don't Smile Until Christmas: Accounts of the First Year of Teaching.* Chicago: University of Chicago Press, 1970. A collection of six exceedingly honest biographical statements by beginning high-school teachers. A concluding chapter on the first year of teaching by the editor.
- Stuart, Jesse. *The Thread That Runs So True.* New York: Charles Scribner's Sons, 1958. An autobiographical account of the famous writer's experience as a teacher in a one-room school. Interesting description of the problems and successes of a beginning teacher, and of life in rural America.
- Updike, John. *The Centaur.* New York: Fawcett World Library, 1964. A novel about a high-school teacher and his son, with parallels from Greek mythology, by a major American novelist.
- Williams, Emlyn. *The Corn is Green.* New York: Random House, 1941. A moving play dealing with the life of a Welsh schoolmistress.

Films

- *Abraham Kaplan* (Indiana University Audio-Visual Center, 16mm, b&w, 59 min., NET). One of a series of five films about "Men Who Teach." Abraham Kaplan, professor of philosophy at the University of Michigan, explains his beliefs and attitudes toward teaching, as well as the differences he sees between instruction and education.
- *Blackboard Jungle* (Films, Incorporated, 16mm, b&w, 101 min., 1955). Although made quite a few years ago, this film's depiction of a large-city vocational training school is still quite interesting. The problems encountered by teachers are not very different from those presented in *To Sir, With Love.*
- *Cloud 9* (EDC Film Library, 16mm, b&w, 25 min.). Documents the reactions of fifth-graders in the Cardozo Model School District in Washington, D.C., to the death of Martin Luther King.
- *The Eye of the Beholder* (Stuart Reynolds, "mood color," 25 min., 1971). This unusual film, accompanied by an equally unusual user's guide, deals with the problem of perception as it relates to human relations in all fields. Twelve hours in the life of an artist provide the fictional motif within which encounters with members of different social groups and races provoke various reactions in the character and the audience. The film has been used by many different professional schools to help students come to terms with attitudes toward other people.
- *For All My Students* (Anti-Defamation League, b&w, 36 min., 1967). In a Palo Alto ghetto high school, students candidly evaluate their teachers who, in turn, probe the reasons for their own successes and failures. This film will help prospective teachers examine methods and styles which may influence their ability to help economically disadvantaged children.

- *Gestalt Series* (Films Incorporated, color, approx. 25 min. each, 1969). These eight films trace Dr. Frederick Perls in an explanation and demonstration of the principles of Gestalt Therapy. He discusses methodology, philosophy, and approach during sessions with a therapy group, and the films include actual group sessions. Two titles are of special relevance to people considering careers in teaching: *Awareness,* in which four group members serve as examples of the Gestalt Method as a learning process with widespread implications; and *What Is Gestalt?,* the introductory film which enumerates basic principles.
- *If . . .* (Films Incorporated, color, 111 min., 1969). Lindsay Anderson's film starring Malcolm McDowell as the leader of a revolution in an English boys' school. From enduring hazing and school discipline, several students unite to wreck the Founder's Day ceremonies. Derived very directly from Jean Vigo's *Zero for Conduct,* the film's violence is a clear result of the date of its production.
- *Incident on Wilson Street* (Contemporary/McGraw-Hill, 16mm, b&w, 51 min., 1964). A documentary on one school's special program to deal with the learning

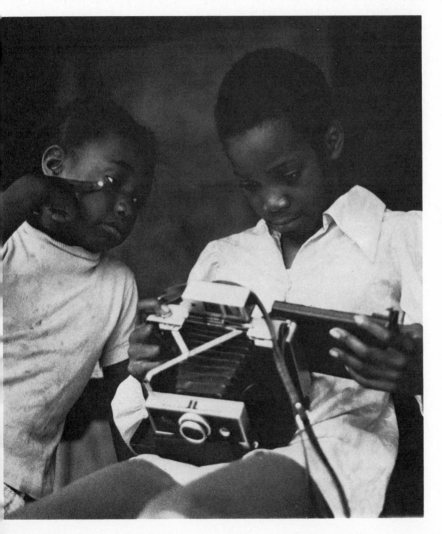

Why teach?

problems of emotionally disturbed children from a poor neighborhood. The film focuses on Angela, a fifth-grader, and the school's attempt to get her back into "regular" classes.

- *Journey Into Self* (Western Behavioral Sciences Institute, b&w, 47 min., 1968). This film is a documentary of an intensive basic encounter group. Eight total strangers meet in front of the cameras to share an intimate experience under the leadership of Carl Rogers, founder of client-centered therapy. The film raises for students the awareness of a technique for self-discovery.

- *Kes* (United Artists, color, 109 min., 1970). The story of a child trying to revolt against the drab life of a coalminer, which society has in store for him. On the path to deliquency, the boy is diverted by a baby hawk (kestrel) as wild and free as his dreams. He takes care of the bird and tries to protect it from his vicious older brother, the neighborhood children, and adults.

- *Men Who Teach Series* (NET, b&w, 59 min. each, 1968). This series of five films tries to determine what personal characteristics make up a great teacher. Each features its subject in class, in his research activities, in private life with family and students, and in interviews. These teachers have all been singled out by their students as having found a way to ignite the spark of interest in learning. The series includes films on *Gerald Holton,* professor of physics at Harvard; *Norman Jacobson,* professor of political science at Berkeley; *Abraham Kaplan,* professor of philosophy at the University of Michigan; *Howard Mitchell,* professor of urbanism and human resources at the University of Pennsylvania; *Lloyd Reynolds and William Geer,* lecturer in history at the University of North Carolina and art historian at Reed College, respectively.

- *Norman Jacobson* (Indiana University Audio-Visual Center, 16mm, b&w, 59 min., NET). One of the films from the "Men Who Teach" series, *Norman Jacobson* is an intimate portrait of a professor of political science at the University of California, Berkeley, made up of scenes of him with students at seminars, scenes of student involvement, and filmed interviews.

- *The Prime of Miss Jean Brodie* (Films Incorporated, 116 min., color, 1969). The heroic visions of a Scottish school teacher have unforeseen consequences on her students. Miss Brodie's personal, quixotic view of world events crashes against the realities the girls experience in the era of the Spanish Civil War and the rise of Mussolini. This film illustrates the power a teacher can exercise over students and the dangers of importing too much of a personal attitude into the classroom.

- *To Sir, With Love* (Columbia Cinematheque, 16mm, color, 105 min.). Based on E. R. Braithwaite's award-winning autobiographical novel, this film stars Sidney Poitier as a teacher in a "rough" school in London's East End. The film catalogue claims that he "treats them as adults and imbues them with standards of decency."

- *Warrendale* (Grove Press Film Division, 16mm, b&w, 105 min., 1968). A powerful film study of emotionally disturbed children made at a residential treatment center in Toronto. Many issues are raised and explored during the film, including the essential dynamics of the learning experience.

- *The Way It Is* (Indiana University Audio-Visual Center, 16mm, b&w, 60 min., 1967, NET). Depicts the chaos of the New York City schools, focusing on what is being done in one school in the Bedford-Stuyvesant section of Brooklyn to improve the situation. Participants in a New York University special learning project are shown visiting with parents, teachers, and students.

- *What Makes Man Human?* (University-at-Large, 16mm, color, 15 min.). One of a series on Jerome Bruner's fifth-grade curriculum, *Man: A Course of Study,* this film reveals one teacher's feelings about the curriculum: how it affects her students, as well as her own teaching methods and theories. Bruner himself appears occasionally to interject theoretical descriptions and hopes for the curriculum.

Slide-tape

- *Project Inc.* (Project Inc., 280 35mm color slides, audiotape, 22:22 min.). A "portrait" of a storefront community art center through the voices and images of teachers and students. This slide-tape presents a variety of different "teaching situations."

Audiotapes

- *The Basic Encounter Group* (Big Sur, 6 hours, 1967). Dr. Carl Rogers discusses the basic encounter group as an instrument for constructive personal growth, organizational change, resolution of inner-group tension, and as a new philosophy of science and education. A good introduction to the theory behind this method of self-discovery, with implications both for the prospective teacher and for the practice of education.
- *Can Change Take Place in the Public School Context?* (Pacifica, 35 min., 1970). Herbert Kohl, author of *36 Children,* talks casually with examples from his own experiences of the difficulties of introducing new methods into public schools. The style keeps the subject from being too intimidating, but the message that change in public schools will require energy and skill from teachers comes through clearly.
- *George Leonard: Ecstasy in Education* (Big Sur, reel or cassette, mono or stereo, 60 min.). George Leonard, author of *Education and Ecstasy,* explains why education until the present has had to be repressive, and why it can now involve joy, ecstasy, and positive motivational conditioning forces.
- *Surely You've Heard of Children?* (Pacifica, 30 min., 1970). The next question is, "Can you buy a preschool franchise as easily as you can get into the fast food business?" For many reasons, from drugs to union politics to busing, many parents have looked to alternative educational sites for their children. This tape examines the educational franchise problem and contains warnings for those who think lightly of setting up an independent school.

Simulation game

- *Confrontation: A Human Relations Training Unit for Teachers and Administrators in a Multi-Ethnic Elementary and High School* (Anti-Defamation League, 1968). Four open-ended films make up the core of this unit, illustrating model confrontations and follow-up discussions. A leader's guide and participant workbooks constitute the remaining materials. Through the filmed enactments of actual school problems, would-be teachers can work out their own reactions and develop with others a system of practical solutions.

Refer to Appendix for addresses of distributors.

Who are teachers?

2   What problems does the beginning teacher face?

This chapter is based on the premise that being forewarned is being forearmed. It is meant to be a mental rehearsal for the problems you might encounter as a beginning teacher. The major sources of the beginning teacher's difficulties are identified and described as they are actually experienced by teachers. Commentary is provided to place the problems in perspective.

Chapter contents

Problems! Problems! Who needs problems!?
Categories of teaching problems
The school milieu: the shock of the familiar
The administration: the face of the bureaucracy
Peers: a mixed blessing
Instruction: so much to learn
Students: friends and fiends
Parents: the soon-to-be-differentiated mass
Problems in perspective
The other side of the coin

The first year of teaching has been described as an emotional roller coaster, filled with peaks of exhilaration, dips of depression, and, *always,* intense involvement. It is a year of adult freedom, immense learning, and great satisfaction. And much of the learning and satisfaction it offers is a direct result of working out or learning to live with problems. In this chapter we will examine some of the problems commonly reported by beginning teachers. However, before you read about what we consider to be the major problems encountered by new teachers—and we can't cover them all—we would like you to take a moment to write down several problems that you would expect to be most common among beginning teachers. After you have done that, write down the two or three problems you feel you might be most concerned with as a beginning teacher.

Common problems encountered by beginning teachers:

1 _____

2 _____

3 _____

4 _____

5 _____

6 _____

7 _____

8 _____

9 _____

10 _____

Possible problems I might experience:

1 _____

2 _____

3 _____

A summary of a research study on the problems generally encountered by beginning teachers appears on page 53.

Problems! Problems! Who needs problems!?

It might well be asked why we are devoting an entire chapter to the problems and difficulties experienced by beginning teachers. At face value, it seems a rather negative approach. Even sadistic. Aren't we running the risk of giving the reader a one-sided view of teaching? If we recount a series of demi-horror stories, are we liable to frighten away potential teachers? Perhaps we are. We believe, however, that there is a pervasive tendency in much writing about education and teaching to oversell. Joys and satisfactions abound. The teacher is portrayed in these writings as a modern-day Pied Piper leading a procession of happy, devoted students out of the Cave of Ignorance into the Light of Wisdom and Happiness. This kind of inspirational literature, in combination with our own tendency to kid ourselves, can be very misleading for the aspiring teacher. One of our aims in discussing the problems of the beginning teacher is to present a corrective to this rose-colored vision of teaching.

Another more positive reason for examining common problems is to give the reader time to develop solutions or responses before encountering them directly. The old chestnut about locking the barn door after the horse has been stolen has special applicability to many teachers. Only after they have made a mistake do they begin to seek a solution. On the other hand, a realization that he will have problems and an attempt to identify them and develop solutions in advance may save the prospective teacher and his students much grief.

Yet another reason for encountering common problems of beginning teachers is to provide the reader with grist for his intellectual mill. It is our hope that these problems will provide the reader with background material to use in the rest of his professional training. Educational theories and points of view can be enlightened by, or tested against, these slices of life from the real world of teaching. We hope, then, that they can be used to enrich the reader's study of educational theory.

What problems does the beginning teacher face?

It is important for the reader to realize, however, that he is not encountering in this chapter a balanced picture of the first year of teaching. Intentionally, we have presented a one-sided, negative view of teaching. Joy and satisfaction we do not need preparation for. Problems, we do.

Categories of teaching problems

"Problem" is one of those all-purpose words that can be applied to situations as different as the threat of nuclear holocaust and chronic bed wetting. Even when limited to aspects of teaching, it can be assigned to widely varying phenomena. There is the problem of having a quiet voice and not being heard by all the children. And then there is the problem of an irreconcilable philosophical disagreement between you and the school authorities about how you teach. Problems are also quite subjective. A problem that might drive one teacher out of the profession and into the expensive hands of a therapist can be a stimulating challenge to another teacher.

To help us deal with this troublesome characteristic of problems, we have organized our discussion around six aspects of the teacher's experience: the school setting, administration, fellow teachers or peers, instruction, students, and

Cartoon by Samuel H. Gross, copyright © 1969, Saturday Review, Inc.

S. GROSS

problems of beginning teachers

In 1964, Frank Broadbent and Donald Cruickshank conducted a study at the State University College at Brockport, New York, on the problems of the first-year teacher. They sent questionnaires to 282 graduates of their institution who had just completed their first year of teaching in elementary and secondary schools. Fifty-eight percent of the teachers responded to the 117-item questionnaire. The results were grouped into six problem area categories and scored for frequency and intensity. According to this study, first-year teachers are troubled by the following problems, listed in descending order:

Methods of teaching
Evaluation of students
Discipline
Parent relations
Classroom routines and materials
Personal problems (primarily lack of self-confidence)

These findings conflict with earlier studies which indicate that discipline is the most troublesome problem area for first-year teachers.

F. Broadbent and D. Cruickshank, The Identity and Analysis of Problems of First Year Teachers, ERIC (October 19, 1965).

parents. We have drawn heavily on reports of actual experiences by beginning teachers to add flesh and some blood to our abstractions.[1]

The school milieu: the shock of the familiar

One of the oddest phenomena related to becoming a teacher is the new teacher's sense of strangeness in what is, after all, a very familiar setting. A person who becomes an insurance salesman or a psychiatric social worker knows he is moving into a strange environment, and expects this new work world to present him with very different experiences than those he has had as a student. The new teacher, however, is reentering a familiar setting, even if it is not the same school in which he was taught. The school routine of classes, periods, bells, tests, homework, and report cards is in his blood. The hierarchical system of principals, teachers, and students is taken for granted. The rituals and pageants—assemblies, Thanksgiving class presentations, honor society induction, sports rivalries with other schools—are all instantly recognizable. The existence of cliques, in-groups, and out-groups among both students and faculty is no secret either. But despite all their experience and sophistication, beginning teachers are commonly overwhelmed by their initial exposures to school.

The beginning teacher's shock at the familiar is sometimes manifested in visible signs of mental and physical stress. In the early months of the school year it is not uncommon for the new teacher to experience depressions and self-doubt, outbursts of crying, physical exhaustion, insomnia, crankiness, inability to control

[1] A large number of the problem cases in this chapter are drawn from a book one of the authors edited. Being a deeply modest chap, he is somewhat uncomfortable about all these references to his book. Nevertheless, these problem cases are the cases with which we are most familiar. Modesty loses to expediency.

What problems does the beginning teacher face?

his temper, and even fits of vomiting before going to school in the morning. The anthropologist Estelle Fuchs has studied the world of the beginning teacher. In her words,

Most of us are aware of the tensions and strains accompanying unfamiliar routines or activities. However, the symptoms expressed by beginning teachers . . . go far beyond the ordinary fatigue associated with a new mode of employment. They are surprisingly similar to the phenomenon described by anthropologists as "culture shock." [2]

Culture shock is the feeling of dislocation people experience when they initially encounter a foreign culture. Peace Corps volunteers, foreign students, tourists, and newly-arrived immigrants frequently report that when first thrust into the strange life patterns of a foreign culture they feel numbingly disoriented, forced to assimilate too much too soon and afraid they have made a drastic mistake to have come to a strange country. It is easy to explain culture shock among Peace Corps volunteers and immigrants, but why teachers? Haven't we just said that teachers, as ex-students, are accustomed to the culture of school? It appears, though, that the new teacher's very familiarity with life in schools is a problem in itself. "School" is a very complicated series of structures, people and interactions, and knowing part of it does not imply knowledge of the whole. Being one o twenty-five students sitting and listening to a teacher is very different from standing in front of twenty-five strange children and taking charge of their learning. People learn a great deal about teaching through teacher-watching, bu there is a great deal they do not learn. Besides this, the new teacher has to learn not only a new set of school routines for her particular school, but also how to ad minister them. She has to learn her way around a new building and find out how to requisition the supplies she needs. She has to "learn" her administration, her fellow teachers and, especially, her students. And on top of all this, the first-year teacher has to develop lesson plans from scratch. She has to build complete units, design bulletin boards, devise an evaluation system and make up tests. The pressure of all this newness causes strain.

As attested to by the following account by a first-year teacher,[3] intellectual understanding of "culture shock" is not always an effective antidote.

Linda Corman/English: "Considering myself sophisticated enough to survive any experience the outside world was pleased to offer, I lent a deaf ear and bored spirit to academic discussions of the severe 'cultural shocks' we, who then dwelt in University of Chicago ivory-towerdom, were likely to undergo on the job. I had attended the only public high school in my small midwestern hometown and had therefore been exposed, I thought, to the social, emotional, and intellectual lives of a socioeconomic cross-section of teenagers and to the academic dispositions of variously talented young students. I had also known urban youth, black and white, in college and before. I had known and liked very well the blacks with whom I became acquainted in college. Certainly, I asserted, I was altogether sympathetic with the

[2] P. 21 of *Teachers Talk* by Estelle Fuchs. Copyright © 1967 by Hunter College of the City University of New York. Copyright © 1969 by Estelle Fuchs. Reprinted by permission of Doubleday & Company, Inc
[3] All the cases in this chapter which are not accompanied by specific citations are slightly altered or fictionalized accounts of situations and problems experienced by the authors or by beginning teachers with whom the authors have worked. The names have been changed to save us all from embarrassme

plight of minority groups and totally without so-called prejudice. And I had traveled a lot on my own, and, after, had lived in Chicago's liberal melting pot, Hyde Park, for a year. On the whole, I concluded, I had met a varied lot of people and should no doubt find very little new — certainly nothing surprising — in anyone whom I should hereafter encounter.

"Perhaps I had simply forgotten these people of my past. For it turned out that I was thoroughly shocked by a large portion of the high school community with which I sought to involve myself. Only now can I see that these people should have been familiar from the beginning. I had read about them in books — in novels and poems, in psychology texts and anthropological studies. And most of them I had indeed known very well before.

"But I did not know myself, and I did not know the role I haphazardly tried to play. I had known tyrant-teachers and pushovers, bright ones and ignorant ones; but I had not known them as colleagues. I had known mischievous students and helpful ones, vicious ones and apple-polishers, but I had not known them as students in a class I was supposed to teach. I had known principals and assistant principals, and counselors and truant officers, but I had not known them from the viewpoint of one who expected to be treated as the college graduate, the lady, and the professional I wanted desperately to be. In short, I saw strange faces because I looked out through the strangely new eyes of a teacher."[4]

Of course, not every kind of shock is equally overwhelming. Some teachers-in-training who are preoccupied with problems related to instruction forget how much clerical and administrative work is required of them.

John Canfield/History: "I couldn't believe all the paperwork that was required (in duplicate, if you please). Most of it was related to the home room. There were a thousand forms to be passed out, to be filed, to be passed to the student to be filled out, or simply to be read aloud. Late in the year one got the feeling that they all should be thrown out.

"The first day of real school was a bookkeeper's nightmare. There were absence reports, homeroom size reports, class size records, tardy slips, and cut slips to be passed out; and there were three schedule cards per student to be passed out, filled out, returned, and filed. Then there were parents' voter registration cards to be collected to prove that the students lived within the school district. Half the students didn't have these, and even if they had, I wouldn't have known which addresses were in the district anyway. Add to this the physical and dental exam forms to be collected, the bus cards to be filled out, lockers to be assigned, and the locks to be sold.

"Lockers! For thirty-eight students I was assigned sixteen lockers, twelve of which worked."[5]

Many new teachers have never come in contact with the rough-and-tumble, occasionally violent, aspect of school life. They may have attended schools where

[4] Kevin Ryan, *Don't Smile Until Christmas* (Chicago: University of Chicago Press, 1970), pp. 104–105. Copyright © 1970 by the University of Chicago. Reprinted by permission of the publisher.
[5] Ryan, p. 30.

What problems does the beginning teacher face?

there was very little fighting and roughhousing, or they may have been smart enough, or timid enough, to stay out of the way. Whatever the explanation, their initial encounters with fists, screams, and hairpulling can be, to say the least, unsettling.

Gail Richardson/
Mathematics:

"Near the end of the period, four of the girls who sat in the back were talking, and from the expressions on two of the faces, I knew that something was wrong. I walked over as the bell rang, but nobody would tell me anything, and all left the room for their next classes. I returned to my desk to gather my things when I heard shouting in the hall and saw a crowd of students outside the door. As I rushed out, Mary and Cathy's shouting match became a shoving match; so I grabbed one girl, and someone else restrained the other. I talked to Cathy for ten minutes until she was more calm, then sent her to the counseling office with a note explaining the incident. The counselor talked to both girls, and they were friends again the following day.

"There were several reasons why this was one of the most upsetting incidents of my first year. In the first place, it was the first fight I had witnessed since I was a freshman in high school, and that had involved two boys; I do not remember ever having seen girls fight before. I was afraid that the trouble would continue after school and involve the friends of each; this was compounded by the fact that one girl was white and the other was black. Even though this had nothing to do with the cause of the dispute, it would certainly worsen the character of any continuation of the disturbance in a school where there were many racial tensions beneath the surface.

"I went to my next class in a daze, trying desperately to stop my knees from shaking and to concentrate on the lesson. My nonviolent, pacifistic nature was greatly shaken by the sight of two girl students screaming at one another with such hatred, especially since both were from my class. By the end of the period I had regained my composure.

"At the end of the year this incident looked as trivial as it really was, and I was amazed that I had been so deeply affected by it, even for a time."[6]

Then there is the straw that breaks the beginner's back. If the teacher had been sure of herself, and of the support from the principal, and if she had been rested and understood her students better, the following would not have happened.

Mrs. Bender/Grade 5

" . . . Bobby, my 'friend,' has been taken from my class. He was transferred to a 5/4 class.

"From the beginning of the term I have had discipline problems with him. I didn't call his mother because she was in the hospital having a baby. I don't know who the father is; I don't believe she does either. Anyway, I haven't been able to contact her. I did, however, speak to the guidance counselor, Mrs. Rogers, about him and she's been watching him for a while. She's started a file on him but I haven't seen it yet.

[6] Ryan, pp. 70–71.

What would you do?

You are a first-year female teacher, in a ninth grade English course. As the first semester proceeds you notice that Fred has a crush on you. He is constantly volunteering to help you pass out papers, and lingers after class each day to talk to you. He found out your home address and came to visit you one Saturday morning. His actions are becoming obvious to the other students, who are starting to kid him about his infatuation.

What would you do?

You are generally recognized as one of the most popular teachers on campus. The students look upon you as a friend who can be trusted, and you have told them that if they ever have problems, school-related or personal, they should feel free to come to you. One day Maryanne, a junior in one of your classes, seeks you out. She is close to hysteria, and tells you that she is ten weeks pregnant. You are the first person she has told. She begs you for advice, but insists you do not tell her parents.

What would you do?

The school in which you are teaching has recently been integrated. There are seven black students in one of your classes. Because you fear alienating the blacks and being accused of prejudice, you make special efforts to treat them fairly. One day three of your white students come to see you and accuse you of coddling the blacks and discriminating against whites.

What would you do?

You teach in a school that uses a letter grading system. You have assigned your students a term paper. You know that one of your students has spent hours and hours on his report, but its quality is quite poor. The student has already expressed his hope that you will take effort into account when grading the reports.

What would you do?

You are the same teacher described in case number four. When you assigned the term paper you distributed a sheet containing all the necessary information about the assignment, including the due date. All but two of the reports were handed in on time, and those were both a week late. Adequate time was allowed for the completion of the paper.

What would you do?

Your seventh-grade students are all reading silently in their seats. Suddenly you notice that two of the boys are pushing and shoving each other. One of the boys, obviously very angry, shouts out a string of obscenities at the other. By this time all of the students are watching the incident. When the swearing is over, all eyes turn toward you.

What would you do?

What problems does the beginning teacher face?

"Tuesday was an impossible day for me. I just didn't know what I was going to do with him. *I came home. I was hysterical. I cried all afternoon, all evening, and all night. I really felt that this was the end. I was not going back and what was the sense of knocking myself out? It wasn't worth it. Here I was trying to help people. They don't want to accept you and this is exactly what I felt, very useless* [author's emphasis]. I felt that I was not a teacher; I was a policeman. What did I need this aggravation for?

"Wednesday, everything was fine. The class was marvelous. There was no problem.

"Thursday, again, because of Bobby, everything went wrong. He had stolen . . . well, I didn't actually see him and couldn't accuse him . . . but paper clips were missing from my desk and while we were going up the stairs at lunchtime Bobby was throwing paper clips at the other children. I was afraid that one of these clips would end up in someone's eye. But, too, it was just one of those things. Everything that he did really got under my skin. I'd gotten to the point where I just wanted to take him and throw him down the flight of stairs we were on. He was just impossible!

"On that same day, Mrs. Rogers, the guidance counselor, passed by my room to observe Bobby. He was in his seat so she just really couldn't understand what my fussing was all about. It just so happened that when she came in, he was in his seat taking a diagnostic test in math that I had prepared. She questioned me as to what was wrong and why I was so upset. I explained exactly what he was doing and told her that I just couldn't take it any more. 'It's either him or me. I won't continue this way any more,' I said, 'because I'm becoming a manic-depressive. Monday, I go home; I'm fine. The next day I'm just very, very upset. I can't deal with my feelings any more.' Well, she sent me out of the room and said that I should take a rest. She said she felt that I was very upset. She knew it! I'm sure she could see it!

"I went down to the office to rexograph some stencils I had prepared and the principal walked in. All he had to do was say something nice to me! And that's exactly what he did. He said, 'Well, Mrs. Bender, how is it going?'

"I just started to cry. I could not control my feelings. I couldn't control anything. He asked what the problem was and all I had to say was, 'Bobby.'

"'Is it just Bobby?' he said.

"'Yes, it's just Bobby.'

"He said, 'Well, if this is truly the problem, Bobby will be taken out of your class tomorrow. There is no need for you to feel so upset about it.' Then he sort of scolded me saying, 'Why didn't you come to me before and tell me about this? Don't let things go so far. You are a human being; you have feelings. This isn't the way to react.'

"Now I was so upset that I just wanted to be left alone. I didn't want him to come near me. I didn't even want to go back to the classroom. I just wanted to go home.

From Herbert Kohl's 36 Children

My alarm clock rang at seven thirty, but I was up and dressed at seven. It was only a fifteen-minute bus ride from my apartment on 90th Street and Madison Avenue to the school on 119th Street and Madison.

There had been an orientation session the day before. I remembered the principal's words. "In times like these, this is the most exciting place to be, in the midst of ferment and creative activity. Never has teaching offered such opportunities . . . we are together here in a difficult situation. They are not the easiest children, yet the rewards are so great—a smile, loving concern, what an inspiration, a felicitous experience."

I remembered my barren classroom, no books, a battered piano, broken windows and desks, falling plaster, and an oppressive darkness.

I was handed a roll book with thirty-six names and thirty-six cumulative record cards, years of judgments already passed upon the children, their official personalities. I read through the names, twenty girls and sixteen boys, the 6-1 class, though I was supposed to be teaching the fifth grade and had planned for it all summer. Then I locked the record cards away in the closet. The children would tell me who they were. Each child, each new school year, is potentially many things, only one of which the cumulative record card documents. It is amazing how "emotional" problems can disappear, how the dullest child can be transformed into the keenest and the brightest into the most ordinary when the prefabricated judgments of other teachers are forgotten.

The children entered at nine and filled up the seats. They were silent and stared at me. It was a shock to see thirty-six black faces before me. No preparation helped. It is one thing to be liberal and talk, another to face something and learn that you're afraid.

The children sat quietly, expectant. Everything must go well; we must like each other.

Hands went up as I called the roll. Anxious faces, hostile, indifferent, weary of the ritual, confident of its outcome.

Reprinted by permission of The World Publishing Company from p. 13 of
36 Children by Herbert Kohl. An NAL book. Copyright © 1967 by Herbert Kohl.

"I did go back to the classroom, however, and handed out the stencils I had run off and we did a music lesson. But my heart wasn't really in it because I felt that I was never going to come back. What's the sense?"[7]

When problems and failures occur during the first year, the beginner has no backlog of successful teaching to reflect on and draw succor from. He feels swamped, as if he were sinking.

[7] Fuchs, pp. 17–19.

What problems does the beginning teacher face?

John Canfield/History: "It got so that I hated eighth period. I looked forward to it with apprehension and self-doubt. In the eyes of the school, I was not failing. None of my kids were in the hall, and there were no 'undue disturbances.' But I knew I was failing.

"I brought in movies, had exercises with the newspaper, had the class write their own newspaper, did map exercises, and had them work on problems I brought in, but I felt that I was only occupying them—a sort of military holding action. I sensed no growth. I felt like Mr. Jonas, the teacher I had observed the year before on the West side. What a disappointing self-image! I began watching the clock, hoping the minutes would race by. They never did. It seemed like an eternity before the bell would ring. It would finally come, and I would drag myself to the first floor and prepare to get away from it all. Thank God it was my last class. I would be completely drained of emotional and psychic energy. Some days I would come home and fall asleep from four o'clock to ten o'clock. I am sure it was a symbolic return to the womb.

"The next morning I would be reborn again and I would trudge off to school to face another day of trying to be a teacher."[8]

Many beginning teachers think of teaching as an intellectual and genteel profession that will make few physical demands on them. Before they develop the necessary stamina and learn how to pace themselves, many discover that sleep is the only healer.

Linda Corman/English: "Exhaustion—the exhaustion from endless improvisation, endless emotional torment, all too violent plunges and flights between rational and emotional extremes—this was my overwhelming reaction to this first year of teaching. Indeed there was shock—the shock of having a ninth-grade girl announce calmly to her homeroom teacher that she was tardy because she had slept with her boyfriend that night and, consequently, required an unexpected morning bath; and shock at the rage and disbelief I incited in an older student whom I had innocently befriended, when I tried to explain that the reason I wouldn't go out with him was that I was married, not that he was black. And I was often frustrated—when I used subject material too difficult or methods too boring, when class uproars prevented academic progress, when I had spent hours preparing a lesson the night before and nobody else in the class had read the assignment, when the audiovisual department refused to cooperate and confounded my plans for the day. Frustrations were endless, shocks enormously frequent! But beyond the shock and the frustration lay the final state: I was exhausted."[9]

Teachers who teach children from a different culture or subculture than their own experience an especially intense type of culture shock. This feeling is particularly common in this country among middle class Americans who teach poor blacks, Latinos, or Indians. All of the turmoil of learning to teach is compounded by lack of understanding; all too frequently one loses appreciation of the style and values of the students one is teaching.

[8] Ryan, p. 43.
[9] Ryan, p. 126.

Miss Kooper/Grade 6: "I really can't explain why Jimmy is particularly more troublesome than the other children. It's just that he calls out all the time. He calls out in Spanish; he speaks Spanish. He shows no respect for me. So far, two weeks in a row, I've given a spelling test and he doesn't take it. He just sits there with the paper. He creates a disturbance. He dances in the halls, he dances around, he sings, he calls out. He's always talking! He's always doing something wrong!

"On Monday . . . well, Monday is always just a bad day. We have library on Mondays and somehow or other they're quiet while they're in the room. I don't have much of a discipline problem while they're in the room but the minute we go outside someplace it's just bedlam.

"We went down to the library and Jimmy was his usual talkative self. He just talked and talked and talked the entire period. I yelled at him. The library teacher yelled at him; she threatened him that he was not going to be able to come to the library any more. It didn't make a bit of difference. He rambled on and on and on in Spanish. He didn't pay any attention to what anybody told him.

"Then later, as we were coming up the stairs he was talking and talking and dancing around. He's the second person in line and the first boy was holding the door, so he was right under my nose. I was standing there waiting for quiet and he was dancing around and running up and down the stairs just making a general nuisance of himself.

"I got so mad at him at that moment! I've never really gotten as mad as I did that time. I grabbed him by the tie to make him stand still and he said, 'Man, let go! Man, don't do that!'

"I just held his tie. I think I probably might have even choked him but he kept on saying, 'Go ahead! Choke me, man! I don't care. I don't care.'

"Finally, I said, 'When you stand still, I'll let you go.'

"He wouldn't, just in spite! He just kept pulling away and leaning back. Oh, I was so mad! Finally he just loosened his tie and took it off his head and I was left standing there with his tie in my hand.

"This kept going on. As we walked through the halls Jimmy talked and talked. I said to him, 'Jimmy, do you remember what Mr. Stark said about putting you back into the fifth grade? Don't think I wouldn't do it!'

"He said, 'Man, you wouldn't send me to the fifth grade. Nobody sends me to the fifth grade. I don't care.'

" 'Well, we'll see,' I said.

"He was imitating me now and he said, 'I don't care. I'd rather go to the fifth grade anyway. I'd rather have a man teacher; men teachers are more fun. I wish you could put me in the fifth grade.'

61   What problems does the beginning teacher face?

"This continued on and on in front of the whole class and I was really mad.

"Finally, Mr. Stark came along. I just looked at him and said, 'I don't want this boy in my class!' "[10]

It is possible that if Miss Kooper had had some understanding of the Hispanic concept of *machismo*—a sense of pride associated with one's masculinity—she would have realized why Jimmy was acting as he was and certainly would not have offended his budding sense of manhood by laying hands on him in front of his friends.

Although the beginning teacher's culture shock is an intense and troubling experience, it is usually a one-time event confined to the first year of teaching. It can be painful, but it doesn't last forever. This is perhaps the reason why people who are contemplating teaching are told, "If you decide to become a teacher, promise yourself that you will teach for two years before making a definite decision about leaving or continuing in the profession."

The administration: the face of the bureaucracy

Most of us, as elementary and secondary school students, had rather simplistic notions of administrators. The superintendent was a vague presence we occasionally glimpsed in the hall talking to one of the staff or in front of a microphone on ceremonial occasions. The principal was much more a part of our school lives as someone beloved or feared, and occasionally both. Even though the principal was near at hand, our student's-eye view of him was rather one-dimensional. He represented AUTHORITY. In all but the rarest instances he stood directly beyond the teacher, supporting the teacher and the system. When as students we saw the principal in his office on official business, it usually meant we were in trouble.

The new teacher's relationship with the principal is not so simple, however. The school principal looms quite large in the life of a beginning teacher, and the teacher-principal relationship (and to a lesser degree the teacher's relationship with vice-principals, department chairmen and master teachers) is many-faceted. The principal is, first of all, a colleague, a fellow educator[11] joined with you in the common task of bringing civilization to the young. You are both professionals. You are part of a common tradition. You automatically share common goals (i.e., improving the educational opportunities of children) and attitudes (i.e., people engaged in the important work of educating the young need more support from the public than they get).

The principal is the official leader. He makes decisions, or acts as the funnel for the decisions of higher authorities. Decisions made by teachers or students are

[10] Fuchs, pp. 27–28.
[11] One of the little curiosities of educationese, the official language of schools, is that administrators refer to themselves as educators—as in "leading educator" and "innovative educator"—and teachers are simply called teachers. Occasionally, when the principal attempts to rally the teacher-troops, he broadens it to "we educators. . . . " Some few, guilty, perhaps, for having left the classroom, insist that they are still "just teachers." One thing you can count on, though: "educators" invariably make more money than teachers.

*A young social studies teacher was applying for a job in a small rural commu-
nity. He was asked by one of the board members whether he thought the world
was round or flat. He replied, "Sir, I can teach it either way."* The Young Sage

normally checked with him. He speaks for the school community to the superintendent, the press, and the local citizens. While he is not necessarily the *de facto*
leader, the most influential person in the school community, he frequently is.
Nothing is ever quite "official" unless the principal has been involved.

He is a helper. He can dispense information and materials, and as an experienced teacher, he is source of tips, shortcuts, and helpful suggestions. The
teacher can directly request his help. He also visits teachers' classrooms and,
ordinarily, holds conferences with them. He is there to aid the beginning teacher
encountering difficulties and confusion.

He is the initiator. A school system is a bureaucracy whose long arm extends
from the State Commissioner of Education to the local district superintendent of
schools to the individual school principal. The principal, in effect, acts in behalf
of the bureaucracy by introducing you into the bureaucratic life of school and
teaching you how to behave.

He is the crisis manager. When something happens which you cannot handle,
the principal's office is where you naturally turn for help. Besides being a potential source of help, the principal needs to know about crises in the school in
order to stay in touch with its problems.

He is the facilitator. Schools run on things—pencils, books, paper, heat, hot
lunches, sanitary toilets, lights, construction paper, window poles, money, and
keys. It is the principal's job to keep you supplied so that you, in turn, can carry
out the aims of the school.

He is the reward-dispenser. He is frequently the person who actually hires you.
Later, he can give or withhold compliments on your performance and give or
withhold extracurricular duty assignments. It is he who assigns classes to you,
deciding what kind of children you will teach and whether or not they will be at
the level or in the subject for which you are prepared.

He is the judge. His is the official view of "how you are doing." The first-year
teacher is neither a permanent member of the faculty nor a permanently-certified
member of the teaching profession. The principal makes decisions about your
qualifications that can have a profound effect on your future in education. He can
enhance or destroy your reputation as a teacher in his school. He can write recommendations for or against you. He can insure that you are not rehired. He can
block certification. And, of course, he can judge you positively and be a very
positive influence on your entire career. Obviously, the principal derives a great
deal of power from his roles as reward-dispenser and judge.

He acts as a buffer between the teacher and angry parents (or, occasionally,
angry students). Teachers can be quite vulnerable to public attack. Parents hear

tales from their children or from other parents and, if they have a question or a complaint to make against a teacher, either go directly to the principal or to the teacher herself. If they do not get satisfaction from the teacher, they then go to the principal. The principal is thus the official "complaint department." This is a delicate position, requiring him to be open and responsive to complaints and at the same time to support the position of the teacher involved. Such situations call for the skills of high diplomacy.

He is the sacrificial lamb. If the community, the teachers, or the school board become dissatisfied with what is going on in his school, the principal, who usually does not have tenure in that position, is vulnerable. The tenured staff cannot be dismissed. The community cannot be substituted for another. Thus the principal, who may or may not be responsible for the reported problem, is likely to be chosen to pay the penalty. The ease with which he can be dismissed is, incidentally, a position he shares with beginning teachers.

Having to perform all these roles makes for a complicated existence. The principal of a school today has a most difficult job, and to do the job well requires the strengths of a field general, a philosopher, a psychiatrist, and a saint. In light of the general shortage of these strengths, it is not surprising that the new teacher often finds herself in conflict with her principal. He has to make large numbers of quick and difficult decisions, frequently with insufficient information or time, and he is sometimes wrong. A factor which contributes to conflict between the administrator and the beginning teacher is that the administrator is often playing several roles at once. When he appears in your room to observe your class, he is both helper and judge. He may say that he is there only as a source of aid, but some day in the future he must make recommendations about you to his superiors and he cannot help but be influenced by what he has seen during his "helping" observations.

Teachers

Another potential source of difficulty is that the administrator must be like a ship's captain, concerned with keeping the ship afloat, running and moving in a particular direction, while the teacher, who is there to stimulate learning and creativity, has a different set of concerns. Bizarre or random activity, questioning and occasional chaos frequently play an important part in learning. And it is at this juncture that the administrator who puts too great a value on order most often collides with the teacher.

Therefore, it is to be expected that there will be confusion and the potential for conflict between the administration and the new teacher who is being initiated into the system. The following accounts may paint a picture that is unrealistically depressing. Again, remember, first, that you are hearing only one side of the conflicts. Second, harmonious relations between beginning teachers and administrators don't receive much attention, but they are by no means rare. You should bear in mind that the administrator wants an effective and happy faculty. He wants you to succeed, because his own success depends on your success and that of the other teachers. Nevertheless, some beginning teachers and administrators encounter problems. What follow are reports from beginning teachers.

The beginning teacher sometimes does not know how to work in a bureaucracy (that is, make it work for her ends) and sometimes is anti-bureaucracy. This can lead her into direct conflict with her administrator, one of whose jobs, again, is to train the beginner in bureaucratic procedures.

Linda Corman/English: "The first unsettling relationship I experienced was between myself-as-book-keeper and the assistant principal, who was chief disciplinarian for teachers as well as for students. . . .

"Playing private secretary to thirty-five students was an exasperating but eye-opening experience. For who would have guessed that blanks requiring a guardian's name or a home address might constitute for some young people a legitimately difficult, perhaps impossible task? One boy had moved around from aunt to friend for the past two years, never quite sure where he would be wanted or want to stay. A girl didn't really know if the cousin with whom she had lived since her mother's disappearance a year ago was her guardian or not. And I had never known anyone who refused to reveal his phone number because his mother's welfare payments would be jeopardized if knowledge of her having a telephone fell into the wrong hands. But I did not have time to digest these strange new things, for unfilled blanks kept flowing in. The censure I received for my shortcomings in this role of private secretary was the final humiliation—and a useless one at that, for indeed, I was trying very hard.

"This completely unexpected burden occupied more time than class preparations, or rather usurped the time allotted for class preparations during the first few weeks of school and frequently thereafter. And the assistant principal was the living symbol of this burden to me, since it was usually he who stalked furiously in and out during class or homeroom periods to chastise me for my errors and delays in fulfilling my clerical duties. He also made a practice of sending for me while I was teaching, requesting that I come immediately to his office, where he would point out a mistake I had made in signing a readmission blank. By the time I returned to my class, the always tenuous state of readiness

65   What problems does the beginning teacher face?

for learning had wholly dissolved into a chaos that I could not hope, at least that day, to subdue. Later I discovered that all teachers were treated precisely the same way—and all parents and students as well! I was not being singled out and I was not particularly inefficient. But in the beginning I did not know this and was not confident enough to oppose the assistant principal as, I learned later, everyone, to some extent, must do."[12]

Mrs. Bender/Grade 5:   "Thursday was the day when I almost handed in my resignation. I just felt that there was no place for me to turn.

"Dr. Frost had come into my room after Freddy and Thomas had had a fierce fight in the classroom, and he asked me about Freddy's record. Now, Freddy had just been transferred into my class; he was just admitted three weeks ago. I received his records only last week and I have not had the time to go through them. I told him, also, that I didn't like to make a practice of reading records before I knew the child. He told me that I was supposed to read them and I said that I disagreed. Then he said something to me which really made me feel very, very bad. He said, 'When you have had twenty years' experience, then, perhaps, you can disagree with me.'

"This was the first time I had ever said I disagreed with him. I always went along with what he said because he was the principal and he had feelings and he had experience where I didn't. I felt that he was very wrong talking to me like this and I was very upset. New teachers sometimes see things that are hackneyed or that are in bad need of change and . . . oh, this wasn't a case that he had any right to . . . true . . . I should read the records but I feel that the opportunity will arise where I will read them. Until such time I feel that I really don't want to know, because every child is an individual and he's just justified on his own. I don't want to have in the back of my mind comments made by other teachers. Dr. Frost said to me, 'Well, that's the purpose of the record card. You should know what the other teachers thought about him so that you will know how to handle him.'

"I really feel that by reading a record card you cannot understand how a child reacts."[13]

One of the principal's tasks is to combine teacher talents, student interests and aptitudes, and school resources in such a way that important learnings take place. Sometimes it doesn't happen that way, though.

Ed McGrath, Jr./ High School Science: "I really wanted to teach in an innovative school and one that would allow me a good deal of freedom. I don't mean freedom of speech so I can use my classroom as a political forum, but freedom to try out-of-the-ordinary things, like independent study projects for low-track kids, field trips, visiting speakers, students being given the chance and some responsibility to help other students. Since I'm a science teacher, it was all very safe, it seemed.

"When I went around interviewing I tried to make crystal clear what I wanted to do and what I thought I would need by way of support. A couple of principals

[12] Ryan, pp. 105–107.
[13] Fuchs, p. 65.

told me directly that my aims were a little advanced for them. I respected their frankness. My future principal, however, got all excited about my ideas and said I was 'just the kind of new blood the school needed.' I was really turned on. He told me that he would set aside some money for some of my projects and that field trips would be no problem. The district had plenty of station wagons and busses. With that encouragement and more, I signed on the dotted line.

"Come September, the tune changed. On a lovely fall day I took some of my classes outside and around the school grounds. I was trying to get them to describe the phenomenon of autumn. They discovered that a lot more was going on in nature than they were fully aware of. At the end of the day there was a rather sharp note in my box from the principal informing me that he hadn't granted permission to conduct classes outside. Also, such nature studies must be reflected in the weekly lesson plans. A few weeks later, I got my classes ready for a field trip to the big river basin about twelve miles away. It was originally the students' idea and it fit in beautifully with the unit on marine biology we were doing. I checked with the other teachers and they all agreed to release the kids. Then I wrote to the principal explaining the field trip, its purposes and the transportation needed. I wrote the note ten days before the date. Well, you guessed it. I was asking too late. Such requests have to be in three weeks ahead of the proposed trip, and there are special forms which I should have used (news to me!). Shot down again. After a while, I got my kids (oops! students) all fired up about independent study. They really came up with some great projects. Some needed special materials and equipment, which when added all up came to thirty-eight bucks. I went in personally to see the principal and ask him how to go through channels and order things correctly. I didn't want to lose the money he had set aside for me. 'What money? Oh, yes. I did set aside a little money for your classes, but when you failed to make application for it at the beginning of school, other priorities came into play.' And so it went all year. We kept on good terms, and the principal gave me a great evaluation. My main complaint is that he guards the district's money and materials rather than letting them loose to do some good. Also, he does a lot of talking about innovation, but it stops at words."

A good quarterback is one who can get the best possible performance from his team. A corporate executive succeeds on his ability to make use of the talents of his subordinates. The principal, similarly, tries to encourage the abilities of his faculty. Sometimes, though, the faculty members feel more exploited than enhanced.

Miss Gould/Grade 5:

"As far as the principal and the assistant principal sometimes taking advantage of the teachers and myself, I'd like to give three examples. First of all, there is one teacher who just came into the school this year, Miss Smith, and somehow or other the principal found out that Miss Smith was a professional dancer at one time. This was a big mistake on her part, to let him know this. I don't know if she did or not, but what happened was he told her he wanted her to start a dancing class for the children after school, of course without being paid, and that she would have to be responsible for a program in dancing for the assembly. This was an example of how the principal takes advantage of the teachers.

"Another example is Mrs. De Peuw, who is my buddy teacher and was my cooperating teacher last term. She also is given an awful lot of assignments. She

What problems does the beginning teacher face?

has special course work in library, so she is given the job of ordering all the books for the library and taking care of the library when the librarian is not there. She also, being a very good teacher and being able to get the most out of her children, was given the added responsibility of the science fair. In other words, she is completely in charge of the science fair and has to make sure that everything is going according to what is expected.

"Now, as far as I am concerned, I am in charge of the music assembly and the glee club. My principal went to a meeting with other principals at the superintendent's office and he heard other principals talking about a glee club, so he figured he had to have one to show off too, and I am not kidding, this is just how he feels. Everything for him is show, so he came to me and he insisted in quite harsh words that I have a glee club. Now, I never worked with a glee club before. I didn't know what to do. And besides that, my class is not that bright that they can afford to lose me for an hour.

"I was very annoyed over it, but there was nothing I could do, because he insisted and he said he would make it hard for me if I didn't do it. In this respect this is how the principal and the assistant principal as well try to take advantage of the teachers in the school, and this is why many of the teachers who can do other things do not. For example, the principal put up a notice saying that he would like someone who could teach Spanish. Now, I know Spanish, and I wanted to teach Spanish before I went into elementary school teaching, so that I could teach Spanish, but I would never let my principal know that I can even speak Spanish, because that's all I would have to do and I would get that position, which I cannot afford to do."[14]

The new teacher is ordinarily observed regularly by the principal during his probationary period. These observations, which bring into play the principal's antithetical roles as helper and judge, can be nerve-racking when handled badly.

Anonymous/ Elementary:

"One thing that happened this week was a trip we had taken on Friday to the museum. The trip worked out much better than I thought it possibly could. . . .

"The least successful lesson during the last week, as was pointed out to me by my principal, turned out to be my trip to the museum. I had not had enough time to really motivate the children and tell them why we were going to the museum and what they were to see and really give them the background. I figured we had so many things to cover, and we would get to this after the trip was over. But as it turned out, the principal came up about ten minutes after I got back to the classroom and questioned the children on what they had seen, and where the museum was located and other things like that. The children knew where the museum was located, naturally, but he had asked what they had seen. One girl got up and said that she had seen armor and this was what he hit upon. He's a history bug, and he asked, 'When did people wear this?' The child said, 'Oh, when King Arthur . . . they worked for King Arthur.' He asked, 'What age in history is this associated with?' I knew this was way above their heads, and they just had no perception of what he was talking about. So it turned out he did a

[14] Fuchs, pp. 115–117.

time line with them, starting with the early Egyptians and the Romans and the Greeks, through the Middle Ages, which was what he was asking for—from 1200 to 1600, 1700, and through the modern ages.

"Now this I would have gotten to if he had given me a free hand, but as it turned out he told me that I should definitely have a time line in the class. Yet I feel that these children have no conception of time, and what is the purpose of having it up in the room if the children don't understand? I sort of told him that we'd do it as soon as possible, but my heart is not really in it, and I feel that he's being very unfair. . . . Then he told me, also in front of the class, which upset me no end, that I should have this time line and a corner of my room devoted to our trip. He wanted to know if I had assigned homework, and I said that the children were doing a composition and art work on what they had seen. He walked out without any further comment, but left me quite upset."[15]

Very infrequently, a beginning teacher is foolishly or shabbily treated by an administrator.

Paul Klein/Grade 3:

"During the special orientation meeting for new teachers, the principal told us all that whenever we have a problem to come and see him. He didn't expect us to be perfect and he felt his major job was to help new teachers. Later that week he stopped me in the hall and warmly repeated his offer of help. I really took him at his word. So in early October when I started having trouble planning and finding materials, I just went to see the principal. He was very cordial and, although he talked a lot about himself, he did give me some fairly helpful advice. I went to see him for three short visits. Just talking the problems out seemed to help. I started finding good materials and my classes really improved. I felt I was really doing well and I couldn't wait to get to school in the morning. Then in early December I started getting treated in an odd way by some of the senior teachers. They were always asking me whether or not they could help. Sort of like I had some incurable disease and could they get me a glass of water. It was weird. Finally, I asked two of them in the lunch room, 'Why all the concern?' Well, it came out that the principal had told them that I was having big trouble and he had told a number of the senior teachers to do what they could for me. He had not been in to observe me once. Later in the year he came in for two brief observations (to conform to minimum standards in our district) and he never had time for a conference. He did, however, write up supervisor conference reports. They were lukewarmish and had no specifics. He did mention in both reports that I was improving and overcoming early problems. What improvement? What problems? All he had to go by was what I told him. I got so mad I wrote him a little note to the effect that my self-reported problems had cleared up some time ago and that I felt my teaching was better than that reflected in his report. I could see the handwriting on the wall, though. I started looking for another position, and got one without too much trouble. I liked the kids in my first school and many of the teachers. Somehow, though, I put myself in a box for the principal and he wasn't going to let me out."

---

[15] Reprinted with the permission of the publisher from Elizabeth M. Eddy's *Becoming a Teacher* (New York: Teachers College Press), © 1969. Pp. 53–54.

What problems does the beginning teacher face?

Peers: a mixed blessing

The new teacher is vulnerable to many outside forces and also to his own insecurities. In the same way that a supportive administrator can turn a potentially disastrous year into a year of growth, so too can one's professional peers. In learning how to teach and how to survive in the classroom, one's peers can be even more important. The following account attests to their importance.

Miss Samson/Grade 4:

"I was quite depressed this week and down in the dumps. It was personal, and also felt that the thought of the principal coming in to watch me this week sort of set me off, because he speaks very highly of me and every time I ask him a question he tells me how well I'm going to do and what great potential I have, how well everyone else thinks I'm going to do, and here he is coming into my classroom. He says all these things and, you know, he has never really seen me teach before. I'm afraid to really think of what he's expecting. So I developed this great feeling of insecurity.

"I didn't know if I was teaching correctly. Nobody had come in to see me and I resented this now. I was just on the brink of tears on Monday and Tuesday.

"I had a talk with Mr. Julian. I started to complain to him about how badly I felt and everything, and he started talking to me, helping me with suggestions of what I should be teaching, what they were covering and how he was doing it, and that I shouldn't feel like that, that all new teachers feel like that and that I really can do it. I haven't got such a bad class and I'll be able to manage with them. He gave me a few tricks and shortcuts. I told him what I was doing, and he was telling what I was doing wrong. I have two groups in spelling, and he said I should eliminate that because it's a great waste of time, and both groups could do the same work. He threw a suggestion at me for social studies on different people and the reasons that they come to New York. I don't even know if it's the suggestions or just the fact that he sat and talked to me that made me feel better. I was in such a blue mood and so afraid. The fact that he might just have sat down, that somebody was helping me and caring, I think, might have set it straight and helped me a lot."[16]

Although there are trends toward increasing cooperation among teachers, for the most part they work independently, in their own classroom and with their own students. When they are engaged in their professional work, teachers are isolated from one another. Still, though administrators are the official source of support and help for the beginner, his teaching peers are a much more accessible and much less threatening source of support. A teacher's peers can have a powerful influence on him, especially if he is at the beginning of his career. This influence can, of course, be positive or negative.

On the positive side, peers can be an ever-ready source of ideas and teaching tips. They can initiate the newcomer to the customs and folklore of the school. For instance, they can tell the beginner which administrative requests must be responded to promptly and which can be done late or ignored completely. Their friendship and reassurance can support one over rough days and weeks. They can suggest to the new teacher materials that "work" with his particular class.

[16] Fuchs, pp. 165–166.

They can help with problems like making transitions from one part of a lesson to another without letting the lid blow off the class. They can share their planbooks, and suggest new approaches and insights on how to make up a planbook that will pass inspection. And, most important, they can be an inspiration to the new teacher seeking to gain mastery of his new role. By their example, they can demonstrate what the phrase "teacher as professional" means.

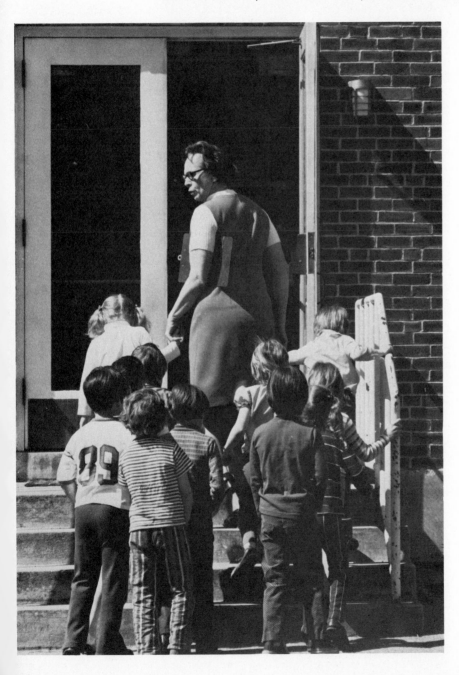

What problems does the beginning teacher face?

And, on the other hand, peers can have negative influence, undermining one's idealism, lowering one's standards, and offering no help at all. Perhaps some capsule portraits will clarify this sad phenomenon. All organizations have people like these. They are a living witness to man's fall from the sublime.

Miss Pyrotechnics: She is a special effects expert. She and her students spend all their time decorating her classroom. The displays are beautiful and ever-changing. The desks and charts are always just right! Even while the class is decorating, the room is spotless. The principal loves to bring visitors to her classroom. She has four special lessons (or routines) she can perform for these occasions.

The Mouth: His hobby is gossip. His arena is the teachers' lounge. He thrives on the trade of secrets, and no morsel is too small to be shared with his colleagues. Nothing is too personal not to be passed on. He should have gone into advertising . . . or broadcasting.

Mrs. Coaster: She has had twelve years of teaching experience. Or, to be more precise, she has had one year of teaching experience which she has repeated twelve times. She still uses lesson plans from her first year of teaching. She knows not the words "outside preparations." She puts in time and nothing else. She has eighteen more years to go before retirement.

The Hoarder: His desk and cabinets are a veritable goldmine of goodies. He has chalk and paper enough to make it to the year 2000. He has materials that make the other teachers drool with envy. He is like a squirrel preparing for the long winter. Nothing is safe from his acquisitive hands. He is exceptionally nice to the office secretary and it pays off. He does not share.

The Big Planner: He is at his best in faculty meetings. He can create out of thin air the most exciting projects and is a champion for all innovative plans. He disappears when volunteers are asked for.

The Sex Bomb: Appropriately, the Sex Bomb comes in two varieties. SHE: In the lunchroom with the girls she is rather quiet, even dull. But when he—any "he"—comes within range, she is transformed. Her clothes suddenly look too tight. Her conversation becomes animated, to say nothing of her flashing eyes. As the situation dictates, she is in desperate need of help or the font of all succor. It seems that he and she need to meet after school for some more private discussion. HE: He begins to stop by your classroom after school to check on "how things are goin'." He's helpful at first. He has a tendency to stand too close. His breath is hot, his hands moist. He knows a great deal about the proximity of intimate little cocktail bars where the two of you could talk about school in a more relaxing atmosphere. (Everyone on the faculty hopes that SHE and HE find each other soon.)

Mr. Up, Up and Away: He dresses nicely. Carefully, that is. His shoes are shined. He volunteers for all committees. It is difficult to tell whether he is bright or dull. He is beautiful to watch. He never makes a false move. He never tells a joke. He never makes a wave—unless the tide is running in his favor. There is never any noise from his class. His students are always busy doing seatwork, but they seem a little glassy-eyed. He, obviously, is going someplace, but his students aren't.

The Ally Seeker: She courts new teachers. Shortly after you have met she tells you about The Great Injustice that was done her. She is telling you for your own good, she says. While it happened to her seven or was it eight years ago, it could be happening to you now. It seems it would be better for everyone if you approach the injustice-doer and slap him/her in the face before he/she does anything to you. Also, you would be proving that you are on the side of Justice. Avoid her. She bites.

The beginning teacher rarely has a dramatic clash with one of his peers. Peer influence is strong, but it is also subtle. Contact with peers only gradually shapes attitudes toward school, toward what constitutes good instruction, toward administrators, and toward the children themselves. The following is from an account of a beginning teacher's first weeks of teaching.

"The older teachers who have been there three or four years usually sit together. Yesterday I had yard duty, which meant I had to eat lunch a little earlier than the rest of the teachers, so I ate with two of the older teachers. . . . We discussed some of the idealism behind teaching. I was told they wouldn't advise someone to come into the school system. When I asked the reason, they told me that the children were getting too hard to handle. . . . They also told me how in a couple of weeks my idealism would have been worn off. It's easy to work with a slow class that is well behaved because you don't have to work too hard. I should not expect too much from these children whose I.Q.'s are in the high 60's and low 70's, and I should just try to teach them as much as I could. . . .

73   What problems does the beginning teacher face?

"Mrs. Holtzman was a teacher last term, and now she's the library teacher. She usually takes my class if I have yard duty or a conference. . . . She told me, 'I feel sorry for you having those kids for the whole term because they're a wild group.' . . .

"There's a teacher whose line is always behind me. . . . She's an experienced teacher. I don't know how long she's been teaching, but she's another one who reassures me that I'm doing well, and I have a bad class, and I have to make the best of it. . . .

"Then an older teacher started in telling me that soon I would start getting letters with four-letter words. The kids start writing letters to the teachers using obscenities, and I shouldn't be surprised when I get these and think they are sending them just to me, because the older teachers get them.

"And there's another teacher, Phoebe Epstein, who teaches the last fifth grade in the level. She's a lot of help to me because she encourages me. . . . We have yard duty together, and we talk. And I always say, 'I just don't know what I'm going to do. I can't seem to cover anything during the day. I just do reading and arithmetic, and that's all I get to cover during the day.' She encourages me. She's really terrific. She tells me, 'Just do what you can; don't be disappointed. Everybody has the same thing. It's not only you.'"[17]

When new teachers join a faculty, the other teachers are understandably curious about how they are going to fit in. Since we all secretly want other people to be like us, it is not surprising that some people get anxious if an energetic newcomer tries to introduce new ideas.

John Canfield/History: "Students were not the only people that I confused during the course of the year. When one is a new teacher, he is looked upon as some kind of threatening animal that is ready to prey upon the older teachers, to turn the students against them, and to subvert the social order that they have carefully constructed over the many years that they have been there. Any innovation that one tries in the classroom or in operation of the school is looked upon as incompetence, negligence, or what is even worse, treason.

"If one wished to take his students on a field trip, he was cross-examined at various levels as to the nature and purpose of the trip and was usually discouraged from its undertaking with stories of control problems, transportation difficulties, and substitution difficulties. If one wished to eliminate a portion of the curriculum for something he felt was more relevant to the particular needs of the students at that time, he was reprimanded for not performing his task properly, or was questioned (even by . . . other departments) as to what he was doing.

"I remember once when I showed an award-winning movie on the concentration camps in Germany during World War II to illustrate a point about man's inhumanity to man during times of war, my students reacted to the movie with what I felt was the proper amount of repulsion and shock. The older teachers, on the other hand, were up in arms about the showing of this film and made it a point at

[17] Eddy, p. 111

one of our very infrequent teachers' meetings. With the exception of the few Jewish teachers on the faculty, who supported my showing of the film, the other teachers either supported the attack or stood by in quiet acquiescence."[18]

Teachers sometimes get in the way of one another. They can grate on one another's nerves. They sometimes find ways of avoiding one another. And occasionally they annoy one another professionally. One teacher may teach another's "specialty," thus spoiling the opportunity for his colleague. Or a teacher may assign so much homework that his students have no time to do the work assigned by a less demanding teacher. And sometimes a teacher may be so relaxed about rules that he makes another look like an ogre.

Linda Corman/English: "I declare at the outset that, though a teacher, I am altogether human: I want to be accepted, to be liked, to succeed, to feel strength or, perhaps, power. One way to do this—the quickest way, I found—is to appeal directly to the students. This doesn't necessarily mean turning one's classroom into a carnival, but it does mean seeking and taking seriously student feedback. A teacher who plays the role, consciously or otherwise, of an overgrown adolescent, a 'with-it' hippie, or the like, often enjoys quite a headstart on the academic, theory-befuddled graduate. Once when I was playing a Donovan recording of Shakespeare's lyric 'Under the Greenwood Tree,' a student observed: 'When we listened to this record in Mr. Krick's class, we turned the lights out and he let us smoke so we could really groove it; this is a drag.' Thinking that I had been quite clever and appealing in bringing a popular folk ballad to my English literature class, my hopes fell painfully at this remark and I turned my disappointment into resentment against the other teacher, who had broken school regulations, I felt, at my expense, making my job even more difficult. Such feelings, I soon realized, were not unusual among teachers."[19]

While we strongly believe that the teaching profession has a larger percentage of dedicated, selfless people than any other profession (excepting, perhaps, the ministry), it nevertheless has its share of rogues and fools. The beginner should pick his way among this field of new colleagues with some care.

**Instruction:
so much to learn**   In an ultimate sense the teacher's only real problem is the failure of the children to learn and to develop. All other conflicts, worries, and defeats pale in significance if the children are learning and developing their human potential. The degree of the children's success as learners is the measure of our success or failure. Although the closeness of the relationship between a teacher's instruction and his students' learning is frequently overstated, it is a crucial relationship. And teaching effectiveness, as we have said earlier, is an area where there are few naturals. The new teacher normally has a number of problems in the area of instruction.

A major difficulty is the sheer newness of the role. There is little in the way of gradual immersion into the role of teacher. After a little student teaching, you suddenly find yourself in charge of your own class and responsible for taking it from the first day of school to the last.

[18] Ryan, p. 45.
[19] Ryan, pp. 117–118.

What problems does the beginning teacher face?

Maxine Bell/Grade 2:

"Now that it is over this whole first year seems unbelievable. So much has gone on. I have changed so. So many of my cherished beliefs about myself and education have gone down the drain or been drastically reshaped. I was so confident, but so ignorant when I started. There were so many little things that I didn't know how to do . . . like passing out papers or assigning them work. I had so many hot ideas and most of them I didn't have the foggiest about putting into actual operation. I was a bug on the importance of individualized instruction. I wrote two or three papers on it during teacher training. I knew all the right words to say about individualized instruction, but I *couldn't do it in my class.* I still believe in it . . . perhaps even more, but I'm just not able to make it operational, to make it go with my kids. Whenever I think back on this year, the image that keeps coming to mind is of a farmer plowing a new field and breaking fresh ground. I didn't have any old furrows to follow. I never knew when I was going to hit against a rock . . . and I did hit some rocks. Sometimes when I expected the plowing to be toughest, it was easiest. And the reverse was equally true. I have to be on my toes every minute of the year it seems. So much planning and adjusting and replanning. I'm glad it is over, and I'm tired. It's been a lot of trouble, this first year, but deep down I'm really proud of myself."

Funny thing about problems. They hurt, but they also make us strong.

During stable periods in the life of a society, there is little disagreement about what should be taught and how. These are not such gentle times. We appear to be in a transitional stage and, while it is not yet clear what kind of curriculum we need, it is increasingly apparent that the standard curricula of the fifties and sixties will not do. The search for effective curricular materials is engaged in by all conscientious teachers, but it is a special problem for the new teacher.

Marion Krug/Grade 8:

"The overriding question of this year has been, 'What works?' I'm in a constant search for materials. It is never-ending. My kids aren't that bright, but they devour material and look at me as if to say, 'Well, what's next?' Our school has a curriculum guide that is only five years old, but it is terribly dated already. The students know a lot of the stuff already. They learned it in lower grades or just picked it up. They are bored by a good bit of the rest, too. I'm constantly squeezing ideas and tips from the other eighth-grade teachers. They are helpful, but they are in the same box I am. Then there is the problem of getting a big buildup on a particular workbook or special unit by a teacher who has had fabulous success with it. I try it and I fall on my face with it. Then there are the kids. They are so fickle. A couple of times I took their suggestion on things they wanted to study and work on. After much work and many late hours, I'd get these classes prepared and the very same kids who were so anxious to make the suggestions now couldn't care less.

"My school district has curriculum specialists. Some of them are very good, too. Particularly the math specialist. He would give me too much material. I'd spend hours deciding about which approach to use to teach ten minutes worth of material. The language arts specialist was a sweet lady, but very rarely available and most of her ideas were really out to lunch. I was on my own there. When you get right down to it, you have to make the curriculum and the materials *yours* before they are any good to you. Someone else's brilliant materials are nothing until you have made them your own. This is hard to do the first year."

Jim   *What exactly do you mean by "the closeness of the relationship between a teacher's instruction and a student's learning is frequently overstated?"*

Kevin   *People often speak as if there were a one-to-one relationship between teaching and learning. This just isn't true. Teachers be-have—question, lecture, joke, drill—in front of their students, but how much of this teacher activity results in student learning? I suspect, not as much as we'd like to think.*

Jim   *We both know that there is little research that conclusively relates the instructional skills and behaviors of teachers to intended student learnings. But are you implying that emphasis on closeness of the teaching-learning relationship keeps teachers from letting kids learn from one another or from other adults or independently?*

Kevin   *Yes, I think we have been overemphasizing the importance of the teacher actively engaging in teaching students. Our schools are organized on that teacher-dominated model, and it just doesn't work that well. It's sometimes valuable, but is overdone. Perhaps we ought to give more attention to the teacher as the creator of a rich and varied learning environment.*

Jim   *I couldn't agree more.*

As the following illustrates, neither homemade nor prepackaged materials are completely satisfying.

Eleanor Fuke/Social Studies:

"My advisor hit upon what sounded like the ideal solution. To relieve some of the pressure, he suggested I use only already-prepared materials. So far I had been creating my own course materials. These I would painfully extract from scholarly books on the subject in question, and then edit down to the vocabulary level of a particular class. These attempts at creativity didn't always stem from a reformist zeal; often there simply were no materials available on the subjects that I wanted to teach and that my students wanted to study. The students suffered a double handicap in this respect. Not only were there no materials already prepared, but I am not an especially creative person, and what I came up with on my own wasn't the most stimulating work.

"My advisor's plan, then, wasn't such a good one after all. To follow it, we would have to forget about drugs and other current topics, because there just are no materials available in cheap, easy-to-read, multiple copies. . . ."[20]

It is not uncommon for the beginning teacher to find himself in conflict with administrators and other teachers over the appropriateness of certain materials or instructional procedures. Often excellent curriculum materials formulated in the universities or by publishing houses are unknown or not accepted in the real world of schools.

[20] Ryan, pp. 140–141.

Men must be taught as if you taught them not,
And things unknown propos'd as things forgot.
Alexander Pope, *Essay on Criticism,* III, 15

No man can reveal to you aught but that which already lies half asleep in the
dawning of your knowledge.
Kahlil Gibran, *The Prophet*

Miss Peters/Grade 4:   "When I went downstairs for lunch the principal came over to me and he took up most of my lunch hour telling me about the observation. He criticized me on two things. Number one, the way that I teach the words—which is by teaching both groups' words to the whole class. This is what I've been told to do in the reading course and this was what the assistant principal told me to do and this is what I myself have found very effective. He criticized this, and the other thing he criticized is one of the drill games which I use and which I have also learned from this course. In short, the only things that he criticized me for were things that the assistant principal had told me to do and things that I had gotten from the reading course."[21]

Another order of problem develops when the teacher begins to doubt the importance of what he has to teach. The prescribed high-school curriculum in American literature is jocularly questioned by this young teacher.

Gary Cornog/English: "My first few weeks of futility with *Macbeth* in the junior classes and with Puritan thought in the senior class were not relieved when I contemplated the prospect that lay ahead of me. After Edwards, American literature seened like a vast, hideous wasteland sparsely covered with stunted trees and unrelieved desolation—an intellectual Nevada—before an author of interest would provide us with an oasis. (Hawthorne, alas, seemed more like a mirage.) I would first have to slog through my colonial literati, then Irving and Poe, then Bryant (I decided to skip him), then Emerson (poor Waldo—so profound, so uptight on Nature, so uncool—I would have a hard time justifying the ways of Emerson to my seniors), then Thoreau ('He must be a communist!' they'll say, I know it; at any rate he's subversive), and finally to Melville. Oh, and of course the *Scarlet Letter;* I almost forgot that one. The menu of our literature would not be complete without that entrée: one has not had a high school education in America unless one has had a pinch of Prynne and a dollop of Dimmesdale."[22]

The actual skills and strategies of instruction can be another problem area. Few teacher education programs have adequate staff to ensure that their graduates have mastered the teaching skills they will need in the field. Most programs are forced to rely on a rather academic study of the teaching process. As a result, the beginning teacher may know *what* to do, but not *how to do it.*

Rita Hodges/Grade 5:   "I'm living proof that teaching is harder than it looks. I've always been a good student. I did very well in my education courses. In fact, I got an A in methods!

[21] Fuchs, pp. 148–149.
[22] Ryan, pp. 6–7.

However, I just about flunked once I had my own class. I really like working with the children independently and in small groups, but once I had to be up front, before the entire class, I'd have trouble. Little things that I had taken for granted became quite difficult to do well. I'd always admired teachers who can ask a lot of good questions and keep things really moving without having to step in and monopolize. Admiring is not doing, believe me! I discovered that asking questions is tricky business. First, it isn't that easy to come up with good ones. Then, calling on someone who you think can answer it or explore the question in an interesting way. Now, the tricky part. Listening carefully to what the student is saying and at the same time evaluating what he is saying and thinking of an appropriate response to his remarks *and* on top of that trying to figure out what the next move should be. Should I ask him another question? Should I call on Lois, who is falling asleep in the back? Should I try Sue who is so eager with that waving hand and always so painfully wrong with her answers? Where should I go? Should I correct what the first student said or get a student to . . . meanwhile losing the train of thought I was trying to develop. It's very complex, this teaching game."

Jean Piaget (1896–   )

Jean Piaget is approaching his eightieth birthday. He is still developing and elaborating on theories that he started to work on as a young man nearly 55 years ago. This man's life work, which is reflected in over fifty books and several hundred articles, has become the pivotal point upon which educational thought and the practice of schooling has begun to turn.

Jean Piaget was born in Neuchâtel, Switzerland in 1896. Both of his parents were intellectuals, and young Jean displayed his own scholarly promise at a very early age. As a small boy, he was intensely interested in nature. He was an active birdwatcher and a collector of fossils and seashells. At the age of ten, after spotting an albino sparrow in a local park, he immediately went home and wrote up his observations and sent them to a natural history journal. His report was published, and, as he later reported, "I was launched."

Once started on the path of investigation and study, he never wavered. Still a young boy, he became assistant to the curator of the local natural history museum. At the same time he became a widely published collector of and expert on mollusks. Upon entering the university, Piaget broadened his basic interest in biology and natural history to include philosophy and mathematics. His interest then expanded from these subjects to the still young field of human psychology. He went to the University of Paris and in the course of his study met Alfred Binet, who developed the first intelligence tests. Binet asked young Piaget to work for him. Piaget's job was to ask children of various ages questions in order to establish standards of responses to the questions. Instead of just recording their answers and going on to the next question, Piaget went further. He probed the students for the reasons behind their answers. This modification led to his major contribution to learning: stages of intellectual development. What Piaget observed was that children at different ages answered questions and seemed to see the world in characteristic and predictable ways. Children at different ages seem to reason in strikingly different ways. From these observations Piaget developed his basic theory of cognitive or mental development. He sees the process of mental development for all people as one composed of four main stages: the sensorimotor (infancy or birth to two years), the preoperational stage (two to six), the period of concrete operations (seven to eleven), and the period of formal operations (eleven through adulthood). Individuals at each stage have a predictable way of thinking about things. Further, the development of each stage is a necessity for advancement to the next stage. For instance, the three-year-old (having passed through the sensorimotor stage) is very busy learning language as a means of representing the environment in which he must function. Whereas a year or so earlier he could only interact directly with the immediate environment, he now can represent in his mind various elements in his world and store them there for later use. However, there are still many things he cannot do. For instance, when he sees certain operations, such as water being poured from a tall, thin glass into a short, wide glass, the act of pouring seems to him to have an effect on the quantity of water. Older children immediately recognize that the amount has remained the same and only the appearance has been changed. This is but one example of a thought process that is characteristic of a particular developmental stage.

Piaget used this basic theory to shed further light on the issue of heredity vs. environment, particularly as it relates to learning. Rejecting the extreme positions that denigrate either heredity or environment, he steers a middle path. He sees nature providing each of us with a predetermined, genetically programmed mechanism that directs us to go through the specific stages of mental development mentioned above. In a way, the child unfolds according to a schedule and in accord with a general plan. Environment plays a key role, in that the child needs a certain kind of environment at each stage of development. In order to mentally progress through the stages he needs to manipulate and interact with variety of environmental elements. To eventually learn to conceptualize the conservation of water as it goes from a tall, thin container into a short, wide one, the child needs to have had a variety of concrete experiences where he sees this principle worked out in his environment.

Jean Piaget has made a startling impact on educational thinking. Specifically, he has helped us see that the child is not a passive agent to be impressed with knowledge. Rather, the child is a stimulation-seeking being for whom action is a direct link to thought. Further, his ideas have provided the intellectual underpinnings for the increased attention to the period of early childhood, as demonstrated by day care centers, preschools, and nursery schools, and the open, active learning environment of the British infant schools.

Both the teacher and the student need to know if learning is taking place. This aspect of instruction is accomplished by means of evaluation. Having been on the receiving end of grades for years seems to be inadequate preparation for the job of evaluating the performances of one's students. The marking periods during the first year can be times of confusion and turmoil.

Wylie Crawford/
Science:

"At our school, however, the policy has been to give a non-weighted grade to all students. This meant that a B was a B was a B, no matter what brand of science was being studied. After the first marking period it became clear that few of the new teachers understood this policy, for it was discovered that there were an excessive number of failures in the A and B [advanced] tracks. The question that naturally arose was, how can a teacher be expected to compare a student's scientific savvy in, say, mechanics, with another's competence in general ecology? Even worse, since none of us had any contact with the student in the C track, we were poorly qualified to judge the difference between a D and an F, since we had no idea how most of the students receiving these grades were doing. An experienced teacher, of course, has a better idea of the range of achievement of his students and is capable of grading any one student against a composite picture of all past classes. But I had no such scale to go by, and so had to rely on a somewhat mathematical approach. Since the science grades for all the juniors would theoretically yield the proverbial bell-shaped curve, and since by the junior year most students had presumably been placed in the right track, the vast majority of the C's should fall in the middle track. This group should also contain a moderate number of B's and D's and very few A's or F's. On any given test, then, the clump of students around the average score would receive a C. Medium-sized clusters above or below this C group would receive B's and D's. Then what about the stragglers? How far below the D range would still be a D, and how far below would be an F? Here, we were told, the teacher could be subjective (as he is in all grading, after all). Well, after much soul-searching , I was usually capable of justifying failing grades for students who really deserved them; but this was an unpleasant process, and the sort of thing that should only happen to a teacher once every few months, just in time for report cards."[23]

Becoming an "evaluator" is easier for some than for others. For a few the evaluation process is a source of great anguish and self-doubt.

Mary Cornog/English:

"So absorbed was I in the day-to-day crisis that it came as a great shock to me to discover, close to the end of the first grading period, that I really did not have much data upon which to base a fair evaluation of my students. Having been some six years removed from the high-school environment myself, and having in the interim become accustomed to the mid-term exam, final exam, term paper routine of college course work, I had not given much thought to the matter of tests and papers when I began to teach. More because of a desire to vary routine class activities than to discover the effectiveness of my teaching, I had given quizzes to the juniors on *Macbeth* and one or two short theme assignments to the seniors. I recall noting with some embarrassment the sparseness of little red marks in my grade book in comparison with the handsome display of the same in the grade books of other teachers. The end of the first grading period, consequently, was a very trying experience for me.

"It was puzzling to me how experienced teachers could grade as much student work as their grade books indicated. I found it extremely difficult at first to grade just one theme. Just as I feared making students mad at me by taking disciplinary action, so I also feared their ire as a result of the low grades I might give them on papers and tests. I think I rationalized this scruple (if that is what it was) by saying to myself, 'Who am I to judge the excellence of a student's work?' Obviously the consequence of carrying this sort of philosophy to various logical conclusions would be complete withdrawal from all evaluative activities—i.e.,

[23] Ryan, pp. 90–91.

What problems does the beginning teacher face?

who am I to judge the worth of this presidential candidate; who am I to judge the sourness of this milk, etc. But at the time, that way of thinking had a definite appeal to my propensity for self-doubt."[24]

Students: friends and fiends

What schools are all about is children. They are at the core of the teacher's sense of achievement or dissatisfaction. They are her victory and her defeat. So much of a teacher's work involves children that it is impossible that she *not* have problems with them. It is difficult, if not dangerous, to deal with such a complex and important topic in the space we have allotted. The subject involves so many variables: the personalities of different teachers; the ages of the children, all the way from nursery schoolers to high-school seniors; differences in the amount of contact a teacher has with her students, which can vary from all day every day to the once-a-week visits of a specialist teacher. In short, the complexity of the topic is outweighed only by its importance to the teacher's success and satisfaction.

The Minnesota Teacher Attitude Inventory, a test frequently given to college students planning to become teachers, is designed to measure attitudes that

[24] Ryan, pp. 8–9.

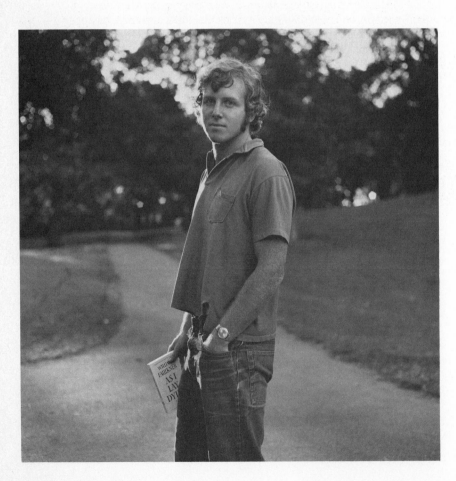

Teachers

predict how well they will get along with students in interpersonal situations. Indirectly, it attempts to indicate how well satisfied the test-taker will be with teaching as a vocation.[25] The test has been a very popular instrument for research on teaching, and has been used in over fifty research studies. One of these studies had curious results:

Large numbers of college students in teacher education programs and a group of over 100 beginning teachers were given the test. The test asks many questions dealing with positive attitudes and feelings of warmth toward one's potential students. The test results show—and they show this very clearly—that the longer college students stay in teacher training programs the more positive and warm their attitudes toward students become. But among beginning teachers there is a sharp drop in positive attitudes toward students. In fact, beginning teachers' scores are significantly lower than those of students just entering teacher training. In other words, as people enter training, their attitudes toward students are positive and become increasingly so until they enter their own classrooms, when their attitudes become sharply less positive.

Why does this happen? How do you explain this phenomenon? As at a number of other points throughout this book, we would like you to stop reading for a moment and jot down some hypotheses about why beginning teachers' attitudes change this way.

_____

_____

_____

_____

_____

_____

_____

_____

_____

What happens between the time one is a college student preparing to teach and the time one actually becomes a teacher is undoubtedly a complicated series of events. We would like to offer our own hypothesis on the issue. College students alternate between being highly idealistic and highly realistic in their outlooks. However, when they enter teacher training, most become very idealistic (thank God!) about children and education. They believe deeply that teachers should have warm relations with students, making the classroom more relaxed and more responsive to the needs of students than it normally is. As the college student takes more education courses and observes in classrooms, his views of children

[25] N. L. Gage, ed., *Handbook of Research on Teaching* (Chicago: Rand McNally, 1963), p. 509.

What problems does the beginning teacher face?

become more idealistic and, as a result, more positive. By graduation, the rose-colored glasses are firmly affixed.[26] Also, he has usually managed to completel shut out some of the more realistic memories of his own childhood and adolescence. He forgets that he joined with the other seventh-graders to put four tacks on Miss Derriere's chair. He blots out all the juicy stories, most of which he knew were untrue, about the young home economics teacher. He forgets about how he enjoyed reading (writing?) obscenities about his math teacher on the lavatory wall. They all forget how cruel kids can be to kids.

"Alice, we've decided that from now on we're going to call you Fatso Alice. . . . Why are you crying, Fatso Alice?"

"We started this club, Roger, and it's called the Red Devils. But you can't be part of it because you smell real bad, Roger."

"Pimples! Pimples! Earl has lots of pimples. . . . Boy, look at old Earl run. An he's crying, too. What a sissy dope."

"My mother's a *what?!!*"

"I can always spot a fruit. I can tell Paul's one just by the way he walks."

Need we say more? Just think back over your experiences with, and as, children in and out of schools. Children are a mixed bag. So is the behavior of an individual child. One day he is eligible for canonization and the next day cannons should be aimed at him. Somehow, though, the dark side of human nature recedes from view during teacher education. Fear not. It reappears. The beginning teacher rediscovers human fallibility, in her children and in herself, and the result is that her affirmative attitudes toward children plummet. Normally positive attitudes make a comeback, although they rarely regain the heights they reached during the latter stages of teacher training.

A thorough discussion of the teacher-student relationship would take several vol umes. Because of space limitations, we will restrict our attention to three areas: discipline, social distance, and sex.

Discipline

Classroom control, classroom management, or discipline (pick your euphemism is one of those problems that shouldn't exist. After all, school is an opportunity fo children. The teacher works hard to help them. It's simple: the teacher is there to teach and students are there to learn. Unfortunately, though, things do not work out this way.

The great majority of schools—whether kindergartens or high schools—are organized with the expectation that the teacher will be "in charge" of her class.

---

[26] This analysis does not, we fear, account for the Lundquist Effect, named after our good friend, Ernie Lundquist. Ernie deviated (as is his habit) from the normal. As Ernie progressed through teacher trainin he began to dislike children more and more. By the time he graduated he had a well-developed distas for, as he called them, "the little creeps." So Ernie decided not to become a teacher. He became an ad ministrator. However, Ernie found sitting in his office quite lonely. The only people who came to see hir were children. As Ernie talked to the children about what his school was really like, he gradually came to like, and eventually, to love children. But as for the teachers . . .

You may not like this, and there are things you can do about it.[27] But it is still what is generally expected of a teacher by the children, the administration, and peers. (We will return to this matter of expectations in the section on social distance.) Few (and lucky) are the teachers who do not have to come to grips with their role as disciplinarian.

A discipline problem occurs when the expected pattern of classroom behavior is violated. Normally, a breach of discipline is an overt act by one or more students that distracts attention from or interrupts the performance of the task at hand. Discipline problems are endemic to the first-year teacher. High-school students report that discipline is the most serious weakness of first-year teachers.[28] Most supervisors and administrators (not to mention elementary students) would agree. The basic explanation for this phenomenon is simply that first-year teachers have had little practice in being "in charge." Few college students have had much opportunity to give orders, coordinate the activities of a group of people, or tell others to do such things as "Quiet down," or "Stay in your seat!" Young women are often particularly unaccustomed to leadership roles. Students, on the other hand, are accustomed to being taught by experienced teachers who know how to control them, usually rather effortlessly. Further, students can sense inexperience and hesitancy in a new teacher. Finally, school is not all fun and games for children and they can get restless and bored. (Remember when you were in elementary and secondary school. Remember how long the school day was, how long you had to sit still at a stretch, and how much you had to do that didn't interest you.) These conditions, plus the potential for friction in any group of so many people, make it almost inevitable that the first-year teacher have some trouble establishing the kind of productive relationship with students that she seeks.

nonymous/
ementary:

"I had trouble with Roberto at the first of this week. He sits right in front of me . . . and he can talk to me. I'll be sitting at my desk, and he'll look over and take something from my desk. If I'm standing up and put something on my desk, he'll have to see what it is. He talks out constantly if I'm giving a lesson, without raising his hand, and he'll have the answers. He'll have wisecracks—like if I yell at someone to do something, he'll turn around and yell. I have my own little assistant teacher in there, and I keep saying, '*I'm* the teacher, not you. . . . Why are *you* telling them what to do?'"[29]

ylie Crawford/
cience:

"In the beginning, my fears about discipline and class control were abated. Instead of finding students who were organized for an all-out, massed offensive, I found students who wished for the most part to be left alone; instead of finding students who were outspoken and arrogant, I found students who were yielding and eager not to 'make waves.' For the first week or two, the vast majority of my students just sat, seemed to listen attentively, and asked questions when called for. . . .

". . . my ideal classroom was one in which everyone was happy, where everyone felt free to speak out when he had something important to say, without fear of

[27] See Herbert Kohl, *The Open Classroom: A Practical Guide to a New Way of Teaching* (New York: New York Review/Vintage Books, 1969).
[28] Roy C. Bryan, *Reactions to Teachers by Students, Parents and Administrators,* Report of Cooperative Research Project No. 668, U.S. Office of Education (Kalamazoo, Mich.: Western Michigan University, 1963).
[29] Eddy, p. 89.

What problems does the beginning teacher face?

Jim   *I wish we could take care of this sticky topic of discipline with a few well-chosen clichés. For instance, "Well-planned and well-executed lessons are sure-fire insurance against discipline problems."*

Kevin   *Or "There is no such thing as a bad child, only bad teachers."*

Jim   *Or "Be fair, firm, and consistent."*

Kevin   *These sayings may be good advice, but this approach skirts the real problem. New teachers normally have discipline problems, and pretending they don't exist doesn't help.*

Jim   *The problem is that if we talk about discipline and control of students, we sound as if we're supporting the authoritarian-teacher model. On the other hand, we probably made our bias clear earlier.*

Kevin   *I'm sure, too, that even teachers in open, more democratically-run schools have discipline problems.*

Jim   *I think you're right. Let's get to it.*

harsh criticism or ridicule from me or from his fellows. To create such a situation it was only natural to smile, and so I did. And eventually, the class did too, but in a slightly different way. As the first month passed, the routine and boredom of even this school began to set in. Many of the students did not understand why they were required to take four years of science (or English, or physical education, for that matter). The happy, relaxed, loosely-disciplined class which I had seen developing began to take strange and subtle turns in the wrong directions. The students were not just happy and relaxed, they were content and almost asleep. I started to get the message: their natural curiosity had not been aroused. I tried to spice up my presentations and asked more questions of individuals in the class, but this seemed to no avail. The symptoms persisted—one student would be looking out the window; another student would be sitting on a table when there were chairs still available; two girls would be gossiping just a little too loud, and would continue even when I approached and finally stood right next to them. While these were noticeable changes, no one of them was objectionable enough to make a big fuss about. After all, my own concept of the ideal classroom atmosphere was broad enough to allow for occasional disinterested students. There would be days when they, too, would become involved and some other students would lose interest. Besides, in the cosmic view of things, the state of the world today was not going to hinge on the fact that a few minor infractions were tolerated occasionally. Treating the students as adults, I felt that they knew they were pushing my patience a bit and that a gentle reminder would be sufficient to set things straight. And it did, for a while. But soon I found myself giving mild admonishments more and more often, and always to the same small group of offenders. Now, instead of just looking out the window, they were waving to passing cars while my back was turned. Instead of just sitting on the tables, a few were sprawled out on them. My resolve was still not shaken. They would soon tire of such shenanigans, and I could win them back through my artfully-designed presentations. After all, I had expected much worse, and we were still getting used to each other. When they saw the folly of it all, our little testing period would be over.

"In reality, as far as the students were concerned, the testing period was already over, and they had won the game. I was going to be a pushover. And, since the other students had been watching the events of the first month, my list of offenders got longer as my blood pressure got higher. The situation got to the point where I had to brace myself before walking into certain particularly 'liberated' classes."[30]

ocial distance

Establishing an appropriate social distance with students occupies a good deal of the attention and energy of a beginning teacher. Like disciplinary techniques, a correct social distance does not come with a teaching certificate or one's first job. Beginning teachers frequently take refuge in the two extremes of behavior. Many hide their insecurities by acting strict and businesslike, sometimes bordering on being hostile. Others attempt to be completely "natural." They reject the stiff "teacherish" image and seek to break down all barriers between themselves and their students. The first extreme, the overly strict teacher, can give rise to long-term difficulties, while the "natural" teacher usually has short-term problems.

The problem with playing the role of the overly strict, aloof teacher is that it might become a permanent habit. Acting like a Prussian officer might appeal to a hidden need for submission in others. Also, one might begin to believe that "a quiet class is a good class," education's version of "the only good Indian is a dead Indian."

[30] Ryan, pp. 85–87.

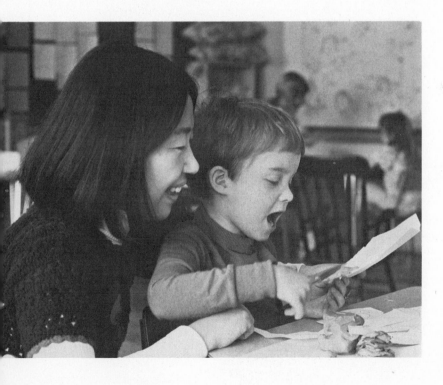

What problems does the beginning teacher face?

Eighth grade rebel

Our actions are like pebbles dropped in a pool. After the in tial splash, the ripples go on and on. The young teacher in this true account acted to solv a problem and the effects of her efforts are still reverberating.

Eighth grade was my rebellious year, a year of testing authority to its breaking point. For Miss B., a young and inexperienced teacher of English, the battle was lost before the fighting began. After several weeks, I was determined to humiliate her, to destroy what little domination she had over the class and over me. I talked loudly to my neighbor during grammar lectures, handed in assignments only when the mood moved me, and popped chewing gum into my mouth every day before class, despite almost daily requests to throw it in the wastebasket.

My relationship with Miss B. grew more and more strained and finally reached a crisis in early May when each pupil was required to write an autobiography for the permanent school record. Since it was to be a major production, Miss B. gave us several weeks to plan, prepare, and write. At first I had great plans for my life story. It was to be full of drama and humor, eloquence, and symbolism.

But it was spring and my mind always seemed to slip out the window with the first lazy flies. Besides, I kept telling myself, I didn't care. The day before the papers were due, Miss B. called me up to her desk.

"Well, how's your autobiography coming? I haven't seen you working on it much during class."

I shrugged my shoulders. "Oh, it's O.K."

"May I see what you have, please?"

I found a rough outline I had made two weeks before and defiantly presented it to her.

"Is this all you have?"

I nodded. She gazed out the window for a long time, then sighed and turned to me, "I want to see you at 3:30. Be prepared to stay a while."

War was finally declared.

When I came in that afternoon, she was working at her desk. She motioned me to a seat, sat up a little straighter, then put her pen down and looked straight into my eyes. "Do you have any idea what a disappointment you have been to me? Or how you've cheated yourself this year?"

I stared back at her, unfazed, and waited for her to continue.

"I have tried hard to understand what's bothering you, why you have completely rejected all my efforts to teach you. Frankly, I'm at my wits' end."

I was silent, determined not to show a hint of emotion. She tried again.

"The tragedy is that you could be one of my best students. You know as well as I that you have both the interest and aptitude for English—if you'd only use them. Why do you refuse to?"

She was hitting hard. I stared at my chipped fingernails. "I don't like English," I finally blurted out, angered at my own sheepishness.

Miss B. countered quickly, "How do you know when you've never given it a try?" More silence.

"Laurie," she said, "I desperately want to instill in you a desire to learn, but I can't force you to do what you won't. Don't you see that you're only fighting yourself? I realize some of what we do in class is boring and repetitious for you, but some of it is important—like the autobiography. It will be a record of the feelings, thoughts, and events of your life up until now. It will be a reflection of you, something that will tell you years from now exactly what you were like at this stage of your life. Don't you think you're worthy of such a record? If you do, I think you should take some time and effort to write one. If not, I'm not going to say any more. I realize that the decision must be yours. What's your answer?"

I gave a hollow little "Yes" that came from deep inside me and barely escaped as a whisper. Suddenly, to my mortification, I found I was crying. I don't know whether they were tears of self-pity, relief, or anger; but I remember exactly how the white circle of Miss B.'s face began running at the edges into her hair and how I bumped into the corner of a desk on the way out.

I never really learned much in Miss B.'s English class. I did write my autobiography, and I stopped chewing gum. But this young teacher's words and our relationship left its mark on my self-centered world. I had seen what was for me a new side of education—that of giving, of honesty, and, most of all, of respect. I don't know exactly when I started regarding education as much more than a one-way funneling tube or when I realized that learning was, in the final analysis, a highly personal decision to give and work and care. I think it might have been in Miss B.'s English class.

Laurie Hedgecock, student, Pembroke College, Providence, Rhode Island.

The problem confronting the overly "natural" teacher is that his view of "natural behavior" is frequently not the same as the children's. The students expect their teacher to interact with them in certain recognizable ways—that is, they expect a certain degree of social distance. They are confused or put off when the teacher acts like "one of the gang." The crux of the problem, then, is that the beginning teacher often wants to be a friend or a pal, while the students expect and want the teacher to be an adult. Students, because they are uncertain and striving to be adults themselves, seek strength and maturity from their teachers. Often they interpret the beginning teacher's efforts at naturalness and informality as weakness.

What problems does the beginning teacher face?

| Joan Poster/
Grade 7: | "Most of my year was spent alternating between being Wanda the Witch and sweet little Miss Muffet. I started out determined to be different from all those cold teachers I had had. I was going to be everyone's sweet Big Sister. I really was surprised when this didn't work. The children didn't respond. If anything, they seemed to be confused. Some of them started treating me like their big sister and I found myself getting annoyed. They became very familiar and started asking me all sorts of embarrassing questions—both in and out of class. The final straw came when one of my boys—one of my favorites, too—came up to me in the hall while I was talking to a senior teacher. Smiling, he patted me on the back and said, 'How's it goin', Miss Poster?' I was mortified.

"After that little incident, I became tough. I was all business. If anyone got close to being familiar, I cut them off at the knees. I really said some nasty things. I was just so uptight that I overreacted. I guess I was hurt that my Big Sister routine didn't work. Later I realized that one reason behind my wanting to be Big Sister was simply that I wanted to be loved . . . at any cost. I guess my insecurities led me to seek love from my students. Anyway, I spent most of the year going back and forth on this issue. One week Wanda and the next Miss Muffet. It was really a strain . . . for me and the kids. Finally, toward the end of the year things began to straighten out and I stopped playing a role. It was much more fun that way. I think everyone was relieved." |
| --- | --- |

Sex

Sex is one of the great unacknowledged issues in the American school. Sexual attraction and romance between students, and even, believe it or not, between teachers, is recognized. But the idea that there might be sexual attraction or romance between a teacher and a student is taboo. It simply is not talked about. This doesn't mean it doesn't exist. Beginning teachers are more likely than others to be faced with this problem. For one thing, they are nearer the students in age. Another factor that makes beginning teachers more vulnerable than experienced teachers is that they are often single, new to the community, and lonely. The strain of the new job may increase their need for affection, and this need may find expression in their relationships with students. In the same way, students often become attracted to their teachers. They sometimes attach themselves to young teachers, greeting them in the morning and walking them to their cars after school. This, too, can be a very awkward situation, in that the student wants to be treated as special and to feel that his affection is reciprocated. If the teacher rejects or embarrasses the student, he can hurt the student deeply.

Besides the platonic attachments teachers can have to young children, it is quite conceivable that a 22-year-old teacher would find a 16-year-old student sexually attractive. As the following account indicates, high-school teachers are particularly vulnerable to sexual attraction or manipulation. Our only advice in this area is *don't*.

Gary Cornog/English: "In one class there dwelt a fair young creature who found me to be an easily flustered appreciator of her many charms. She was a coquette and, to my way of thinking, a dangerous one. She had me at a great disadvantage. While she could liltingly ask special favors of me (such as my continued toleration of her misbehavior in class), I could not cope with her in anything like a spontaneous way. Unless I was in a phenomenally commanding mood, I could expect to hear such daily entreaties as 'Oh, Mr. Cornog! Mr. Cornog! Could you come here and help me?' 'Mr. Cornog, I just don't understand!' (All this spoken in a voice of tender urgency.) She would have her left arm raised, her right arm aiding it, and would be leaning forward and upward from her desk so that (I thought) I would not fail to notice her finer endowments (I didn't).

"'What is it, Julie?' I would reply, hoping the fear in my heart would not be evident in my voice. It nearly always was.

"'Mr. Cornog, there's something here I don't understand. Could you come here and look at it?'

"*Don't,* I tell myself. *Don't.*

"'Read it to me and I'll explain it.' (*From here,* I almost added, but that would be too obvious.) No. She's getting up.

"What's my new teacher like? Oh, she's a tall, willowy blonde, about twenty-five, with green eyes and a husky, sexy voice."

What problems does the beginning teacher face?

" 'I'll bring it up there.'

"She approaches. She arrives at my left side. I note a scent of lemony perfume an attempt at make-up about the eyes. She leans over to place the book in front of me, and some of her long dark hair grazes my shoulder. By this time I feel thoroughly unwilling to answer any question regarding syntax. *What about private tutoring?* I hear my lecherous innards suggesting. Heaven forbid! My frustration causes me to blurt a response to her query, hoping that she'll return to her seat. The class by this time has observed me melting into a limpid pool behind the desk. She must be smiling triumphantly above me, her glory reflected in my devastation. If only she had been as innocent of malice in her manipulations as had been tender in my innocence, then all would have been well. Alas, she was not. She thought it great sport to exercise her arts for the benefit of her friends, and I could think of no way to break the spell. I could not ignore her, because then the class would notice my attempt and think that she had really gotten to me. I could not allow her to continue to dominate me, for then the respect I sought would never appear. Who could respect a hen-pecked English teacher? The befuddled teacher doing battle with the temptress every day — what a tableau! What a cliché. It pained me to see myself in such a humiliating posture. It was so absurd."[31]

Some first-year teachers become terribly discouraged by their relationships with students. Most of us teach because we like young people and want to work with them. When we are rejected or make fools of ourselves, it is painful. Most problems with students are a result of inexperience, and the majority of second-year teachers find that most of their previous problems disappear and they feel very much at ease with their students. Developing satisfying relations with students usually involves some initial uncertainty. However, previous experience with children as a camp counselor, settlement house worker, or tutor can ease the transition. Contacts with children and adolescents before beginning teaching helps you learn about how you relate to children best.

Parents: the soon-to-be-differentiated mass

The parent and the teacher are natural allies. Both are concerned about the child. They are both working to help the child develop his potential as a person, and both want the child to be happy, sensitive, intelligent, and well-balanced. Frequently, though, the relationship between teacher and parent runs amuck and natural allies become enemies. Instead of devoting their energies toward understanding the child and aiding him, they waste them on conflict with one another.

For most prospective teachers, the parents of future students seem very remote. They do not seem particularly important in the light of all the more obvious issues and sources of difficulty. If you try to picture them, what probably comes to mind is a huge, undifferentiated mass of faces. Once you begin to teach, however, certain personalities and types come quite vividly to life. In an effort to speed the process of differentiation, we offer the following capsule portraits of some of the more troublesome types.

Mrs. Mysonthegenius: She has a nice boy. He seems to have average intelligence and he's rather nervous. After meeting her, you know why. If he doesn't

[31] Ryan, pp. 18–19.

you have threatened that if there is one more sound in the classroom you will personally call every parent to complain—and there is a sound.

the principal comes in to observe your teaching and you hear him snoring in the back of the room.

the principal asks you what you plan to be doing next year.

your students chip in at Christmas to buy you a book on careers in the foreign service.

you have your students correct their own tests and the lowest mark in the class is 96 percent.

it is 10:15 and the class has ripped through three-quarters of the work you have prepared for the day.

you return after being sick for three days and the students chant, "We want the substitute!"

it feels like February and it's only late September.

the teacher across the hall comes in and offers to show your kids who's boss.

the parents of eleven of your students ask to see the principal and you are not invited.

unsolicited, your principal offers to write a recommendation for your placement file.

you are convinced you have finally come up with challenging and interesting work for your class and when you present it they chorus, "We did that last year."

after sitting in your class for five minutes, your supervisor starts to shake his watch.

make it to Harvard, she will be shattered. When she is not busy telling him to work harder, she is trying to convince you how lucky you are to have a future Supreme Court Justice in your class.

Mrs. Putdown: The first thing she tells you is that she was once a teacher. She then finds innumerable opportunities to indicate how much she knows and how good she was . . . and still is. She questions you about your "rationale" for teaching this content or using that procedure. When you answer her, she informs you that she prefers the old ways, the tried and true ways. She has dozens of ways of reminding you that this is only your first year of teaching. You wish she would go back to teaching.

Mrs. Latecomer: Her daughter has really been a problem. The girl is obviously unhappy and seems to have made little progress all year. You have looked for the mother at PTA meetings and Open House nights, but she has never shown up. You have written notes home, but they haven't been answered. You have called to make appointments, but she has missed them, having forgotten that she had to go to her Garden Club those days. You send home a failing report card. She complains to the principal that you don't like her daughter.

Mr. Heavyhands: You are at your wits' end with one student and you need help from his parents. He's picked three fights this week and his work is dropping off badly. Other teachers have been complaining about him. You call his father, who

What problems does the beginning teacher face?

roars that he will be right over to school. He arrives breathing fire. You explain your concern, and he keeps socking his fist into the palm of his hand and describing what will happen when he gets his hands on "that no-goodnik." He is embarrassed and hurt by his son's behavior and he has a very old and simple solution. You are sorry you called him.

Mrs. Youthinkyouvegotproblems: She attends all the school functions. However, she never wants to talk about her child. She wants to share her trials and tribulations with you. She heard you took a psychology course once and has chosen you as her therapist. She goes on and on and on. You get a tight feeling in the pit of your stomach.

Mrs. Specialhelp: Her son is doing very well in your class. She doesn't think so. He is always happy and carefree. She reports that he feels school-work is no challenge. She is convinced that he needs special attention. How about after-school tutoring? Maybe Saturday morning? All his other teachers gave him special attention. Aren't you "dedicated"?

The sources of teacher-parent problems are the same as those involved in any human relationship, but encounters are more highly charged than in most relationships. This is to be expected since a child and his future are at issue.

As we point out in Chapter Six differences in perception frequently cause disagreement and conflict between people. A parent and a teacher are quite likely to perceive the same phenomenon in very different ways. The nerve-frazzled teacher perceives a child as a wild, undisciplined, raucous menace. The mother perceives her child as energetic, spontaneous, and sociable. Differences in perception are enhanced by the different circumstances under which they see the child. An apparently quiet, shy child is frequently a chatterbox in the security of his home.

Evaluation is another area of difficulty. It is part of the teacher's job to make judgments on a child's performance, a process which can touch on some deep insecurities. It can wound the hopes and aspirations of parents. That this is the Age of Anxiety becomes very apparent to the teacher in her contacts with some parents who look to the school as the royal road to success for their children. In our competitive society, being average is taken by some as failure. If a child is average, something must be wrong with him. Or with you, his teacher. "How can he get over being 'average'?" The thought that their child could be *below* average is more than some parents can bear. For these reasons, the teacher needs to be especially sensitive when dealing with issues of evaluation, and would do well to stay away from what are, after all, meaningless terms like "above average" or "below average."

Social distance can be a source of difficulty in relations with parents as well as with students. Issues of social distance have been at the nub of much parent-teacher antagonism in recent years. Since most teachers are middle class or aspiring to the middle class, they have little intrinsic trouble communicating with middle class people. But when they deal with parents from a lower or higher class or a different ethnic group, or both, the potential for communications difficulties is heightened. Upper class parents can look down on public schools and treat teachers condescendingly. Poor parents often have had unfortunate and unpleasant experiences with schools and, as a result, regard them with suspicion. Often these parents speak a different language or dialect than the teacher. They are put off by educational jargon. What the teacher sees as his humble classroom is to them part of a huge impersonal bureaucracy. In many urban areas this impression of the school as a cold, unfriendly, and impersonal institution is supported by the evidence: the school doors are locked, and parents have to pass by policemen and assorted hall guards before they are given a pass to see the head secretary in order to see the teacher. The fact that many lower class parents have as children encountered prejudice in schools and found attendance at school more discouraging than helpful makes communication even more difficult. Since they have neither wealth nor connections, these same parents are forced to rely heavily on the schools to provide their children a way out of the deprivation and futility that characterizes so much of their own lives.

Going to school changes children. It exists to help children change in specified ways: to read, to speak a foreign language, to solve problems. And, students do change. They master things. They acquire confidence. And they become increasingly independent of their parents. Some parents rejoice at the child's growing freedom from them. For others, this process of independence is painful. Hearing her little girl talk about how much she loves her teacher may arouse jealousy in a mother, and cause her to act hostile when she meets the teacher. When a high-school student comes home from school with political or social or religious views that conflict with those of his parents, it can cause resentment and confusion. Thus it is not uncommon for a parent to approach a conference with the teacher with a sincere mixture of appreciation and hostility.

The great majority of parent-teacher conferences are cordial, constructive, and characterized by mutual respect. While there may be initial problems of perception or communication, the shared interest of parents and teacher in the child is enough to overcome these minor blocks. However, problems do develop—and they are not always the fault of the parent.

Miss Bender/Grade 5: "This week was Open School Week. Parents visited the school on Thursday morning. Four parents showed up in my class. They started coming in at ten in the morning. They observed the reading lesson and then we moved on to our regular seats and we started social studies oral reports.

"One of the girls, Roberta, gave her oral report and then William gave his. I noticed that the reports started serious oral discussion. Children whose parents were not there wanted to be recognized to answer questions—to do extra things. They wanted recognition. That was the entire thing. It is obvious to me at this point that these children definitely lack love and affection and I only wish I were able to divide myself into so many people and to just work with each one individually and give him the attention that he needs. As far as the children whose parents were there were concerned, they, of course, were interested in showing their parents exactly what they do in school and of course those are the children who are actually my good children, the ones who very rarely give me any problems. . . .

"It was just four parents and I was very, very upset after the parents left, realizing that all of these children are actually lacking love and attention and they put on

What problems does the beginning teacher face?

a good show, so to speak, only because there were parents in the room and they resented the fact that it was not their parent who was there to see what was going on in the school."[32]

It is common teacher folklore that the teacher always sees the parents of the good students, while the parents of underachieving or troublesome children never show up. The implication is that these unseen parents lack real concern for their children (which is rarely the case) and are major contributors to their child's difficulties (which may or may not be true). The young teacher quoted above is guilty of making some harsh judgments and unwarranted assumptions about parents who probably have to work and would find taking a day off to visit the school very awkward.

John Luke/History:

"In the late winter we had our Annual Parents Night. It was a big public relations show, timed about three weeks before the bond issue was to be voted on. All the teachers were to work with students on displays and projects. And, of course, we had to get lots of student work up on the board. The drab old school building looked like the Rose Bowl Parade by the big night. We met the parents in our rooms and gave them an overview of what we were doing for the year. I thought I would be nervous, but somehow I wasn't. I was so distracted and fascinated by their faces. I never suspected that they would look so much like their kids! Or vice versa. And the way some features from one parent and some from the other found their way into their child's face was so absorbing! In the midst of my opening soliloquy in bounced the principal with his flash camera to take a picture of all the gay decorating I had done. Well, he just looked around the room, decided to save a flash bulb and headed for the door. My classroom had all the gay carnival atmosphere of a men's locker room. We 'chatted' about this a few days later.

"When I finished my talk, I handed out folders of their children's work and told the parents I would be happy to talk with them individually. Most of my students had been doing fairly well, so most of the evening went well. The parents of my two prize ding-a-lings didn't show, an event I greeted with mixed emotions. Although I had been quite apprehensive about talking to these strangers, things were going well. I had been trying to be as direct and honest as possible. Looking back on it, I think I was especially intent on being honest because I felt the whole showboat atmosphere and intention of the Parents Night was dishonest. My over-reaction got me in trouble, though. One set of parents hung back. I hadn't met them yet, but I knew immediately who they were. They were Kenny Prewitt's parents. He, poor kid, had gotten the worst features of both parents. Kenny is a great big happy kid. He is not bright and he is quite lazy. All he likes to do is play his guitar, which he is pretty good with. The only time I have gotten any work from him was during a unit on the Civil War. I got him to look up the folk songs and marching chants of the Civil War. He gave a 'singing and strumming' report to the class. But, after that . . . nothing! I'm an easy grader and he was carrying about a C— at that time. Well, the Prewitts asked a lot of questions and I stayed with my straight-facts approach and avoided generalizations. Then Mr. Prewitt glanced anxiously at his wife, looked over his shoulder to see that none of the other parents was within earshot and said, 'Tell me, Mr. Luke. We're both college men. My son, Kenny. Is he . . . you know . . . college material?'

[32] Fuchs, pp. 132–133.

"I didn't know what to say, so I said, 'What do you mean?'

" 'We just want to know if we should be saving to send him to college. Does he have it for college?'

"All I thought of was that here was a guy who really wanted a straight answer, so I said, 'No.' Then I looked at Mrs. Prewitt. I should have looked at her before answering. Her calm face just seemed to break up, to dissolve before my eyes. After the tears came the hostility. 'How dare you prejudge my boy! Admit it, you don't like Kenny. You are trying to ruin his chances. We work hard to raise our only son and then some young know-it-all teacher ruins everything!' Underneath the hysteria, which subsided in about five long minutes, she was right. I had no right to make that judgment. Also, I didn't have enough data. Well, I made another appointment with them. During this I saw that frightening intensity behind their desire to get my class's number one guitar player into college. Some good things came out of this conference, though. Kenny's work picked up. I learned a good lesson, too. Somewhere T. S. Eliot says that human nature can stand just so much reality. I believe him."

Occasionally, the teacher is involved in bizarre misunderstandings. A parent hears something from her child or from another parent which troubles her. Instead of going to the teacher directly, she handles it "indirectly."

nda Meehan/Grade 3:

"I was having a great first year. Everything was going well. I was especially pleased by my rapport with parents. That is why I was so shocked when the principal, Mr. Carnes, called me into his office and told me he had just received a visit from two parents complaining about me. They were the parents of two of my boys. They claimed that I favored the girls. As evidence of this they charged that I systematically assigned excessive homework on the nights the boys had Little League games. I was stunned. Homework! When I did give it, there was only about fifteen minutes' worth. I only gave it about twice a week, and there was no special day. Just when I thought it was needed. I was furious. Why hadn't they come to me! They had told him that they were afraid I would take it out on their children. That was even worse! I couldn't believe my ears. I left the office, stopped for a cigarette to calm myself and went back to my room. I certainly wasn't going to bring this up with my children, but I had to know one thing. I asked the boys what evening they played Little League baseball. Almost exactly half the class chimed out 'Monday and Wednesday' and the other half said 'Tuesday and Thursday.' I went right to the principal's office and brought him back with me. I asked the question again. The boys chimed out like last time, but all—boys and girls—were very confused. The principal burst out laughing and after a few seconds so did I."

Contact with parents can lead to insight and growth or it can lead to sorrow and disappointment.

ohn Canfield/Social Studies:

"It is very easy to forget how concerned these parents are about this matter; however, there are times when it is brought home very painfully. One such incident occurred after several social studies teachers had taken a group of students to

What problems does the beginning teacher face?

the state capital at Springfield. The trip had cost each of the students eleven dollars. This paid for the busses, the guided tour, and the food, and it left about three dollars to help defray the cost of books for the history department that were not provided for in the budget.

"During the beginning of the year, I had thought that eleven dollars would have been too great a strain on the budgets of most of the kids. But after I had seen all of the souvenir buying that went on during that trip, I didn't feel so bad about the eleven dollar cost. However, as we arrived home that night, about eleven o'clock one bus was late. As we were explaining to the waiting parents why the other bus had been delayed, one of them began to talk about the trip. 'I hope these kids learned something today,' he said. 'I hope the sacrifices that we parents make have some effect on what these kids learn. Eleven dollars is a lot of money. I hope they learned something as a result of this trip.' I wasn't really at all sure that they had learned something; in fact, I was sure that there were several who hadn't. I began to feel very bad at that moment. Suddenly all of the fun had been taken out of the trip. But here I was reassuring the man that they had learned quite a bit about the history of the state and about the important things that take place in the state government. For several days I was very depressed by this whole incident.

"Unfortunately, not all parents are as concerned about the education of their children as the man was that night. On the contrary, many are so unconcerned that they make the education of their children virtually impossible. I remember one girl in my homeroom who was very brilliant according to the battery of tests that the students submit to during their twelve years of education. However, she had what teachers commonly refer to as 'a home problem.' Her parents were less than cordial to her and to each other. This was caused by a drinking father and a promiscuous mother. The child, who was a freshman, was just beginning to discover the great potential that she herself had for getting into trouble. And she was beginning to emulate the behavior of her mother in very specific terms. As her school attendance record became a problem, the parents were called in for the customary parent conference with the personnel of the attendance office. The parents did not appear at the designated time. After a second appointment was made and not kept, the child was declared truant. The parents were contacted by a truant officer who informed them of their legal responsibility. Then a new conference was scheduled — this time with the parents and the child's counselor. At this meeting it became quite apparent that the parents looked upon the child as a mere liability, something that was in the way rather than something to be loved and cared for.

"The parents of the child offered her no guidance or direction. The mother wanted no part of the girl. The father was a little different. In his more sober moments he felt a great deal of guilt about his neglect of the child, and he promised to take her to live with him. This never materialized. Meanwhile, the girl was getting deeper into trouble. Her circle of friends was becoming worse all the time, her grades were terrible, and her attendance was falling off even more. The father was finally induced to enroll her in a private school where she would get more individualized attention and where her activities would be more carefully supervised.

"Even after all of this, one cannot help but feel sorry for the girl and somehow resent the parents for their lack of care for the child. Although one can intellectually understand the forces in our society that cause these situations, it is very difficult for one to face objectively the consequences of them."[33]

Problems in perspective

Now, after having had a preview of some of the problems of teaching, you are probably giving serious thought to a career as a social worker or business executive. If you are vaguely apprehensive about becoming a teacher, count yourself among the fortunate few. If you are downright scared of the problems you may encounter, you are in the great majority. All but a handful of people are plagued by fears and worries. One of the authors, in addition to having the more common fear that the children just would not respond when he asked them to do something, was afraid to write on the blackboard because his handwriting was illegible.[34] Perhaps we fear teaching because we know school so well, and because it has been for us a place where we have known fear: fear of being wrong; fear that the teacher would punish us; fear of getting hurt or beaten up; fear that the other kids wouldn't like us. It is to be expected that some of our childhood school-related fears become associated with our thoughts about an adult career as a teacher.

[33] Ryan, pp. 47–49.
[34] Then there is the case of a friend, Jack Shay, who as a teacher education student was petrified by the thought of being in front of a class and discovering that his pants were unzipped. Overcome by this worry Jack finally decided not to be a teacher. The last we heard from him was that he was the star in an X-rated movie.

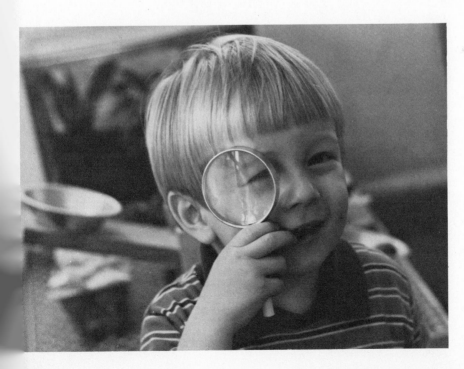

What problems does the beginning teacher face?

What can we do with fears and uncertainties? The worst thing to do is to deny them and hope they will go away. To decide not to become a teacher because of them is unfair to yourself. You may be denying yourself a rich and satisfying career as a teacher. The best approach to these worries is to use them creatively. Explore them. Bring them out into the light. Grow and gain strength from them. Talk about them with your friends. (If you do this you will be surprised at how many friends who seemed the very essence of self-confidence are insecure in certain ways.) As practice in staying responsive to problems and fears, make a list of what you feel, after reading this chapter, will be your major problems as a teacher and then compare it with what you wrote at the beginning of the chapter. Like the other things you've written in response to questions, you may wish to save this and keep reexamining it. You may find as you work with children in student teaching and other capacities that the list changes and begins to shrink.

_____

_____

_____

_____

_____

_____

_____

_____

The other side of the coin

It would be misleading to leave the reader with the impression that problems dominate the life of the teacher—but it is much more difficult to write about joys and satisfactions than about problems. Problems, like an unresponsive class or a bullying supervisor, are concrete and identifiable. Joys, on the other hand, are personal, gossamer-like, and seldom bear sustained scrutiny. The English novelist Joyce Cary has written that joy is not in the great events of our lives, but in the little everyday things, like a good cup of tea, which we easily overlook. So, too, with teaching. Its joys and satisfactions lie in everyday events and small surprises. As a teacher, you may find joy in

- those rare electric moments when you can *feel* the children thinking and *see* them making new connections.
- watching two lonely kids whom you brought together walking down the hall together, now friends.
- getting your planbook back from the supervisor with the comment, "These appear to be excellent lessons."
- a note in your box on a rainy Friday afternoon, written in a childish scrawl, "You are my most favorite teacher. Guess who?"
- correcting test papers and being surprised at how well your students know their work.

- shopping downtown and meeting one of your students, who proudly introduces you to his mother as "my teacher," and being able to tell by the way she responds that you are respected in their household.
- having a former student call to tell you that he has a problem and needs to talk with you.
- getting a note from the parents of the student you have been most worried about that makes you realize your concern is beginning to pay off.
- chaperoning a dance and having your most hostile student smilingly introduce his girl to you.
- hearing in the teacher's lunchroom that your supervisor called you "a real professional."
- dragging yourself back to school at the end of Christmas vacation and being enthusiastically greeted by your students as you enter your classroom.
- agonizing in advance over a conference with your most troublesome child's parents, only to have them back you up all the way.
- being observed by the principal and having your students make you look terrific.
- seeing the look of pride in a child's eyes as he brings up his artwork for you to see.
- surviving until June, being bone-tired, but proud of what you and your kids have been able to do.
- cleaning out your desk on the last day of school after the kids have been dismissed and finding a box of candy with a card signed by the whole class.
- knowing all the time that what you are doing with your life *really makes a difference.*

What problems does the beginning teacher face?

Discussion questions

1 Think of an occasion when you have experienced "culture shock"—abroad or in another part of this country, in an unfamiliar social milieu or, perhaps, on first entering college. Try to remember in as much detail as possible how it made you feel. Did you eventually overcome it? How? Can you trace the progression of your feelings and behavior from the first encounter to the final adjustment? What, if anything, does this suggest to you about ways to minimize the possible effects of culture shock when you begin teaching?

2 Learn to identify the psychological mechanisms people draw on to minimize feelings of anxiety: intellectualization, reaction formation, suppression or denial, rationalization, projection, regression or dependence. Try to characterize the outlook represented by each in one sentence, i.e., "Look what you made me do!"

3 Can you remember or imagine any common types of teachers, like Mrs. Coaster or The Big Planner, whom we have neglected to describe? Try writing a short description of one or two.

4 How do you explain the attitudinal differences between prospective and first-year teachers revealed by the Minnesota Teacher Attitude Inventory?

5 Where do you stand on the issues of discipline and social distance? Do you believe the school should be concerned with discipline? What is your concept of an effective degree and method of discipline? How much social distance do you feel is appropriate for you? Is there anything about these topics that frightens you? What can you do to prepare yourself?

6 If you were to begin teaching tomorrow, and were free to evaluate your students in any way you chose, or not to evaluate at all, what would you do? Be prepared to defend your position.

7 What do you expect to be the major problems you will encounter as a beginning teacher? What can you do now to begin solving them? What can you do after you begin teaching? What do you envision as the joys and satisfactions of a career in teaching?

For further reading

- Braithwaite, Edward R. *To Sir, With Love.* Englewood Cliffs, N.J.: Prentice-Hall, 1960. A British Guianan living in London becomes a teacher in a British secondary school. The book describes his trials and eventual success teaching lower class London teenagers.
- Brembeck, Cole S. *The Discovery of Teaching.* Englewood Cliffs, N.J.: Prentice-Hall, 1962. The book is composed of actual case situations centering on students and teachers.
- Cuban, Larry. *To Make a Difference.* New York: Free Press, 1970. A candid view of the problems faced by teachers in inner-city schools. The book's major thesis is that the individual teacher must match the methods and materials of instruction to the student. The author discusses different learning styles, the teacher as liaison with the community and as curriculum developer, and specific problems such as race, discipline, and expectations.
- Eddy, Elizabeth M. *Becoming a Teacher: The Passage to Professional Status.* New York: Teachers College Press, 1969. A recent study of twenty-one elementary school teachers in New York City. Using research methodologies from anthropology, the author analyzes the transformation from student to teacher.
- Fuchs, Estelle. *Teachers Talk: Views from Inside City Schools.* Garden City, N.Y.: Doubleday, 1969. A collection of teachers' statements about themselves, schools

and learning during their initial four months of teaching in an urban setting. The author analyzes these teacher statements, explicating the underlying assumptions of the teachers and suggesting alternative actions.

- Hersey, John. *The Child Buyers*. New York: Alfred A. Knopf, 1960. A biting satire of American values and of the school as an extension of these values. The author is a major American novelist.
- Herndon, James. *The Way It Spozed to Be*. New York: Simon and Schuster, 1967. A highly personal account of the author's first year of teaching poor black children in an urban setting. Few authors have the sense of the complexity of the human condition and the process of schooling as the author of this book.
- Herndon, James. *How to Survive in Your Native Land*. New York: Simon and Schuster, 1971. This book is a collection of essays of reflections and anecdotes. Different from his first book *The Way It's Spozed to Be,* this book reflects the author's eight years of teaching experience in a middle class suburb. The book is peppered with wit and wisdom and advice on how to succeed in your native land.
- Hilton, James. *Goodbye, Mr. Chips.* Boston: Little, Brown, 1934. A short and sentimental novel depicting the life of a British schoolmaster from youth to old age.
- Hunter, Evan. *Blackboard Jungle.* Cambridge, Mass.: Bentley, 1971 (1st ed. 1954). A very popular novel about a new teacher's uphill struggle in an urban high school. Although quite absorbing, somewhat stereotypic and excessively violent.

What problems does the beginning teacher face?

- Jersild, Arthur. *When Teachers Face Themselves*. New York: Teachers College Press, 1955. Jersild's major thesis is that before teachers can understand students they must understand themselves. He develops a case for this assumption, followed by suggestions as to how teachers can go about better understanding themselves.
- Kaufman, Bel. *Up the Down Staircase*. Englewood Cliffs, N.J.: Prentice-Hall, 1964. An easy-to-read, humorous and poignant semi-fictionalized account of a beginning teacher's experience in a New York City high school. A thoroughly enjoyable book.
- Kohl, Herbert. *36 Children*. New York: New American Library, 1968. A popular account of a Harvard-graduate teacher's first-year experience in a ghetto school in Harlem. The students' initial hostility to Kohl and the ways in which he overcomes their feelings are excellently described. The book also describes vividly the difficult conditions under which teaching is practiced in some sections of New York City.
- Kozol, Jonathan. *Death at an Early Age*. Boston: Houghton Mifflin, 1968. A first-year teacher's account of life in a Boston ghetto school. Tyrannization of the children, cynicism, condescension, racism, and anti-intellectualism are dominant themes in Kozol's account. The book has become a rallying-point for critics and educational reformers.
- Ladd, Edward T., and Sayres, William T., eds. *Social Aspects of Education: A Casebook*. Englewood Cliffs, N.J.: Prentice-Hall, 1962. Approximately twenty detailed cases of actual school experiences involving racial segregation, discipline, school organization, and curriculum reform. Each case is followed by an insightful analysis.
- Leonard, George. *Education and Ecstasy*. New York: Dell, 1968. Based upon the work of advanced innovative schools, brain-research laboratories and experimental communities, this book urges that education become an aesthetic unity of learning and living.
- McGeoch, Dorothy M. *Learning to Teach in Urban Schools*. New York: Teachers College Press, 1965. Accounts by four beginning teachers of their experiences in urban elementary schools. Provides a realistic picture with hard-learned practical tips.
- Patterson, William N. [G. F. Miller]. *Letters from a Hard-boiled Teacher to His Half-baked Son*. Washington, D.C.: Daylion, 1935. Over twenty letters from a veteran teacher to a son who is just beginning his professional life as a teacher. As the title implies, the advice is tough and practical.
- Rasey, Marie Y. *It Takes Time*. New York: Harper & Row, 1953. A novel that focuses on a young woman's choice to become an elementary school teacher. Much valuable description of various teaching methods.
- Ryan, Kevin, ed. *Don't Smile Until Christmas: Accounts of the First Year of Teaching*. Chicago: University of Chicago Press, 1970. A collection of six exceedingly honest autobiographical statements by beginning high-school teachers. A concluding chapter on the first year of teaching by the editor.
- Williams, Emlyn. *The Corn is Green*. New York: Random House, 1941. A moving play dealing with the life of a Welsh schoolmistress.
- Williams, Sylvia, *Hassling*. Boston: Little, Brown, 1970. A teacher's account of two years in the life of her high school. This true story captures a school and its community struggling to deal with student radicalism, civil rights disruptions and the daily problems of keeping a school going.

Films

- *Behavior Modification in the Classroom* (University of California, color, 24 min., 1970). An opportunity to see teachers using operant conditioning and modeling procedures to promote task-oriented behavior. This film shows primary, intermediate, and junior high-school classes before and after the application of behavior modification techniques. It is useful to teachers who feel the need of an organized approach to the psychology of creating a positive classroom atmosphere.
- *Blackboard Jungle* (Films, Inc., 16mm, b&w, 101 min., 1955). Although made quite a few years ago, this film's depiction of a large city vocational training school is still quite interesting.
- *Crowded Out* (National Education Association, color, 29 min., 1967). A dedicated but overworked teacher is no longer able to give students individual attention when a new plant causes overcrowding of a school. Parent-teacher conflicts and discipline problems mount until the teacher is forced to resign. This film is especially directed toward community groups who might help with problems faced by a teacher whose pupil load is too large.
- *The Eye of the Storm* (ABC Media Concepts, color, 25 min., 1970). Mrs. Jane Elliot's experiment in examining the roots of prejudice was based on a hierarchy of eye color. The film suggests one successful method of throwing the problem of prejudice into a new light and forcing students to spend time as both oppressor and oppressed. It should stimulate other approaches to confronting directly problems of racial conflict in integrated classes.
- *The Fish Teacher* (Audio/Brandon, 16mm, color, 1966, France). A delightful fantasy in which a class of French schoolgirls transform their teacher into a fish. A slight undercurrent of "revolution" is evident.
- *Glasser on Discipline* (Media Five, color, 28 min., 1972). Using typical discipline problems as examples, Dr. William Glasser (author of *Schools Without Failure*) reveals some practical solutions, including five basic steps to achieving effective discipline in any school. He emphasizes that discipline is not punishment, but rather the learning of rules with natural consequences for student privileges if they are violated.
- *If* (Films, Inc., 16mm, color, 111 min.). Described as "part humorous, part realistic, and part revolutionary," this film depicts problems which can be generalized to many different school situations.
- *If a Boy Can't Learn* (Lawren, color, 28 min., 1972). A moving film about a seventeen-year-old "senior" who cannot read, this film follows a boy through special therapy at the Pacific Medical Center Learning Disabilities Unit and back to his high school. There, his teachers use special motivational techniques to keep his attention and to reward his progress. They meet regularly to make lesson plans for him and to discuss his case with a Learning Center specialist. This film will convince any prospective teacher that even severe learning problems can be overcome if teachers' attitudes change and expert advice is available.
- *Interaction in Learning* (Indiana University Audio-Visual Center, 16mm, b&w, 29 min.). Different kinds of social interaction which occur during the school years are portrayed through scenes of students in informal group discussions, class presentations and interactions with their teachers.
- *Kids Are People, Too* (Macmillan, color, 43 min., 1973). A cinéma vérité treatment of one teacher's efforts to reach disruptive children. She sets up a special classroom which violates all the traditional rules, and after vivid struggles the children learn to trust her. The whole program is threatened when a supportive

What problems does the beginning teacher face?

principal is replaced by a traditionalist. The film addresses the necessary subject of discipline in what is a humane version of behavior modification.

- *A Little Younger/A Little Older* (NBC Educational Enterprise Code #0034C2, 16mm, b&w, 14 min.). An NBC special report on the youth revolution brought about by the first generation of "television children." The film asserts that the Sixties, characterized by affluence, mobility, political unrest and drugs, will be followed by years when the young will be even more influential.
- *No Reason to Stay* (Contemporary/McGraw-Hill, 16mm, b&w, 27 min.). A look at the school dropout and what he drops out *from.* Through the eyes of a student we are shown both real incidents and fantasies about teachers who "bore to death thousands of innocent students." The film takes a deliberately biased look at the educational system and how it fails.
- *Semester of Discontent* (Indiana University Audio-Visual Center, 16mm, b&w, 60 min., NET). Focuses on the thoughts of faculty, students and administrators at several major universities in order to investigate the issues behind the mounting unrest in the nation's universities.
- *They Call Me Names* (BFA, color, 22 min., 1973). A film to remind teachers that some students may have undetected mental retardation, and that other students who are mentally different will have been accused of being mentally retarded by peers and other teachers. The pain portrayed in the lives of real children who are stereotyped in this way should help make teachers sensitive to different cognitive styles and to the potential damage of labelling students.
- *The Can Do It* (EDC, b&w, 34 min., 1968). Made in the Pastorius School, a public elementary school in Philadelphia, this film illustrates Lovey Glen's progress in teaching a class of six-year-olds in an open classroom setting. By showing five occasions throughout the school year, starting on the second day of class, the film proves that both the students and the teacher can learn fruitfully in the open classroom format.
- *Up the Down Staircase* (Warner Bros., 16mm, color, 123 min.). Adapted from the book by Bel Kaufman, the film portrays a large-city school from the viewpoint of a young, idealistic teacher on her first assignment.
- *What They Want to Produce, Not What We Want to Become* (EDC Film Library, 16mm, b&w, 1 hour). Presents the views of some Canadian high school teachers, students and principals on the problems of "school." The students explain why they are fed up with school, while the principal tries to explain his reasons for running the school the way he does.

Audiotapes

- *Adolescence Is No Time for School* (Center for the Study of Democratic Institutions, 29 min., 1969). For the teacher who thinks that he or she has problems, this tape will come as a necessary reminder that many students are unhappy with school as a learning environment. Kenneth Tollell, Professor of Education at Howard University, argues that students should have experiences and opportunities for learning more consistent with the adolescent period of psycho-sexual development.
- *The Captive Child* (Center for the Study of Democratic Institutions, 53 min., 1970). Peter Marin distills his experiences in the Palo Alto Experimental High School as a lesson in the need to rethink how schools handle the problems of adolescents. Marin argues that educational opportunities in the adult community will be nec-

essary if teachers are to be able to offer meaningful help to their restless or discontented students.

- *The Teacher as Decision Maker* (National Education Association, 3.75 ips, reel or cassette format, 6:40 min.). This brief discussion of the need for teachers to be allowed to take part in instructional decision making is part of a longer tape called "The System." It can be used alone or in conjunction with the other sections.

Simulation game

- *Solving Multi-Ethnic Problems: A Simulation Game for Elementary and High School Teachers* (Anti-Defamation League, 1969). Players adopt the roles of Terry Patterson, a new fifth-grade teacher at Valleybrook Elementary School or of Sandy Johnson, a new teacher at Lakemont High. Among the problems the players encounter are involving black students in predominantly white extracurricular activities, solving conflicts between Puerto Rican and black students, correcting misconceptions of white teachers in an integrated faculty, and easing the concern of parents over an interracial incident. The game kit includes two color films, each approximately 20 minutes long, which begin with orientation talks for new teachers at the two schools and then depict several problem incidents.

Refer to Appendix for addresses of distributors.

What problems does the beginning teacher face?

3

How do people become teachers ?

The purpose of this chapter is to give you an understanding of exactly how an individual becomes a teacher. The chapter takes a womb-to-tomb view of teacher education and explores the forces that contribute to both good teaching and ineffective teaching. Besides giving you a view of how you can be involved in your own transformation into a teacher, the chapter takes a look at teacher education, its problems, its strengths, and some new developments.

Becoming a teacher can be compared to sculpting a work of art from a piece of stone. The difference is that the prospective teacher is both the sculptor and the stone. He begins with a vision of what he wants to be and then sets to work transforming the vision into a reality. The process takes an understanding of the material with which one is working—the self—and the tools at one's disposal. It takes long hours of chipping away at and smoothing surfaces. It takes commitment.

The task of the teacher is to show that time is limited, that in perspective human existence can be condensed into a few climactic moments. Man is a product of limitation and yet always yearns for transcendence. To know our limitations is the foundation of education; to transcend them is the vocation of the teacher (empha-sis added). Frederick Mayer, *The Great Teachers.*

Perhaps this comparison is unduly poetic. We are using it, however, to highlight two points fundamental to this chapter: that becoming a teacher is an active, dynamic process, and that you bear the responsibility for the kind of teacher you become.

In Chapter Four we discuss our ideas about the special skills, competencies, knowledge, and attitudes the effective teacher should possess. The compe-tencies we prescribe can be considered a blueprint or, to continue the teacher-sculptor analogy, a rough outline of the shape of the potential work of art. This chapter will focus on *the process of becoming,* the process of making yourself a teacher. To make yourself the kind of teacher you want to be, you need to know yourself and to know what tools are available to help you and how they can be used most effectively.

Learning to be a teacher

When a college student enters a teacher-training program, or begins taking courses for certification as a teacher, he is much further along in his training to be a teacher than he ordinarily realizes. He has been in training since he was in diapers, and already knows an immense amount about the field he has chosen to enter. Because most of this training is unstructured or informal, however, we mistakenly tend not to take it seriously. Some aspects of this informal curriculum, as well as the formal curriculum, will be examined below. The major emphasis of this chapter, however, will be on teacher attitudes and behaviors, rather than on the content or subject matter one teaches. As you read about the portion of the informal curriculum that is already behind you, ask yourself, "What effect has it had on me?" and "How have these experiences shaped me and my vision of what a good teacher is?"

Ingrained human tendencies

It seems to be a natural human tendency to teach one another. Humanity has sur-vived because we have this special capacity to pass on what we know, and no one is required to discover everything for himself. Man taught man not to fool around with huge furry cats with sharp teeth and blood-stained claws—unless he carried a heavy club or a sharp stick. Man taught man how to rub sticks together and make a life-preserving fire. Man taught man that he could make marks on stones to represent words and ideas. And so on and on.

From the time we can crawl we are constantly being taught by other humans. "That's a no-no!" "You can hurt yourself putting the steel nail file in the electric socket." "You'll never grow up to be a pro football player if you don't eat your turnips." "Say 'thank you.' " "Nice girls simply don't use language like that!" (The rationality or usefulness of what we are taught is sometimes, in retrospect, open to question.) In this way, children learn to respect electricity, eat their vege-

How do people become teachers?

tables, and curb their language (at least in the presence of adults), and they also learn to be teachers. Have you ever observed three- or four-year-old children playing together? Much of their play is imitative of their parents. One child tells another how do to something, or scolds him for leaving his toys around, mimicking the tone and words his own parents use to instruct him. The child-teacher has learned both his parents' message and the teaching medium.

Thus, human beings have survived as a result of their deeply ingrained habit of correcting one another, reporting what they know, moralizing, and responding to the behavior of others.[1] These behaviors precisely duplicate much of what teachers do in classrooms. Teaching skills, then, are acquired by the vast majority of people in the normal flux and flow of life. They are lodged in the very marrow of the human race.

Teacher-watching

Teacher-watching is a major pastime in American schools. By the time we graduate from college we have spent sixteen or seventeen years observing sixty or seventy teachers. Since most of us have experienced traditional teacher-centered schooling, with the teacher invariably facing the students and all the students facing the teacher, it is difficult to avoid being a teacher-watcher. Teacher-watching is a variety of people-watching, one of mankind's most enduring pleasures—but it is often undertaken with more intensity since it contributes to a student's very survival in school. Trying to understand or "psych out" the teacher can be more crucial (and occasionally more interesting) than mastery of the subject matter. "I just can't figure out my history teacher. What does that man want?"

The result of this none-too-casual teacher-watching is difficult to determine precisely. But when we consider the amounts of time students devote to analysis of their teachers' personalities, motivations, instructional methodologies, and general effectiveness, the suspicion grows that its impact is massive. One obvious effect of watching so many teachers for so long is that the prospective teacher compiles a highly detailed mental catalogue of the teacher behaviors he finds acceptable and unacceptable. He has stored up observations of methods and motivational approaches. He has collected techniques of handling children that he considers workable and with which he feels comfortable. Although it is unusual, we are sure there are other cases like that of the young third-grade teacher who had decided when she was in the third grade that she wanted to be a teacher, and had never wavered from that desire. Having made her career choice at eight years, she consciously spent the next thirteen years preparing to teach her own third-grade class. And, as she reported, she had plenty of good and bad teaching models on which to draw. But even those who decide on a career in teaching during their last year of college have been seriously engaged in teacher-watching and have stored away countless observations of life in classrooms and student and teacher behavior.

Media models

First student: "Who's your favorite teacher?"
Second student: "Mr. Dixon—of 'Room 222'."

---

[1] J. M. Stephens, "Research in the Preparation of Teachers: Background Factors that Must be Considered," in *Psychology in Teacher Preparation*, ed. John Herbert and David P. Ausubel (Toronto, Ont.: The Ontario Institute for Studies in Education Monograph Series, no. 5, 1969), pp. 55–61.

The American people's growing interest in the public schools is manifest, among other ways, in the emergence of the teacher as a stock character in the mass media. In recent years the movies have given us Sidney Poitier in *To Sir, With Love,* Sandy Dennis in *Up The Down Staircase,* Maggie Smith in *The Prime of Miss Jean Brodie,* Joanne Woodward in *Rachel! Rachel!,* and Elliot Gould in *Getting Straight.* On television, it all started a decade ago with James Franciscus in "Mr. Novak." This show was followed by the "Bill Cosby Show" with Cosby as a high-school gym teacher, "Lucas Tanner" with David Hartman as a high-school teacher, and "Room 222" with Lloyd Haynes as a social studies teacher. Nightowls can still see, on the late night show, Jennifer Jones in *Good Morning, Miss Dove* and Glenn Ford as a teacher and Sidney Poitier as a student in *The Blackboard Jungle.*

These media teachers are providing us a new set of role models, whom we experience with a different kind of intensity from that we invest in "live" teacher-watching. For one thing, media teachers are almost uniformly immensely attractive young people, and the viewer gains a more intimate knowledge of their private lives than he does of the lives of his "real" teachers. Second, they are usually models of what is traditionally considered good teaching. Third, dramatized classroom situations are more intense than reality, and thus often tend to make a deep impression. And finally, the media teacher can be observed dispassionately because there is no need to psych him out for survival purposes. One can relate to and learn from the media teacher without complications.

The impact of media teachers on the student of teaching has not been studied but, unfettered by facts, we will make some tentative observations: first, the fact that some media teachers have become minor culture heroes may help to raise the status of teaching and underline its importance. Second, media teachers rarely perform the traditional information-dispenser function of the teacher, that is, to convey to students "the facts." Third, media teachers are often shown responding to the emotional and social needs of children. Fourth, media teachers are portrayed as warm human beings who fall in love, enjoy life, and, especially, gain deep satisfaction from their work—a view of teachers rarely available to the student in the classroom.

d courses

During the Colonial period, and well into the late nineteenth century, a person who wanted to teach simply declared himself a teacher. A high-school or college diploma was considered nice to have but in no way necessary. If you could do readin', writin' and cipherin', there was sure to be a school waiting to hire you. The self-declared teacher competed for a job and, if he got it, continued teaching as long as his clients were willing to pay. Today, however, the nation's institutions of higher education have taken on responsibility for initially training teachers. While this is a well-entrenched practice, it is essentially an arbitrary one. As a society, we could conceivably turn over the job of teacher education to the public schools, private industry or even to public corporations.

By and large, higher education institutions discharge their responsibility for the professional training of teachers through two channels: education courses, which will be discussed here, and practice teaching. At their best, education courses prepare teachers to translate into practice knowledge and principles derived

How do people become teachers?

from such disciplines as psychology, philosophy, sociology, and anthropology. At their worst, education courses offer useless and outdated facts and theories or a potpourri of unrelated anecdotes about schools and children.

Each college or university with a department or school of education offers an array of education courses, some required and some elective, reflecting its own judgments and those of the state legislature on how a teacher should be trained. As a minimum, though, the teaching candidate must take the sequence of courses that leads to licensing or certification. After successfully passing the required education courses, including practice teaching, and graduating from college, the student is eligible for state certification.[2]

Education courses are normally embedded in what is called the professional sequence, which means, very simply, that they are designed to prepare one for work as a professional teacher. Like courses in medicine, architecture, baking, or computer programming, they are vocational. Not all of the material presented, however, is immediately usable or relevant to real world situations. Courses in the history of education are a case in point. Such courses rarely help the teacher who is struggling to find material that will interest her students or who is trying to find ways to get the sullen kid in the back of the room to put aside the chip on his shoulder. They do, however, let the prospective teacher know where her profession has been and what its accomplishments and failures have been. And they may, too, save the teacher from, in effect, reinventing the wheel.

Most of the content of a teacher education program, however, should have obvious transfer value to one's future teaching situation. When students fail to use their courses for that purpose, it is usually for two reasons. First, they are so familiar with teachers and schools that they underestimate the difficulty of teaching well. This is like the boy who sat at the end of a pier all summer watching other boys swim. Finally, convinced he "had it," he jumped in—and, of course, drowned. Education courses are like the swimming lessons the boy should have taken.

A second and related problem is inherent in the nature of courses themselves. We frequently take courses because they sound interesting, or we have heard the instructor is great, or we are required to take them or we don't know what else to do with our tuition money. We "take the course" as if we were taking a pill. While this is always unfortunate, it can have serious consequences for the future professional. Just as no one wants to be treated by a doctor who sat passively through a course in the malady afflicting him, no one wants to send his child to the class of a teacher who inertly and obediently took the course in reading instruction. What we are somewhat laboriously trying to point out is that there can be minimal transfer value from just "taking a course." A much more active approach is needed. The best way for this to happen is for you to go into a course with your own questions about teaching and learning. Incidentally, some teacher education programs are introducing their students into the schools as aides and observers at the beginning of their teacher training experience. One purpose of this approach is to give the students an opportunity to generate their own questions

[2] A word of warning: we live in a very mobile society, and many teachers prepare in one state to teach in another. Efforts are being made to establish national certification standards, but at present what fulfills requirements in one state may not be satisfactory in another. Therefore, it is good to know where you hope to teach so you can meet that state's certification standards.

To erect fine buildings and to seek to meet the needs and abilities of all individuals who desire to avail themselves of the opportunities so generously offered
without providing teachers with qualifications commensurate with the ideal is a
sham. I. L. Kandell

and to recognize their own "felt needs." A course is much more likely to be valuable to a student if he is using it to solve his own questions and problems.
Regrettably, too few people approach education courses (and others) with this
active posture.

Real teaching

When we leave education courses behind and enter the classroom, we move
from words and personal fantasies to real children and hard realities. The major
difference between the traditional ways people learn to be teachers and teaching
itself is the difference between passive and active learning. First, you observe
and think and read about teaching; then, you find yourself actively engaged in
the process, struggling to respond to your unique situation in a constructive way
and working to master many aspects of your role all at once.

Universities ordinarily treat student teaching as a course for which there is credit
and some evaluation procedure. The student teacher is supervised by the university staff and a master teacher from the school. For students it represents an

How do people become teachers?

opportunity to test out their ideas and previously untried skills in the real world. For a great many students, this period is the most meaningful of their college years. For the supervising teachers it is an opportunity to monitor their own profession, screening out those who might be harmful to children—the whackos— and those who don't measure up to minimum standards—the incompetents.

The early years in the classroom are also periods of intense learning. As we saw in the last chapter, this is especially true of the first year of teaching, which differs from student teaching in that the beginning teacher has full responsibility for the class. Although she is typically supervised by an administrator or a department chairman, she is normally on her own. She has to start from scratch, setting the goals, procedures, and tone for the year. Amid all the problems and successes, there is an immense amount of learning and growth going on.

The first real teaching encounters are periods of testing. Primarily, the teaching candidate is testing whether or not he is going to gain satisfaction as a teacher. Then there is a whole range of testing, from alternative ways of handling content to different styles of leadership with one's students. As at no other time in his teaching career, the beginner is continually testing approaches, evaluating what he is doing and refining or discarding on the basis of this feedback. It is a long process, becoming a teacher. And, as we shall see next, it is not without flaws.

Learning how *not* to be a teacher

We have spent the preceding several pages pointing out how much teacher training you have already had. Teaching tendencies are ingrained in you simply as a consequence of growing up in our culture. You have watched dozens of teachers and stored up countless techniques and biases. You have been exposed to media teachers who may have prompted you to look at teaching and schools in a new light. Education courses and real teaching encounters still lie ahead of most of you. It would be wonderful if each of these experiences contributed beneficially to your professional development and each built on each until you achieved a state of flawless excellence. Or if, to put it another way, as a result of these learnings "every day in every way we become better and better." As most of you are profoundly aware, things don't very often work that way.

Ingrained human tendencies

The same experiences from which people learn to be teachers teach them how *not* to be teachers. Or, more precisely, how to be nonteachers. In other words, each of the sources of knowledge about teaching has drawbacks or counterproductive aspects. We need to be aware of these limitations if we are to correct for them, and thus gain more than we lose from each experience. For instance, our ingrained tendency to teach others—that is, to moralize, tell what we know, criticize, correct, and volunteer right answers—gives rise to behavior that may have been very appropriate to a relatively static society. At a time when there was less to learn, and when knowledge expanded less rapidly, these teaching tendencies were more in tune with student needs. Now, however, the task of school is to help children live in the twenty-first century. And since there is no guarantee that the knowledge the teacher possesses will be accurate or useful in thirty years, students can no longer be regarded as empty vessels to be filled by the teacher's words and moralizing. Students need to learn to think independently, to work both independently and cooperatively, and to adopt a fluid approach to learning. They must be helped by the teacher to become liberated human beings who possess the ability to evaluate new information and new situations and come up with independent solutions. Students need to be much more involved in their own learning, and they should be learning skills that transfer from one situation to another, rather than time-bound facts. What we have, then, is a severe conflict between students' needs and our own ingrained tendencies to impose our knowledge, biases, morals, and answers. Normally this is done without giving children the opportunity and, especially, the skills to properly evaluate what they are learning from us . . . and from the rest of the people in society. If the schools do not develop individuals with the skills and habits of independent judgment and action, students will not be able to cope with life. If they don't cope, they are not free. If they are not free, they (we) are slaves. This is a fundamental issue. Our job as teachers is to free people from ignorance. But ignorance can no longer be defined as simple lack of information or awareness. Access to television, magazines, newspapers, and books is making that kind of ignorance obsolete. Ignorance in a fluctuating world is the inability to process information. (For instance, you have or will soon have more than enough information on teaching as a career. The crucial question is, "Do I have the ability to process this information and come up with a good decision?") What this means is that in order to be effective teachers we must in a sense suppress our ingrained tendencies to teach—in the most primitive sense of that word.

A fundamental problem of modern man is that he is trapped in outmoded forms and concepts. Politicians spend huge amounts of public funds on roads for individual cars, when it has been self-evident for a decade that such action is disastrous and that we need better mass transportation. At a time when our energies should be spent on finding ways for nations to live together in harmony, no government in the world has a Department or Ministry of Peace, and many spend massive sums on weapons of war. We have become prisoners of the way things used to be. The same thing happens to prospective teachers. Having sat in classrooms for sixteen or more years, we limit our definitions of what a school is, what a teacher is, and what constitutes being educated to what we are familiar with. Perhaps what all of us who aspire to be teachers (and that very definitely includes the authors) need is new models of what it is to be a teacher.

Teacher-watching

Teacher-watching has its pitfalls too. It is not uncommon for a prospective secondary-school teacher to model himself on a favorite college lecturer who can captivate 300 people for ninety minutes at a time. He goes off to teach in secondary school hoping to duplicate the performances of his idol, and fails utterly because, first, he just isn't as fascinating or effective as his idol and, second, high-school students have different tolerances and motivations than college students. Then there is the problem of the prospective teacher who admires all her mild and gentle former teachers, but who herself naturally exudes energy and enthusiasm. She may try to deny her strengths in a misguided attempt to be something she is not. We may, too, have admired the wrong models. For instance, we may hope to emulate the very clever teacher who was so bright and humorous, but who wasted a tremendous amount of time drawing attention to himself and who controlled students with a sharp tongue.

How do people become teachers?

It is worthwhile to acknowledge explicitly who our favorite teachers are and why we find them attractive. If we consciously choose to emulate a certain teacher, we need to think seriously about how such a choice is likely to affect our teaching. Will modeling myself after Mrs. Y or Mr. X enhance or undercut my strengths? Are our personalities similar? Where should I draw the line between myself and my model?

Media models

Media models don't pose as serious a problem as real teachers can, but they may teach us things about teachers and schools that should be quickly forgotten. The trouble with media models is that they are usually variations on Superman, disguised as a mild-mannered public-school teacher. No matter what the problem, he plunges right in and saves the day for Western civilization. He throws himself into the lives of children with very little background information. He knows no failure. He is a stranger to depression and insecurities. He easily strikes a balance between his family life and his professional life. He never makes a serious mistake that he simply has to live with. As a teacher, he is always up front running the show and dispensing wisdom. Great entertainment—maybe—but not the best model for us poor mortals who can't quite keep up with a speeding bullet.

Another shortcoming of media models is the conventional schools in which they perform. It seems to be a basic tenet of the mass entertainment industry that the characters can be idealized but the settings must be commonplace. If media schools have to be instantly recognizable to a mass audience, the result is that the media will not use their programs to champion or even illustrate educational reform. At least they have not done this so far.

Ed courses

Discussing education courses earlier in this chapter we wrote about *how not to learn* how to teach from education courses, that is, to be a passive recipient. Here we want to talk about the issue of how to learn *how not to teach* from education courses. Many students expect to learn how to teach from observing their education professors, whom they assume to be paragons of pedagogical excellence. Evidently they haven't heard about education professors who deliver impassioned lectures on the evils of the lecture, or about the professor who teaches Principles of Teaching and breaks every rule in the book.[3] Unfortunately, professors of education are just as frail and fallible in this regard as are other teachers.

Loss of perspective is another pitfall. Occasionally prospective teachers embrace a particular principle of teaching so fervently they lose their grip on common sense. For instance, a teacher who adopts the practice of verbally reinforcing or praising student participation in class ("That's an interesting answer, Sara. That's the kind of thinking we should have more of around here.") may overdo it. In excess, supposedly reinforcing statements become meaningless and even embarrassing to students ("You don't say much in this class, Ralph, but when you do, it's really a top-drawer contribution! Keep up the keen thinking!"). Then there is the story—probably not true—of the elementary-school teacher who, as a result of her education courses, is converted to teaching for problem

[3] If you ever come across this elusive book, please send a copy to the authors.

solving and commits herself to using that approach in her classroom. Things go relatively well until a girl asks to go to the washroom and the teacher tries to make a problem-solving session out of it. Remember . . . perspective.

A related issue is extravagant expectations for education courses. It is our view that teaching and learning are very complex phenomena, and that the training of teachers is a more massive task than is typically acknowledged. We find excessive the expectation that nonteachers will be transformed into superior teachers by six or eight courses. Look at the discussion in Chapter Four. To become the kind of teacher we describe there requires the acquisition of considerable knowledge and a wide repertoire of skills and strategies. It calls for a good deal of behavior change in the prospective teacher. What many critics of education courses are really saying is that the magnitude of the task is such that it cannot be accomplished within the traditional course format. More on this later.

Real teaching

"Experience is the best teacher." Maybe, but experience can also be a poor teacher, and teaching is no exception. Real teaching encounters, whether tutoring experiences or student teaching or the first years of full-time teaching, can have a negative effect, too. The fact that poor teaching is not the exclusive province of the beginning teacher is proof enough of this point. The explanation is not that teachers get too little practice. If anything, teachers get too much practice. What is missing is knowledge-of-results, or *feedback*. Years ago the great learning theorist E. L. Thorndike, in the process of formulating his "law of exercise," discovered that in dart-throwing games if the target was hidden from view people could throw darts over and over without improving their performance. The lack of feedback about where their darts were landing made self-correction impossible.

In this sense, dart-throwing seems to be analogous to teaching. Teachers receive relatively little feedback on their performance. Although colleges and universities employ supervisors for student teachers and school districts do so for beginning teachers, the cost prevents both institutions from providing as much supervision as they would like. Also, supervision is a difficult process, which depends for its success on many variables.

The beginning teacher often has trouble making sense of the feedback he does get from his students, such as looks of attention or inattention, questions, responses to questions, and signs of confusion. For instance, it is common for neophyte teachers to be shocked and upset after giving their first test. They had been convinced by the looks on their students' faces and by the silence when they asked, "Do you understand? Are there any questions?" that their students really understood. What little feedback we receive may not be very good—in fact, it may seriously mislead us.

If the teacher does receive accurate feedback, and knows, for example, that the majority of her students are not learning subtraction or that three of her driver education students have racked up cars this week, what does she do about it? How does she remedy the problem? It is not only a matter of knowing the results, but also of knowing the available and constructive alternatives. It is at this point that people learn how *not to teach*. Take as an example the case of a beginning teacher interested in having her students do group projects. After she divides the

How do people become teachers?

Raymond Fleming (1919–1969)

When Ray Fleming died in California three days before Christmas in 1969, much of Palo Alto felt the loss. Ray taught American history at the local high school. He also taught his students, his colleagues, and the community something about what it is to be black in a predominantly white society, and about what it means to be a man.

When he was still a young boy in South Carolina, both of Ray's parents died. A family friend in White Plains, New York, sent for Ray and raised him through his high-school years. Ray wanted to become a labor arbitrator, but couldn't afford to go to college. Instead, he went to work, hoping to save enough to continue his education. However, World War II changed the course of Ray's life. He joined the Army and became a highly decorated combat paratrooper.

Because many opportunities denied Ray as a black civilian were available to him as a soldier, he decided to stay in the military after the war. During his military career he married, rose to the rank of major, spent tours of duty in Japan, Korea, Germany, and the Philippines, and fathered four sons and a daughter. Also, during the service Ray's desire for education became insatiable. He read constantly and took courses at nearby colleges whenever he was stationed in the United States. Finally, Ray earned his B.A. from the Munich branch of the University of Maryland. He was forty-two. Shortly afterward he retired from the military. His own struggle for education had given him a new vocation. He wanted to be a teacher.

Ray took his wife and family to California. He had been accepted in a graduate teacher education program at Stanford University, where he took courses in education and history and became a teaching intern at Palo Alto's Cubberley High School, one of California's fine secondary schools. At the end of a year he was certified as a teacher, earned a master's degree, and was voted the school's most outstanding teacher. Ray was invited to stay on at Cubberley and, since his frequently uprooted family seemed settled, he decided to stay.

Ray Fleming was a passionate man dedicated to rational investigation. He used history as a vehicle to teach his students how to think about the world and about themselves. Ray was always putting books in students' hands and urging them to dig beneath the surface. From his study of history and his own experience as a black man, he knew how standardized textbooks can distort reality, and stressed the value of original sources and the danger of unquestioningly accepting someone else's synthesized view. He worked to develop a spirit of inquiry and a capacity for independent investigation in his students. He presented students with evidence, frequently inconsistent or conflicting, and forced them to come up with their own rational evaluations.

Ray was soon made department chairman and, although he had many obligations at home and at school, he felt a duty to the larger community. He was active on the Human Relations Council. He served on an advisory board for the Office of Economic Opportunity. He spoke frequently to groups throughout California about the inequality of educational opportunities for blacks, Mexican-Americans, Indians, and other minorities. In 1967 the racial tensions that inflamed the rest of the country began to be felt in white, affluent Palo Alto. Blacks from East Palo

Alto began attending Cubberley in search of a better high school education. When these black students demanded fairer treatment from the faculty and more attention to the black experience in the curriculum, tempers flared and communication broke down. The role of arbitrator he had once hoped for was thrust upon Ray. Ray helped the dissident black students shape their anger and disappointment into an instrument for change. He showed the predominantly liberal faculty that their sympathy and leniency were patronizing and insulting to the black students. He made others see the cruelty of their indifference. The combined efforts of teaching and endlessly arbitrating in the troubled school sapped his energy. It was at just about this time that Martin Luther King was assassinated. Ray was deeply discouraged but, realizing the importance of that moment in history, he rallied himself. He had always lectured to church and civic groups on black history and black problems. Now he redoubled his efforts. He established the Martin Luther King Memorial Scholarship Fund to enable Cubberley students to go to college, and contributed his lecture fees to it.

Ray never compromised his academic standards. In the fall after the black students had voiced their demands, Ray offered a black history course. Some students apparently expected an extended rap session. They found, instead, that their teacher expected them to study, learn, and question rigorously. Some dropped the course, but most remained to meet Ray's challenges.

That same fall, Ray's students and friends noticed that the ordinarily strong, energetic man was walking more slowly and often seemed to be in pain. In November Ray entered the hospital, and in less than two months he was dead of cancer. Young and old stopped to mourn; in his death they rediscovered their teacher.

One of Ray Fleming's students wrote in the school newspaper, "If ever there comes a time in one's life where a genuine grasp on living renews itself, let it come now. Just as life comes only at death in the phoenix legend, so must the humanitarian in all of us renew his efforts with the death of Mr. Raymond Fleming. For this hope and toil to benefit mankind were his life work."

---

students into groups, outlines the tasks, and gets them started, things begin to fall apart. She envisions another fall of Rome taking place in her class. Tension begins to build up. She does not know her alternatives and does not know how to proceed. As a result, she does what many teachers do—retreats to what she knows well from her own elementary- and secondary-school experience. She abandons the group work, rearranges the students' chairs in rows, and conducts a highly teacher-directed class. Retreating to the safe and traditional is a common reaction in a teacher who is frustrated and does not know the available alternatives. This attitude of "when in doubt, retreat," coupled with the strong influence of our ingrained tendencies and our own experience with teachers, may account for the very reactionary quality of most instruction.

This is not to say that teachers cannot grow and improve "on the job," or that they cannot use the feedback available to them to help analyze, and gradually eliminate, their weaknesses. We simply want you to put the old cliché about "learning from experience" in balanced perspective.

How do people become teachers?

Some approaches to your education as a teacher

Refreshing winds of change are blowing in higher education. College students have more curricular variety and choice available to them now, and more voice in campus affairs. The foregoing analysis of how people learn to be teachers (or nonteachers) may seem somewhat discouraging, but it is presented in a spirit of hope. By understanding what has already happened to you and what may be in store for you, you are much more likely to be able to transcend the limitations of those experiences. This is particularly true today, because higher education is increasingly responsive to student needs and desires.

In *The World and the American Teacher,* Harold Taylor suggests that deciding to become a teacher is like choosing to become a poet. "The preparation begins in a decision to become something, a commitment made about one's life and the purpose of it."[4] This statement is reminiscent of the analogy to sculpture with which we began this chapter. Both suggest that the process of becoming a teacher requires you to expend energy and imagination, rather than simply sitting back and letting it happen.

Adopting an active, aggressive approach to your education can have some intriguing implications. For instance, you may find it useful and revealing to behave like a critical "consumer" of the education that is offered to you. Analyze the instructional strategies, motivational techniques, human relations skills, and evaluation methods of your professors. If you think it would be helpful, ask them to discuss their teaching methods with you. Look for opportunities to teach someone else what you have learned or are learning. It has been said—and our own experience confirms this—that the most effective way of finding out what you know and discovering how to apply it is to teach it to someone else. You might also look for opportunities to relate your other courses to some aspect of teaching that interests you. For instance, do your sociology term paper on an educationally related topic, such as the correlation between social class and tracking assignments in a nearby school. Or study local Boards of Education for a political science class to determine which political and social groups are represented (and unrepresented) by their members. You might try to arrange an independent study project to visit, and perhaps teach in, experimental schools. If certain experiences which you feel you need for your education are not available on your campus, see if arrangements can be made to acquire them someplace else. You might be able to cross-register at another school or receive credit for an independent study project.

We are not suggesting that you try to make everything you do immediately relevant to your career choice. Rather, we are advocating a more active and creative response to the curriculum and to your decision to teach.

The informal education of a teacher involves many of the factors we discussed earlier—ingrained tendencies to teach, teacher-watching, and the like. We shoulc

---

[4] Harold Taylor, *The World and the American Teacher* (Washington, D.C.: American Association of Colleges for Teacher Education, 1968).

not ignore, however, the importance of the individual teacher's growth and development as a person. The informal education a person gains as he learns to work with other people, to develop his own standards and value system, and to become independent and self-reliant is of central importance to his effectiveness as a teacher. Viewed in this perspective, the discipline one gains from learning to play a muscial instrument, the give-and-take skills one acquires from living in a dormitory, the deepened maturity gained from doing service work—all contribute to one's development as a person and as a teacher. The same thing could, of course, be said about the personal development of an engineer. But it is especially important in the case of the teacher because her "person" is continually on view to her students, and may in the long run be her most important contribution to their search for maturity and personal growth.

There is an old tale about a student who wanted to learn how to live the good life. The student heard that in a distant land there lived a teacher of abundant wisdom, and he decided to travel there to study under the wise teacher. When he arrived in the city where the great teacher lived, he was directed to an opulent mansion. The teacher's servants cringed at the mention of the teacher's name. After a very long wait while the teacher meditated, the student was ushered into his presence. He bowed, sat before the richly dressed teacher and said, "Teacher, I have come a long way to inquire of you how to live a good life." The teacher smiled, saying, "You have come to the right person," and began to hold forth on the "good life." After five or six minutes, the student rose and explained that he had to leave because he could not hear the teacher. "What is this? Why can't you hear me, simpleton, you're right in front of me!" "I cannot hear what you say because *what you are* speaks so loud. I must seek elsewhere."[5] Our students, confirmed teacher-watchers all, are seekers not unlike the student in the fable.

If you are interested in a further discussion of teacher education, particularly its problems and new developments, keep reading. If not, turn to page 131, the closing section of the continuing education of teachers. (If you do skip ahead, we will be a little hurt. But, then again, we'll never know, will we?)

[5] This fable was told to one of the authors on a bitter cold night in Mobile, Alabama. As reported by said author (whose name will be withheld because he was supposed to be visiting a sick friend in Perth, Maine), "On a dingy back street this old man with a heavy foreign accent shuffled up and asked if I would buy him a drink in exchange for a story. Being a seeker of truth and having seen all the movies in Mobile anyway, I agreed. What followed is reported above. When the story was ended, I had a deep intuition that the old man had been more involved in the story than he let on. As he got up to go I looked deep into his watery eyes and said, 'Sir, I have a deep intuition that you are involved in the story more than you let on.' He winced and then replied, 'Look, fella. Three shots of bar whiskey don't give you the right to pry.' With that he shuffled off into the wintry night, in the general direction of Winnipeg, Manitoba."

Some problems in teacher education

A young sage once said, "Everyone cares about teacher education . . . but not very much."[6] The United States of the 1970s has so many more attention-getting problems to grapple with that little public energy is left to expend in sustained attention to teacher education. Compared with the energy crisis, pollution, and dissatisfaction among the young, teacher education is, admittedly, not much of a drawing card. However, it has for some time been a matter of sustained national concern. In the fifty-year period between 1920 and 1970, there were ten major national studies of teacher education, each accompanied by recommendations for action. By and large, these reports have been negative in tone. And the public has by and large responded with apathy. This response has been deeply disappointing to many teacher educators who realize that major change will not occur until the public takes the issue of how teachers are educated much more seriously. If the public were told that its doctors were being badly trained or that bridge-builders were plying their trade in a dubious manner, action would be taken swiftly. The health and safety of the body apparently takes a higher priority than that of the mind and spirit.

The vicious cycle

What, exactly, is the problem? Few teachers are fully prepared before they begin teaching and, once on the job, they are forced to learn by trial-and-error. In other words, our formal system for preparing teachers is not the major influence on their classroom performance. Teacher education is caught in a vicious cycle, which makes significant improvement especially difficult. Its components are so deeply interrelated that the cycle can be entered at any point.

There is a lot of competition for resources—that is, money and personnel—within a university. The university can give only so much of its resources to teacher education without getting itself into political trouble both on and off the campus. As a result, the teacher training program is rarely what the people involved would like it to be, but is "the best we can do *under the circumstances.*" And frequently it is. Field work, clinical exercises, and technological aids like videotape recorders are often too expensive. Therefore the primary modes of professional education become those that are least costly—lectures and student teaching. Because of its limited resources, the professional education program is designed to consume relatively little time. This is particularly striking when teacher education is compared with the training of such other professionals as veterinarians and civil engineers, programs of study that take up much more time and energy. In sum, the education student does not have to put out a great deal. Nor does he risk much, since normally one can acquire a college degree and professional training as a teacher at the same time.

Approximately 50 percent of all trained teachers either never teach or leave teaching by the end of their second year. Although there are many reasons for this high turnover rate, we believe that insufficient training accounts for much of it. The undertrained teacher makes frequent mistakes, knows enough to realize it, and thus feels more frustration than satisfaction at her performance. Familiar with the high turnover rate among beginning teachers, administrators and experi-

---

[6] Modesty keeps us from identifying the young sage.

enced teachers are unwilling to offer much in the way of inservice training to make up for insufficient preservice training. The high turnover rate thus makes it difficult to build a strong professional staff in a school. Furthermore, the local community is understandably reluctant to support expensive inservice training courses if the participating teachers keep leaving, because local children too often do not reap the benefits. And the nation as a whole cannot understand why more money should be spent on long and expensive teacher training programs if teaching is a revolving-door profession. To complete the cycle, lack of strong public support for more rigorous, longer, and more expensive training reinforces the *status quo* in the education of teachers. This brief summary is, admittedly, a simplified version of the situation, and it does not take into account changes that have taken place recently. It may be unduly pessimistic. But these qualifications aside, teacher education appears to be trapped in a vicious cycle of low expectations.

Insufficient commitment

In addition to this massive dilemma, there are a number of more specific difficulties that contribute to the poor state of teacher training. An issue we have already mentioned, but which needs amplification, is the low level of commitment. Thirty percent of the people who are trained as teachers in our nation's universities and colleges never teach a class as an employed teacher. In analyzing this troubling phenomenon, B. O. Smith and his coauthors of *Teachers for the Real World* write:

Perhaps the main reason that so many trained teachers never enter the classroom is a lack of commitment to the profession born of little investment in preparation for it. Not many people who are prepared to practice medicine or law fail to follow their profession: in all probability they would consider their failure to practice a waste of knowledge and training. Apparently those who are prepared to teach but never enter the classroom do not feel this sense of waste. Perhaps they feel that the amount of knowledge wasted is not that great or that valuable. If physicians were trained by giving them only basic liberal arts and science courses and four or five courses in medicine in the junior and senior years, perhaps, they would not feel committed to their vocations or competent to practice. Yet this is the way teachers are now trained.[7]

Smith goes on to state that because prospective teachers take a basic liberal arts program, glossed over with a thin veneer of pedagogy, they have lost next to nothing if they decide not to enter teaching. Their preparation has been essentially the same as that of a liberal arts graduate. Smith suggests that if the prospective teacher were required to make a heavy investment in his preparation, he would either not enter teaching at all or would feel committed to it as a career. Lack of commitment seeps into many aspects of teacher education. Even those who do teach often don't look upon it as a lifetime career. As we have said earlier, many people see teaching as a respectable way to bide time until marriage, as "a good insurance policy," or as a stepping-stone to administration. If people look upon teaching as a transient occupation, something they are traveling through, the intensity of their commitment is bound to be seriously diminished.

[7] B. O. Smith et al., *Teachers for the Real World* (Washington, D.C.: American Association of Colleges for Teacher Education, 1969), p. 24. Reprinted by permission of the publisher.

How do people become teachers?

A related issue is lack of competition and the commonplace image of a career in teaching. The nation's higher education institutions train almost a quarter of a million teachers each year. Given such vast numbers, teacher education programs are bound not to be very competitive. If a person is not admitted to one program, there are around 1200 others to choose from. As a result, the individual who is accepted into a teacher training program does not feel that he has been admitted into a small group of elite and highly dedicated professionals and professionals-to-be. A major consequence of this is the commonplace image of teaching. At many institutions, being accepted into a teacher training program carries about as much prestige as being eligible to take required physical education courses or to pay taxes. (We feel compelled to say that we consider this lack of commitment a reflection of a severely warped system of values. It is difficult to imagine a career whose potential for impact on people is as great or more important to society than the education of its young. We are somewhat cheered, however, by signs that many people are waking up to the importance and significance of a career in teaching. We will be even more optimistic when university professors in the liberal arts actively encourage their best students to enter elementary and secondary education.)

The leader-follower dilemma

There are numerous alternatives to the way we are presently conducting school. Various unorthodox approaches are being experimented with on a small scale, and some are being considered for wider adoption. New curricula and new ways of organizing the school day and the teaching staff are being suggested. Some critics are beginning to question the very idea of schools in such a society as ours. All of this controversy raises a very pressing issue for teacher education: whether to prepare (and again with very little time and few resources) teachers for the way schools are now or for the way they may be in the future. Both alternatives are fraught with problems. If a given program undertakes to train teachers for the future, it must confront the question of what future schools will be like. Dozens of loud voices begin to vie with each other to assert very different views of how the schools will change. The danger, or course, is that a program may train teachers who are ineffective in existing schools and perfectly suited to schools that never come into existence. For example, should teachers be trained for the traditional self-contained classroom, or for team teaching? Or should we assume that all schools will soon have highly differentiated staffs of paraprofessionals, master teachers and education specialists? Should teachers be trained to function in a school that uses individualized self-directed instruction and relies heavily on media for instruction? In sum, should teacher education lead or follow?

We are undergoing a revolution in our thinking about education and schools. Like most revolutions, it will undoubtedly occur sloppily and unpredictably. At the very least, future teachers need to be educated to what is going on in education so that they can play an active part in directing the revolution in our schools.

The producer-consumer relationship

The relationship between the schools and the teacher education institutions is troubled not only by the leader-follower problem, but also by the consumer-producer problem. At present, colleges and universities almost singlehandedly "produce" the teachers for American schools. The schools, on the other hand, act as passive consumers of teachers. The inefficiency of the situation is reminiscent of Russian industry twenty-five years ago, when huge factories blindly turned out suits and dresses, impervious to consumers' desires and needs. The consumers, having no say in the operation, were frequently stuck with outdated styles or shipments of dresses all uniformly extra-large.

Teacher trainees and schools lose a great deal in the isolation of training from practice. For one thing, students of teaching are usually taught to teach in the absence of children. The public schools, too, miss the youthful spirit and energetic service of prospective teachers. This problem has been getting special attention recently. Universities and schools are beginning to develop collaborative teacher training programs which capitalize on the skilled teachers and the availability of children that the schools can offer. This in turn allows the university to focus its efforts on what it can do best.

What's new in teacher education

We have run the risk of depressing you by talking about what's wrong with teacher education, and a corrective is in order. There have been some very encouraging developments within teacher education in recent years. The knowledge base—what we know about teaching—is being expanded. New institutions, such as federally funded research and development centers and regional laboratories, have been created for the purpose of expanding the knowledge frontier. Hopefully, the newly created National Institute of Education will have an

How do people become teachers?

impact here. Universities and industry have shown renewed interest in the education of teachers. While these new efforts have not yet brought about any major breakthroughs, the climate is encouraging. Interest is high, and individual contributions to a solution of our teacher education problem are emerging.

What follows, then, is a brief description of some new approaches to the training of teachers. Some are in an embryonic stage of development. Others have been tried, tested, and found effective. They are very dissimilar. They are more like apples and plums and bananas than a bunch of grapes. All of them, though, represent new directions for teacher education.

Early teaching experiences

For a number of decades the standard method of training teachers has been to rely almost exclusively on university course work and student teaching. The study of education tended to be overly academic, and student teaching was too short and too unpredictable to serve as a satisfactory antidote. A number of universities have attempted to improve their programs by providing their teaching candidates with early, clinical experiences in the schools. Early in their programs teaching candidates are attached to schools, often to perform tasks that contribute to the learning of children. A candidate may be assigned to a particular teacher or team of teachers as a teacher aide, or she may be rotated weekly among a number of positions, assisting behind the main desk in the office, helping the school librarian, working as a tutor in the remedial reading lab, and so on.

Participation in community affairs is a feature of some of these programs. The future teacher is assigned to a community agency or service group and, ideally, has opportunities to meet parents and children in nonschool settings. Also, he is enabled to see from an unfamiliar vantage point how the school fits in the total life of the community.

The purposes of these early school experiences are many. First, by returning to school in an authoritative but nonteaching role, the future teacher can begin to encounter some of the problems of that role without having also to deal with the issues of teaching. Second, through real-life encounters he can deepen his understanding of children and their needs. These experiences provide a reality base on which to draw while studying educational theory in the university. The study of education thus loses its cold, abstract quality. Third, such arrangements allow public-school teachers and administrators to take their rightful place in the preparation of teachers. Fourth, these early experiences can serve as testing grounds enabling students to make more realistic decisions about whether they wish to teach or not.

Teacher education programs vary tremendously in the use of early teaching experiences. Some programs have developed a core of highly structured clinical experiences. Some confine the early experience to a short period of time, linking it to a specific education course. Despite this diversity, all of the programs are motivated by a common belief that experience in school may not be the best teacher, but it does vitalize the study of education.

We should add, too, that there is nothing to prevent the prospective teacher from arranging some early teaching experiences of his own.

Simulation

Since World War II the U.S. armed forces have used "war games" to prepare military men, from privates to generals, for the trials of warfare. War games are designed to reproduce the conditions of battle without its hazards, and are based on the principle of *simulation*. In a simulated situation, real conditions are artificially reproduced, and the participants enact the appropriate roles in problem situations. Simulation has been introduced into teacher education only recently, but it has aroused great interest and high expectations. The principle of simulation can be applied with equal success to the problem of running an entire high school or dealing with an angry parent. One commercially available set of materials simulates an elementary-school classroom in an urban setting. It describes the socioeconomic background of the community and provides test scores, records, and past teachers' reports for each of the teacher's students. A teacher education student plays the role of the teacher, and after the rules of the game and all the information about the school and the class have been introduced, the game begins. Sometimes a problem is introduced by means of a short film. Other times, the problem is presented verbally to the "teacher." Typical problem-solving situations deal with student misbehavior, the teacher's relationship with administrators and parents, curriculum planning, and teaching methods. Although there may be an initial "let's pretend" quality to simulation activities, the participants almost invariably take them quite seriously once the problem-solving situation begins to evolve.

Simulation can have many different uses. Like early teaching experiences, it can be used to introduce the future teacher to some of the issues and problems that must be confronted in the schools. At a later point in training, simulated experiences can be used to see if teaching candidates are able to apply educational principles in teaching situations. Simulation can also serve to initiate discussion of specific issues. For instance, a class studying teaching by inquiry can begin with a simulated lesson, and an analysis of the lesson can be used to illustrate the underlying principles of inquiry.

One of the drawbacks of field experiences for teacher trainees is the reality of making a mistake with real children. Call it what you will, student teaching is real teaching, and the beginner is bound to make mistakes. Simulation allows him to deal with complex issues and to make mistakes in a safe environment. Another of its advantages is that mistakes can be immediately analyzed and constructive alternatives can be presented on the spot. Simulation shares many of the objectives of student teaching, but is more controlled, more open to analysis, and more economical in terms of time and human resources.

Microteaching

Microteaching is a training setting for teachers. The normal complexities of the classroom are reduced, and the possibilities of providing immediate growth-producing feedback are increased. A teacher, either beginning or experienced, can use microteaching to practice a particular skill or strategy. The impact of microteaching lies in the fact that it provides actual classroom practice *and* instantaneous feedback on one's performance. First, the normal dimensions of classroom teaching are reduced. The length of the lesson is reduced, frequently to only five minutes, its scope is narrow, and the teacher works with only a few students. At the same time, the feedback or knowledge-of-results mechanisms are maximized. The trainee reflects on his own performance immediately after the lesson. A supervisor who has watched his performance helps him think about

127   How do people become teachers?

what he did and how it might be improved. The students who have been taught (unless they are very young children) provide feedback on the teaching. Also, the lesson is videotaped and the trainee and supervisor later analyze the tape and, of course, search for ways to improve the performance. The cycle is repeated until the trainee and his supervisor are satisfied with his performance.

A typical microteaching session would proceed as follows: first, the trainee would receive some initial introduction to a specific approach or strategy or teaching skill. For example, if he is trying to master the skill of asking probing questions, he might watch a demonstration film, read about the uses of the skill, and then prepare a brief lesson. The lesson is, primarily, a vehicle for the teacher to practice a particular skill or approach, rather than a learning experience for the students. While it is important to have an interesting lesson, his major focus is on improving his skill in this one area. Arrangements having been made, the teacher teaches the lesson to a small group of students. After the lesson is over, feedback forms are handed out to the students. The teacher and the supervisor may also fill out these rating forms. The trainee and the supervisor then enter the critique phase. Normally, they both examine the written feedback forms and review the videotape. The critique sessions are not aimed at across-the-board improvement of the trainee's performance. Rather, the intention is to focus on the specific skill being practiced. Normally, a trainee would go through a full series of microteaching experiences to gain competence in an array of teaching styles, strategies, and skills.

By design, microteaching is not "real world" teaching. Instead of learning by trial and error (or not at all) the trainee acquires new skills in an environment that is safe both for him and for the students. Like the other teacher-training approaches described in this section, microteaching should not be interpreted as *the* approach, but as one of many approaches needed to train the highly competent professional teacher.

Human relations training

All of us have known teachers whose personalities or ways of interacting with people undercut their effectiveness as teachers. You may have had a teacher who reacted defensively to questions and, in turn, put students on the defensive. Or you may have known a teacher who was so shy that students either wanted to protect her or continually challenged her authority. Human relations problems not only limit a teacher's effectiveness, but also sap any satisfaction he might get from working with people. Such problems are the concern of a new movement in our culture, known by various labels such as T-grouping, encounters, the bod biz, sensitivity training, and therapy for normals. The most common label, however, is human relations training. Its aim is to help us to become more sensitive to ourselves and to the ways in which we interact with others.

Interest in human relations training is not confined to teachers. However, it can be argued that it is particularly pertinent to teaching, since effective leadership and communication are essential components of the teacher's role. The aim of human relations training is to clear away communication difficulties and leadership problems. To accomplish these rather straightforward objectives, a variety of techniques, some quite unorthodox, are employed. Typically, individuals join a group organized by a trained leader. Through a series of exercises and games whose purpose is to break through superficial communication, individuals gain a greater understanding of the way they are perceived by others. They also become involved in helping other group members see themselves accurately and adopt more fruitful methods of communicating. It is difficult to speak with any precision about the human relations training movement because it is new and highly diverse. Also, its effectiveness depends both on the skill and sensitivity of the trainer and on the mental health of the group member. It is no cure-all for someone who is emotionally unstable. It resembles microteaching in that it is an environment created to enable people to learn some things about themselves which they can later apply in real life.

Some educators regard human relations training as an antidote to what they consider the schools' excessive attention to cognitive matters. In their view, teachers have been overly concerned with the mind and minimally concerned with the body, and have largely ignored the emotional life of children. Human relations training, therefore, attempts to make the future teacher aware of the interdependence of his own mind, body, and emotions and then of that of his students. When a particular human relations training encounter accomplishes these goals, it is undeniably enriching the training of a teacher.

New media

The primary mode of most formal education is the spoken word. While words have great power, they can have severe limitations as well. For instance, the word "radical" may be decoded by two different people in entirely dissimilar ways. Some words, such as "mother," carry so much emotional weight that a person cannot respond to them objectively. And, again, some uncommon words are devoid of meaning for many individuals. "Flagellation" is a meaningless sound to many people. These and other difficulties with words often make verbal communication, both written and spoken, imprecise and incomplete. This is always unfortunate, and it can be particularly so in teacher education when theories, concepts, and principles are being discussed. Also, words can have limited value when a supervisor is attempting to talk to a student teacher about his teaching performance. The new communications media are a way of alleviating this problem by making the education process less exclusively dependent on words.

Film is hardly a new medium in teacher education, but promising new ways of using it are being devised, among them the development of protocol materials for teaching. Protocol materials are slices of life that have been captured on film or videotape and are used to analyze and gain understanding of people's behavior. Since all of a child's experience bears on his life in school, protocols are not restricted to classroom episodes.[8]

Instead of talking or reading about the way children behave in certain classroom situations, a protocol may be shown in a teacher education class. The students might first watch it to identify the behavior occurring in the class. After a second and, possibly, third viewing, students make tentative hypotheses about the teaching-learning strategies exhibited. Finally, they may discuss and arrive at an evaluation of what is taking place in the class. One of the major benefits of protocol materials is that they capture life in the raw in a form that allows it

[8] Listings of available protocol materials may be obtained from Dr. Donald Orlosky, College of Education, University of South Florida, Tampa, Florida.

How do people become teachers?

to be analyzed over and over again. This, in turn, enables the student of teaching to look deeply into classroom events and to develop a precise vocabulary to talk about the complex phenomena of the classroom. Further, protocol materials allow abstract principles to be presented in the context of concrete situations, enhancing the potential for learning.

In teaching, understanding is not enough. Theory must become part of the teacher's practice. Making the transition from theory to practice is the job of training. The new media are making an important contribution to training in that they provide the means to present models and to provide feedback. In order to bridge the gap from theory to practice, it is helpful to have an explicit model of the behavior we want to acquire. This is especially true in the acquisition of complex teaching skills and strategies. Films and videotapes can make models of teaching excellence readily available to beginning and experienced teachers. Understanding the principles behind a five-step problem-solving strategy, for instance, may not be enough to enable you to put it into practice. However, if you were able to observe repeatedly one or two models of this problem-solving technique, the chances of your being able to perform it would be greatly increased.

Feedback, the other important ingredient in the acquisition of new behaviors, has been enhanced in efficiency and effect by the wide distribution of videotape recorders. The videotape recorder, or VTR, can provide instant or delayed feedback in such varied training settings as tutoring, simulated and microteaching sessions, and student teaching. The teacher-in-training can see his own behavior as it appears to others. He can observe it repeatedly, analyzing it for weaknesses and ways to improve. He can show it to others to gain their insights and observations. And, finally, he can use videotape recordings as a record of his progress over a period of time.

The new media have significantly extended the potential impact of teacher education, and have pointed teacher education in new directions. In addition, the new media have a second-level impact of some importance. For many years critics have complained that teachers do not use the media and audiovisual aids available to them in the classroom. Overhead projectors, films, and records commonly sit in the corner gathering dust. Sometimes teachers do not even know how to operate the equipment. If there is any truth to the old saying that teachers teach as they were taught, the use of new media in teacher training could help break this dismal cycle. Marshall McLuhan claims that the medium is the message. If the medium of teacher education is a rich use of media, the message—that they can enhance instruction—will be taken seriously. Unfortunately, not all teacher education programs have the size and staff and the financial resources to take advantage of these new media.

Competency-based teacher education programs

Most teacher education programs have rather nebulous goals, i.e., educating the effective teacher. The means of achieving the goal—courses and student teaching—are explicit enough, but exactly how it is achieved usually remains decidedly vague. Also, the customary way of assessing whether a goal has been achieved is dubious. The usual criteria are satisfactory grades on paper-and-pencil tests at the ends of courses and the ability to survive student teaching. The impreciseness of this approach keeps teacher education in the dark about what it actually is accomplishing.

In the last few years a new approach to teacher education called "competency-based teacher education" (CBTE) has been developing and offers promise to improve teacher education. A CBTE program specifies the competencies to be demonstrated by the teacher trainee, makes explicit the criteria to be applied in assessing the trainee's competencies, and holds the trainee accountable for meeting those criteria. There are three types of competencies which can be measured: 1) teacher knowledge—facts, principles, generalizations, awareness, and sensitivities that the teacher is expected to acquire and demonstrate (quite possibly measured by paper and pencil tests); 2) teacher performance—behaviors that the teacher is expected to demonstrate that are believed to help foster desired outcomes in children; and 3) teacher consequences—outcomes that the teacher is expected to bring about in the emotional and intellectual growth of his pupils.

The major point to emphasize is that in a CBTE program certain competencies and criteria for judging those competencies are unambiguously specified and are made public to the trainees in advance. Rather than leaving the competencies and criteria vague, they are made as explicit as possible. Thus, the important consideration is whether the trainee demonstrates competency on specific criteria rather than whether he has taken a particular course. By specifying the knowledge, performance, and competencies expected of trainees, learning experiences can be specifically designed to help the trainee acquire and demonstrate the competencies. Courses, or other instructional units such as modules, become the means by which trainees acquire competencies.

At the present time there is no evidence that CBTE programs produce more effective teachers than traditional programs, but the CBTE emphasis on specific outcomes offers the opportunity to test the effectiveness of these programs that the more traditional programs that emphasize courses instead of outcomes do not.

The teacher's continuing education

After the mortarboard, what?

To become a teacher is not only to commit yourself to your students; it is also a commitment to yourself to be a continuing learner. The idea that one's education ends with graduation from college is foolish for anyone. For the teacher, it is tragic. To be a teacher in the last quarter of the twentieth century is to try to make comprehensible to children a world that is constantly changing, and that many adults have difficulty making sense of. What is known is expanding moment by moment. New information and theories are replacing yesterday's ideas. Society's needs and those of the individual (which are frequently contradictory) are shifting and evolving. What is useful and relevant to life in a post-industrial society will not remain constant. In quieter times, just a few decades ago, the teacher did not need to know as much—and what he did know seemed quite stable. To fulfill his commitments to society and self, today's teacher must be a continuous learner.

From one point of view there is nothing new in this. It has always been true that when someone stops learning himself, he cannot deal effectively with other learners. He loses the sense of what it's like to learn, and thus loses touch with what his students are experiencing. The nonlearning teacher becomes a mechanic. He may give out valuable information and aid people in acquiring needed skills, but he also exudes intellectual sterility. He is telling his students, "I really don't find learning exciting. I really don't enjoy the life of the mind."

<table>
<tr><td>

Types of continuous learning opportunities

</td><td>

One of the aims of education, according to school constitutions and college catalogues, is to develop the ability to engage in independent study. Independent study is jargon for being able to go it alone. Although it is much discussed by educators, students seem to get little actual practice in choosing their own areas of interest and systematically investigating them. Independent study, though, is one of the most important means available to the teacher for his continual self-renewal. The teacher is daily confronted with things he does not understand about children and knowledge and their interaction. "What are children really doing when they yell out answers to homework problems?" "What are the fundamental skills of composition that children should know?" "How can I help my students to use history for their own benefit?" Such questions are daily grist for the teacher's independent study mill. Of course, the teacher's study should not be confined to professional problems. His own interests may lead him into such areas as organic gardening, physical fitness, old movies, politics in colonial America, or the humanizing of the corporate state. Not by professional problems alone doth the teacher live!

</td></tr>
</table>

Group study is another common mode of continuing learning for the teacher. It frequently takes the form of committee work. Problems arise in the school for which there is no apparent solution, so a group of people take on themselves the task of exploring the problem with a view toward recommending an enlightened course of action. In recent years, teachers and administrators have begun inviting community residents to these study groups in order to have the input of opinions from outside the confines of the school. Typical issues these study groups might take on are "Alternatives to the present second-grade reading program," "An analysis of the unused educational resources in a particular community," and "The potential benefits and cost of using paraprofessionals in our high schools."

A third way of continuing to learn is to take courses or work toward an advanced degree. Most colleges and universities offer courses suitable and interesting to teachers. Special and regular courses are offered in the evening and during the summer vacation. These courses and degree programs not only allow teachers to gain a deeper understanding of their work, but also make it possible for some teachers to train for other jobs in education, such as guidance counseling, administration, or college teaching.

Besides personal satisfaction, there are very real incentives for teachers to participate in continual schooling. In most school districts with a salary scale, the two major variables that affect a teacher's salary are his years of teaching experience and his formal education. A teacher with a master's degree frequently makes as much as a thousand dollars more than a fellow teacher with equal experience and no master's degree. While this is a rather crass reason to pursue graduate study, it does indicate the taxpayers' belief that teachers should be continually upgrading themselves. Many states require teachers to do advanced graduate work to keep their initial certification. Some require the master's degree for permanent certification.

In addition to the general categories of continuing education mentioned above, there is a considerable variety of activities that can enrich the professional life of a teacher, such as participating in a teacher education program, writing a new curriculum, joining an encounter group, working on a research project, taking summer employment in an entirely different field, taking a sabbatical year of travel and study, or making a film. Not only can such activities be personally satisfying, but they can also make us more stimulating teachers.

Any human activity, even one as challenging and ever-changing as teaching, can lose its excitement. A commitment to continuing education is a way of dealing with this condition of life. Besides the activities suggested above, the habit of daily asking yourself, "What am I trying to do?" and "What is this about?" will help make you a continuous learner and an effective teacher.

Discussion questions

1 There is a proverb that "teachers are born, not made." What arguments can you marshal for or against it?

2 What are some of the outstandingly effective and ineffective teacher behaviors you have observed in your years of teacher-watching? What have you learned from the media models you have seen? What experiences have you had or do you expect to have in the teacher education program at your college or university?

3 What kind of educational experience would you like to design for yourself? Can you carry it out? Why or why not? How can you use your current courses to help you explore some aspect of education that interests you? What else can you do to make your education relevant? What will you do?

4 How does our statement that "we have become prisoners of the way things used to be" relate to teaching behavior, both personally and culturally? What's wrong with the traditional notion of a professional sequence of courses as the major vehicle of teacher education? What's right with it?

5 Can you think of any explanation other than those we proposed for the defection from teaching of many trained teachers?

6 Do you want to be trained for schools as they are or as they might be? What might be done to alleviate the isolation of teacher training institutions from the schools that will employ their graduates?

7 What are the advantages of practical experience early in teacher training? What are the disadvantages? Do you think that the principle behind simulation is valid? What are the advantages and disadvantages of simulation as a training method? of microteaching?

8 Which of the new approaches to teacher education we have discussed are available in your school's program? Would you like to experience some that are not currently available? What can you do about it?

9 What possible implications do you see in our suggestion that you become a critical consumer of your education? Try to imagine the attitudes, tactics, and traditions of the marketplace, and of the consumer movement, applied to education. Suppose this idea were adopted in the schools?

How do people become teachers?

For further reading

- Allen, Dwight, and Ryan, Kevin. *Microteaching.* Reading, Mass.: Addison-Wesley, 1969. This book describes the microteaching approach to teacher training. In addition to the rationale and mechanics of microteaching, a number of practical applications of microteaching are described.
- Conant, James B. *The Education of American Teachers.* New York: McGraw-Hill Paperbacks, 1964. This book is based on a study of teacher education in this country. It analyzes the problem and proposes sweeping changes. Although over ten years old, it still has much to say to the field.
- Eddy, Elizabeth. *Becoming a Teacher.* New York: Teachers College Press, 1969. This slim book analyzes the process of becoming a teacher from the point of view of an anthropologist. The author finds many parallels between becoming a seasoned professional and being initiated into adulthood in primitive tribes.
- Fuchs, Estelle. *Teachers Talk: Views from Inside City Schools.* Garden City, New York: Doubleday, 1969. A collection of teachers' statements about themselves, schools, and learning during their initial four months of teaching in an urban setting. The author analyzes these statements, explicating the underlying assumptions of the teachers and suggesting alternative actions.
- Koerner, James. *The Miseducation of American Teachers.* Gretna, La.: Pelican, 1963. A somewhat dated, but still biting, critique of our institutions and practices for the training of teachers.
- Ryan, Kevin, ed. *Don't Smile Until Christmas: Accounts of the First Year of Teaching.* Chicago: University of Chicago Press, 1970. A collection of six exceedingly honest biographical statements by beginning high-school teachers. A concluding chapter on the first year of teaching by the editor.
- Silberman, Charles E. *Crisis in the Classroom.* New York: Random House, 1970. Sponsored by the Carnegie Foundation, Silberman's book argues that American schools are grim, joyless places—oppressive, intellectually sterile, and aesthetically barren. This condition, Silberman argues, is due primarily to the mindlessness of American education. However, he finds hope in the implementation of concepts borrowed from British primary schools.
- Smith, B. Othanel; Cohen, Sol B.; and Pearl, Arthur. *Teachers for the Real World.* Washington, D.C.: American Association of Colleges for Teacher Education, 1969. A major report by a high-level committee on teacher education. Building on what is already known about the preparation of teachers, it charts a sound and workable plan for the future. A milestone book.
- Stephens, J. M. *The Process of Schooling.* New York: Holt, Rinehart & Winston, 1967. A distinguished educational psychologist presents a unique view of the effects of schooling and how children learn.
- Waller, Willard. *The Sociology of Teaching.* New York: Wiley, 1965. This book first appeared in 1932 but is surprisingly fresh and alive. Waller describes the life of a teacher and the forces within his school and community that impinge upon his work.

Films

- *Blackboard Jungle* (Films, Inc., 16mm, b&w, 101 min., 1955). Although made quite a few years ago, this film's depiction of a large-city vocational training school is still quite interesting. The problems encountered by teachers are not very different from those presented in *To Sir, With Love.*

- *Education for Psychological Maturity* (Indiana University Audio-Visual Center, 16mm, b&w, 29 min.). Featured personality in this film from the "Philosophies of Education Series" is Arthur Jersild, professor at Teachers College, Columbia University. The film explores theories presented in Dr. Jersild's book, *When Teachers Face Themselves.*
- *The End of a Morning* (EDC, 16mm, b&w, 1969). Made at the Hilltop Head Start Center in Roxbury, Mass., this film shows a classroom of four-year-olds completing their morning's activities. A final segment illustrates the teachers' comments to one another about how the day has gone.
- *Good Morning, Miss Dove* (Twyman Films, 16mm, color, 106 min.). Based on the novel by Frances Patton, this film tells the story of a small-town geography teacher. As Miss Dove reminisces about her life, the viewer is presented with many amusing examples of "how people become teachers."
- *A Lot of Undoing To Do* (Philadelphia Board of Education, 16mm, b&w, 15 min., 1967). Another film from the series in the 1967 Philadelphia Cooperative Schools Program. Rather than describing the development of a particular curriculum, this film documents an attempt to train teachers in the general philosophy of a "process curriculum" by having them participate in sensitivity groups, improvisational drama, and the like during a summer training program. The film effectively juxtaposes the reality of the school situation with the ideas explored during the summer program.
- *Making Things to Learn* (EDC Film Library, 16mm, b&w, 11:27 min.). A film on the workshop process. Filmed in public, private, and Head Start classrooms in the Boston area, *Making Things to Learn* shows adults building various kinds of educational materials and children using the materials in their classrooms.
- *Minicourses* (Macmillan, 1973). These kits, consisting of film sequences and workbooks, are a sample of the kind of instructional training available to beginning teachers. Offered at different grade levels, the courses deal with such problems as asking effective questions in mathematics and individualizing instruction in oral language. They are designed to be self-teaching and self-evaluative, and they rely on the supplied films as well as on videotaped microteaching lessons.
- *Personalizing Educational Programs* (Oakland Community College, Michigan, color, 20 min., 1972). This film reports on the progress of Oakland Community College's program to develop an educational plan for each student based on individual cognitive strengths. It is listed here primarily as an example of the kind of analytical tools available to teachers for individualizing instruction.
- *Psychology Film Series* (CRM Productions, color, approx. 30 min. each, 1969–   ). This series of films provides a general background in many fields of psychology and includes a number of titles of interest to teachers who want to understand the learning process. Most of the films include a segment of documentary behavior followed by an analysis from a scholar in the field. Relevant titles include *Learning, Development, Cognitive Development, Emotional Development, Moral Development,* and *One Step at a Time: An Introduction to Behavior Modification.*
- *This is Marshall McLuhan: The Medium is the Message* (Contemporary/McGraw-Hill, 16mm, color, 53 min., 1968, NBC News). This discussion by Marshall McLuhan dramatizes his belief that electronic media are orienting society toward an "all-at-once" mode of perception. McLuhan's views on the effects of mass media have strongly influenced the "media movement" in education.
- *To Sir, With Love* (Columbia Cinematheque, 16mm, color, 105 min.). Based on E. R. Braithwaite's award-winning autobiographical novel, this film stars Sidney

How do people become teachers?

Poitier as a teacher in a "rough" school in London's East End. The film catalogue description claims that he "treats them as adults and imbues them with standards of decency."

- *Up the Down Staircase* (Warner Bros., 16mm, color, 123 min.). Adapted from the book by Bel Kaufman, this film portrays a large-city school from the viewpoint of a young, idealistic teacher on her first assignment.
- *The Workshop Process* (The University of California, 16mm, 12 min.). Documents the organization, operation, and evaluation of a teachers' workshop in the Montbello School District in California.

Audiotapes

- *Education, Technology, and Values* (Canadian Broadcasting Corporation, 30 min., 1971). A discussion of the impact of new technology—its practices, theories, and goals—on the teacher and on pupil expectations. The use of computers, television, and portable tape equipment will change both the social content and the methodology of education, according to Dr. Fred Rainsberry, former head of the CBC Youth Division; Graham Scott, Univac employee and school trustee; and Murray Shukyn, the prime mover behind the experimental SEED school in Toronto.
- *Intensive Group Experience* (Big Sur Recordings, 3.75 ips, reel or cassette, mono or stereo). The history and development of the encounter group method is explained by Carl Rogers.
- *On Staying Awake: Talks With Teachers* (National Education Association, 3.75 ips, reel or cassette). These taped addresses to teachers are based on a written

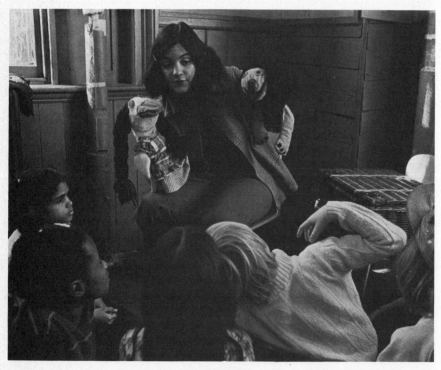

work by Ole Sand called *On Staying Awake,* which describes a multilevel approach to humanizing education.

- *The Person of Tomorrow* (Big Sur Recordings, 3.75 ips, reel or cassette, mono, 90 min., 1970). Carl Rogers presents his views on rock music, violence on campus, and the encounter group movement, and in so doing discusses some changes necessary in education.
- *Principles and Philosophy of Open Encounter* (Big Sur Recordings, 3.75 ips, reel or cassette, mono or stereo, 1 hour). William Schutz informally discusses, with participants at the Esalen Institute, an overview of the encounter group movement, its philosophy, and some underlying premises on which open encounter is based.
- *Psychology and Education for the New Age* (Noumedia, 3.75 ips, $\frac{1}{4}$ track, mono or stereo, 5 hours). This long tape was made at the Menninger Foundation in Topeka, Kansas, in 1970, and covers a great deal of ground for teachers, therapists, and others interested in psychology and education.
- *Rules of Thumb of Open Encounter* (Big Sur Recordings, 3.75 ips, reel or cassette, mono or stereo, 1 hour, 1968). In this second tape, Dr. Schutz outlines his own guidelines for running encounter groups.
- *Seminar on Encounter and Education* (Big Sur Recordings, 3.75 ips, reel or cassette, mono or stereo channeling, 4 hours). Carl Rogers lectures on the use of encounter methods in education and, in an informal seminar, develops the question, "How would we plan a college based upon encounter methods?"

Videotapes

- *Motivating Children to Learn* (Great Plains National ITV Library, b&w, 15 30-min. videotapes or videocassettes, 1968). Dr. Rudolf Dreikurs addresses teachers in this series of lectures on techniques for overcoming reluctance to learn. Case studies and group discussions are part of the presentations, which always center around the child's view of the world.
- *Catalog of Video Tapes for Teacher Education* (Carleton College, various formats, b&w, 1971). This catalog lists an enormous collection of protocol materials from classrooms at different grade levels and in different curriculum areas. Although the administrators of the videotape project warn that the tapes were not made for the purpose of criticizing any particular teaching style, the collection as a whole becomes almost a taxonomy of behaviors, allowing education students to observe the variety of means that can be used in the classroom.

Mediagraphy

- *Mediated Teacher Education Resources* (American Association of Colleges for Teacher Education, 1970). Under headings by medium, this book lists a rather thin sample of the films, slides, audiotapes, videotapes, and simulation games available to teacher education programs. Many of the materials included are designed to help prospective teachers anticipate and confront behavioral and attitudinal problems in the classroom. Catalogs from the distributors listed in the back of the present volume would probably constitute a varied and valuable collection of teacher education media resources.

Refer to Appendix for addresses of distributors.

How do people become teachers?

4　What makes a teacher a teacher?

This chapter describes what we believe to be the essential attributes that distinguish teachers from other educated persons. Effective teaching is much more than an intuitive process. A teacher must continually make decisions and act upon those decisions. In order to do this effectively the teacher must possess theoretical knowledge about learning and human behavior, demonstrate a repertoire of teaching skills that are believed to facilitate student learning, display attitudes that foster learning and genuine human relationships, and possess knowledge in the subject matter to be taught.

"Teaching! What a deal!"

"That's the life—two weeks off at Christmas and three months' vacation every summer."

"What're you getting paid for, anyway? Just talking to kids!"

"*Anybody* can do that. . . ."

But *can* just anybody teach? Is "just talking to kids" the essence of teaching? What should a teacher know and be able to do that will make him more capable and effective than a nonteacher? This question is the central focus of this chapter. It is our goal that while reading you continually ask yourself what kind of teacher you would like to be, and what you can do to make your ideal self-image as a teacher a reality.

The teacher's role is much more complex than it appears to the casual observer. Colleges and universities, however, generally operate on the assumption that knowledge of the subject matter is all that is necessary to become a teacher. This is undoubtedly why so many college professors—despite their Ph.D.s and expertise in their fields—have difficulty communicating their knowledge.

Until recently, almost nothing has been known about what constitutes effective teaching or about how one could be trained as an effective teacher. Thus, historically, colleges did not neglect pedagogy out of contempt for the subject, but because so little reliable data existed about teaching that it was not considered a subject at all. Although we are still far from having all the answers, educational research during the last decade has brought us much closer to understanding teaching and learning.

Most observers would agree that elementary and secondary teachers require knowledge and skills unique to the teaching profession. A teacher must ask himself not only "What am I going to teach?" but also "What should my students be learning?" "How can I help them learn it?" and "Why is it important?" To answer these questions the teacher must be familiar with children and their developmental stages. He must know something about events occurring outside the classroom and about what society needs and requires from the young. He must have enough command of the subjects he is going to teach to be able to distinguish what is peripheral from what is central. He must have a philosophy of education to guide him in his role as a teacher. And he must know something about how human beings learn and how to create environments that facilitate learning.

What are the specialized skills and attributes of the effective teacher? As mentioned in the introduction, the four areas of competence that we consider essential for a teacher are:

1 command of theoretical knowledge about learning and human behavior
2 control of technical skills of teaching that facilitate student learning
3 display of attitudes that foster learning and genuine human relationships
4 sureness and adequacy of knowledge in the subject matter to be taught

The rest of this chapter will examine these four areas of competence in depth.

What theoretical knowledge does the teacher need?

Teacher education programs are frequently criticized by prospective teachers on the grounds that they overemphasize theory at the expense of practice. Experienced teachers commonly tell beginners, "Forget all that theory they're giving you at the university. Here's what works in the real world. . . ." The problem, though, is not that theory is wrong or unworkable, but that many teacher education programs offer students no opportunities to apply theory to practical situations; it is usually up to the neophyte teacher to translate theory into practice on the job. But theory is no less important for the failure to apply it effectively. As has often been said, "Nothing is as practical as a good theory."

Theoretical knowledge about learning and human behavior equips the teacher to draw on concepts from psychology, anthropology, sociology, and related disciplines to interpret the complex reality of the classroom. The teacher who lacks theoretical background will be obliged to interpret classroom events according to commonly held beliefs or common sense, much of which is, unfortunately, based on outmoded notions of human behavior. As Josh Billings said almost a century ago, "The trouble ain't that people are ignorant; it's that they 'know' so much that ain't so." Consider the following statements:

- The more content a person knows, the better a teacher he is.
- Content is best kept pure by departmentalizing instruction.
- Content or subject matter has a logical structure or logical sequence that dictates how it should be taught.
- Bigger schools are better than smaller schools.
- Smaller classes are better than bigger classes.
- Homogeneous grouping (grouping pupils of comparable intelligence or ability for instructional purposes) makes learning more efficient.
- Classes must last for about an hour for optimal learning to take place.[1]

All of these contentions are commonly believed among educated people, including educators, yet there is no evidence to verify any of them and considerable evidence to refute them.

Every teacher should be familiar with currently respected theoretical knowledge about human behavior and social systems. In addition to such general knowledge there exists specialized theoretical knowledge, which is the unique province of the effective teacher. Teaching is neither static nor a matter of intuition; it has given rise to a body of theoretical knowledge that is constantly growing.

What is theoretical knowledge?

Theoretical knowledge that relates to teaching has been described by B. O. Smith as data that makes up a large part of the content of the disciplines and consists of concepts and laws that are conditional propositions; that is, a set of conditions is stated and a set of consequences associated with the conditions is also stated.[2] An example of relevant theory derived from psychology is the concept of *reinforcement,* defined as any event that increases the strength of a given response. A student who is praised for a certain behavior is likely to repeat it; the praise functions as reinforcement. Psychologists also state that frequent reviews immediately after initial learning, followed by relatively widely spaced reviews over a period of time, are likely to increase retention of knowledge. Thus, a teacher who consciously refers to a concept discussed earlier in the week and continues to draw parallels to it throughout a unit is likely to help the students grasp and remember the concept. (See page 141 for some of psychology's contributions to what we know about learning.)

How does one acquire theoretical knowledge?

Theoretical knowledge relevant to teaching is derived from courses or disciplines such as educational psychology, educational sociology, educational anthropology, linguistics, foundations of education, tests and measurement, and classroom management. But because the relationship of theoretical knowledge to a given occupation is typically indirect, as Smith emphasizes, it is not enough for you simply to take the appropriate courses. Theory develops within a dis-

[1] Adapted from Neil Postman and Charles Weingarter, *Teaching as a Subversive Activity* (New York: Dell 1969), p. 144.
[2] B. O. Smith et al., *Teachers for the Real World* (Washington, D.C.: American Association of College for Teacher Education, 1969), p. 42.

What do we know about learning?

Behaviors which are rewarded (reinforced) are more likely to recur.
Sheer repetition without indications of improvement or any kind of reinforcement is a poor way to attempt to learn.
Threat and punishment have variable and uncertain effects upon learning; they may make the punished response more likely or less likely to recur; they may set up avoidance tendencies which prevent further learning.
Reward (reinforcement), to be most effective in learning, must follow almost immediately after the desired behavior and be clearly connected with that behavior in the mind of the learner.
The type of reward (reinforcement) which has the greatest transfer value to other life-situations is the kind one gives oneself—the sense of satisfaction in achieving purposes.
Opportunity for fresh, novel, stimulating experience is a kind of reward which is quite effective in conditioning and learning.
Forgetting proceeds rapidly at first—then more and more slowly; recall shortly after learning reduces the amount forgotten.
The most rapid mental growth occurs during infancy and early childhood; the average child achieves about half of his total mental growth by the age of five.
Not until eleven years of age do most children develop the sense of time which is required for historical perspective.
The most effective effort is put forth by children when they attempt tasks which fall in the "range of challenge"—not too easy and not too hard—where success seems quite possible but not certain.
Children are more apt to throw themselves wholeheartedly into any project if they themselves have participated in the selection and planning of the enterprise.
Reaction to excessive direction by the teacher may be: (a) apathetic conformity, (b) defiance, (c) scapegoating, (d) escape from the whole affair.
Over-strict discipline is associated with more conformity, anxiety, shyness and acquiescence in children; greater permissiveness is associated with more initiative and creativity in children.
What is learned is most likely to be available for use if it is learned in a situation much like that in which it is to be used and immediately preceding the time when it is needed. Learning in childhood, forgetting, and relearning when needed is not an efficient procedure.
If there is a discrepancy between the real objectives and the tests used to measure achievement, the latter become the main influence upon choice of subject matter and method.

Goodwin Watson, "What Psychology Can We Feel Sure About?"
Teachers College Record (1960), pp. 253–257. Reprinted as a separate pamphlet under the title *What Psychology Can We Trust?* (New York: Bureau of Publications, Teachers College, Columbia University, 1961).

cipline and is formulated in terms suitable to that discipline but usually unsuitable or inadequate for a learning situation. For teachers this means that principles derived from psychology must be adapted to a classroom before they become useful. A classroom is always subject to a number of variables

What makes a teacher a teacher?

absent in the experimental situation. In the late afternoon of a school day, for instance, both teacher and student are likely to be tired, and their behavior then is likely to differ from what it would have been in the morning. In contrast, the laboratory experiments from which theory is derived are controlled to eliminate such variables. Thus, a teacher must have a command not only of the theoretical knowledge but also of the learning situation, in order to make the necessary adaptations.

Perhaps an example will clarify the need for adaptation. A student teacher "knows" from her educational psychology course that any behavior that is reinforced will be strengthened. Yet she deals with a noisy student by calling his outbursts to the attention of the rest of the class. What she doesn't realize is that by publicly acknowledging his behavior and attracting other students' attention to him, she may be reinforcing his noisemaking. The student teacher, of course, is at a loss to explain why the boy persists in his behavior despite her reprimands. Her theoretical knowledge has not been internalized to the point that she draws on it instinctively in the classroom. Many apparently inexplicable events of the classroom will make sense only when they are related to theories of human behavior. Make no mistake about it—this is a difficult task and does not come easily. It requires practice, insight, and the advice and assistance of colleagues. You should view real or simulated classroom situations in conjunction with your courses in theory, and practice applying the appropriate concepts to your observations. It is also valuable to exchange ideas, interpretations, and solutions with other teachers, both to verify your own views and to gain insight into other valid interpretations of the same events.

How can theoretical knowledge be used?
A teacher's theoretical knowledge can be used in two ways: to interpret situations and to solve problems. (Practical knowledge, on the other hand, is more limited in applicability and is used primarily to respond to familiar situations.)[3] For example, a teacher may see a child acting like a bully and interpret the child's aggression as a reaction to some frustration the child had experienced. In doing so the teacher would be drawing on theoretical knowledge about frustration and its possible consequences to interpret the child's behavior. To solve the problem, the teacher would avoid shaming the child but would seek the causes of his frustration and try to channel the child's energy in a more constructive direction. Adults lacking theoretical knowledge would be likely to attribute the child's aggression to "bad character" and be unable to deal with the situation.

Problem solving is a primary aspect of the role of the teacher. He is constantly required to make diagnoses and decisions about problems related to learning and to human relations. In order to do this effectively the teacher must possess a high degree of theoretical understanding. He applies this understanding by formulating hypotheses both about the interpretation of problems and about the actions he should undertake in response to them. But there should be no air of finality about his proposed solutions. If the actions the teacher has chosen do not solve the problem, the situation should be reinterpreted and alternative responses sought and tested.

Classroom problems are rarely entirely original, except in the case of the new teacher, to whom nearly all are unprecedented. As a result, once a teacher has

[3] Smith, p. 44.

developed and incorporated a solution to a given problem, he will tend to use the same solution, with appropriate modifications, when confronted by similar situations; a solution that worked once in a particular situation is habitually relied upon as the "correct" way to handle all related problems. One teacher's means of handling disruptive outbursts might be to separate the offending child from the others by putting him in the corner. This solution deals only with the symptom, rather than the problem itself, which might vary from insecurity due to parental neglect to dislike of the school environment. Single-solution behavior is dangerous because it fails to take into account all the variables of individual situations. Also, a solution that is overused tends to become ineffective. Teachers must guard against the "single-solution rut."

Because of their insecurity and lack of theoretical knowledge, beginning teachers often seek "recipes" to solve certain categories of problems. "What do I do when one child hits another?" Questions of this type are requests for pat answers which can be automatically "plugged in" when needed. Unfortunately, this approach rarely works because the reasons why one child hits another are as numerous as are the possible and appropriate teacher responses. As a teacher you should not only refrain from using "single solutions" but also avoid seeking them; instead, you should acquire knowledge about learning, patterns of behavior, how children from different cultural backgrounds behave, and what values they possess, and familiarity with such concepts as motivation, self-concept, feedback, reinforcement, attitude formation, perception, and peer approval.

Let's consider an example of how theoretical knowledge can help a teacher interpret classroom events and solve the problems arising from them. In psychology, *self-concept* is defined as the sum of a person's beliefs about and evaluations of himself as a person. Every individual has an image of the kind of person he is, derived from previous experiences, and he tends to behave in ways that are consistent with that image. A child's self-concept is an important factor in both his ability to learn and his interaction with other children and his environment. For instance, if a child views himself as likeable and outgoing, he is apt to respond in a friendly manner when meeting new children. If a child is insecure because he views himself as weak, ugly, or unwanted, he will not respond easily to a group of new children.

Suppose a teacher observes that a particular child is doing poorly in science. The problem at issue is how to help this child improve his performance in that subject. A number of factors may be influencing his performance—he may possess inadequate scientific concepts; he may not be interested in science; he

What makes a teacher a teacher?

may not be very intelligent; or he may view himself as poor in science and as a result not try as hard as he might. Several of these factors may be interrelated in complex ways.[4]

A teacher who functions as a problem solver would hypothesize that the child's poor performance could result from any of these factors and proceed to investigate further by collecting information about the child's previous performance in science, his intelligence level, and his self-concept. In this way the teacher can determine whether the child's self-concept is an important determinant in his poor science performance.

If the child's intelligence level is high and his previous experience indicates that he should be doing reasonably well in science, it might be hypothesized that the principal reason for the child's poor performance is his conception of his own abilities. What can the teacher do? Can a teacher help change a child's self-concept? The answer is an unequivocal maybe. If the teacher is one of the child's major sources of self-information, he may be able to encourage a revised self-concept through a guidance program designed to help the child gather reliable information about himself. Sometimes children lack self-understanding to such an extent that they must be referred to specialized professional help before progress can be made. Again, the teacher may have to make that decision on the basis of his own observations and knowledge.

If the child's problem does not seem serious enough to require referral to a specialist, the teacher himself might try any of several approaches to improve the child's self-concept in science. Discussing his abilities with him, helping him view his abilities more realistically, and arranging for a successful experience are among the potential ways to change the child's self-perception. The teacher proceeds throughout as an hypothesis-maker, forming tentative ideas about experiences that might improve the child's self-concept, and testing those ideas. The teacher's hypotheses will become more perceptive and accurate as his understanding of the variables influencing a child's self-concept increases.

A teacher needs much more than common-sense understanding of human behavior. The capable and effective teacher uses theoretical knowledge drawn from various education-related disciplines to formulate and test hypotheses about human behavior in the classroom. In our opinion, the translation of theory into practice cannot be left to chance; you must constantly seek experiences that allow you to apply theoretical concepts to classroom situations and to receive guidance and feedback about their application.

What teaching skills are required of an effective teacher?

Knowing vs. doing

Simply knowing something does not guarantee the ability to act upon that knowledge; there is a profound difference between *knowing* and *doing*. A teacher may know, for example, that he should ask his students questions that require more than mere factual answers, but he is not always able to act upon that knowledge.

[4] The authors are indebted for this example to Frederick J. McDonald, *Educational Psychology* (Belmont, California: Wadsworth, 1965), pp. 439–441.

No teacher education program can afford to focus exclusively on theoretical knowledge at the expense of the practice, or "doing," dimension of teaching, just as no individual teacher can rely solely on knowledge of subject matter. Every prospective teacher needs to develop a repertoire of teaching skills to use as he sees fit in varying classroom situations. In contrast to the theoretical knowledge component of a teacher's preparation, which focuses on the situation in which the teacher finds herself, the teaching skills component focuses on the trainee herself—the observation, analysis, and modification of her teaching behavior.

Research has not yet conclusively identified the teaching skills that have the most beneficial impact on student learning (the results of some very revealing studies, however, are reported in Chapter Six), but many educators have independently defined the skills they believe essential to good teaching, among them the following:

- the ability to ask different kinds of questions, each of which requires different types of thought processes from the student
- the ability to effectively reinforce certain kinds of student behavior
- the ability to diagnose student needs and learning difficulties
- the ability to continually vary the learning situation in order to keep the students involved
- the ability to recognize when students are paying attention and to use this information to vary behavior and, possibly, the direction of the lesson
- the ability to utilize technological equipment, such as motion picture projectors
- the ability to judge the appropriateness of instructional materials
- the ability to define the objectives of particular lessons and units in terms of student behaviors
- the ability to relate learning to the student's experience[5]

A repertoire of teaching skills

This list is far from complete. It does make clear, however, that teachers need a large repertoire of skills to work effectively with students with varying backgrounds and different educational goals. There is some evidence that the outstanding characteristic of a good teacher is flexibility,[6] since varied approaches are necessary to meet the multiple needs of students.

We believe strongly that a teacher education program should train candidates in the performance of selected teaching skills. Many teachers and teacher educators, however, blanch at the term "teacher training." They regard training as something one does with animals, not human beings; human beings, they say, should be educated, not trained. We don't agree. We believe that a teacher's preparation must consist of both education and training. The objection that training a teacher makes him a robot and prevents the release of his creative energies is contradicted by what we know of training in other occupations. Surgeons and pilots, for example, are trained to perform certain operations

[5] Partially adapted from Smith, *Teachers for the Real World*, p. 71.
[6] Donald Hamachek, "Characteristics of Good Teachers and Implications for Teacher Education," *Phi Delta Kappan* 50 (February 1969): 341–344.

proficiently and even automatically. This level of mastery enables them to turn their attention and energy to tasks more worthy of their creativity. As B. O. Smith says, "A trained individual has relaxed control, which frees him from preoccupation with immediate acts so he can scan the new situation and respond to it constructively. Training and resourcefulness are complementary, not antithetical, elements of behavior."[7]

The skills in which a teacher is trained should depend upon the age level and cultural background of the children he will teach, the subjects to be taught, research evidence on the effectiveness of certain skills, and other factors. Once the necessary skills have been selected, a training procedure is developed. Smith argues that the training process must have the following six components:

- establishment of the practice situation
- specification of the behavior
- performance of the specified behavior
- feedback of information about the performance
- modification of the performance in the light of the feedback
- performance-feedback-correction-practice schedule continued until desirable skillfulness is achieved[8]

Probing questions—
a representative
teaching skill

Before teaching skills can be acquired they must be specified. The specific behaviors or components that must be learned to master the skill must be described explicitly—vague or general descriptions will not provide adequate guidelines for the trainee. Consider the following material that was designed to teach the skill of asking probing questions. This skill description was developed as part of a training experiment that utilized beginning teachers at Stanford University.[9]

Today you will have an opportunity to develop skills in basic classroom questioning techniques. The session is designed to help you extend the range and quality of your questioning techniques in such a way that the pupils you teach are led to think more deeply about problems raised in class.

The techniques outlined below are designed to be used in discussion, review, and inductively organized lessons where active pupil participation is prerequisite to the realization of the goals of instruction. Any given technique may be appropriate in one situation but not in another. The selection of a particular technique depends upon the extent to which, in your judgment, it requires the pupil to analyze critically a problem or to justify rationally his answer. Do not use a given technique unless you feel it contributes to the educational relevance of the lesson.

Your goal is to ask penetrating and probing questions that require pupils to go beyond superficial, "first answer" responses.

[7] Smith, p. 80. Reprinted by permission of the publisher.
[8] Smith, p. 71.
[9] Frederick J. McDonald and Dwight W. Allen, *Training Effects of Feedback and Modeling Procedures o Teaching Performance* (Palo Alto, California: Stanford University, 1967), pp. 188–191.

Henry David Thoreau (1817–1862)

Henry David Thoreau, the American writer, naturalist, and dissenter, spent a relatively short period of his life as a teacher. In the opening chapter of *Walden,* he writes, "I have thoroughly tried schoolkeeping. As I did not teach for the good of my fellowman, but simply for a livelihood, this was a failure." Although Thoreau was passionately interested in education, he quickly recognized that he was not personally suited to teach in conventional schools.

Nevertheless, education remained one of his absorbing preoccupations. Thoreau thought of his entire life, and particularly the twenty-six months he spent at Walden Pond, as an educating act, undertaken not only to teach himself how to live but also as an example to his fellow men who had lost the art of living.

After graduating from Harvard, Thoreau applied for and was appointed to a position as teacher in the Concord village school. He had not yet been teaching for two weeks when a church deacon came to complain about his class and to warn that if he did not apply the rod, he would spoil the school. The story is that the same afternoon Thoreau selected six male students at random, beat them, and walked abruptly out of the school and to his lodgings to write a resignation.

The following year Thoreau and his brother John founded a school in Concord in which they could teach on their own terms. They began the year with four pupils, but the school was an instant success and they soon had as many students as they could handle.

Contrary to the common practice of the day, there was no corporal punishment in Thoreau's school; nevertheless, discipline was strict. One afternoon a week, the school went on a nature-study walk as a regular part of the curriculum. Here "the Captain of the Huckleberry party," as his friend Ralph Waldo Emerson called him, was in his element. A student later wrote that Thoreau could tame the fishes in the pond, feed the mice from his fingers, and keep up a fire of conversation while birds lighted on his head and shoulders. Pupils were amazed to discover that he knew every spot where wildflowers grew and every sheltered nook where climbing ferns hid. They found Thoreau a winning combination of the Pied Piper, St. Francis of Assisi, and Daniel Boone.

But this wonderful school was short-lived. After two years, John became ill and died. Henry was so deeply shaken by his brother's death that he made no effort to carry on the school.

Throughout his lifetime, Thoreau chided the schools, colleges, and general populace for their failures to improve education. His favorite target was Harvard, because of the remote-from-life quality of its curriculum. He claimed astonishment when he was informed upon leaving college that he had studied navigation. "One turn about the harbor would have given me more knowledge than four years as a student," he wrote.

What makes a teacher a teacher?

Thoreau set great store by the educative powers of physical labor. He argued that students should not play at life, or merely study it while the community supported them, but should work at and live through a profession from beginning to end. He proposed that colleges be built by students and teachers, not by contractors and laborers.

Thoreau was also concerned with the lack of educational opportunities for adults. He pioneered the cause of adult education, becoming enraged when the town of Concord spent sixteen thousand dollars on a town hall and nothing to educate adults. He saw no reason why the townspeople could not spend less for big barns and set aside something for works of art, journals, books, and scientific instruments. Every village, he said, should have a fine museum.

Thoreau was an ardent ecologist, convinced that nature should be the source of education. He begged townspeople to preserve the rivers, waterfalls, and meadows, both for their beauty and because he believed them more capable of educating than hired teachers and school systems. He admired American Indians for conceiving of education as learning to live within nature. The Indian's life, he suggested, was in harmony with the nature of man and the universe.

For all his praise of Indians, however, Thoreau never proposed that man give up booklearning. He imagined education as the process of achieving the best of both worlds: intimacy with nature and with the finest creations of civilization, the classics.

Basic questioning techniques: There are two ways of achieving the above goal: 1) The teacher asks penetrating questions that require pupils to get at the heart of the problem. This forestalls superficial answers. Whether you are able to do this largely depends upon your knowledge of relevant content; 2) The second approach is based on specific techniques that may be used after the pupil has responded in some way (i.e., a question, a comment, an answer to a teacher's question). The goal here is to get the pupil to go beyond his first response. You are attempting to produce greater critical awareness and depth by probing. Your cue is the pupil's response—once it has occurred, don't immediately go on with the discussion yourself. Probe his answer by means of one of the techniques outlined below.

1 Teacher seeks further clarification by the pupil: *You may ask the pupil for more information and/or more meaning. You may respond to the pupil's responses by saying such things as:*
    "What do you mean?"
    "Could you put that in other words to make clearer what you mean?"
    "Can you explain that further?"
    "What do you mean by the term . . .?"
2 Teacher seeks increased pupil critical awareness: *Here you are requiring the pupil to justify his response rationally. You may say:*
    "What are you/we assuming here?"
    "Why do you think that is so?"

"Have we/you oversimplified the issue—is there more to it?"

"Is this one or several questions?"

"How would someone who took the opposite point of view respond to this?"

3 Teacher seeks to refocus the pupil's response: *If a pupil has given a high quality answer, it may seem unnecessary to* probe *it. However, you can refocus his or the class's attention on a related issue.*

"Good! What are the implications of this for . . .?"

"How does this relate to . . .?"

"Can you take it from there and tie it into . . .?"

4 Teacher prompts pupil: *In prompting you are giving the pupil a hint to help him go on and answer a question. Suppose a pupil has given an I-don't-know or I'm-not-sure type of response. Rather than giving him the answer or redirecting the question to another pupil, you may give the puzzled student a hint.*

Teacher: "John, define the term 'polygenesis.'"

John: "I can't do it."

Teacher: (Prompting) "What does poly mean?" or, "Well, genesis means origin or birth, and poly means . . .?"

This technique allows you to probe *even though at first it appears that the pupil can't answer the question.*

5 Redirect: *This is not the* probing *technique per se. It helps you bring other students into the discussion quickly while still using* probing *techniques. In redirecting, you merely change the direction of interaction from yourself and the first pupil to yourself and the second pupil.*

Teacher: "What is the relationship between pressure and volume?"

First Pupil: "As the pressure goes up, the gas is condensed."

Teacher: (to Second Pupil) "Can you tell us what is meant by condensed?" Or, "Can you restate that in terms of volume?"

To sum up, the techniques outlined above have two things in common:

1 *They are initiated by the teacher immediately after the pupil has responded.*

2 *They require the pupil to go beyond the information he has already given.*

Concluding remarks: *Try to use the techniques as frequently as you can. Do not stay with one given technique for too long at one time. In addition, don't forget to reinforce when you* probe—*if you are not at ease you may otherwise behave like a "Philadelphia lawyer."*

If you prefer to run through the first five-minute lesson as a warm-up, this would be fine. You may teach the same lesson over two or three times. We will focus more on probing *than on transmitting new or complex material. The maximum amount of time for the session will be two hours.*

Many skills can be acquired in a simulated teaching situation in which the trainee is presented specific information and asked to take appropriate steps to solve the problem. Similarly, many teaching skills, such as the ability to ask probing questions, can be acquired through a relatively new training procedure called microteaching. Both simulation and microteaching have been discussed in Chapter Three.

What attitudes does the effective teacher possess?

Many people believe that the teacher's personality is the most critical factor in successful teaching. If the teacher possesses warmth, empathy, sensitivity, enthusiasm, and humor, he is much more likely to be successful than if he lacks these characteristics. In fact, many people argue that without these attributes an individual is unlikely to be a good teacher.

For years educational researchers have sought to isolate the characteristics essential to good teachers. In a massive study, David Ryans concluded that effective teachers are fair, democratic, responsive, understanding, kindly, stimulating, original, alert, attractive, responsible, steady, poised, and confident. Ineffective teachers were described as partial, autocratic, aloof, restricted, harsh, dull, stereotyped, apathetic, unimpressive, evasive, erratic, excitable, and uncertain.[10]

But this information is not very useful. After all, what human interaction wouldn't be improved if the participants possessed only positive traits? Getzels and Jackson, summarizing fifty years of research on teachers' personalities and characteristics, conclude: "Despite the critical importance of the problem and a half-century of prodigious research effort, very little is known for certain about the nature and measurement of teacher personality, or about the relation between teacher personality and teaching effectiveness."[11]

A person's *attitudes,* or predispositions to act in a positive or negative way, toward persons, ideas, and events, are a fundamental dimension of his personality. Although little empirical evidence exists relating specific attitudes to teaching effectiveness, almost all educators are convinced of the importance of teacher attitudes in the teaching process. Attitudes have a direct—though frequently unrecognized—effect on our behavior in that they determine the ways we view ourselves and interact with others.

We believe that there are four major categories of attitude that affect teaching behavior: 1) the teacher's attitude toward himself; 2) the teacher's attitudes toward children and his relationship with them; 3) the teacher's attitudes toward peers and parents; and 4) the teacher's attitude toward the subject matter.

If the teacher is to help a student have meaningful experiences, discover his aptitudes and abilities, face his inner difficulties, and accept himself as a person, he needs to know and understand that student. But before a teacher can do that, he must work at knowing and understanding himself. Empirical evidence from psychology indicates that a person who denies or is unable to cope with his own emotions is unlikely to be capable of respecting and dealing with others' feelings. A person who never admits to feelings of anger and hostility, for example, may overreact to, ignore, or deny the legitimacy of another person's anger. He may consider it "bad" to feel anger. The same is true of fear, feelings of inadequacy, and most other natural human emotions.

[10] David Ryans, *Characteristics of Teachers* (Washington, D.C.: American Council on Education, 1960).
[11] J. W. Getzels and P. W. Jackson, "The Teacher's Personality and Characteristics," in *Handbook of Research on Teaching,* ed. N. L. Gage (Chicago: Rand McNally, 1963), p. 574.

Thus if a teacher is to understand and sympathize with a student who is hostile, he must face hostile tendencies in himself, and recognize their implications for his students and others with whom he has dealings. Unless the teacher recognizes his own anxiety, he will be unlikely to understand and empathize with his students' expressions of anxiety. He may not recognize that a student's inability to learn, inattentiveness, impudence, or irritability may be the result of anxiety. The teacher also needs to recognize that his own anxiety may make him irritable, causing the students in turn to feel anxious and display similar symptoms. As Arthur Jersild has said, "A teacher's understanding of others can be only as deep as the wisdom he possesses when he looks inward upon himself. The more genuinely he seeks to face the problems of his own life, the more he will be able to realize his kinship with others."[12]

The question remains, "How can one achieve understanding of self and, after achieving it, accept it?" Jersild suggests that "to gain knowledge of self, one must have the courage to seek it and the humility to accept what one may find."[13]

There are a number of potential sources of increased self-understanding. Jersild suggests that books by sensitive and compassionate people who have made progress in their own struggles to know themselves can be a valuable aid in self-examination. For prospective teachers, such books might include Sylvia Ashton-Warner's *Teacher,* an account of her teaching experience in a Maori Infant School in New Zealand, and Herbert Kohl's *36 Children.* Another method he suggests is "participant observation," the process of observing a class and

[12] Arthur Jersild, *When Teachers Face Themselves* (New York City: Teachers College Press, 1955), p. 83.
[13] *Ibid.*

          What makes a teacher a teacher?

recording what you hear, see, and feel as you observe. Your record is then compared with the records of other observers. This experience may demonstrate to
you that what you notice in any given situation is determined in large part by
habits of thought which you take for granted. It may also illustrate that your
"objective" perceptions are often projections of your own subjective state, and
thus may tell you more about yourself than about the people you have
observed.

As previously noted in Chapter Three, in recent years a number of techniques
have been developed to help individuals better understand themselves and their
relationships, feelings, and attitudes toward other people. These processes,
which include sensitivity training, T-grouping, awareness experiences, and
encounter sessions, share no standard format or common set of experiences,
but all emphasize introspection, self-evaluation, small-group activities, and a
"here and now" existential orientation. They are usually characterized by strong
emotional interaction. A more detailed discussion of human relations training
appeared in Chapter Three.

While at one time group sessions were considered "freaky" or of dubious value,
more and more people are recognizing their validity and effectiveness in helping
people gain self-understanding. Jersild's survey of 1,032 teachers revealed that
over 40 percent thought they would need personal help, such as group therapy, if
they were to put the widely endorsed concept of self-understanding into practice
in their teaching.[14] In group therapy sessions, a person may be helped to see his
anger, fear, and self-protective maneuvers as others see them. The way others
respond to him may help him perceive facets of his personality or behavior of
which he was previously unaware. A structured exercise in which someone
mimics his conduct, for example, might illuminate for him certain aspects of his
behavior.

Self-examination can also grow out of day-to-day relationships with others. The
procedures by which one gains self-understanding are less important than the
courage and desire to do so. We constantly find ourselves in new situations with
new people who challenge us in new ways, and as a result understanding oneself is a continuous process. Because teachers interact with and influence so
many young children, they must work particularly hard to understand themselves
and their actions in order to understand the children in their charge.

Your college years are likely to be a time of protracted self-examination. As you
gain new independence from your family, examine values you may have taken for
granted, test yourself against rigorous academic standards, encounter new
ideas, and live in close quarters with others your own age, you probably find
yourself experiencing new feelings and recognizing unfamiliar things about yourself. College is also likely to offer you more leisure than any future period of your
life (believe it or not!) to explore and learn about yourself. Some colleges offer
sensitivity sessions run by trained leaders, as well as personal counseling sessions, to help you face and cope with feelings of limitation, insecurity, inferiority,
or confusion, the need to be liked and approved of, lack of direction, and other
problems. We urge you to regard self-examination as a serious commitment, and

[14] Jersild, p. 84.

to undertake it *as a prospective teacher,* in an effort to make a good decision about whether to teach and to become the best teacher you are capable of becoming.

Consider for a moment a need basic to most people—the need to be liked. Teachers, too, especially beginners, need to be liked by their pupils and their peers. Many teachers do not realize how strong their need for approval is; a teacher may approve particular student actions not because they are in the student's best interests but for fear that if he disapproved he might lose their affection. Unfortunately, the teacher rarely recognizes his own motivations when such incidents occur. Unless the teacher is aware of the strength of his own need, he will be in no position to examine and judge his actions correctly.

Another configuration of needs that can influence classroom behavior is represented by the teacher who needs to have students depend on him. This teacher feels pleasure when the students demonstrate that they need him. Thus the teacher habitually engineers situations in which the students have to depend on him in order to accomplish the assigned tasks. This teacher usually behaves like a benevolent dictator in the classroom, kindly but relentlessly building a "cult of the individual." The novel, play, and movie of *The Prime of Miss Jean Brodie* depict this type of teacher very well. In order to be considered one of "Miss Brodie's girls," a student must adhere to a code of Miss Brodie's invention. This type of teacher is potentially very damaging to her students. Instead of producing students who are self-directed and who can make choices for themselves, such a teacher inhibits growth. She may not behave consciously in this fashion; she is probably unaware of her own need for others to be dependent on her. This teacher needs counseling to make her aware of her need and of its negative effect on students. The situation may even be serious enough to warrant psychotherapy.

As we stated earlier, a person's attitude toward himself has a direct influence on his attitudes toward others. If, for example, a teacher sees himself as friendly but is not considered friendly by his students and does not, by every objective criterion, behave in a friendly manner, he is not likely to change his behavior until he acquires some insight into his inaccurate self-image. He will be perplexed when his students do not respond warmly to what he considers friendly behavior, and will probably form negative attitudes toward them. If, on the other hand, he is able to adopt a more realistic self-concept—to recognize that he is not naturally friendly and that he will have to change his behavior patterns—he will be on the road to changing his attitudes toward his students and improving his relationship with them.

We hope that these examples illustrate vividly how a teacher's personal needs and attitudes can influence his behavior, and how self-knowledge can deepen insight and even change behavior.

The teacher's attitudes toward children

Children are sensitive observers of adult behavior, and they frequently recognize, and become preoccupied with, aspects of the teacher's attitude toward them of which the teacher may be unaware. There is a variety of attitudes or feelings toward students that can decisively reduce the teacher's effectiveness; the teacher may have:

- strong dislikes for particular pupils and obvious fondness for others
- biases toward or against particular ethnic groups
- low learning expectations from poverty-level children or those with certain ethnic backgrounds
- a bias toward certain kinds of student behavior, such as docility or aggressiveness

Few teachers are entirely free of such attitudes at the outset, and self-awareness can be the crucial factor distinguishing a biased teacher from a fair one. Thus, it is important that the prospective teacher confront his own attitudes early, perhaps through group discussions, role-playing, or simulated and real experiences. It is necessary to acknowledge one's attitudes in order to change them, but even then change is neither easy nor automatic. Any attempt to change attitudes must take into account both of their components, feelings and cognition. Attitudes may be based almost entirely on feelings, as when a teacher's dislike for a particular student causes her to refuse to let the student participate in a particular activity. Or, if a teacher feels strong rapport with a certain child, he may have a tendency to let the child "get away with" more than other students are allowed. An example of cognition as the primary component of an attitude is the assessment of a student's needs causing a teacher to require the student to participate in particular activities, even those the child might dislike.

If an attitude is based on a negative feeling, it is usually amenable to change through counseling or role-playing techniques. In a role-playing situation each of the participants is asked to portray as realistically as possible the behavior and feelings of another person, perhaps a member of a minority group. Rather than intellectualizing his feelings, the role-player attempts to suspend his own feelings and to draw on his capacity to feel what the other person is experiencing. The result is that the individual playing the role begins to project himself imaginatively into the identity of the other person. Role-playing as a technique is based on the belief that one of the most effective ways to change attitudes is to participate in experiences in which one can observe the effect on others of attitudinal behavior; the process creates the content.

If, on the other hand, an attitude is primarily based on cognition, new information may be effective in producing attitude changes. An excellent illustration of this effect involves the notion of *teacher expectancy*. If a teacher expects a student or group of students to behave in a certain way, the teacher's attitude may serve as a *self-fulfilling prophecy*—that is, the students may behave in the predicted manner in response to the teacher's attitude and not as a result of the other factors on which the teacher's expectations are based. A teacher who is told that his students are "slow" will have different expectations for their performance than he would if he were told the students were "fast."[15] Regardless of their innate ability, students deemed "slow" may respond poorly precisely because of the teacher's low expectations. Many teachers have low expectations of poor children. This phenomenon is cited by many educators as a major cause of low student performances in urban schools attended by poor children. The teachers' expectations can be changed by providing proof that their ability is not inherently inferior to that of other children. The teachers' attitudes toward these youngsters are likely to change somewhat as a result of their raised expectations.

At this point let us consider the position, most eloquently expressed by Carl Rogers, a noted counselor, psychologist, and therapist, that significant learning depends on certain attitudinal qualities that exist in the personal relationship between the facilitator and the learner. Note that Rogers uses the term "facilitator," rather than "teacher," because he believes it puts emphasis on what happens to the learner rather than on the performance of the teacher. The term "facilitator" also implies significantly different functions than does the term "teacher."

The attitude most basic to the learning relationship, according to Rogers, is realness or genuineness. Instead of playing a role or presenting a front, the facili-

---

[15] For further discussion of teacher expectations, see Thomas L. Good and Jere E. Brophy, *Looking in Classrooms* (New York: Harper & Row, 1973), pp. 68–112.

© 1970 United Feature Syndicate, Inc.

What makes a teacher a teacher?

Excerpts from a diary of a beginning teacher

As you read these excerpts try to identify what attitudes the teacher is mani-festing toward self, children, peers, and subject matter.

September 7. I'm exhausted today. I gave them all back their papers which, thank goodness, took up part of the class time. I also assigned them four questions to do for homework. I didn't write the questions on the board, which was a mistake; I ended up repeating everything five or six times.

I feel so pushed, preparing and correcting papers; hope things calm down soon.

September 9. I tried playing a game with them in class today. It didn't go very well. One of the biggest problems was that I didn't have a firm enough control over the class to do it. I had them asking one another questions. They were divided into two teams and all that. I even set up a panel of judges who decided whether the answer to a question was right.

I also gave them a pop quiz at the beginning of the period. I tried it in one class at the end, but that didn't work as well; they were too excited from the game to settle down.

One real catastrophe today. The map fell on my head during fourth period. The class went wild, luckily the assistant principal was right outside the room and came in and rescued me.

September 13. I gave the quiz today and they did pretty well and then I finished up discussing geography — I hope. I only gave them twenty of the spelling words and left off the longest and most difficult. They were very upset because they said they had all learned that one.

The day has finally come. Despite all of the work and how tired I am, I think I am really going to like teaching.

September 26. I'm having a problem getting the classes to keep quiet now. For a while they were pretty good, but now they're beginning to get to me. Even the good students are starting to talk during class. I don't think it's because they're not interested because the talk is almost always about what I'm discussing, but still they're talking without permission. If it was only a little I wouldn't mind, but it's beginning to get to the point where I can't go on because of the talking.

September 27. The assistant principal came and visited one of my classes today. Before class I was talking at my desk with one student and all of a sudden I heard this deathly silence hit the class. (I guess that's not the right way to say it, but anyway.) I looked up and there he was. I started the class. I'd ask a question and there was absolute silence. Nothing. It was terrible! It's bad when they're all talking at once, but it's horrible when they're afraid to move.

September 29. I've been getting bored, teaching the same thing over and over and so today I did different things in different classes. I discussed with some, gave some a quiz and had others writing. I tried discussing with my sixth-period class but they're just impossible after about ten minutes. I got really mad at them and told them to take out their books and study quietly for ten minutes and then I would give them a quiz. While they studied, I made up the quiz and it was a dilly—only four people passed. I suppose it isn't good educational psychology to do that but it made me feel much better, and at that point it was either them or me.

October 14. *I have now firmly and purposely gotten my classes separated. That is, I am no longer doing the same thing five times a day. At first it was a big help being able to prepare only one lesson each night. But I realized that it was terribly boring for me, and my boredom would be reflected in the kids. Once I felt that I had my bearings, I decided to change all that. Well, it's taken me this long to carry out my plan. Although I use much of the same material in all of my classes, I do not use it all at the same time or in the same manner. I can really see the difference in the classes.*

October 19. *Tonight was the PTA open house. I was pleased at how well it went. I guess that parents are not really ogres after all. But it was an awfully long day. I really do love teaching and I look forward to all of my classes, but I often feel that I am not doing my best for these kids. Teach and learn—and have I learned a lot in these seven weeks!*

November 4. *Teacher's Convention—WHAT A FARCE!*

November 9. *Every day I learn so much. I hope that the children are learning some too, but they couldn't possibly learn more than a fraction of what I have. I think there is hope for me yet. I already know so much more than I did in September. Sometimes I feel the huge mountain of things yet to learn pressing down on me but I think I've made a significant dent in the mountain. I may live through the year. But then again, it seems overwhelming.*

November 30. *Beautiful day! Introducing a new unit and the kids were great—love it. Everything went well.*

December 8. *Ugliness! Nothing went well at all. Jabber, jabber, jabber—I don't know. Sometimes I get so upset and depressed it's horrible. They don't listen or follow instructions, or learn anything. I guess it's a normal feeling for new teachers.*

December 12. *Almost the end of the period before vacation. I guess not really but it seems like it must be. Happiness!! They announced that all evaluation meetings are cancelled until after Christmas. Hurray! Except for the faculty meeting Thursday.*

Jean Morris, "Diary of a Beginning Teacher," *National Association of Secondary School Principals Bulletin* 52 (October 1968): 6–15.

---

tator must enter into a relationship with the learner. He must be a real person, one who " . . . is *being* himself." He is free to be enthusiastic, bored, interested, angry, sensitive, and sympathetic. As Rogers says,

Because he accepts these feelings as his own he has no need to impose them on his students. He can like or dislike a student product without implying that it is objectively good or bad or that the student is good or bad. He is simply expressing a feeling for the product, a feeling which exists within himself. Thus, he

What makes a teacher a teacher?

is a person to his students, not a faceless embodiment of a curricular require-
ment nor a sterile tube through which knowledge is passed from one generation
to the next.[16]

Another essential attitude Rogers describes as valuing the learner—his feelings, his opinions, and his person—as he is and as worthy in his own right, and accepting both his imperfections and his potentialities. The facilitator who possesses this attitude can accept a student's occasional apathy, fear of failure, or hatred of authority, as well as his more positive characteristics. In short, this attitude is an expression of the facilitator's confidence and trust in the capacity of the human being.

A third attitude that Rogers considers essential to the establishment of a climate for self-initiated, experiential learning is empathic understanding. "When the teacher has the ability to understand the student's reactions from the inside, has a sensitive awareness of the way the process of education and learning seems *to the student,* then again the likelihood of significant learning is increased.[17] Empathic understanding implies that the facilitator understands the learner, but does not judge or evaluate him. Rogers urges that a teacher initially set himself the goal of making one nonevaluative, accepting, empathic response per day to a student's demonstrated or verbalized feelings. By doing so, he believes, the teacher will discover the potency of this approach.

Rogers' approach is intended to create classroom environments conducive to self-initiated learning. He maintains that the teacher's skills, his knowledge of his field, his curricular planning, his lectures, and his selection of books and other learning aids are all peripheral; the crux of the learning situation is the relationship between the facilitator and the learner, which should be characterized

[16] Carl Rogers, *Freedom to Learn* (Columbus: Charles E. Merrill, 1969), p. 106.
[17] Rogers, p. 10.

by the three attitudinal predispositions described above. Unless the learning environment is characterized by *realness, valuing,* and *empathy,* according to Rogers, it is sterile and cannot produce significant learning.

It is interesting to compare Rogers' ideas with the findings of Martin Haberman, who studied the teaching behavior of students in the Intern Teaching Program at the University of Wisconsin.[18] The interns, under the dual supervision of the university and the school, had been given a minimum of theoretical knowledge prior to instructing full-time in the classroom. The teaching behavior of the more successful interns was compared with that of the less successful interns. Haberman's studies indicated that academic achievement at the graduate level, communication skills, and positive attitudes toward children, as measured both verbally and on written instruments, were all irrelevant to success as an intern. There were, however, five factors which significantly distinguished the successful

[18] Martin Haberman, "The Teaching Behavior of Successful Interns," *Journal of Teacher Education* 16 (June 1965): 215–220.

                 What makes a teacher a teacher?

and unsuccessful interns: belief in the youngsters' potential, ability to organize the classroom situation, genuine enthusiasm for the subject matter, ability to set appropriate standards, and willingness to listen to the youngsters and utilize their comments in teaching. The results of this study seem generally to support Rogers' theories, except that Haberman found a positive attitude toward children to be insufficient for success in teaching; belief in their abilities must be demonstrated by continual use of student input in the classroom.

In any case, there is little question that if you have empathy for your students, value them as unique individuals, and are secure enough to be yourself without playing a role, you will be a more successful teacher; and the atmosphere in your classroom will make possible for you and your students a joy, excitement, and closeness absent from many classrooms.

The teacher's attitude toward peers and parents

The teacher is not isolated in his classroom. He interacts daily with fellow teachers, administrators, and other school personnel, and he must often have very sensitive dealings with parents. It can happen that a teacher who is very gifted in his work with children has a disastrous professional life because of his uncontrolled attitudes toward the adults he encounters. However, most teachers do not have significantly different attitudes toward adults than they would toward children possessing the same characteristics. Therefore, much of what we have already said about the teacher's attitudes toward himself and toward children also applies to his attitudes toward peers and parents.

Authority

The teacher's attitude toward those who represent authority (ordinarily administrators, but for prospective teachers the university supervisor or the cooperating teacher) is often a source of conflict. A teacher may find it hard to be himself while dealing with people who outrank him in position or prestige, though he may feel perfectly comfortable with people who are his equals or in a lesser position. Sometimes a teacher finds that he yields too readily to demands from others, especially those in positions of authority, and as a result feels guilty about complying rather than standing on his own convictions. When this occurs, the result is often a continuing undercurrent of resentment toward the person making a request.

These responses to authority are dysfunctional in that they impede communication and understanding. A teacher must examine his reactions to persons in authority positions and strive to overcome predispositions to hostility or anxiety unwarranted by reality.

Competition

Some teachers develop a strong drive to compete with other teachers for recognition from both authority figures and students. They strive to have the best lesson plans, to be the "most popular teacher" or to maintain the friendliest relationship with the administration. Such persons are striving to be recognized and rewarded. As a result of this attitude, they sometimes cut themselves off from much-needed help and severely limit their ability to be of help to others. They are unable to recognize the need for cooperation and sharing of ideas for the benefit of both staff and students.

Superiority and prejudice

One attitude which never fails to cause trouble for the teacher is a feeling of superiority to his fellow teachers and the parents of his students. He may feel intellectually superior to his colleagues or socially superior to his students' parents, or both. Some teachers simply have little tolerance for people who differ from them in values, cultural background, or economic status and, as a result, treat others with disdain and contempt, rather than patience and respect. Consider the following description of a teacher's meeting with lower-class Negro parents who have come to the school to lodge a complaint about their child being teased:

. . . the point was made by the Reading Teacher that this little girl actually was not so much teased by other kids as she was something of a troublemaker herself. It happened that this was not the truth. . . . The Reading Teacher then delivered an excellent and persuasive assessment of the little girl's incorrect behavior and she was so persuasive that the child ended up by apologizing to the Reading Teacher for all of the things that she had done wrong.

. . . The parents come up with a just and proper reason to place blame, and they get it instead. Up they come angry and with proper outrage. Off they go, humbled, sad, and weakly, having as it were apologized for the stupid thing they've tried to obtain. The look of embarrassed humility.[19]

Had the father been a lawyer or doctor, the scenario described above would undeniably not have taken place. Feelings of personal superiority can cause teachers to treat people in an offensive and humiliating manner.

The teacher's attitude toward the subject matter

This section is short because our message is simple—it is most important, whatever subject matter you teach, that you feel *enthusiasm* for it. Just as students can usually discern the teacher's attitude toward them, they are also very sensitive to the teacher's attitude toward the subject matter. One of the most striking characteristics of the excellent teacher is her enthusiasm for what she is teaching or "facilitating." The bored teacher conveys her feeling to the students—and who can blame them for failing to get excited if the teacher, who knows more about the subject than they do, doesn't find it engaging?

Some teachers find it difficult to feel enthusiasm for a curriculum they haven't constructed themselves, or don't identify with, or don't want to teach. The surest way to guarantee that the teacher is enthusiastic about what he is teaching is to allow him to teach what he is enthusiastic about. And we do not mean this as a mere play on words. We would much rather see an enthusiastic teacher teaching Turkish military history or macramé than an uninspired teacher teaching Shakespeare.

One of the reasons we advocate the development of new curricula that concentrate on the problems of mankind, rather than the traditional disciplines, is that we believe most teachers can generate more interest and enthusiasm for problems dealing with mankind's survival than for mathematics or history *per se.* We also believe that students will feel more enthusiasm for this kind of curriculum. The teaching profession contains many individuals who don't care about what they are teaching and don't care much more about the students. As one student put it, "Teachers should be more enthusiastic about their subject. There is nothing worse than sitting in a lesson knowing full well that the teacher is

[19] Jonathan Kozol, *Death at an Early Age* (Boston: Houghton Mifflin, 1967), p. 92. Reprinted by permission of the publisher.

What makes a teacher a teacher?

dying to get rid of you and rush back to the staff-room to have her cup of tea."[20] A thirteen-year-old boy expressed himself similarly: "I feel there is nothing like a teacher's enthusiasm for his subject to make learning a pleasure, and I am sure that a computer cannot show enthusiasm."[21]

Or, in the words of a teacher, ". . . the main hazard a teacher runs is to get bored and complacent. He teaches the same things the same way and pretty soon all of the kids begin to look alike, too."[22]

Don't allow yourself to be pressured into teaching something you care little about. Make sure you have a positive attitude toward the subject you teach. Enthusiasm—if the teacher has it, life in the classroom can be exciting. If it is missing, there is little hope the students will learn much of significance.

What subject-matter knowledge does the teacher need?

The prospective teacher's subject-matter preparation can be seen as having two facets: study of the content of the discipline itself, and familiarity with the knowledge derived from it to be taught to the pupil.[23] In some fields, such as biology, the discipline is the same as the subject to be taught; other teaching fields, such as social studies, draw on many subject-area disciplines. In all fields, though, the knowledge to be taught is less extensive and advanced than the content of college disciplinary courses; the content of the school curriculum is selected from the available knowledge on the basis of the students' prior learning and the limitations of time. This is one reason why expertise in a discipline is not a guarantee of success at teaching the same subject at the elementary- or high-school level. Another is that, in addition to the two kinds of subject-matter preparation described above, the teacher must possess *knowledge about knowledge.* By this we mean sufficient perspective on a subject to be able to analyze and convey its elements, logic, possible uses, social biases, and relevance to the needs of the students. When a teacher can assert that a process for solving a particular problem is correct or incorrect, or identify a certain ethnic bias in a literary passage, the knowledge he draws upon to make these assertions is what is meant by *knowledge about knowledge.*

We have assumed that the educated man is one who knows; *yet knowing about literature may give one little sense of human tragedy or of belonging to humanity, little compassion. Knowing some science—let us say physics—may do little to help one sense the spirit of science. If we really believe in a liberal education, we must be more concerned with what students are and are becoming than with what they know and are learning in fact and skill. This does not mean that knowledge is unimportant but rather that the true teacher sees knowledge as a means, not as an end.*[24]

---

[20] Edward Blishen, ed., *The School That I'd Like* (Harmondsworth, England: Penguin Books, 1969), p. 141
[21] Blishen, p. 143.
[22] Myron Brenton, *What's Happened to Teacher?* (New York: Coward-McCann, 1970), p. 147.
[23] The authors are indebted to B. O. Smith, author of *Teachers for the Real World,* for many of the ideas expressed in this section.
[24] Ernest O. Melby, "The Contagion of Liberal Education," *Journal of Teacher Education* 18 (Summer 1967): 135.

It is precisely this concern for the uses of knowledge that many teachers lack.

Let's turn to the teacher's preparation in the disciplines that will comprise his teaching field. Most teacher education programs draw heavily on the disciplines. We consider training in specific disciplines as essential to a teacher's general education as it is to that of a doctor or a lawyer; and we are not advocating the total dissolution of disciplinary study. However, we feel that one of the major faults of existing teacher education programs is that the disciplinary approach fails to prepare teachers for the second facet of subject-matter preparation—the knowledge to be taught to the pupil. For instance, a teacher who majored in mathematics might find that his college courses, however rigorous, simply didn't prepare him to teach elementary mathematics or algebra. The mathematics courses required of a prospective teacher probably differ little from those prescribed for a mathematics major planning on a career in industry. As a rule—despite the involvement of many scholars in the curriculum reform movement— university professors are not concerned about preparing teachers to teach the subject matter that elementary- and secondary-school students are expected to learn. Most college courses are designed to prepare students for more advanced study within the discipline. The methods courses offered in schools of education represent an attempt—not always successful—to remedy this situation. In short, much of what the prospective teacher learns from his study of the disciplines is not taught to children, and thus it is not directly applicable to teaching. This is particularly true for the elementary-school teacher, who is called upon to teach content virtually ignored by the academic departments of the universities.

In Chapter Seven, we express our belief that the discipline-oriented approach to the public-school curriculum must be replaced by a curriculum organized around societal problems and the concerns and interests of the students. If a teacher's college education should include the study of various disciplines, and

What makes a teacher a teacher?

if the disciplines in themselves are inadequate preparation for teaching young-sters, what then do we propose? The teacher education program should offer opportunities for prospective teachers to develop curriculum units that are apt to be of interest to students, drawing on concepts and approaches from several dis-ciplines. In addition, the courses taken by the prospective teacher should serve as models of the issue-oriented inquiry approach, thus requiring the prospective teacher to experience the same mode of learning he wishes his students to expe-rience.

The mode of study should focus on problem solving, with the prospective teach-ers themselves assuming a major share of the responsibility for analyzing the problems, selecting and organizing the materials, and carrying on discussion. Through this process they would learn to think through problems on their own and would acquire the skills necessary to identify and locate relevant materials. By experiencing the same kinds of difficulties that their own students will be likely to encounter, prospective teachers would be better prepared to deal effec-tively with them.

To be prepared in the subject matter of instruction is to know the content to be taught and how the content can be related to the interest and experience of children and youths. To prepare the teacher in this subject matter will require courses oriented to the teacher's need for knowledge that can be tied in with the life of children and youths rather than discipline-oriented courses.[25]

Translating the content of discipline-oriented courses into a more appropriate mode of instruction will be a difficult undertaking. But we are convinced that allowing the prospective teacher to organize materials to focus on meeting the students "where they're at" will make the job of translation easier.

We thus urge that the prospective teacher know intimately the content he is to teach, and that this content be centered around man's physical and social problems and issues relevant to the students' lives. It is equally important for the teacher to be well-versed in the disciplines from which the instructional subject matter is derived. In Smith's words, "The first is necessary for teaching anything at all. The second supplies a depth of knowledge essential to the teacher's feel-ing of intellectual security and his ability to handle instructional content with greater understanding."[26] Finally, a teacher must have knowledge about knowl-edge as a whole, so that he can bring perspective and a command of the logical operations used in manipulating information to any subject-matter content. These three types of knowledge, we believe, are essential for the effective teacher.

Summary
You may have found this to be a difficult chapter because of its theoretical emphasis. We think it is an important one, however, because it provides you with an overview of what a truly effective teacher needs to know and be able to do. It may have been a frustrating chapter if you concluded that there was no way that you could achieve the ideal that we described. We share that frustration since we

[25] Smith, pp. 121–122.
[26] Smith, p. 122.

ourselves have not measured up to this ideal in our own teaching, and we're not certain that we ever will. Nevertheless, we continue to aspire toward being the type of teacher we have described in this chapter. If you too can fix your sights upon this conceptualization of what makes a teacher a teacher and continually work toward this ideal, you are certain to observe the positive results in your classroom.

Discussion questions

1 Which of the theoretical principles listed on p. 141 strike you as simple common sense? Which are new to you? If any surprise you, to what do you attribute the surprise? Which seem most important to you as a prospective teacher? For what kind of theoretical knowledge do you feel the greatest need?

2 Which of the skills listed on p. 145 seem most important to you? What skills would you add to the list? subtract?

3 We say on p. 155 that teachers' low expectations of poor children can be changed by providing proof that their ability is not inherently inferior to that of other children. What might constitute such proof?

4 Is there any group or type of people toward whom you have negative feelings? Can you identify the basis of those feelings? Do you want to change them? How might you try?

5 Carl Rogers argues for a teacher who "is *being* himself" and shows his feelings. Do you agree? Have you known any teachers who did so? Do you think children can cope with any reaction from the teacher as long as it is honestly expressed? Do you think this kind of teaching requires any particular prior training?

6 Analyze the five factors that Haberman found to characterize successful interns (p. 160). Which seem to you the result of training? which of individual attitudes? which a result of combination of the two?

7 Do you agree that it is preferable for an enthusiastic teacher to teach an irrelevant subject than for an uninspired teacher to teach a crucial subject? What implications do you see in this remark? On what assumptions about teachers, students, and subject matter is it based?

For further reading

- Borton, Terry. *Reach, Touch, and Teach.* New York: McGraw-Hill, 1970. Focuses on the affective concerns of teachers and students. Borton believes that what a student learns in school and what he eventually becomes are significantly influenced by how he feels about himself and the world outside. Thus, the teacher's goal should be to help each student increase his understanding of his feelings, and expand that self-awareness by utilizing his intellectual resources.
- Fuchs, Estelle. *Teachers Talk.* New York: Doubleday, 1969. A collection of teachers' statements about themselves, schools, and learning. The author analyzes these teacher statements from the perspective of an anthropologist.
- Ginott, Haim. *Teacher and Child.* New York: Macmillan Co., 1972. An application of Dr. Ginott's philosophy concerning children as applied to teachers and their relationships with children.
- Good, Thomas L., and Brophy, Jere E. *Looking In Classrooms.* New York: Harper & Row, 1973. An excellent book that provides a teacher with concrete skills that enable him to observe and interpret classroom behavior of both teacher and student.

What makes a teacher a teacher?

- Greer, Mary, and Rubinstein, Bonnie. *Will The Real Teacher Please Stand Up?* Pacific Palisades, Calif.: Goodyear Publishing Co., 1972. A refreshingly entertaining potpourri of cartoons, short articles, human relations exercises, and games designed to help teachers humanize education for children.
- Holt, John. *How Children Fail.* New York: Pitman, 1964. Holt insists that schools often teach children to think badly, to give up a more natural way of thinking in favor of one that does not work for them and that we rarely use ourselves. As a result, he maintains, most of them get humiliated, frightened, and discouraged. Very readable and enjoyable.
- Holt, John. *How Children Learn.* New York: Pitman, 1967. In the sequel to *How Children Fail,* Holt tries to describe situations in which effective learning occurs. The reader will take away new perceptions, techniques, and, possibly, even a new philosophy.
- Holt, John. *What Do I Do Monday?* New York: Dutton, 1970. A book of practical suggestions for classroom activity.
- Jersild, Arthur. *When Teachers Face Themselves.* New York: Teachers College Press, 1955. Jersild's major thesis is that before teachers can understand their students, they must understand themselves. He develops a case for this premise followed by suggestions as to how teachers can go about better understanding themselves.
- Joyce, Bruce, and Weill, Marsha. *Models of Teaching.* Englewood Cliffs, N.J.: Prentice-Hall, 1972. A useful book for both teachers and teacher educators that describes numerous teaching models that are built on different assumptions about teaching and learning.
- Neill, A.S. *Summerhill.* New York: Hart, 1961. A personal account of one man's philosophy of education, based on freedom for the learner, and of the school he established in England to implement his philosophy. For those concerned with expanding the student's freedom and allowing him choice in the direction of his education, this book is a must.
- Passow, A. Harry, ed. *Education in Depressed Areas.* New York: Teachers College Press, 1963. A collection of research-based articles that focus on culturally disadvantaged learners and their special educational difficulties. Written by leading sociologists, educators, psychologists, and teachers, the selections cover such topics as teaching techniques, strategies, and devices that appear effective in this area of education.
- Raths, Louis E.; Harmin, Merril; and Simon, Sidney B. *Values and Teaching.* Columbus, Ohio: Charles E. Merrill, 1966. This very useful book presents techniques to help the teacher assist students in clarifying their own values. Focuses not on instilling values, but on helping students recognize how the values they hold influence their decision making.
- Rogers, Carl. *Freedom to Learn.* Columbus, Ohio: Charles E. Merrill, 1969. The major theme is that students can be trusted to learn and to enjoy learning when a facilitative person creates a responsive environment and encourages responsible participation in the selection of goals and ways of reaching them. Includes case studies of three facilitators at three levels of education, all of whom have, in quite different ways, provided their students with freedom to learn.
- Sanders, Norris. *Classroom Questions: What Kinds?* New York: Harper & Row, 1966. Designed to help teachers develop the ability to ask questions that are not limited to factual recall. Through the use of discussion and examples, the author helps the reader recognize how different types of questions can stimulate various levels of thought processes on the part of students.

- Schutz, William C. *Joy.* New York: Grove Press, 1967: Focuses on helping people expand their awareness through a number of theories and exercises. The book emphasizes openness and honesty and assumes that joy will result when our feelings are expressed and explored.
- Smith, B. O., et al. *Teachers for the Real World.* Washington, D.C.: American Association of Colleges for Teacher Education, 1969. Focuses on the knowledge, skills, and attitudes teachers need to possess.

Films

- *The Best of the Real: Teaching in the Inner City Elementary School* (Center for Urban Education, 1st film 28 min., 2nd film 22 min., 3rd film 40 min., all 16mm). A series of three films documenting the classroom work and techniques of a New York City fifth-grade teacher who was identified as "effective" by students, teachers, supervisors, and parents. The first film shows him teaching an elementary algebra class; the second, a humorous short poem; and the third records an analysis of his teaching techniques.
- *Change — Training Teachers for Innovation* (IDEA, color, 29 min., 1970). This film employs two techniques for involving the classroom teacher in making effective change, techniques that were pioneered by training personnel in industry. It helps education students to visualize the steps by which change in the classroom can win support from administrators and parents.
- *Children Without* (Mass Media Ministries, 16mm, b&w, 30 min., 1964). This film documents the efforts of teachers in a school in an economically substandard area of Detroit. Through a dramatization of the experiences of one little girl who attends the school, the viewer is shown how these teachers are concerned not only with the mental development of their students but also with their emotional, psychological, social, and physical needs.
- *Critical Moments in Teaching Series* (Holt, Rinehart, and Winston, color, approx. 10 min. each, 1970). Dramatizations of problems that arise in elementary and secondary classrooms. Children pose problems such as inattention, inability to do written work, social withdrawal, and the like, forcing teachers to invent imaginative solutions to what used to be considered simple situations. All films in this series of sixteen titles are open-ended, allowing for discussion, and all assume that problems arise not only from students but also from parents and administrators.
- *Education for Psychological Maturity* (Indiana University Audio-Visual Center, 16mm, b&w, 29 min.). Featured personality in this film from the "Philosophies of Education Series" is Arthur Jersild, Professor in the Department of Psychological Foundations and Services at Teachers College, Columbia University. The film explores theories presented in Dr. Jersild's book, *When Teachers Face Themselves.*
- *Four Teachers* (National Film Board of Canada, 16mm, b&w, 59 min., 1961). Although a little dated, this film presents an interesting comparison of classrooms, student-teacher relationships, and of the importance placed on education in four parts of the world — Japan, Poland, Puerto Rico, and Canada, with intermittent comments by a university professor and a grade-school teacher.
- *I Have an Egg* (Contemporary/McGraw-Hill, 16mm, b&w, 15 min., 1966, Poland). An award-winning documentary film about an extraordinarily patient teacher and a group of blind children. The students are being taught how to answer a very difficult question using only the tactile sense: define an egg.

What makes a teacher a teacher?

- *Lloyd Reynold/William Geer* (Indiana University Audio-Visual Center, 16mm, b&w, 59 min., NET). This film from the "Men Who Teach" series presents an interesting comparison between two people with very individual teaching styles. Portraits of William Geer, lecturer in modern civilization and history at the University of North Carolina, and Lloyd Reynold, art historian at Reed College, are built from scenes of their lectures, their methods of counseling students, their philosophies, and interviews with present and former students.
- *My Name Is Children* (Indiana University Audio-Visual Center, 16mm, b&w, 1967, 60 min., NET). This film presents scenes of children and teachers at Nova Elementary School in Fort Lauderdale, Florida, to show how one school uses an "inquiry approach" to motivate students. A montage of activities is accompanied by natural, spontaneous dialogue by students and teachers.
- *The Prime of Miss Jean Brodie* (Films, Inc., 16mm, color, 116 min.). Although it takes place in Scotland in the thirties, this film deals with relevant and provocative issues in comtemporary society: the relationship between teachers and students, and the responsibility of a teacher toward her students.
- *Robin Pitman, Art Teacher* (Peter M. Robeck for the BBC, b&w, 16 min., 1968). In a studio-like classroom, Robin Pitman starts discussing art by drawing a simple dot. With students he investigates the strength of materials, the meaning of shapes, and the utility of various tools. Pitman then discusses his unorthodox teaching techniques, saying in summary, "I try to strip from my students preconceived notions of how things *should* look. I want them to look for new approaches to their own creativity."
- *Sir! Sir!* (McGraw-Hill, b&w, 20 min., 1970). Impromptu role-playing at the Duke of York School in Canada illustrates the effects of a role reversal between teachers and students. Teachers' favorite clichés come home to roost in an amusing and provocative way and are recorded with feeling by the National Film Board of Canada.
- *The Tutors of Fernald* (Special Purpose Films, b&w, 30 min., 1972). Teachers must utilize the skills of their students, argues this moving film about cross-age tutoring at the Fernald School, University of California at Los Angeles. Examining the differences in attitude and technique that allow students to succeed where teachers have failed will reveal helpful insights, especially for teachers of integrated groups of children with learning problems.
- *What Teacher Expects . . . (The Self-fulfilling Prophecy)*. (National Film Board of Canada, b&w, 26 min., 1969). A film presenting a provocative theory of interest to educators and parents: that how well a child performs in school is often the close result of what his teacher expects of him, rather than what objective tests might indicate him capable of. Dr. Robert Rosenthal discusses this film account of his experimental results in self-fulfilling teacher expectations. The theory is demonstrated in teacher-pupil situations where the subject is word recognition.
- *Who Teaches Them* (Indiana University Audio-Visual Center, 16mm, b&w, 30 min., NET). Part of the NET "Radical American Series," this film examines through on-location reports and interviews the differences between schools with a radically left- or right-wing orientation. Among the people interviewed are the director and faculty of the Free University of New York; the President of Harding Colle Searcy, Arkansas; and the Dean of Rampart College, Larkspur, Colorado.

Audiotapes

- *Abraham Maslow: Self-Actualization* (Big Sur Recordings, 3.75 ips, ½ track, mono, 60 min.). A one-hour tape made at the Esalen Institute in which Maslow defines "self-actualization," discusses his own extensive research on the motivations of self-actualized people, and makes observations on the "business organization."

- *R. D. Laing: Politics as Experience* (Big Sur Recordings, 3.75 ips, ½ track, mono, 60 min., 1970). This tape, excerpted from a longer discussion, presents Laing's views on the "binds" and "double binds" that can prevent a person from knowing who he really is.
- *Non-Authoritarian Teaching Series* (Pacifica, approx. 60 min. each, 1969–71). This series of four tapes features experienced teachers and educators recounting their efforts to manage classrooms successfully without exercising traditional teacher-student power relationships. Paul Goodman leads off the discussion at a workshop on nonauthoritarian teaching at Berkeley. John Holt follows with a general inquiry into the idea of schools and the role of the teacher. In the third tape, a junior high-school teacher describes a course in black history she offered in unusual approaches. James Herndon then addresses specific procedures and possibilities for a more democratic and unified classroom.
- *Scott Buchanan, Teacher* (Center for the Study of Democratic Institutions, 27 min., 1970). Through reminiscences of his life's work as a Socratic teacher, Scott Buchanan explains his view of the teacher's role in the learning process. He discusses the program of completely required courses (no electives) which he created at St. John's College in Annapolis, Maryland. An unusual approach to the problem of how to exercise beneficial influence over students, this tape mixes views commonly considered "radical" and "conservative."
- *A Sixth Grade Teacher Reports: Two Approaches* (National Education Association, 3.75 ips, reel or cassette format, 14 min.). One section of an hour-long tape on *The Teacher,* this report tells how a sixth-grade teacher uses both "hard" and "soft" approaches with her students in order to help them understand themselves and one another in relation to society.
- *Student-Teacher Relationship* (Canadian Broadcasting Corporation, 30 min., 1970). James Ross, a community college teacher, discusses the student-teacher relationship and the classroom atmosphere. He raises the intriguing question of how one can define a "student."

Filmography

- *Films in the Behavioral Sciences* (Behavioral Sciences Media Laboratory, 1970). An annotated catalogue of educational films, classified into many topics within the general fields of behavior and learning. Teachers can become aware of new research into the processes of learning and the motivational factors of behavior. Although most of the titles indexed are relatively technical, the teacher is addressed specifically in sections on human learning, attitude and attitude change, communication, and motivation and emotion.

Refer to Appendix for addresses of distributors.

What makes a teacher a teacher?

Schools

5   What is a school?

This chapter is an examination of the nature of schools and schooling. A number of different avenues for reaching an understanding of schools will be presented. In addition you will be confronted with different views of a school and models of schooling. At the end of the chapter, your role in the reform of schooling will be discussed.

Chapter contents

Education and schooling
What is the relationship between education and schooling?
Discovering the purposes of school
Formal statements
Personal experience
Models of schools
The need for objectivity
The function of the school: an anthropologist's analysis
The unfinished work of the schools

"What is a school?" This may not strike you as a particularly profound question. In fact, it probably seems rather tame. School is an everyday thing. We have all spent vast stretches of our time there. Much of what we are—intellectually, socially, and emotionally—can be traced to our experiences in school. School is just . . . school. However, behind the familiar words and images lie thorny issues which have baffled theoreticians and practitioners of education for years. Quiet communities have been split into warring camps because of their inability to agree on an answer to this question. Let us see if you can answer the question, "What is a school?" In the space below, jot down a definition or two of school.

_____

_____

_____

_____

_____

Your answer to the question, "What is a school?" reflects who you are and what your experience with school has been. Perhaps you responded in one of the following ways:

- A school is an agency that weans the child from the protective warmth of the family and gets him ready to contribute to the world of work.

- A school is a bunch of bricks and mortar, chalkboards, and water fountains (usually with wadded gum in them) arranged in a predictable way.
- A school is a place where they fix your head so you think like everyone else.
- A school is where children fall in love with learning.
- A school is a tax-supported babysitting agency.
- A school is a place where young savages become citizens.
- A school is where we learn how good or bad we are compared with a lot of people our own age at a lot of different skills and tasks.
- A school is a place where we explore who we are and how we can become full, creative human beings.
- A school is where children learn to be virtuous.
- A school is a place where the children of one generation come together to unite against the generation in power.
- A school is a fun palace.
- A school is a fact factory.
- A school is a tax-supported institution where the dead wisdom and worn-out skills of the past are force-fed to the young.
- A school is where education takes place.

Each of these descriptions says a great deal about the school experience of the person who formulated it. What does your definition say about you and your experience?

Education and schooling

It is commonly believed that school is where people go to get an education. On the other hand, Marshall McLuhan, one of the sages of the sixties, has quipped that today children interrupt their educations to go to school. The distinction between "schooling" and "education" implied by this remark is important. Like "school," "education" has myriad definitions. We have sprinkled a few such definitions here and there throughout the book for you to sample. For the moment, however, let us say that education is a process of human growth by which an individual gains greater understanding and control over himself and his world. It involves our minds, our bodies, and our relations with the people and the world around us. Education, while taking many institutional and sometimes rigid forms, is strictly speaking a process, an activity characterized by continuous development and changes. The end product of the process of education is learning.

If a school is a physical location, schooling is the specific process that takes place there. It is a formalized process, and its basic pattern varies little from one setting to the next. Throughout the country, children arrive at school at approximately the same time, take assigned seats, are taught by an adult, use the same textbooks, do homework, take exams, and so on. The slices of reality that are to be learned, whether the alphabet or an understanding of English metrics, have usually been specified in advance. What is learned as a result of schooling is also limited by subject: if a little boy wants to learn what a girl *really* looks like, he just knows that school is not the place to make his investigations. In the same way, the high-school student knows she is not likely to find out in her classes how practical politics really operates or what contemporary *avant-garde* writers are up to. Finally, schooling tends to be limited to the young. There are, then, definite conditions surrounding the formalized process of schooling.

Education is much more open-ended and all-inclusive than schooling. Education knows few bounds. It can take place anywhere, whether in a tavern or on a tractor. It includes both the formal learning that takes place in schools and the whole universe of informal learning, from hooking a worm on a line to burping a baby. The agents of education can range from a revered granddad to the guests on a late-night television talk show, from a retarded child to an acorn. While schooling has a certain predictability, education takes us by surprise. We go to the movies to relax and come home with a vivid sense of poverty's corrupting influence on the human spirit. We get into a casual conversation with a stranger and discover how little we know about other religions. People are engaged in education from the cradle to the grave. The child learns how to satisfy himself by putting his thumb into his mouth. A retired businessman picks up a book on prison life and goes on to become involved in penal reform. In its all-inclusiveness, education, as a term or label for human activities, is similar to the word "life." In the same unspecified way everything is part of life, almost everything can be called education.

What is the relationship between education and schooling?

The relationship between education and schooling is not always a positive one. While education is essentially a process of growth, schooling can provoke growth, stagnation, or even deformation. Another related issue has to do with the teacher's place in the schooling–education relationship.

Schools are created for the express purpose of providing a certain type of educational experience, which we call the curriculum. Teachers are trained and hired to fulfill the purposes of the curriculum. In simpler societies, when a boy could learn to be a man by following his father around and imitating the men of the village, schools were not necessary. Formal schooling became a social necessity when the home and the community were no longer effective or competent at training the young for adulthood through informal contacts. Societies have realized that education is too important to be left to chance. While important things are sometimes learned on street corners and grandfathers are excellent teachers, they are simply not as reliable as the formal educative process. There

> *. . . if we divorce schools and their curriculum from the guts and hopes of human beings, we can expect students to find them gutless and hopeless.* Dr. Mark Shedd, commissioner of education for the state of Connecticut.

is an excellent possibility that if education is randomly acquired the young will grow up with a lopsided understanding of the world and poor preparation for adult life. The chance schooling of the street has educated many in such skills as how to exploit one's fellow man, and produced many a champion penny-pitcher who can't read. Occasionally we see families with the intellectual resources, skills, and time to educate their own young, but this is all too rare amid the complexities of modern life. Also, for each individual set of parents to educate its children, even with the help of older children, grandparents, and neighbors, is wasteful and socially inefficient. So schools are established.

The distinction between education and schooling is often blurred because the two concepts are undifferentiated in most people's minds. Keeping the differences between these two concepts clearly in mind is often particularly difficult for the people who should be most sensitive to them, that is, teachers who "do" education "in" schools. People enter teaching because they wish to educate. However, the everyday experience of working in a school inevitably causes their allegiances to shift from abstract educational ideals to the network of personalities and ideas surrounding the particular schools where they teach. Often teachers find themselves doing things that are contrary to their ideals, such as behaving in extremely authoritarian ways, because such practices suit the institutional demands of their school. This is a particularly dangerous tendency at times like the present when many of society's institutions need to be changed or adjusted to new cultural realities. Teachers have a strong tendency to invest themselves in what the school *is* rather than what it should be. Much of the unrest on faculties can be traced to their confusion about the relationship of education to schooling.

Discovering the purposes of school

By distinguishing between education and schooling we may have clarified the question, "What is a school?", but we have not yet answered it. We need to think further about the goals of a school. The following are some means of searching out its purposes and functions.

Formal statements

The most direct method is to read official statements of purpose. Like most institutions, our schools have occasioned many official attempts to explain what they are all about. A few illustrations may suffice. In 1960 John Gardner, the founder of Common Cause, contributed the chapter on education to the report of the President's Commission on National Goals. Discussing the purposes behind our society's support for schools, he wrote, "Our deepest convictions impel us to foster individual fulfillment. We wish each one to achieve the promise that is in him. We wish each one to be worthy of a free society, and capable of strengthening a free society."[1]

---

[1] American Assembly, *Goals for Americans: Programs of Action in the Sixties,* ed. President's Commission on National Goals (Englewood Cliffs, N.J.: Prentice-Hall, 1960), p. 81.

What is a school?

A year later, The Educational Policies Commission of the National Education Association issued a statement entitled "The Central Purpose of American Education," whose last paragraph reads:

The purpose which runs through and strengthens all educational purposes—the common thread of education—is the development of the ability to think. This is the central purpose to which the school must be oriented if it is to accomplish either its traditional task or those newly accentuated by recent changes in the world. To say that it is central is not to say that it is the sole purpose or in all circumstances the most important purpose, but that it must be a pervasive concern in the work of the school. Many agencies contribute to achieving educational objectives, but this particular objective may not be generally attained unless the school focuses on it. In this context, therefore, the development of every student's rational powers must be recognized as centrally important.[2]

Both these statements by high-level groups are representative of official views of the purposes of the schools. They are eloquent, but they are also highly abstract. They may point a teacher in the general direction he should be traveling, but such statements have little value in the fast-moving world of the classroom. When a teacher is struggling to come up with an approach to a map-reading lesson, statements of purpose such as "to foster individual fulfillment" and "to develop the ability to think" are not specific enough to be helpful. However, expecting that kind of relevance may be asking for too much.

There is, however, the question of accuracy. To what degree do these statements reflect the real purposes and functions of school? Terry Borton, an affective educator, doesn't think they are very accurate. He writes:

There are two sections to almost every school's statement of educational objectives: one for real and one for show. The first, the real one, talks about the academic excellence, subject mastery, getting into college or a job. The other discusses the human purpose of school: values, feelings, personal growth, the full and happy life. It is included because everyone knows that is important, and that it ought to be central in the life of every school. But it is only for show. Everyone knows how little schools have done about it.[3]

Another factor limiting the value of statements of purpose is their after-the-fact quality. Purposes and goals are determined for public consumption, not as guides to moment-by-moment behavior. They are not intellectual cornerstones for real curricular decisions about what should be taught and how it should be taught. They do not affect a school's decision to teach the children to read or not to push other children or not to talk while the teacher is talking. These lessons will be taught in schools that have opposing goals, and in schools that have

---

[2] Educational Policies Commission, *The Central Purpose of American Education* (Washington, D.C.: National Education Association, 1961), p. 15.
[3] Terry Borton, "Reach, Touch, and Teach," *Saturday Review* 52 (January 18, 1969): 56.

no written statements of purpose at all. In other words, schools do not come into existence to fulfill their stated purposes. Educational psychologist J. M. Stephens speculates that "the very existence of schooling may stem not from a deliberate decision of groups or societies, but from blind, spontaneous tendencies which are developed by evolutionary demand and which are found to be prevalent in human beings, although more pronounced in some people than in others."[4]

A final point about statements of purpose is that they may mask completely contradictory practices. For instance, it is common for schools to espouse in their charters the idea, also proposed in the Educational Policies Commission's statement, that the schools should develop the child's ability to think. While many schools do this and much more to help students develop into adulthood, some children, on the other hand, come away from their schooling believing, in fact, that they cannot think. Many children, as a result of what they are made to learn and how they are taught, leave school believing they are "dumb-dumbs" and that the life of the mind is not for them. For them, school is an intellectually discouraging place where they learn what they are not capable of rather than what they can do. But these schools, too, repeat noble phrases attesting to their dedication to teaching children to think.

Personal experience

If the formal statements by commissions and individuals can be misleading, why cannot we simply rely on our own experience? We have all spent a large percentage of our lives in schools, and each of us has a rich store of ideas and impressions to draw on. Personal experience is undeniably a very important source of data to help us come to know what a school is. Understanding the school from personal experience has, however, two limitations. One is the angle from which we have seen our own schools; the other is the narrowness of that angle. The position from which the student observes, experiences, and comes to know the school is just one of several vantage points. Teachers have another very different point of view; administrators another; parents another; students actively involved in school affairs another; and foreign visitors to our schools another. For instance, the students in a seventh-grade American history class finish the year confused and upset because their teacher has raised serious and unanswered questions about the administration of justice in our country. But the

[4] J. M. Stephens, *The Process of Schooling, A Psychological Examination* (New York: Holt, Rinehart & Winston, 1967), p. 8.

Miss Peach by Mell Lazarus. Courtesy Publishers-Hall Syndicate.

What is a school?

teacher feels that unsettling the students, and goading them to asking new questions, is exactly what he is trying to accomplish. The principal, on the other hand, is worried about all the calls he has received from the children's parents, some challenging what the teacher is doing and threatening to withdraw their support of the school. Many of the parents think their children are too young to deal with complex social issues. One community group has condemned the teacher as un-American, unprofessional, and a troublemaker. Another organization has come to his defense for making education socially relevant and for personifying American idealism. A foreign visitor may be confused by all the uproar, shocked by the lack of respect afforded the teacher, and disturbed that the teacher told the students so little and asked them so many questions. The angle from which we perceive, then, affects what we see of school and the judgment we make about it. We have somehow to make up for the limitations of our angle of vision if we are really to know what a school is.

Reproduce your school in words

Spend a few minutes reflecting on one of the schools you attended before coming to college. Recall its physical characteristics, the dominant colors, how it smelled, the architectural imagination it reflected. Think of the moods you associate with this school. Then write down all of the descriptive words and phrases that have come to your mind. Don't be concerned with order or form, but try to write at least twenty such phrases.

_____

_____

_____

_____

_____

_____

_____

Now that you have recorded these bits of description, pick out the five you feel to be most important. Write them below in order of importance.

_____

_____

_____

_____

_____

The angle of perception is not the only limitation of personal experience; the narrowness of the slice of experience we observe is also a factor. You have just composed a word picture of a school you have attended. Contrast your word picture with these two:

- strong smell of disinfectant and human sweat in the air / gritty sound of chalk scraping blackboard / fear of getting beat up on way home / drab, greenish paint everywhere / hundreds of broken windows
- bright colors and sunny rooms / same alphabet cards as grade school on top of board / knowing everyone—all 105—in the school / bonfire pep rally for whole community before regional football championships / two-year-old desks with carved up tops!

Certainly, the two word pictures differ immensely. It is quite doubtful that their authors went to the same school. The first sounds like a rather run-down school in a slum. The second could be a relatively new school in a rural area. The point is that the same word, "school," conjures very different images in two minds. This is because schools, and the experience of going to school, vary radically within this country. The public school in a small citrus-growing town along the Rio Grande River, serving mainly Mexican-American children, is worlds away from the private boys' preparatory school on the outskirts of New Haven, Connecticut. The newly integrated elementary school in a tense working class neighborhood can be profoundly different from the busy, innovative elementary school in a quiet suburb just fifteen freeway minutes away. When we call on our own experience to answer the question, "What is a school?" we must remember that each of us has had quite limited experience. A great variety of people, motives, activities, and outcomes are covered by the simple word "school." Nevertheless, there *are* many points of commonality in the school experiences of people in this country, which we will explore throughout this volume.

Models of schools

A model is a representation of reality. All of us create mental models to help us sort out the hundreds of thousands of sounds and sights we encounter daily and to organize them into sensible patterns. Scientists, in particular, use theoretical models in their efforts to predict events and to explain why certain things have occurred. Models can be similarly useful to us as we attempt to answer the question, "What is a school?" A number of descriptive models have been developed

Washington Star Syndicate.

Many schools are still storage bins, twelve year warehouses for the young where, ideally, very little is supposed to happen and where all events are subject to intensive control. Organized from the outside in, they were created on the basis of buildings, budgets, administrative efficiency, pupil head counts, accounting procedures and rigid structures. Variety, flexibility and originality are untolerable because they make administration difficult, they ruin normal accounting and scheduling systems, and they make the citizens suspicious. Thus the textbook and syllabus become the academic analogs of fenders, or tail-lights and spray paint on the assembly line: they are added to the kids as they move through on the curricular belt. It is easy to teach 'facts' not only because the culture is fact-ridden, but because it is easy to test for learning when 'facts' are to be regurgitated. Peter Schrag, *Voices in the Classroom.*

to explain the purposes and functions of a school. A few such models are briefly described below.[5] As you read, think about how well each one describes the schools you know.

The school as an acculturator	The school brings together people of divergent backgrounds to accommodate themselves to and share one culture. The school's role is to teach "the American Way of Life," and to pass on the customs, values, and social patterns of the dominant group to immigrants and others who have been excluded from full participation in this society. According to this view, the school is a melting pot, whose function is to minimize the influence of minority ethnic, racial, and religious influences and to teach "Americanism."
The school as a factory	The school prepares children for industrial work. The modern school, which was In fact designed during the Industrial Revolution, pre-adapts children to the world of work by immersing them in a crowded, noisy environment ruled by a time clock and dominated by the production mentality. Large numbers of students (raw material) are brought together to be processed by teachers (workers) who are overseen, in turn, by administrators (foremen). As in a factory, regimentation, lack of individualization, and systemization (seating, grouping, grading) are the major operating principles. The final product of the school is "a good worker." A variation of this school is seen in the new stress on career education. The purpose of the school here is not to produce a worker, but for the potential worker to have a productive job in society. Great attention is given to the job possibilities and the necessary training.
The school as a preparer for college	The school prepares the student for more schooling. The goal of the school is to ready the boy or girl for admission to college. As a result, the here and now is not nearly as important as the future. Using this model, the curriculum of the secondary school is justified to the degree it prepares students to do college-level work. Likewise, the elementary-school curriculum is justified to the degree it prepares students for success in secondary school. In this model, the "prestige" of a school as a stepping-stone to a "good college" is an important consideration.

[5] Several of the models described below are adapted from Bernard Spodek's "Early Learning for What?" *Phi Delta Kappan* 50 (March 1969): 394–396.

The school as a bureaucracy	The school is a training ground for life in a bureaucratized society. According to this model, the school is a set of experiences that wean the child from the protective and highly personalized care of his family so that he can deal with the governmental and economic bureaucracies he will encounter in later life. School teaches us how to cooperate and interact easily with large numbers of people we do not know well. We learn how to live by rules in whose formulation we had little or no voice. According to this model, the school helps to modify the individual so that he will not oppose the bureaucracy, thus assuring the safety of the system.
The school as babysitter	The school relieves the parents of full-time responsibility for their children. The school is valued as a repository or "dumping ground," which enables parents, particularly mothers, to pursue new alternatives. In an industrial state such as ours, releasing women from extended childrearing frees them for other work. A variant of this is the mean babysitter model: the parents are free to be continually loving and permissive to the child, while the school dispenses discipline and, sometimes, punishment.
The school as developer of human potential	The school attempts to insure that each individual develops his capacities— intellectual, social, and physical—to the fullest possible measure. The teachers are specialists in identifying students' strengths and needs and matching the instructional program to these strengths and needs. The cornerstone of the school is the uniqueness of each child, and the school is designed to be flexible and have a positive impact on the child. By aiding each child to develop his human potential the school sees itself being a major contributor to a richer, more humane society.

A phenomenon as varied and widespread as a school cannot be explained by a single model. And a model is only as good as its ability to explain reality to us. Therefore, a model of a school has value to the degree that it helps us understand what we already know about schools and to make sense of the new information we receive.[6]

The need for objectivity	Our attempt to find out what a school is can be greatly aided by the objectivity that characterizes scientific investigation. We can avail ourselves of such objectivity in two ways: we can acquire it ourselves by studying and using the scientific method, and we can familiarize ourselves with the work of scientists from various disciplines who have studied education and the schools.

Throughout this book we call upon a large number of sources to further understanding or, at least, to strengthen our grasp on the questions we have posed. Besides teachers and children, and an occasional novelist and poet, we have selected from the research and theories of philosophers, psychologists, economists, computer scientists, and scholars from several disciplines. Since we have borrowed rather heavily from psychology, sociology, and anthropology, a page or two of introduction may be helpful to readers who have not yet studied these disciplines. Let it be understood, however, that these are very abbreviated and incomplete descriptions. Readers familiar with the intellectual approaches of these disciplines are urged to skip ahead to the section entitled, "The Function of the School: An Anthropologist's Analysis."

[6] For a fuller discussion of this issue, we suggest you read Joseph C. Grannis' "The School as a Model of Society," which is reprinted in the accompanying book of readings, *Kaleidoscope*.

What is a school?

The 23rd Century scholars made another exceptionally interesting observation. They pointed out that 20th Century institutions were caught in a savage crossfire between uncritical lovers and unloving critics. On the one side, those who loved their institutions tended to smother them in an embrace of death, loving their rigidities more than their promise, shielding them from life-giving criticism. On the other side, there arose a breed of critics without love, skilled in demolition but untutored in the arts by which human institutions are nurtured and strengthened and made to flourish. Between the two, the institutions perished. John W. Gardner

The psychologist's view

A psychologist studies the mind and human behavior. An educational psychologist specializes in the relationship between the human mind and education. There are several types of educational psychologist, and different schools of thought within the discipline, but broadly speaking they all concern themselves with human development and the conditions that foster it. Among the areas on which they focus are the development of concepts, the formation of attitudes, stimulation of creative behavior, the use of instructional strategies in the classroom, and the motivation of the learner. Because of the nature of his field and the questions with which he is dealing, the educational psychologist is especially interested in the question, "What is a school?" He is not satisfied to regard the school simply as the setting where the activities that interest him happen to take place. The school and its characteristics have a pronounced effect on the phenomena he studies. In attempting to answer our question, the trained psychologist would ask such questions as the following: What changes is the school attempting to make in the child? How is it known whether these

Maria Montessori (1870–1952)

Maria Montessori became a proponent of preschool education, an urban educational reformer, and a believer in equal opportunities for women sixty years before any of these issues were matters of widespread concern.

As a child, Maria Montessori excelled in mathematics and thought of becoming an engineer. Later she developed an interest in medicine, and overcame tremendous criticism to become the first woman to enroll in the University of Rome's medical school. After graduating, she lectured on anthropology at the university, and became associated with the psychiatric clinic. She developed an interest in retarded children and, suspecting that they were far more capable of learning than was commonly believed, founded and headed the Orthophrenic School, where she achieved remarkable results with mentally deficient children.

But it was not until she was 36 years old that Madame Montessori found her life-work. Believing her methods could be even more effective with normal children, she opened her first school, the Casa del Bambini (Children's House), to the preschool-age street urchins of Rome. Madame Montessori's school was run on the principle of allowing children freedom within a carefully designed environment and under the sensitive guidance of a trained directress. The materials and toys available in the school were prescribed, but the children were allowed freedom to handle or ignore them as they wished. Self-learning and individualization were stressed, but there were definite limits on freedom: students were required to come to school clean, and even their free play was structured. However, a child was never forced either to play or to learn. The teachers were instructed simply to wait until the child became interested in a particular game or project. A child who was concentrating deeply on a ritual with a toy was not aided or corrected by a teacher unless he asked for help.

Madame Montessori discovered that certain simple and precise educational materials evoked sustained interest and attention in the young child. Children under five years old would concentrate on a single task, oblivious to distraction, for periods of from fifteen minutes to an hour, and afterward seem refreshed rather than tired. Madame Montessori's close observations of children led her to conclude that, from birth to age six, every child possesses an "absorbent mind," which equips him to learn more quickly and easily than at any subsequent period in his life. Throughout these years, she found, the child experiences periods of specialized sensitivity, during which his interest and mental capacity are particularly suited to the acquisition of particular knowledge, such as colors, language, and textures. Montessori recognized that small children learn through their senses, and developed methods of stimulating the child's senses in ways that would enhance learning. For instance, children were taught the alphabet with sandpaper letters which they could manipulate with their fingers. Montessori was the first to use flashcards as a sensory stimulus, and she even introduced the hula hoop, which became a fad in the United States in the fifties. She was severely criticized for ignoring discipline; she replied that, in the conventional schools she had visited, children were "not disciplined, but annihilated."

Madame Montessori's teaching methods have aroused considerable interest in the United States as a result of recent psychological research verifying many of her theories. Psychologists and educators have come to agree with her that the period of early childhood is critical in determining a person's intellectual potential.

Before her death, Madame Montessori travelled widely, establishing schools, teaching teachers, and promoting her still unconventional ideas. A typical Montessori classroom today is a beehive of activity, each child pursuing an independent task at his own speed. A two-and-a-half-year-old carries a tray holding a jug of water and two glasses across the room. On reaching the other side he begins to fill the glasses with dry grains of rice. He is joined by a little girl who sweeps the spilled rice into a pile. A third child appears with a brush and dustpan to collect the deposit. A group of children is busy using colored pencils to shade designs they have made themselves using geometric forms cut out of metal. The teacher dictates words to some boys who compose them on a mat with large moveable letters.

New Montessori schools have recently sprung up in this country in response to the demands of parents. Teachers of underprivileged or minority children, in particular, claim great success with Montessori techniques, and the day care center movement and day care programs and the early childhood movement, in general, have been significantly influenced by her views.

changes have been made? How are the components of the school — teachers, learning materials, and physical phenomena like heat and light — organized to help the student learn, and thus achieve the goals of the school? What principles of learning pervade the school's activities? In what ways is the school hindering learning? What unconscious or incidental learnings are acquired by children who attend school? And then there is the overriding question: is the school experience nurturing the intellectual, social, and emotional potential of the children?

Before a psychologist would attempt to answer such questions, he would observe and record much of the behavior that takes place in the school. He would also administer tests to ascertain the students' capacity to learn and how well they are actually learning. The educational psychologist does not try to explain all the phenomena of the school, but only those that bear directly on the mind and its development.

The sociologist's view

Sociologists investigate how people live together in groups — how groups are formed and how they function, how individuals behave collectively, and how they organize themselves to get things done. The educational sociologist looks at the school as a specialized agency for the socialization — that is, the adaptation to society — of the young. The educational sociologist perceives the school as one of society's institutions, like the family, the church, or the occupational group, and studies the school as purposeful collections of human and nonhuman resources.

Trying to understand the school on these terms, the educational sociologist asks such questions as: What does the school provide a society? Do the schools furnish the same services to the lower and the upper classes? If not, what are the effects of these discrepancies on individuals and on the society? What are the characteristics of a school as an institution? If an institution is defined as a network of rewards and punishments, how does this definition apply to the school? How are teachers rewarded? How are they punished? How do they reward and punish students? How do students reward and punish teachers? Does the culture of the school reflect the multiracial, pluralistic nature of American society, or is one set of values predominant? How does the school impose this culture on the young? If every institution has a social structure, what is the school's structure? What is the flow of authority in a school? Who has power? Under what circumstances? What are the various student subcultures? How do teachers and administrators react to these subcultures?

Sociologists have been called people with a compulsion for organizing common sense. While this is a left-handed and unfair definition, it is true that sociologists examine what is right around us. Frequently, however, when sociologists organize common sense observations, we are startled by a new insight. An example is the assertion of the great sociologist Talcott Parsons that the primary concern of the school is motivating the child to *achieve*. While some were arguing that the school teaches the 3 Rs, and others that it trains children for American citizenship, Parsons pointed out that a school is a social agency

There is nothing on earth intended for innocent people so horrible as a school. To begin with, it is a prison. But it is in some respects more cruel than a prison. In a prison, for instance, you are not forced to read books written by the wardens and the governor. G. B. Shaw, *Parents and Children.*

The object of the common school system is to give every child a free, straight, solid pathway by which he can walk directly up from the ignorance of an infant to a knowledge of the primary duties of a man, and can acquire a power and an invincible will to discharge them. Horace Mann, 1837.

that teaches achievement and competition, virtues which are highly prized in an industrial society.

The anthropologist's view

The popular image of an anthropologist is someone who spends time on South Sea islands taking detailed notes on the behavior of the exotic inhabitants. This is a dated notion, since the anthropologist is increasingly applying his trained powers of observation to urban society. Essentially, the anthropologist is a student of man, and focuses on man's customs, social relations, and culture. He normally lives among the people he is studying so that he can observe first-hand and in intimate detail their manner of life. From this immersion in the flux and flow of everyday life, and analysis of the data he has collected, the anthropologist is frequently able to identify and explain the complex patterns inherent in the behavior of a group of people.

Anthropologists are bringing a fresh perspective to the study of the school. By training, anthropologists are equipped to observe and study relatively small communities of people, and their methods are proving effective in the investigation of classroom procedures and cultures. They have the added advantage of a cross-cultural perspective, which enables them to compare and contrast the ways education is conducted in different societies. Most of us are hyperopic—that is, unable to see clearly what is nearby—about our own culture, and particularly so about schools. For instance, schools have been characterized by rituals, in which we have all engaged more or less unquestioningly. Here are just a handful, some of which have faded from the educational landscape.

- We had to stand when we recited, even though sometimes neither visibility nor audibility were relevant factors.
- We had to be ready to account for our behavior to the teacher, but were not allowed to ask the teacher to account for his behavior.
- We had to do homework that no one ever examined, for reasons never made clear to us.
- We had to bring notes from home if we needed anything or wanted anything that was different from what the others generally needed.
- When bells rang, we had to stop what we were doing and what we were thinking and go to other places.

What is a school?

- We had to participate in air raid drills that everyone knew were absolutely worthless.
- We had to refrain from talking in class, in the halls, in the lavatory, and in the auditorium.[7]

To the anthropologist, with his ability to discern patterns and meanings beneath the surface of events, a culture reveals itself in its treatment and training of the young. Therefore, he has many questions to ask about the schools: What are the culture's core values and how are they modified by the schools? Does the school reinforce the traditions of the culture? What is the meaning and importance of school rituals (the fall weekend football pageant, graduation ceremonies) and customs (pre-holiday assemblies and school dances)? How do they prepare people to fit into the larger culture? What is the language of the classroom and how does it differ from the language of the street?

The anthropologist is, then, a "culture watcher," and as such he can help us analyze the schools to overcome our blindness to what is most familiar.

**The function
of the school:
an anthropologist's
analysis**

The reason for disciplined inquiry into the nature of the school and other issues raised in this book is to transcend commonplace, and frequently faulty, conclusions. To illustrate, let us examine a particularly penetrating analysis of the function of the school, one which surpasses common sense. Earlier we claimed that it is a task of the school to interpret the world to the young. This assertion is faulty

[7] Adapted from Robert Goldhammer, *Clinical Supervision* (New York: Holt, Rinehart & Winston, 1969), pp. 26–29.

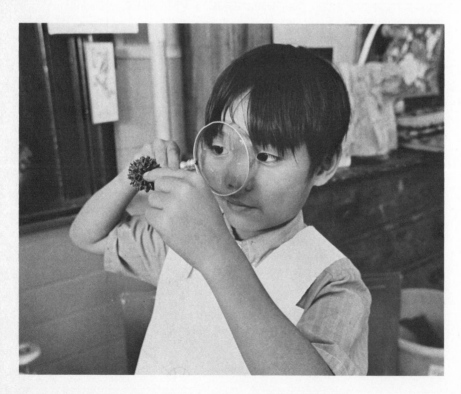

on two counts. First, obviously, the world in all its variety—people, ant-eaters, floods, eggplants, newspapers, logarithms—is just too much with which to deal. Schools have to be selective. They must choose fragments from the universe of knowledge. The goal, of course, is to select those bits and pieces that can be used by people to discover more and more. The second error is more subtle: while educators may think they are interpreting the world to the young, what they are ordinarily doing is transmitting their own culture and its values.

By "culture," we mean the system of norms and standards that a society develops over the course of many generations and that profoundly influences their everyday behavior. More simply, culture is as people do. The implication, clearly, is that American public schools teach the American way of looking at the world and the American way of doing things. By and large, this is not a conscious process. It was not consciously introduced into the curriculum. If we ask educators what, broadly speaking, they are trying to do, they are likely to reply that they are teaching reality and how to deal with it. But, in fact, our schools teach our version of reality and our way of handling the real world. And so, too, do the schools of other countries. Schools in Northern India differ markedly from those in Ghana, and neither have much in common with American public schools. However, the schools of each country are attempting to perform a similar function: to transmit the unique culture of the country to its newest members, the young. This desire to insure that the young share the common culture may explain why in many school systems we teach American history in the third grade, the seventh grade and again in the eleventh grade, and why we give very little attention to the history of China. China is the most populous nation in the world, with one of the oldest and richest cultural heritages. China may have introduced the first formal schooling. Most scholars and foreign policy experts are sure that China will loom large in the future of this country. Nevertheless, until recently the American people had developed the habit of ignoring China, and as a result its existence is hardly acknowledged in schools.

There is danger inherent in this tendency of schools to concentrate on transmitting the dominant culture. Just a few decades ago there was little apparent need for different cultures to understand and appreciate one another, but electronic communications, nuclear weapons, and jet travel have changed all that. If schools offer the young an understanding only of the prevailing culture, the result may be an attitude of smug cultural superiority, a phenomenon that frequently leads nations to foolish actions. In cultural terms, what we do not know we frequently do not respect. Without mutual respect people easily become enemies.

This tendency of the schools—of all schools everywhere—to modify reality by filtering it through the lens of a particular culture is not all bad. A society's culture is, perhaps, its most precious gift to its young. A culture is a structure for ordering the chaos of raw existence. It provides a framework—a language system, rules for interacting with other people, ways of solving problems—within which to know oneself and the world. It assures the individual that life is worthwhile and defines for him what constitutes the good life. A person's culture, whether he is an Australian Bushman or a Swiss banker, is his compass and anchor in his day-to-day existence. According to the anthropologist's analysis, then, the school's major function is to transmit this precious and necessary heritage to the young.

The unfinished work of the schools

It is probably clear by now that there is no single satisfactory answer to our question, "What is a school?" This and many other questions we will ask in this book are too large and complex to be adequately answered here—if, indeed, they can be answered at all. We pose them and talk about them anyway to aid you in your investigations into the issues behind the questions. People contemplating a career in education must commit themselves to working out answers to these questions. It seems unlikely that you can make a good career choice lacking an understanding of the institution you are considering entering. And if you hope to survive and be happy within an institution, you will need to know how it works. You need to know what the institution says it is doing ("we are training future citizens," or "we are educating well-rounded citizens prepared to excel in college") and what it actually does. You need to know what a particular school's expectations of you, as teacher, will be, so you can decide how to respond or if you wish to respond at all. Finally, if you hope to improve the schools, that is, make them better because of your involvement with them, you need a realistic view of what is now going on in the schools and a vision of what the schools can become.

Schools are a human invention. As we established earlier, people bring schools into being for social purposes. The overall purposes of school are to advance the common good and to help people live better and happier lives. However, if schools are to serve society, they must at least keep pace with the society. Many people who are concerned about our schools feel that they are moving very slowly while the rest of society experiences dynamic change. In effect, the schools are out of phase with and lagging behind the society they are supposed to be serving. The result is tension. As happens frequently in times of tension, views polarize in the manner suggested by John Gardner's statement on page 182. Nevertheless, the purposes for which schools are brought into being are still vital. People still desire good schools for their children. And, as you will see later in this book, many excellent ideas are being generated and movements are underway for the renewal of our schools.

Some readers may be uncomfortable with the idea that it is their job to renew the schools. Many may feel that becoming a good classroom teacher is enough. The teacher, however, is more than a worker. As professional people he and his colleagues *must* have a voice in deciding how their services are rendered. It follows that the teacher is not responsible simply for his own performance, but bears responsibility for the total educational enterprise. To live up to this responsibility requires a deep understanding of the schools and much hard work, but it is the very critical nature of the problems confronting the schools that makes teaching such an exciting occupation today. Schools are becoming increasingly important in the life of each individual and in the health of the society. Pressures are building for changes in public education. In the immediate future, education is where the action will be. Society is inviting us to complete the unfinished work of the schools.

Discussion questions

1   Can you think of some pieces of information you picked up on the street that you later "unlearned" in school? Can you think of some things you learned in school that your experience later taught you were untrue? Which has happened more often? How do you react to this?

2   To what extent did the schools you attended serve the purposes suggested by the various models we described? Can you suggest any models we have overlooked?

3   Which of the models of the school we have discussed is illustrated by the cartoon on page 179? Is it inappropriate to any of the models we have discussed? Does it seem to you an apt comment on your own education?

4   How do you react to the remark, "Children enter school as question marks and leave as periods"? Is this desirable? Is it necessary? How would its meaning be changed if the statement were changed to, "Six-year-olds are question marks and seventeen-year-olds are periods." Would that statement be equally true?

5   What are the dangers inherent in the schools' tendency to transmit their own culture? What gaps did this tendency leave in your own schooling? What purpose does this tendency serve?

6   Think about Marshall McLuhan's statement that children interrupt their education to go to school. What kinds of things does the school expect children to learn on their own, outside of school? What kinds of things does society expect children to learn in school and make no effort to teach elsewhere?

7   Think about Bruno Bettelheim's statement that education is man's oldest and best means of shaping future generations and perpetuating his past society. Is this true? What about our economic system? What about the family? What does "best means" mean in this sentence?

For further reading

- Broudy, Harry Samuel. *Paradox and Promise: Essays on American Life and Education.* Englewood Cliffs, N.J.: Prentice-Hall, 1961. A collection of fifteen essays by one of America's leading educational philosophers on major issues confronting the schools.
- Cremin, Lawrence A. *The Transformation of the School.* New York: Alfred A. Knopf, 1961. An award-winning history of the progressive education movement from 1876 to 1954. The book carefully traces the origins, development, and finally the effect of the progressive education movement on our schools.
- Dewey, John. *Democracy and Education.* New York: Macmillan, 1916. The key work, and certainly the most widely read book on education, by America's foremost philosopher and contributor to educational thought. (See also biography on p. 26.)
- Dreeben, Robert. *On What Is Learned in School.* Reading, Mass.: Addison-Wesley, 1968. This book offers us a sociologist's perspective on the nature of schooling and its link to the surrounding institutions of family, occupations, and

politics. It focuses on the relationships between the school structure and the learning outcomes and the relevance of those outcomes to the surrounding institutions.

- Gardner, John W. *Excellence: Can We Be Equal and Excellent Too?* New York: Harper & Row, 1961. A challenging analysis of the problem of fostering both excellence and equality. Major attention is given to the role of the schools.
- Grannis, Joseph. "The School as a Model of Society." *Harvard Graduate School of Education Association Bulletin* 21 (Fall 1967): 14–27, reprinted in the companion book of readings to this volume, *Kaleidoscope: Readings in Education,* 2nd ed., edited by Kevin Ryan and James M. Cooper. Boston: Houghton Mifflin, 1975. In this article the author describes three different models of schools and their effect on children. The major point is that the hidden curriculum of the school is the structure of the school and the way human beings are organized within it.
- Henry, Jules. *Culture Against Man.* New York: Random House, 1963. A distinguished cultural anthropologist writes vividly of the weaknesses of complex urban and industrial cultures. This book contains some withering analyses of what goes on in the American schools.
- Hutchins, Robert M. *Education for Freedom.* Baton Rouge, La.: Louisiana State University Press, 1943. A distinguished American educator argues the case for a conservative approach to education if we are to preserve and extend freedom.
- Mayer, Martin. *The Schools.* New York: Harper & Row, 1961. A provocative, stimulating description of life in American classrooms and the controversies affecting them, by a literate and sophisticated journalist. The book is extremely well written and filled with interesting anecdotes and personal impressions.
- Peddiwell, J. Abner [Harold Benjamin]. *The Saber-Tooth Curriculum.* New York: McGraw-Hill, 1939. A satirical spoof on the origin of schools, the inadequacies of the curriculum, and the reluctance of educators to keep the curriculum relevant to societal needs. Humorous and entertaining reading.
- Sarason, Seymour B. *The Culture of the School and the Problem of Change.* Boston: Allyn and Bacon, 1971. An examination of school cultures and the problems inherent in attempting to bring about change. The author particularly highlights the important role of the principal in any change process.
- Schaefer, Robert J. *The School as a Center of Inquiry.* New York: Harper & Row, 1967. A short, highly readable description of how the schools might more adequately serve children by returning to their central task of stimulating inquiry.
- Spindler, George D., ed. *Education and Culture: Anthropological Approaches.* New York: Holt, Rinehart & Winston, 1963. This book was written by anthropologists and social scientists whose studies relate to education. The tools and techniques used by anthropologists offer the reader a number of fascinating insights into American education.
- Thelen, Herbert A. *Education and the Human Quest.* New York: Harper & Row, 1960. An insightful book which addresses major questions about the relationship between man's development and education. Many questionable practices are analyzed by a writer of immense sensitivity and wisdom.

Films

- *Abraham Kaplan* (Indiana University Audio-Visual Center, 16mm, b&w, 59 min.). One of a series of five films about "Men Who Teach." Abraham Kaplan, professor of philosophy at the University of Michigan, explains his beliefs and attitudes toward teaching, as well as the differences he sees between instruction and education.

- *Free Growth* (University of California, 16mm, b&w, 36 min., 1971). This essay on freedom in education uses a wide range of case histories, and it shifts through such sites as a Hopi reservation and the Los Angeles Free School. Man-in-the-street interviews are included to illustrate the traditional belief in compulsory education. The film treats education as part of the larger question of self-fulfillment and choice of life direction.
- *Friday* (Judith Pacht, 16mm, b&w, 5 min., 1972). The problem posed by this film is whether the opportunity exists for children to discover who they are within the school institution. It begins with a roll call and ends with a children's folk song asking "What is your name?" With examples of depersonalization, suppression of basic impulses, and the use of shame as a means of control, the film reports on the effects a teacher can have on children who are trying to discover their own identities in a "learning" environment.
- *How Children Learn* (NBC, 16mm, color, 23 min., 1972). From traditional elementary schools to experimental junior high schools without walls, changing methods and attitudes toward the individual needs of the children are illustrated in this film.
- *Learning About Thinking and Vice Versa* (Film Bureau, 16mm, b&w, 32 min., 1972). This film documents a workshop held for teachers and administrators in two Philadelphia inner-city schools. It recommends practices, especially one-to-one interviews, by which teachers can learn more about children's thinking.
- *No Little Hope* (Center for Urban Education, 16mm, color, 28 min.). Documents the meaning of education to various people in New York City. Through the words of the people interviewed, many of them parents, it becomes clear that "the process of education" cannot be fully understood without taking into account parents, the community, mass media—and, of course, the schools.
- *Rubin on Schools* (American Documentary Films, 16mm, 15 min.). Jerry Rubin speaks on the antihuman institutional oppression of modern educational systems.
- *Summerhill* (Contemporary/McGraw-Hill, 16mm, color, 28 min.). A visit to a coeducational English boarding school founded by A. S. Neill forty-five years ago. The school's objectives are explained by filming the students and faculty in various activities.
- *The Mind of Man* (NET and BBC, 16mm, color, 119 min., 1971). Major research clinics all over the world were visited in order to film this survey of current mind research. Areas treated include mind development in children, effects of drugs, dreams, brain structure, sexuality, and reasoning. Interviews with Richard Fineman, Sir John Eccles, Noam Chomsky, and B. F. Skinner.
- *What Makes Man Human* (University-at-Large, 16mm, color, 15 min., 1969). This film concerns Jerome Bruner's innovative curriculum for fifth-grade social studies. Bruner and several teachers discuss the structure and scope of the course and explain why they advocate an educational approach that views man and his social life as the constant focus of curriculum.
- *What They Want to Produce, Not What We Want to Become* (EDC and CBC, 16mm, b&w, 60 min., 1970). In a series of interviews with Canadian students, teachers, and administrators in all school levels, expectations of school and frustrations are discussed. The structure of a highly traditional and disciplined school is contrasted with such alternative school situations as Summerhill and the Everdale Place School.

Audiotapes

- *Education for Freedom* (Center for the Study of Democratic Institutions, 44 min.). Dr. Alexander Meiklejohn was writing a book on how to educate for a free society. Before he died the Center recorded his first two chapters, in which Meiklejohn posed the question of what kind of education a John F. Kennedy needed to fit himself for the Presidency.

- *Education: For What and for Whom?* (The Center for the Study of Democratic Institutions, 3.75 ips, ½ track, 30:15 min.). This tape of a talk given at the Tenth Anniversary Convocation of the Fund for the Republic, presents Robert Hutchins, head of the Center for the Study of Democratic Institutions; Rosemary Park, former president of Barnard College; and Admiral Hyman Rickover in an analysis of educational problems.

- *George Leonard: Ecstasy and Education* (Big Sur, 60 min., 1970). George Leonard describes the history of education and why it has had to be repressive, and why it can now include joy and other positive motivations.

- *George Leonard: Seminar on Education* (Big Sur, 6 hours, 1968). Leonard postulates the theory that schools have stopped the learning process in favor of training to fill essential niches in a self-perpetuating society. True education, he says, should focus on individuality and creativity.

- *Ivan Illich on Educational Alternatives* (Canadian Broadcasting Corporation, 30 min., 1971). Illich contends that the ideology of consumerism casts a false perspective on schools. This tape is especially concerned with the impact of this viewpoint on schools outside the United States but within its economic and ideological sphere.

- *The Role of the University in a Democratic Society* (Pacifica, 39 min., 1967). John Kenneth Galbraith, Harvard economics professor and government advisor, defines his concept of the university in a speech at the University of California in Berkeley.

- *The School: An Empire Transmitting Technological Verities* (Noumedia #N7004, 3.75 ips, ¼ track, mono or stereo, 1 hour, 1970). In the second of three lectures given at Yale University in 1970, Ivan Illich discusses in depth the inhibition and perversion of human growth by institutionalized schooling, as well as the high costs and illusory goals of schools.

- *Schooling Today* (Noumedia #N7003, 3.75 ips, ¼ track, mono or stereo, 1 hour, 1970). In the first of the Yale lectures, Illich discusses what he considers to be the problems of schooling today. The sound is poor, but audible.

- *Schooling vs. Education: Rx for Junior Colleges* (The Center for the Study of Democratic Institutions, 3.75 ips, ½ track, 56:20 min.). W. H. Ferry of the Center for the Study of Democratic Institutions and James D. Finn of the University of Southern California School of Education argue about the gap between schooling and education. Using the California schools as his model, Ferry offers a prescription for junior colleges to correct the gap. Finn follows with a dissent.

- *Schools Against Children* (Pacifica, 29 min., 1970). John Holt talks on education at a conference held at Berkeley. This tape constitutes a good discussion of how the public schools in this nation have worked against the needs of children.

- *Yesterday I Could Not Sleep Because Yesterday I Wrote My Name . . .* (The Center for the Study of Democratic Institutions, 3.75 ips, ½ track, 42:09 min.). Ivan Illich tells John Cogley, editor of *The Center* magazine, "in the name of education, we must get rid of the school." Illich goes on to claim that instead of liberating people, school reinforces and widens the gap between rich and poor.

All audiotapes available on both reel and cassette unless otherwise noted.

Filmstrip

- *The Right to Education* (UNIPUB [UNESCO], 98 frames, b&w). This filmstrip shows projects in fundamental and technical education being pursued by the United Nations, but it focuses on the improvements in quality of life that education can bring to everyone.

Refer to Appendix for addresses of distributors.

What is a school?

What did you do in school today?

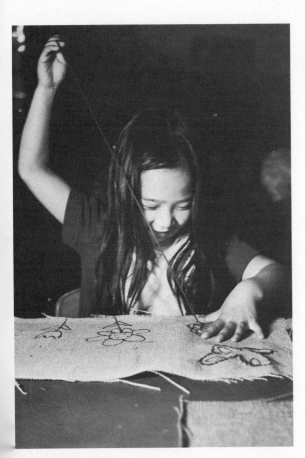

6   What is life in schools like?

This chapter attempts to describe school environment and classroom life as reported by a number of social and behavioral scientists. It examines some of the characteristics of student life, the language of the classroom, relationships among students, and the school as a social system. In addition, descriptions of two innovative schools are presented to illustrate environments that differ considerably from more traditional schools and classrooms.

Teachers are overworked and underpaid. True. It is an exacting and exhausting business, this damming up the flood of human potentialities. What energy it takes to make a torrent into a trickle, to train that trickle along narrow, well-marked channels! Teachers are often tired. In the teachers' lounge, they sigh their relief into stained cups of instant coffee and offer gratitude to whoever makes them laugh at the day's disasters. This laughter permits a momentary, sanity-saving acknowledgment, shared by all, that what passes for humdrum or routine or boring is, in truth, tragic. (An hour, of which some fifty minutes are given up to "classroom control." One child's question unanswered, a hundred unasked. A smart student ridiculed: "He'll learn better." He learns.) Sweet laughter, shooting up like artesian water, breaks through encrusted perceptions and leaves a tear in a teacher's eye. A little triumph.[1]

Is this an accurate portrayal of classrooms and teachers? Many observers of American education—and many teachers and students—would insist that it is. Others might not recognize much truth in it. Generalizations of this sort are necessarily inexact, for no single observer has seen more than a tiny fraction of American schools, let alone tried to concoct a description that does equal justice to every school. As a result, some characterizations of the schools are criticized

[1] From p. 1 of *Education and Ecstasy* by George B. Leonard. Copyright © 1968 by George B. Leonard. Reprinted by permission of the publisher, Delacorte Press.

on the grounds that the schools sampled are not representative—but in what sense can one school really be representative of another? Different socioeconomic groups, different communities, and different sections of the country produce schools that are dissimilar in certain respects. Even two schools in contiguous neighborhoods may be markedly different, and a single school can change radically in a few years' time. It is also important to remember that observers are no more interchangeable than schools are. Each of us perceives reality differently. As you read this chapter, for example, you will undoubtedly react to particular passages by thinking, "That's just what life in my school was like," or "It wasn't like that at all." Someone else who attended the same school, but whose background and experiences differ from yours, may remember the school in an entirely different light. There is no certified version of reality. But, despite these important qualifications, the authors—and other observers—believe that certain conditions are more typical of schools than they are idiosyncratic and that some observations are authentically generalizable. Let's look at life in the schools, and see what we can find out about the school as an environment.

The school as an environment

The relative importance of heredity and environment is an old issue among philosophers and educators, and one that seems unlikely to be resolved in the near future. Perhaps it's insoluble. But one thing seems clear—both heredity and environment deeply influence an individual's capacity to learn. We all feel intuitively, though we'd probably have trouble proving it, the crucial importance of environment in shaping who we are. John Dewey, the American philosopher and educator (see p. 26 for his biographical sketch), contended that environment

leads [an individual] to see and feel one thing rather than another; . . . it strengthens some beliefs and weakens others . . . it gradually produces in him a certain system of behavior. . . . In brief, the environment consists of those conditions that promote or hinder, stimulate or inhibit, the characteristic activities of a living being.[2]

Environment and learning

If school represents a major aspect of the environment of every child, how important is the school environment in facilitating or impeding learning? The work of psychologist David Krech[3] may give us some clues.

Environmental richness

To determine the effect of environment on rats, Krech is rearing matched sets of rats in sharply contrasting environments. One set of rats is kept in a sealed room, where each animal lives in a separate cage, in darkness and silence. The second set of rats, littermates of the first, lives together in a large cage with an abundance of playthings. They are taken out each day and handled; they learn to explore mazes; their environment is rich.

Krech has discovered that the enriched rats develop a higher concentration of an important brain enzyme than do the deprived rats. As a result of the lives they

[2] John Dewey, *Democracy and Education* (New York: Macmillan, 1916), p. 13.
[3] As reported in Leonard, pp. 36–37.

What is life in schools like?

live, the enriched rats develop larger and heavier brains, particularly the cortex or outer bark, which is associated with higher learning. The deprived rats are markedly inferior to the enriched rats in learning ability; they are mentally crippled.

It is dangerous to equate the deprived condition of the rats in the experiment with the deprivations of children in certain of our schools and communities. And yet it is almost impossible not to draw inferences about schoolchildren who are deprived of affectionate physical contact, denied playthings, strictly regimented, and not allowed freedom to interact with other children and with their own environment. What kind of brain atrophy might be occurring in this situation?

Interactive environment

The environment of the advanced rats has two distinct characteristics: it is rich in physical objects and it is interactive. That is, it allows the individual rat involvement with other rats, with playthings and mazes, and with human beings. It is highly unlikely that the rats would show comparable advancement if they were allowed only to look from a distance at a rich and varied environment. In this respect, the setup of the experiment is undeniably relevant to human beings: mere physical proximity to a stimulating environment does not stimulate; interaction must occur for the learning process to be affected. This is why taking a group of children from an inner-city ghetto to an art museum to "expose" them to cultural riches usually has little or no impact. As Leonard states:

No environment can strongly affect a person unless it is strongly interactive. To be interactive, the environment must be responsive, that is, must provide relevant feedback to the learner. For the feedback to be relevant, it must meet the learner where he is, then program (that is, change in appropriate steps at appropriate times) as he changes. The learner changes (that is, is educated) through his responses to the environment.

Within these constraints, the human organism is incredibly flexible. If there are limits on the human ability to respond to learning environments, we are so far away from the limits as to make them inconsequential. Throughout human history to date, it has been the environments, not the human beings, that have run up against limitations.[4]

An environment must, then, be interactive in order to exert a strong influence. A teacher-dominated classroom in which lecturing is the standard mode of instruction obviously does not encourage or permit effective interaction. Yet, as we will see later in this chapter, teacher dominance and teacher talk are the rule rather than the exception. Consider, for example, these observations of depressing school environments:

What a bore school is nowadays, the same as it has been for hundreds of years. What we get is the same old thing—teacher, outdated textbooks, and a class fed up to the teeth with the teacher and the school. What we need is one vast change in the educational system of this country. Children do not want to be taught at, but want to find out things for themselves. If a child is interested in the way a dogfish's heart works, let him go and find out, by cutting one up. Robin, 16

[4] As reported in Leonard, pp. 39–40.

. . . the basic premise is that the teacher and the school have unlimited faith in the capabilities of the pupil. The children must exist in an atmosphere where they can fully and entirely respond to the people and objects around them. A child who is blandly presented with a difficult English text to precis, or who has to copy a mass of fact concerning fossils covering a blackboard, will in the majority of cases react unfavorably. How much better it would be to let this child write a vivid description of some deep and moving experience, or to go out and discover for himself some interesting rock or fossil.[5] Kenneth, 17

The room in which I taught my Fourth Grade was not a room at all, but the corner of an auditorium. The first time I approached that corner, I noticed only a huge torn stage curtain, a couple of broken windows, a badly listing blackboard and about thirty-five bewildered-looking children, most of whom were Negro. White was overcome in black among them, but white and black together were overcome in chaos.They had desks and a teacher, but they did not really have a class. What they had was about one quarter of the auditorium. Three or four blackboards, two of them broken, made them seem a little bit set apart. Over at the other end of the auditorium there was another Fourth Grade class. Not much was happening at the other side at that minute so that for the moment the noise did not seem so bad. But it became a real nightmare of conflicting noises a little later on. Generally, it was not until ten o'clock that the bad crossfire started. By ten-thirty it would have attained such a crescendo that the children in the back rows of my section often couldn't hear my questions and I could not hear their answers. There were no carpetings or sound-absorbers of any kind. The room, being large, and echoing, and wooden, added resonance to every sound. Sometimes the other teacher and I would stagger the lessons in which our classes would have to speak aloud, but this was the makeshift method and it also meant that our classes had to be induced to maintain an unnatural and otherwise unnecessary rule of silence during the rest of the time.[6]

The environments described above are clearly not designed to stimulate the learner, to meet him where he is, to interact with him, or to provide relevant feedback as he responds to his surroundings. But it did not take a long and arduous search to find such descriptions; these are situations in which millions of students find themselves daily. Is it any wonder that so many students fail to learn when the environment specifically intended to facilitate learning—the school—has the opposite effect on many who spend time there?

Schools also tend to suffer in comparison with other learning environments that are a part of children's lives. At one time in history school was the child's major source of learning about the world. Just the fact that schools possessed books about the world made schools a rich source of information. But today the schools are competing with other learning environments, such as those provided by television, records, transistor radios, and improved recreational and social facilities. As a result of interacting with these other environments children are far more

---

[5] The schools described here are not American. These are reports by English children which appear in a fascinating book, *The School That I'd Like*, edited by Edward Blishen (Harmondsworth, England: Penguin Books, 1969), pp. 59, 64. Copyright © Penguin Books and the contributors, 1969. Reprinted by permission of the publisher.

[6] Jonathan Kozol, *Death at an Early Age* (Boston: Houghton Mifflin, 1967), pp. 29–30. Reprinted by permission of the publisher.

Students talk about schools

Schools usually have one thing in common — they are institutions of today run on the principles of yesterday. 15-year-old girl

I am tired of hearing that the hope of my country lies in my generation. If you give me the same indoctrination as a child, how can you expect me to be any different from you? 15-year-old girl

Give me the school where discipline, regimentation and good manners are not everything. We would rather have a school where we can talk on equal terms with our teachers on sex, morals, ethics, loyalty, religion, etc. We want the school where teaching will be equated with a perpetual quest for truth, beauty, integrity. A school where personality and brain-building come first and diplomas or certificates last. After all, a diploma or degree is not the perfect vaccine against stupidity. Cosette, 17

In my view, the sooner we all get out of the stuffy classroom, the better it will be for everybody. Life is much more interesting if you can go out and see something instead of just sitting in a desk and being loaded with information about it. Lynne, 15

*A school where the teacher is regarded as a friend and yet respected;
Where the barrier of the desk is overcome,
And learning is a series of discussions and experiments;
Where the formidable word "lesson" is incomprehensible,
For there are no lessons as such,
And yet we learn more willingly than before.* Susy, 17

History and geography are dealt with adequately, but psychology and politics, drug-taking and smoking and love and death are not mentioned in the school syllabus at all. Kari, 13

A teacher can be very rude and cruel to a child, but any objection on his part is treated as impertinence. Education is a search after the truth, and to find the truth one must be humble. This is impossible if teachers are too proud to admit when they are wrong. Janet, 16

sophisticated and knowledgeable. Schools that ignore this fact and do not provide a stimulating, interactive environment for children will continue to produce discontented students.

Conflicting environments

It is often argued, in defense of the schools, that they are not the children's sole environment. In fact, the home and the street are ordinarily more influential in a child's life. This is of particular concern when the school environment is in direct conflict with the rest of the child's experience. The value system of the school is likely to honor work for its own sake and to stress obeying rules and preparing for the future by delaying gratification. The culture of the neighborhood, on the other hand, may regard work as exploitation or as a necessary evil, hold the law in low regard, and value action and excitement above order. The child's parents may have adopted a philosophy of "eat, drink, and be merry" as a defense against despair. How fully are neighborhood values assimilated before the child even begins school? How are children affected by inconsistency in their environments?

Nevertheless, psychiatrist William Glasser argues that when children do not learn it is the school, not the parents or the neighborhood, that has failed; the students have not been taught in school to gain and to maintain a sense of identity and self-worth through social responsibility. The student, Glasser maintains, has learned a lot about the world by the time he enters school and has, within the limits of his age, learned to cope with it; whatever his environment, he is optimistic about the future.

Very few children come to school failures, none come labeled failures; it is school and school alone which pins the label of failure on children. . . . *Whatever their background, children come to school highly receptive to learning. If they then fail to continue to learn at their rapid preschool rate, we may if we wish blame it on their families, their environment, or their poverty, but we would be much wiser to blame it on their experience in school.*[7]

Studies of life in classrooms

While the total environment of a school is highly significant, some educators are more concerned with specific dimensions of life there. An excellent perspective on how time is typically spent in the elementary classroom is provided by Philip W. Jackson's *Life in Classrooms*.[8] Before describing Jackson's findings, let's try

[7] William Glasser, *Schools Without Failure* (New York: Harper & Row, 1969), p. 26.
[8] Philip W. Jackson, *Life in Classrooms* (New York: Holt, Rinehart & Winston, 1968).

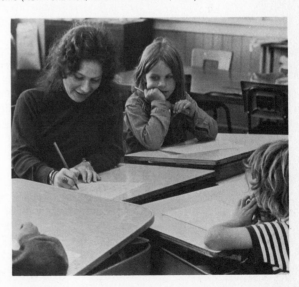

What is life in schools like?

an experiment. Listed below is a series of words representing the opposite extremes of a continuum, each pair connected by a row of boxes. Place a check in the box which you think best represents the child's experience of life in an elementary classroom. Do this quickly, giving your immediate responses rather than thoughtful consideration.

distraction	☐ ☐ ☐ ☐ ☐ ☐ ☐ ☐ ☐ ☐	concentration
delay	☐ ☐ ☐ ☐ ☐ ☐ ☐ ☐ ☐ ☐	promptness
boredom	☐ ☐ ☐ ☐ ☐ ☐ ☐ ☐ ☐ ☐	excitement
postponing	☐ ☐ ☐ ☐ ☐ ☐ ☐ ☐ ☐ ☐	doing
unexpressive	☐ ☐ ☐ ☐ ☐ ☐ ☐ ☐ ☐ ☐	talkative
confusion	☐ ☐ ☐ ☐ ☐ ☐ ☐ ☐ ☐ ☐	order
restriction	☐ ☐ ☐ ☐ ☐ ☐ ☐ ☐ ☐ ☐	freedom
interruption	☐ ☐ ☐ ☐ ☐ ☐ ☐ ☐ ☐ ☐	continuity
denial	☐ ☐ ☐ ☐ ☐ ☐ ☐ ☐ ☐ ☐	satisfaction
repetition	☐ ☐ ☐ ☐ ☐ ☐ ☐ ☐ ☐ ☐	freshness

Check back later to see how your responses compare with Jackson's findings. Do your perceptions of life in an elementary classroom agree with his?

The significance of routine

Anthropologists have taught us that the humdrum aspects of human existence have cultural significance, and Jackson asserts that we must look at the most routine events in an elementary classroom if we are to understand what happens there. Are certain trivial acts repeated innumerable times? How frequently do they occur? What is their cumulative effect on the child? What do they teach him? Jackson's observations of elementary-school classrooms demonstrate how revealing the answers to these questions can be.

Have you ever figured out how many hours a child spends in school? In most states the school year is 180 days. The day typically begins at nine and ends at three, a total of six hours. Thus, if a child doesn't miss a day of school, he spends over a thousand hours in school each year. Including kindergarten, the average child will spend over seven thousand hours in elementary school. How are those hours typically spent?

You may think first of the curriculum — so many hours of reading and language arts, so many hours of mathematics, science, play, social studies, music, art, and so on. But what do students really *do* when they are studying these subjects? They talk individually, to the teacher and to one another. They read silently and aloud. They yawn. They look out the window. They raise their hands. They line up. They stand up. They sit down. In short, they do a number of different things, many of them commonplace and trivial.

And what about the teacher? Jackson has observed that the elementary teacher engages in as many as a thousand interpersonal interchanges each day. What is the nature of these interchanges? The teaching-learning process consists, for the most part, of talking, and the teacher controls and directs discussion. The teacher acts as a gatekeeper, deciding who shall and who shall not speak. (One may debate whether or not this *should* be the teacher's role, but clearly most teachers function this way.)

The teacher also acts as a dispenser of supplies. Since both space and resources are limited, and the number of students wishing to use them at any one time is likely to be greater than the supply, the teacher must dole them out. A related function is the granting of special privileges to deserving students— passing out the milk, sharpening the pencils, taking the roll, or operating the movie projector. Although little teacher time is involved in the awarding of these special jobs, they are important because they help structure the classroom socially as a system of rewards and punishments.

Timekeeping is another teacher responsibility. It is the teacher who decides when a certain activity ends and another begins, when it is time to stop science and begin spelling, and when to go outside for recess. In some schools the teacher is assisted in timekeeping by bells and buzzers which signal when a "period" is over. As Jackson observes, things happen because it is time for them to occur and not because students want them to.

These teacher functions can all be seen as responses to the crowded conditions in the classroom. If the teacher were dealing with one student at a time in a tutorial situation, gatekeeping, granting special privileges, dispensing supplies, and timekeeping would become superfluous. But since this is not feasible, much time and energy are spent keeping order. The resulting atmosphere has unavoidable effects on the students. What are some of the consequences for students of crowded classroom conditions?

What students
experience

One of the inevitable outcomes for the student as a result of what Jackson calls these "traffic-management" functions performed by the teacher is the experience of delay. Since a student's actions are limited by space, material resources, and the amount of teacher attention he can command, there are definite limits on his freedom in the class. In addition, since the class ordinarily moves toward a goal as a group rather than as individuals, the pace of progress is often determined by its slowest members. Waiting is a familiar activity for elementary-

What is life in schools like?

school children—waiting in line to get a drink of water; waiting with arm propped at the elbow to be called upon to answer a question; waiting to use the paper cutter; waiting until others have finished their work to go on to the next activity; waiting until four other students have finished reading aloud for his chance to do so.

Denial of desire is another common experience for elementary students. His question goes unanswered, his raised hand is ignored, talking out of turn is not permitted, relief of bodily functions is allowed only at specified times. Some denial is necessary, and some is probably beneficial, but one thing is certain—delayed gratification and denied desire are learned in school. Though you as a teacher will invariably be kept busy, it is important to recognize that this is not the case for your students and that a certain amount of student frustration is bound to develop as a result of delay and denial.

Students also experience frequent interruptions and social distraction. Interruptions are of many sorts—interruptions of seatwork by the teacher to give additional instructions or to clarify one student's question, mechanical interruptions when the motion picture film starts to flicker, interruptions when messages from the principal's office are read aloud to the class, interruptions for fire drills, interruptions when the teacher is working with one student and another student misbehaves, and so on. Students are expected either to ignore these intrusions or quickly to resume their activities. The emphasis on an inflexible schedule contributes to the sense of interruption by frequently making students begin activities before their interest has been aroused and stop at the height of their interest when the schedule dictates that they must begin another task.

A related phenomenon is social distraction. Students are often asked to behave as if they were in solitude when in fact they are surrounded by thirty or so other people. At certain times during the day students are assigned seatwork and required to work on their own. At such times communication among students is often discouraged if not forbidden. To be surrounded by friends, sometimes seated across from them at a table, and not allowed to talk is a difficult and tempting situation. As Jackson remarks, "These young people, if they are to become successful students, must learn how to be alone in a crowd."[9]

Delay, denial, interruption, and *social distraction,* then, are characteristic of life in elementary classrooms. How are children affected by these classroom facts of life? It is difficult to measure their effect, because they are present to a greater or lesser degree in every classroom. Also, different students have different levels of tolerance for these phenomena. It would seem, however, that the student who either possesses or quickly develops patience will find school more tolerable than the student who lacks it. The ability to control desires, delay rewards, and stifle impulses seems to be necessary to the "mature" student. Jackson explains:

Thus, the personal quality commonly described as patience—an essential quality when responding to the demands of the classroom—represents a balance, and sometimes a precarious one, between two opposed tendencies. On the one hand is the impulse to act on desire, to blurt out the answer, to push to the front o

---

[9] Jackson, p. 18.

the line, or to express anger when interrupted. On the other hand is the impulse to give up the desire itself, to stop participating in the discussion, to go without a drink when the line is long, or to abandon an interrupted activity.[10]

The necessary balance is achieved by the majority of students. Others may respond in either of the two ways described above, or in still another manner. If you as a teacher are to understand why children act as they do, an understanding of the dynamics of the classroom is a necessity. Jackson's book offers considerable insight into life in elementary classrooms.

The language of the classroom

In any elementary, junior, or senior high-school classroom, at any given moment, the chances are very good that someone will be talking. Who will it be? Will he be talking about something related to instruction, or to management of the classroom, or about something extraneous to the lesson? These kinds of questions have been asked by researchers for years, but only recently have effective techniques and instruments for analyzing the language of the classroom been developed.

Interaction analysis

One of these instruments, developed by Ned Flanders and called Flanders' Interaction Analysis, enables the observer to categorize both teacher and student verbal behavior.[11] Developed to facilitate extensive research into teacher influence on student attitudes and achievement, Flanders' system measures a primary component of teacher influence: verbal directness or indirectness. The amount of intellectual freedom the teacher grants to students can be estimated by determining the proportion of directness and indirectness in the teaching. Direct verbal behavior on the part of the teacher—lecturing, giving directions, reciting facts, criticizing—tends to minimize the variety of possible student responses. Indirect behavior—eliciting student statements, accepting and making use of student ideas, praising, encouraging, varying strategies in response to the situation—increases the freedom of the student.

[10] *Ibid.*
[11] Flanders' instrument, coupled with Galloway's nonverbal communication recording instrument, may be found on pages 214–215.

What is life in schools like?

Kevin   Do you think we're drawing an overly depressing portrait of American schools?

Jim   Well, yes and no. I can think of scores of good schools that I have visited or taught in. I hope we're not giving the impression that such schools don't exist or are so few and far between that they're inconsequential.

Kevin   I'm afraid we may be giving that impression.

Jim   Then I hope we've clarified that point—there are hundreds or thousands of excellent classrooms and schools in this country. But, on the other hand, I think our descriptions are far more typical of the majority of schools. So many schools are what Charles E. Silberman has described in the Carnegie Report, " . . . grim, joyless places . . . oppressive . . . intellectually sterile and aesthetically barren."

Kevin   Jim, you're lapsing into gloom again! I think we should emphasize, however, that what is, is not what should be or necessarily what will be. There are many efforts being made by people both within and outside the educational system to change the picture.

Jim   We ought to say, also, that if we didn't think the new people entering education could have a meaningful impact in changing the system, then we wouldn't have made the effort to write this book.

Kevin   Amen.

Flanders' initial research project involved 147 teachers, representing all grade levels, six different school districts, and two counties.[12] In summarizing his findings, Flanders discovered the "rule of two-thirds": during about two-thirds of classroom time, someone is talking. About two-thirds of that time, the person talking is the teacher. Two-thirds of the teacher's talk is spent giving directions, expressing opinions and facts, and occasionally criticizing students. Flanders also discovered that superior classes—those that scored above average on constructive attitudes toward the teacher and the classwork—also scored higher on content achievement tests, after test results were adjusted for initial ability.

In studies of seventh-grade social studies and eighth-grade mathematics classes, Flanders found that the teachers in superior classes talked only slightly less than the teachers in the other classes, 50 to 60 percent of the time, but that only 40 to 50 percent of their teaching was directive. In other words, the teachers whose classes had constructive attitudes and scored higher on content achievement were more flexible than others in the quality of their verbal influence.

By contrast, the analysis of classes below average in constructive student attitudes and in content achievement showed that their teachers spoke over 75 percent of the time, and that over 75 percent of their talk was devoted to giving directions, expressing opinions and facts, and, occasionally, criticizing students. For these teachers, the rule of two-thirds becomes the rule of three-fourths plus.

[12] Ned A. Flanders, "Intent, Action and Feedback: A Preparation for Teaching," *The Journal of Teacher Education* 14 (September 1963): 251–260.

The implications of Flanders' research are that much teaching is directive, and that directive teaching tends to make students dependent on the teacher. Interestingly enough, Flanders has found that preservice and inservice teachers trained in the use of Interaction Analysis have been able to become more indirect, to accept more student ideas, and to criticize less than teachers not so trained.[13]

Language moves

In another study Arno Bellack used a totally different conceptual framework to study classroom language patterns. Utilizing 15 teachers and 345 pupils in "Problems of Democracy" classes in high school, Bellack viewed classroom discourse as a game played with language.[14] His analysis of classroom language yielded several valuable insights:

1 *Teachers dominate verbal activities. The teacher-pupil ratio in terms of lines spoken is 3:1; in terms of moves, the ratio is about 3:2.*
2 *Appropriate teacher and pupil moves are implicitly but clearly defined — the teacher is responsible for structuring, soliciting, and reacting, while the student is ordinarily limited to responding. (This evidence corroborates Flanders' finding that teachers dominate classrooms in such a way as to make the students dependent.)*
3 *Teachers initiate about 85 percent of the cycles. The basic unit of verbal interchange is the* soliciting-responding *pattern. Verbal interchanges take place at a rate of slightly less than two cycles per minute.*
4 *In approximately two-thirds of the moves and three-fourths of the lines, talk is content-oriented.*
5 *Fact-stating and explaining account for between 50 and 60 percent of the total discourse in most classrooms.*

Bellack's empirical evidence suggests that the classroom is teacher-dominated, subject-matter-centered, and fact-oriented. The student's primary responsibility seems to be to respond to the teacher's soliciting moves. Thus, student initiative does not seem to be characteristic of the high-school social studies classes sampled. It is, once again, dangerous to generalize from a limited sample. Yet evidence from studies such as Bellack's indicates that, for a large number of classes if not the majority, this is the case.

Questioning

In a third study of classroom language, James Gallagher investigated the kinds of questions that teachers ask. His study involved 235 boys and girls in 10 different classes for gifted children at the junior and senior high-school level.[15] Gallagher differentiated between four categories of questions:

1 *Cognitive-Memory* questions require the student to reproduce facts or other remembered content through the use of such processes as recognition, rote memory, and selective recall. An example of a cognitive-memory question would be: "Can you tell me where Christopher Columbus first landed in the Americas?"
2 *Convergent* questions require the student to generate new information which

---

[13] Edmund J. Amidon and Evan Powell, "Interaction Analysis as a Feedback System in Teacher Preparation," in *The Nature of Teaching*, ed. Lois N. Nelson (Waltham, Mass.: Blaisdell, 1969), p. 82.
[14] Arno Bellack et al., *The Language of the Classroom* (New York: Teachers College Press, 1965).
[15] James J. Gallagher, "Expressive Thought by Gifted Children in the Classroom," *Language and the Higher Thought Processes* (Champaign, Ill.: National Council of Teachers of English, 1965), pp. 56–65.

leads to the correct or conventionally accepted answer. Given or known information usually determines the correct response. An example of a convergent question might be: "Could you summarize for us the author's major point?"

3 *Divergent* questions require the student to generate his own data independently in a data-poor situation, or to take a new perspective on a given topic. Divergent questions have no "right" answer. An example of a divergent question is, "How might the history of the United States have been different if the Pilgrims had landed on the west coast instead of the east coast?"

4 *Evaluative* questions require the student to make value judgments and decisions regarding the goodness, correctness, or adequacy of information, based on a criterion usually set by the student. For example, the evaluative question, "Which president did more to enhance the office of the Presidency — Jefferson or Jackson?" requires the student to decide on criteria to judge what enhancing the office of the Presidency means, and then to compare Jefferson and Jackson with respect to those criteria.

The results of Gallagher's study show that in practically all class sessions, Cognitive-Memory questions comprise 50 percent or more of the total questions asked. The more the class tended toward a lecture mode rather than a discussion mode, the more often teacher questions and student responses fell into the Cognitive-Memory category. Convergent questions were the second most frequent category, with very few Divergent or Evaluative questions and responses. In fact, Gallagher surmises that class discussion could operate normally if only the first two categories of question were available.

Gallagher also found an extremely close relationship between the type of teacher questions and the pattern of thought expression observed in the students' responses. To a large extent, he observed, the teacher controls the expressive thought patterns of the class.

Nonverbal communication

When we think of language we ordinarily think of words. A number of researchers have recently become interested in another kind of language — the silent language of gestures, facial expressions, bodily movements, and other means of nonverbal communication. In his book *The Silent Language*,[16] anthropologist Edward Hall maintains that much of the content of a culture is communicated nonverbally. Hall has helped train American diplomats to understand how gestures and expressions that communicate one thing in our culture may be interpreted quite differently in another culture. He uses as an example the differences between American and Arab culture regarding the appropriate distance between two conversing people. If two Americans are carrying on a conversation at a distance of twenty feet, they will consider the distance unacceptable and will move closer together until both are more comfortable. The exact distance they choose will vary, depending on how well they know each other, but about three feet is the norm. However, in Arab cultures the appropriate distance is less than three feet. Therefore, when an American and an Arab are conversing, the Arab is trying to get closer while the American is trying to move backwards in order to establish the "appropriate" distance. Hall reports that he has seen this situation occur with the result that the Arab wonders what is wrong with him since the American seems repelled, while the American *is* repelled by what he considers pushy behavior.

[16] Edward T. Hall, *The Silent Language* (Garden City, N.Y.: Doubleday, 1959).

An interesting story, but what does it have to do with teaching? The answer: a great deal. Most teachers are totally unaware of their nonverbal communication patterns. That they may be saying one thing verbally and communicating the opposite nonverbally does not even occur to most teachers. For instance, the third-grade teacher who puts her arm around the white students in her class, or pats their heads fondly, yet maintains a certain distance with the black students, is definitely communicating a message. Yet, if asked if she discriminates between her students, she would be likely to reply indignantly in the negative. In fact, research indicates that lower class youngsters rely heavily on nonverbal communication to understand meanings in the classroom.[17] The authors maintain that, if there is a discrepancy, the message a teacher communicates nonverbally is probably more valid and truthful than the verbal message, because it is much easier to conceal real feelings in words than in actions.

Since nonverbal communication is more difficult to conceptualize, define, interpret, and measure than verbal communication, very little work has been done to date in this area. Charles Galloway has, however, developed guidelines for observing a teacher's use of *space, time,* and the *body.*[18]

Space. A teacher's use of space can convey meaning to the students. For example, when and where a teacher chooses to travel in a classroom has significance. A teacher who never ventures far from her desk at the front of the room may convey insecurity to the students—she seems reluctant to leave "home base." Some teachers rarely venture into the students' territory except to monitor their seatwork. A teacher's unwillingness to mingle with students will certainly be detected by them.

Time. How a teacher uses classroom time is often an indication of the value he places upon certain activities. The elementary-school teacher who spends a great deal of class time on social studies but very little on mathematics is conveying a message to the students that they will almost surely detect.

Body maneuvers. Teachers frequently use nonverbal tactics to control students' behavior. The raised eyebrow, the finger to the lips indicating silence, the hands on hips, and the silent stare all communicate unmistakeable meanings. Galloway notes that when the teacher's verbal and nonverbal communications are in contradiction, the students read the nonverbal cues as a truer reflection of the teacher's real feelings and act accordingly. You can see this happening when a teacher verbally reprimands a student for talking but acts in such a way that the student knows the teacher doesn't really feel strongly about it. Shortly thereafter, the student begins talking again.

How can a teacher analyze or become more aware of his nonverbal communication? Perhaps the best and most accessible cue the teacher receives is feedback from students, though teachers vary considerably in their ability to recognize student responses and to utilize this information to analyze their own behavior. You can also make a videotape of yourself teaching and analyze the tape to pick out inconsistencies between your verbal and nonverbal behavior. The videotape recorder is a tremendous boon to teachers in that it allows them to evaluate their own performances relatively objectively.

[17] Basil Bernstein, "Social Structure, Language and Learning," *Educational Research* 3 (1961): 163–176.
[18] Charles Galloway, "Nonverbal Communication," *Theory Into Practice* 7 (December 1968):172–175.

What is life in schools like?

Table 6.1 Summary of categories for interaction analysis using nonverbal categories

	Verbal (Flanders)	Nonverbal (Galloway)	
		Encouraging	*Restricting*
Teacher talk	1 Accepts feelings	1	11
	2 Praises or encourages	2 Congruent: nonverbal cues reinforce and further clarify the credibility of a verbal message.	12 Incongruent: contradiction occurs between verbal and non-verbal cues.
	3 Accepts or uses ideas of student	3 Implement: im-plementation occurs when the teacher ac-tually uses stu-dent's idea either by discussing it, reflecting on it, or turning it to the class for consideration.	13 Perfunctory: perfunctory use occurs when the teacher merely recog-nizes or ac-knowledges stu-dent's idea by automatically repeating or restating it.
	4 Asks questions	4 Personal: face-to-face con-frontation.	14 Impersonal: avoidance of verbal inter-change in which mutual glances are ex-changed.
	5 Lectures	5 Responsive: change in teacher's pace or direction of talk in response to student behavior, i.e., bored, dis-interested, or in-attentive.	15 Unresponsive: inability or un-willingness to alter the pace or direction of lecture disre-garding pupil cues.
	6 Gives directions	6 Involve: stu-dents are in-volved in a clarification or maintenance of learning tasks.	16 Dismiss: teacher dis-misses or con-trols student behavior.

Verbal (Flanders)	Nonverbal (Galloway)	
	Encouraging	Restricting
7 Criticisms or justified authority	7 Firm: criticisms which evaluate a situation cleanly and crisply and clarify expecta- tions for the situation.	17 Harsh: crit- icisms which are hostile, se- vere, and often denote aggres- sive or defen- sive behavior.
Student talk 8 Student talk- response	8 and 9 Recep- tive: involves attitude of lis- tening and inter- est, facial in- volvement, and eye contact.	18 and 19 Inatten- tive: involves a lack of attend- ing eye contact and teacher travel or movement.
9 Student talk- initiation		
10 Silence or confusion	10 Comfort: silences charac- terized by times of reflection, thought, or work.	20 Distress: in- stances of em- barrassment or tension-filled moments, usu- ally reflecting disorganization and disorienta- tion.

Source: Sue S. Lail, "The Model in Use," *Theory Into Practice* 7 (December 1968): 177.

Still another means of analyzing nonverbal communication is by using Galloway's nonverbal analysis instrument (see Table 6.1). Modifying Flanders'
instrument, Galloway concentrates on two major categories of nonverbal communication—encouragement and restriction.[19] His instrument classifies the
teachers' or students' verbal behavior, and then categorizes the teacher's accompanying nonverbal behavior in terms of whether it encourages or restricts
interaction. Unlike Flanders' system, which encompasses all verbal communication, Galloway's does not purport to describe all kinds of nonverbal communication. You might want to try analyzing the nonverbal behavior of one of your
friends using Galloway's system.

We have seen in our brief survey that decoding language of the classroom can
shed considerable light on what happens there. The techniques and systems that

[19] Sue S. Lail, "The Model in Use." *Theory Into Practice* 7 (December 1968): 176–180.

What is life in schools like?

Flanders, Bellack, Gallagher, and Galloway have developed to look at the language of the classroom can also be used by teachers to analyze their own communication processes and messages. How much do you want to dominate discussion when you become a teacher? Do you want to have a direct or indirect influence on students? Do you want the students to become dependent on you, or do you want to foster independence? Do you know when you are communicating one message verbally and another nonverbally? What kinds of thinking do you want your students to practice—recall and recognition, or analysis and evaluation? The kind of thinking they do is in part a product of the kinds of questions that you ask them. If you feel it is important to understand your experience, it would make sense for you to develop competency in one or more of these language evaluation systems during your teacher education program.

The school as a social system

One way to view life in schools is to look at it as a social system to be analyzed. One sociologist, Talcott Parsons, has done an extensive examination of both elementary and secondary classes as social systems.[20] The two main questions he sought to answer were: 1) How does the school class instill in each pupil the commitment to a future adult role and make him capable of performing successfully in that role? and 2) How does the school help allocate the human resources of the students within the role structure of adult society? Since completion of high school—and, increasingly, college—is the minimum educational level that allows much freedom of occupational selection, Parsons also tried to discover how it is determined who goes to college and who does not.

Studying a sample of 3,348 Boston high-school boys, Parsons found that the factor that determines whether a student enters college is his prior enrollment in the college preparatory program. With very few exceptions, this course of action is determined by the ninth grade, and the most important element in the decision seems to be the boy's performance in elementary school. The student's record is evaluated by teachers and principals who advise him for or against enrolling in the college preparatory program, and few students act against their advice. Thus, Parsons concludes, the primary selective process for college occurs in elementary school and the "seal" is put on it in junior high school.

Except for sex differences, there is initially no formal basis for differentiation of student status within the elementary-school class. Differentiation develops gradually in the elementary school along lines of achievement, and extends through high school, where it distinguishes the college-bound from the non-college-bound. As Parsons says:

The essential point, then, seems to be that the elementary school, regarded in the light of its socialization function, is an agency which differentiates the school class broadly along a single continuum of achievement, the content of which is relative excellence in living up to the expectations imposed by the teacher as an agent of the adult society.[21]

[20] Talcott Parsons, "The School Class as a Social System: Some of its Functions in American Society," in *Society and Education,* ed. R. Havighurst, B. Neugarten, and J. Falk (Boston: Allyn and Bacon, 1967), p 122–134.
[21] Parsons, in Havighurst *et al.* eds., p. 126.

In addition to the school class, there are two primary social structures in which the student participates: the family and the informal peer group. Because the school functions as a socializing agency for society, both of these groups have an impact on the child that may either complement or counteract the school's socializing function. We will look at the influence of peer groups later in the chapter. Parsons asserts that the child's learning of achievement motivation is, psychologically, a process of identification with the teacher, and hypothesizes that those students who identify with the teacher will probably go on to college, while those who identify with their peer group instead will probably not go to college.

While the teacher thus plays a role in the child's development similar to that of the parent, there are some important differences between them. The teacher is more concerned with performance than with solicitude for children's emotional needs. A mother, on the other hand, must give first priority to the needs of her child, regardless of his capacity to achieve. A child has only one mother, but many teachers; thus, unlike mothers, teachers are in a sense interchangeable. Parsons sees this as an important distinction, for it means that the child must internalize his relation to the teacher's *role* rather than to her particular personality.

Thus, Parsons sees the socialization and selection process in the elementary school as involving: 1) an emancipation of the child from primary emotional attachment to his family; 2) an internalization of societal values greater than he can learn from his family alone; 3) a differentiation of the school class along the lines both of actual achievement and of the value placed by the child upon achievement; and 4) the selection and allocation of human resources by the school, acting as an agent of society, with respect to the adult role system.

Contrasting the roles of elementary and secondary schools, Parsons states that the elementary-school phase is concerned with the child's internalization of motivation to achieve and the selection of persons on the basis of their achievement, while the secondary-school phase focuses on the differentiation of *qualitative* types of achievement. Those secondary-school students who are relatively high in what Parsons calls "cognitive" achievement but who are not college-bound will seek more or less technical roles as electricians, mechanics, and the like; whereas those students who are relatively high in what Parsons calls "moral" achievement (generally known as citizenship) and who are not college-bound will seek more diffuse, "social" or "humanly" occupations as, for example, salesmen and insurance agents. For those students who are college-bound this distinction will evidence itself in emphasis on intellectual curricular work for the "cognitive" types, and, for the "moral" types, leadership roles in student government and extracurricular activities.

What Parsons has shown us is a way to conceptualize how the school, particularly the elementary-school class, serves as a socializing and selection agency for society. How fully the student identifies with the teacher's role and, in so doing, accepts the values of the school as personified by the teacher, is, Parsons maintains, the factor that determines his future adult roles in society. The students who reject these values, i.e., do not identify with the teacher's role and favor peer-group identification, will be non-college-goers, thus determining to a large extent what roles they will play in society. The crucial criterion in determining future adult roles is student achievement in the elementary school. If Parsons' thesis is correct (remember that his study was limited to boys), the elementary-school years are the crucial period in a student's development.

Peer relationships and social class

In this country virtually all children receive some public education, and children from different socioeconomic levels frequently attend the same schools. When children go to school, they make friends with their classmates and form friendship groups. An interesting question might be: "Is the social class position of the family a contributing factor in determining either a child's choice of friends of his reputation? In other words, do children tend to make friends with children from similar social class backgrounds, or are the schools a melting-pot where children from different social classes meet and become friends?" Another pertinent question might be: "Is the relationship between friendship groups and social class the same in the elementary schools as it is in the high schools?"

These questions were the subject of a study by sociologist Bernice Neugarten conducted in 1946.[22] She selected a community whose status structure was divisible into five social classes. Group A consisted of the "upper crust," the "money crowd," and comprised only 2 percent of the town's population. Group B consisted of professionals, members of the school board, and active community leaders. This group was highly educated, lived in big houses, and had higher-than-average incomes. Group C consisted of the "average man," and constituted the bulk of the population. Group D was the lower income group—poor but honest blue-collar workers. Group E was distinctive primarily on the basis of nonrespectability. This group—all Caucasian—was considered dirty, dishonest, and both biologically and morally inferior by other community members.

The subjects of the study were children enrolled in grades five, six, ten, and eleven. Since hardly any children from Group A were enrolled in the public schools, this category was eliminated. Neugarten administered to the students a sociometric test consisting of a series of short statements or descriptions, each followed by a blank space in which the children were instructed to write the name of the child who, in their opinion, best fit the description. To gather data regarding friendship status, the children were asked for the names of the other children whom they would and would not want to play with or be friends with, and with whom their mothers would not want them to associate.

At the elementary-school level, the results showed that children are selected as friends by children from their own social level more often than by children of

---

[22] Bernice L. Neugarten, "Social Class and Friendship Among School Children," in *Society and Education* ed. R. Havighurst *et al.*, pp. 102–108. The reader should note that this study was conducted about thirty years ago. On the basis of your own school experiences determine whether her findings conform to your own remembrances about your peer relationships.

other social levels. This is not surprising, since neighborhood friendships carry over to the schools, and children from the same neighborhoods are likely to belong to the same social class.

Neugarten found a mutual rejection between groups B (professional background) and E (nonrespectability) greater than that between any other two groups. It might be expected that the greatest divergence of views and values would exist between the two groups at opposite ends of the class axis. The lower the social class of the child, the less often he was mentioned as a best friend. With the exception of the group of lowest status, children tend to select as friends, first, the children of higher status than their own and, second, children of their own status level.

The data on reputation follow the same pattern as the data on friendship. In fact, there is even less variation. All children, regardless of their own social class, agreed that the Group B subjects were well dressed, good-looking, good in school, and leaders. By grade five, the child of the lower class faces a different problem of adjustment in school life than does the child from the middle class, since membership in the lower class is almost certain to result in an unfavorable reputation among his peers.

When the data from the elementary-school children is compared with that from the secondary students, some important differences emerge. While both age groups discriminated by class in their selection of friends, high-school students did not adhere to class lines in rejecting individuals as friends. While at the elementary-school level members of Group E tended to be rejected as friends, particularly by Group B, in high school this rejection did not occur. Neugarten hypothesizes that not being mentioned at the high-school level may be indicative of an even greater degree of rejection than unfavorable mention at the elementary level. Whereas in elementary school Group E children may still be potential playmates, at the high-school level Group B may be so distant psychologically from Group E that students from the latter group do not enter their minds as potential friends. Another possible explanation is that differences in social status may be less recognizable at the high-school age, due partially to the dropping-out of the "most objectionable" members of Group E. A final possibility is that high-school students are more democratic than elementary-school students.

Group B students were found to have the most positive reputations at the high-school level. Group C and D students were not singled out as having either positive or negative reputations. Group B students were in the limelight, while Group E students were isolated and ignored.

Neugarten summarizes her findings in the following manner:

The finding that social-class differences in friendship and reputation are so well established by the time children reach the fifth grade may be of some importance to the psychologist. The child of eleven or twelve soon becomes aware of his reputation and desirability as a friend, and he must make his adjustment in the light of what others think of him. Perhaps one of the reasons that the child of lower class is so often a "behavior problem" in school is that he finds himself rejected by his classmates and enjoys such an unenviable reputation. This may also be one of the reasons why lower-class children often find school unpleasant and unrewarding and why the child of lower class so often welcomes the first opportunity to leave school altogether.

From one point of view the data also raise the general question of the extent to which the school, in communities like Hometown [the site of the study], is encouraging democratic living on the part of its children. It is undoubtedly true that the teacher plays a central role in influencing the opinions of one child toward another. While there is no systematic research on the topic, anecdotes and observations suggest that teachers' behavior toward children of lower class is different from their behavior toward those of middle or upper class and that this discrimination follows the differences in reputation among the social groups.[23]

Peer relationships and values

The studies by another sociologist, James Coleman, of peer relationships among adolescents have resulted in some very interesting observations.[24] Coleman believes that industrial society, by shifting much of the responsibility for the training of a child from his parents to the school and by extending the necessary period of training, has made of high school a social system of adolescents. The values and activities of this adolescent subculture are quite different from those of adult society, and its members' most important associations are with one another rather than with adults. Society has created for adolescents a separate institution of their own; home is merely a dormitory while "real" living consists of activities unique to the peer group.

Coleman asserts that society has not yet recognized the existence of this adolescent subculture; education continues to focus on individuals. Teachers exhort individuals to concentrate on scholarship while the community of adolescents diverts these energies in other directions. If educational goals are to be realized in today's society, Coleman argues, the power of the adolescent community must be taken into account. At present, adults establish goals and create institutions to help students reach those goals. If the adolescent community were allowed to formulate its own educational goals, its very structure would reinforce those goals, rather than hindering them, as is now the case.

Coleman studied ten high schools, all located in the Midwest. To gather his data, Coleman asked the students to respond to a questionnaire. Among the questions asked the boys was, "How would you most like to be remembered in school: as an athletic star, a brilliant student, or the most popular?" In every school the boys showed a greater tendency to select "star athlete" than either of the other choices. In almost every case the leading crowd tended to choose the athlete image, and in all cases they rejected the ideal of the brilliant student. Boys were also asked to name the best athlete, the best student, and the boy most popular with the girls. Boys named as best athlete were identified as members of the leading crowd twice as often as were those named as best students.

[23] Neugarten, p. 108.
[24] James S. Coleman, "The Adolescent Subculture and Academic Achievement," in *Society and Education,* ed. R. Havighurst *et al.,* pp. 109–115. Coleman's findings were reported in 1960. Do you think his observations are still valid today?

Each girl was asked how she would like to be remembered: as a brilliant student, a leader in extracurricular activities, or the most popular. The girls tended slightly less than boys to want to be remembered as brilliant students. The girl who was most often named as best student had fewer friends and was less often in the leading crowd than was the boy most often named as best student—which, remember, was less than half as often as best athlete. The girls in the ten schools were split as to whether the image of activities leader or of most popular girl was more desirable.

Coleman points out that in every social context certain activities are highly rewarded, while others are not. Those activities that are rewarded will attract nearly everyone with some ability to compete. Conversely, those activities for which there are few rewards will not attract the potentially most talented. Interscholastic athletics attract academically talented boys because of the social rewards. Athletes are rewarded because they bring glory to the school and community, whereas the rewards for high grades are usually individual and personal. Good students force their classmates to keep up with them and frequently bring upon themselves such derisive labels as "curve raisers" and a few others we think it safer not to print.

In a school where academic achievement brings few social rewards, few students will excel in scholarship, and those who get good grades will tend not to

What is life in schools like?

be those of greatest ability but those of mediocre ability. The academically gifted will be concentrating their efforts in areas that bring social rewards. Coleman's study thus indicates that the adolescent subculture generally acts as a deterrent to academic achievement, and that high schools actually encourage a diversion of academic talent into other channels.

The adolescent subculture's values and norms thus supersede the school's stated objective of academic excellence. The authors do not agree with Coleman that the adolescent subculture's values differ markedly from those of adult society; we think that adult society also values athletics and popularity over intellectual attainments (witness the huge audiences sporting events attract on television and the use of professional athletes to endorse commercial products). It may be that the high schools accurately reflect not just the adolescent subculture, but a large subculture of adult America. In any case, it is obvious that peer relationships and values exert a tremendous effect on the behavior of adolescents in high school—an effect that teachers frequently forget in the daily instruction of kids.

Teaching patterns, incidental learnings, and ritualism

Just as there is a difference between the scholastic objectives of a school and the behavioral preferences of students, there may also be a disparity between what a teacher thinks she is teaching and what the students are actually learning.

In a provocative book on the supervision of teachers, Robert Goldhammer proposes a thesis with very significant implications for anyone preparing to teach.[25] Goldhammer observes that a kind of learning entirely unrelated to the teacher's intended objectives takes place in the classroom. This learning, which he calls "incidental learning," is not measured or evaluated by the teacher, and the teacher is rarely even aware that it occurs. Incidental learning can facilitate intended learning, impede it, or have very little effect upon it. Goldhammer's thesis is that if a teacher continually repeats certain behaviors, the implications of these "teaching patterns" will be grasped and digested by the students. Isolated teaching behaviors will not have this effect, but behaviors repeated day after day for an entire school year will produce incidental learnings that the teacher may not even recognize. Let's look at some examples of teaching patterns and make some guesses about what the students may be learning in response to them:

- All directions are given by the teacher.
- All questions originate from the teacher.
- All evaluations are performed by the teacher.
- The pace of instruction and all sequences of instruction are determined by the teacher.
- The teacher asserts that he will not call on people who call out, out of turn, but he often does.
- The teacher uses school work as an instrument of punishment:
  Pupils who have committed a disturbance are required to copy the "W" pages from the dictionary for homework.

[25] Robert Goldhammer, *Clinical Supervision: Special Methods for the Supervision of Teachers* (New York: Holt, Rinehart and Winston, 1969), pp. 11–32.

- The teacher takes the entire class to the bathroom at the same time every day.
- The teacher assigns extra work, that is, more of the same thing, to children who finish their assignments quickly.
- A reward pattern: When a pupil has finished reciting, the teacher generally responds, "Yes, but . . ."
- The teacher corrects papers, figures attendance, and so on, while, at the teacher's direction, a pupil is reciting.[26]

These practices are illustrations of negative teaching patterns; that is, they distract pupils from the intended object of study and teach the children perceptions of themselves, of school, or of learning that can lead to distrust, self-deprecation, confusion, or insecurity. What incidental learning might result from the first four examples given above? The students are probably learning that the teacher is the director and that they are dependent on her for their learning. What about the teacher who assigns extra work to those who finish early? Perhaps the students learn to dawdle to avoid extra work. And how about the teacher who responds, "Yes, but . . ." to students' answers? Perhaps the students learn that the teacher has all the correct answers, or maybe they learn not to volunteer answers, since no matter what they say it is never right.

Needless to say, there are many positive teaching patterns as well. For example, the teacher who listens intently to student comments and then builds upon them, without interjecting her own thoughts, may be teaching students that she values their ideas and their participation. Undoubtedly many teaching patterns have positive connotations for some students and negative meanings for other members of the class. The point to remember about teaching patterns and incidental learnings is that the teacher is usually unaware of them and of the power that they possess. In many cases incidental learnings have a far greater impact on classroom environment and overall learning than do the intended learnings—so be on the alert for incidental learnings that may result from your teaching patterns.

Robert Goldhammer is also critical of school practices that he believes foster student dependence on the teacher and a condition of docility. One of the practices that contributes to this condition he labels "ritualism." He has observed that students are required to behave in certain ways to conform to school rituals without knowing why they should do so and without being permitted to question the practice. He further contends that these ritualistic practices serve to infantilize the student, produce conformity, and reduce the student to a state of blind acceptance. A democracy depends on enlightened citizens, Goldhammer argues, and these ritualistic practices subvert the development of the kind of questioning behavior necessary to citizens who think and act for themselves. Goldhammer also offers some good examples of ritualistic practices:

- I must regularly participate in various patriotic litanies, for example ". . . for Richard stands, one naked individual. . ."

[26] From *Clinical Supervision: Special Methods for the Supervision of Teachers* by Robert Goldhammer (p. 15). Copyright © 1969 by Holt, Rinehart and Winston, Inc. Reprinted by permission of Holt, Rinehart and Winston, Inc.

What is life in schools like?

- When bells ring, I must stop what I am doing and what I am thinking and go to other places.
- I must follow lines and arrows painted on the floors when going through the halls, even when I am the only student in the hall.
- I must go up certain stairs and down others.

	Offense		Disciplinary action
1	late to detention	1	1-hour detention
2	disturbance in detention	2	1-hour detention
3	food thrown in cafeteria	3	1-hour detention
4	trays left in cafeteria	4	1-hour detention
5	cutting in cafeteria line	5	monitor asks student to take his proper place in line; if student refuses, a 1-hour detention
6	tardiness because of the following: doctor's appointment funeral college interview	6	no penalty when student shows appointment card for doctor's appointment or note for funeral excuse student must bring in note, sign log in office, and return the attendance verification by 2:30
7	any other tardiness	7	each term a student is allowed to be tardy twice without penalty; the third un-excused tardiness and those following will result in a 1-hour detention
8	no note or doctor's appointment card when tardy	8	1-hour detention
9	truancy	9	1-hour detention for each period cut, served consecutively
10	failure to return absentee note	10	if not returned the day following absence, student is marked NO NOTE by the nurse; the list is sent to the office the second day, the student goes to the office with his note if he does not have the note on the second day, 1-hour detention for each day not returned
11	cutting detention	11	detention is served plus 1 more hour
12	failure to return office forms and documents such as report cards, insurance forms, library notices after 3rd notice, etc. when the student is allowed more than 1 day	12	1-hour detention for each day not returned
13	smoking or suspicion of	13	first offense, 2-hour detention period second offense, internal suspension

Discipline code from a high-school student handbook. What does it tell you about the school?

Appearance requirements at _____ High School encourage the student to follow current acceptable standards of appearance. The following are not considered acceptable:

Men's jeans if stained, bleach spotted, torn or ragged.

Men's T-shirts reminiscent of underwear; differentiation to be made by color, style, and thickness of material.

Flapping shirts -- men's shirts designed to be tucked in the trousers should be worn that way, not left flapping outside.

Any clothing which is too tight or too short.

Students must wear socks or stockings with all shoes except sandals. Safety rules dictate, however, that sandals must not be worn in the shop area.

Gym garments are to be worn only in the physical education area where they are required.

At evening and away from school functions, where the school is being represented, students shall dress in current business attire.

In school, appearance (hair, clothing, footwear, accessories, and make-up) of students should be neat, clean and appropriate.

Dress code from a high-school student handbook.
What values are represented here?
Do you agree with them?
Can you make a case for or against the relationship of such a dress code to student learning?
What are the incidental learnings that might accrue from the enforcement of this dress code?

- I must prove my points by citing evidence (that is, by quoting authorities), even though the teacher never does.
- I must study what I am told to study, whether or not that represents something I would like to study.
- I may not wear my shirt out.
- I may not chew gum.
- I am taught to value freedom, but have little opportunity to experience it.[27]

Goldhammer's point is that school is for many students a place where they must obey certain rules, ask or not ask certain questions, do certain assignments, and take part in certain ceremonies—for reasons which are mysterious to them. They do certain things because they have been told to do so or "because they're rules," without knowing why. The result is tragic when the students no longer even question why they do something; they do it simply because they have been told to do it. Certainly blind obedience to authority and an unquestioning attitude are antithetical to the principles of democratic citizenship. Our schools are charged with the task of preparing citizens for participation in a democracy, but those that emphasize obedience, blind deference to authority, and ritualistic behavior cannot possibly produce enlightened citizens. In such cases, the means surely will not achieve the desired ends.

[27] From *Clinical Supervision: Special Methods for the Supervision of Teachers* by Robert Goldhammer (pp. 26–29). Copyright © 1969 by Holt, Rinehart and Winston, Inc. Reprinted by permission of Holt, Rinehart and Winston, Inc.

Wait! I only call on people who have their hands raised.

The kids were just great; not a sound out of them.

This will all make sense to you later on.

In my class, you earn what you get.

What these kids need is motivation.

Grammar was good enough for me; it ought to be good enough for them.

There are no poor students, only poor teachers.

It's not the answer, but the question, that's important.

The school as potentiality

It appears that life in schools is not the exciting experience it should be for many students. The difference between eager first-graders and blasé teenagers, or even between first-graders and fifth-graders, is an object lesson on the effects of schooling. As students spend time—or do time—in school they are inevitably shaped by it. Many become docile, they question authority less, they learn to think of themselves as successes or failures, they perform rituals without knowing why, they are asked to memorize things they do not care about—and this is called learning.

All schools are not this way, however. There are many innovative and stimulating schools that encourage creativity and independence in a truly interactive environment. Let's look at two of those schools.

Metro High School

What are the alternatives? Can the school environment be humanized and made conducive to learning, or is there something about schools that enforces rigidity, conformity, and boredom? One type of alternative school that is being experimented with in many parts of the country is the "school without walls," and one of the most well known and successful schools of this type is Chicago's Metro High School. Metro does not have a conventional school building. The program was based on the idea that the human and physical resources of the city create the best interactive environment for a high-school education. Consequently, instruction and learning take place in a variety of locations within the city, including museums, universities, and business corporations.

Metro High School is a fully accredited four-year high school operating as part of the Chicago Public Schools. The school has a student body of 350, randomly selected from thousands of applicants, and closely reflecting the high-school population of the city as a whole in terms of race, family income, and previous success in school.

Metro is characterized by close relationships between teachers and students. Counseling groups consisting of 15 students and a teacher meet for two hours each week to plan students' schedules, discuss school problems, and participate in activities designed to foster cooperation.

The formal curriculum is a combination of institutional course offerings and nine-week minicourses called "learning units." Many of these learning units focus on activities not usually covered in a high-school curriculum: exploring probability with a group of insurance actuaries, assisting a veterinarian, learning film techniques from television film producers, viewing the current show at the Museum of Contemporary Art, and studying a neighborhood's problems with a neighborhood organization. Students are allowed great freedom of choice among the variety of learning units. After the nine-week period, students are evaluated and either given or denied credit. There are no letter grades.

How do the students and teachers like this alternative to the traditional high school? Personal interviews conducted by the University of Michigan confirmed that the Metro students have a strong positive identification with the school. Moreover, 80 percent of the first graduating class went on to college.[28] Students who were potential dropouts have published newspaper and magazine articles, organized community action groups, made films, mastered complex skills in industrial laboratories, and acted in professional theater companies. Problems exist, of course—some students find it difficult to assume so much responsibility for their own learning. Time is wasted. Students have not been as involved in formal decision making as the program's originators would like. But the process of solving these problems is viewed by most participants as an important aspect of the learning process.

A part of Metro's basic philosophy is that if schools are to help students grow up and live in the world, they do their students a disservice by isolating them from that world in monolithic school buildings.

The Beloit-Turner Middle School

Although the Metro High School is an exciting alternative to the traditional school, it is unlikely that many of our readers will find themselves teaching in a school without walls. But there is no reason why an interactive, responsive environment cannot exist within a school building. Consider, for example, the Beloit-Turner Middle School in Wisconsin, a school specifically designed for young adolescents rather than for miniature adults.[29] The school consists of three large open classrooms or pods, each serving as a homeroom for 125 to 150 students, and as a classroom for varying numbers of students throughout the day. These pods are arranged around a central core of administrative and special service offices and a large open instructional materials center. Carpeting covers the floors of all the building, including the cafeteria.

The program is based on the assumption that sixth-, seventh- and eighth-graders have special needs, interests, and objectives—and that the school should take these factors into account rather than working against them. It recognizes that early adolescents are in the process of discovering themselves and of defining their relationships with everything and everyone. They are in a questioning stage

[28] Robert C. Riordan, *Alternative Schools in Action* (Bloomington, Ind.: Phi Delta Kappa Educational Foundation, 1972), p. 38.
[29] James Cass, "A School Designed for Kids," *Saturday Review* 53 (March 21, 1970): 65–67, 75.

What is life in schools like?

Sylvia Ashton-Warner

A visitor to Sylvia Ashton-Warner's New Zealand classroom finds it very different from the traditional American school. The Maori children make noise and run around; raw emotion is an integral part of classroom life.

The Maori five-year-old comes to school with unbridled aggressive impulses: he expresses himself in taking, breaking, and dominating. In Miss Ashton-Warner's classroom, however, the destructive child is neither punished nor suppressed, but allowed to vent his frustrations. Having come to believe from her work with the Maori that violent and destructive tendencies can be channelled toward creative ends, Miss Ashton-Warner encourages the children to express themselves in art. She subscribes to Eric Fromm's idea that adult destructiveness is the outcome of an unlived life, and argues that people should be allowed to work out aggressive feelings when they are children. The children in her classes often draw pictures of houses engulfed in flames, make bombs out of clay, and destroy clay figures as soon as they are made.

Twenty-four years of teaching Maori and white New Zealanders have contributed to Miss Ashton-Warner's theory of organic teaching, which she describes as

- the preservation of inner resources
- the exercise of the inner eye and
- the protraction of the true personality

Specifically, she uses the children's own work as the basis for teaching. They write their own readers and draw up their own vocabulary and spelling lists. According to Miss Ashton-Warner, learning should progress from the known—one's own inner feelings—to the unknown—the outer world. Young children are ready for and respond to this kind of learning as they do not to lessons arbitrarily chosen by the teacher. Describing New Zealand as a society in which people's inner resources have atrophied because everything they want is available ready-made, she declares, "I think that we already have so much pressure towards sameness through radio, film and comics outside the school, that we can't afford to do a thing inside that is not toward individual development."

Miss Ashton-Warner believes that her method of teaching can make the human being naturally and spontaneously peaceable. In brief, she argues that education must deal with aggression—the name we give to the expressions of the child's frustrated drives toward self-preservation and sexual gratification. By recognizing and even welcoming their presence in the child, and making them the foundation for "organic learning," these drives can be diverted to constructive and creative ends.

In theory, Miss Ashton-Warner would have children do nothing but creative artwork in school until they are seven. She admits, however, to a gap between theory and practice which requires her to teach some things during this period. Miss Ashton-Warner identifies two "enemies of traditional education": the children's interest in one another and their desire to make things. Instead of telling the children to "be quiet" and "work by yourselves," the traditional refrains in American schools, she has them do all their work in pairs. Each checks the other's mistakes and hurries him up if he is too slow. The children sit cross-legged on mats, fighting, arguing, correcting, and helping each other. As a result, learning becomes an integral part of their relationships with one another.

Miss Ashton-Warner's encouragement of the children to make things can be hard on the visitor's—and the teacher's—ears. If you don't like noise, she warns, don't be a teacher—at least not one like her.

During the last few years Miss Ashton-Warner has been teaching in schools and universities in North America. Just recently, however, she has returned home to New Zealand.

---

and need to draw upon various disciplines to explore social issues and problems and to develop individual interests, values, and attitudes.

The school day is divided into three large blocks of time, each of which is spent in the pursuit of a different major objective. One-half of the day is devoted to "Developing Social Sensitivity and Understanding" (which draws on the social studies, English, and foreign languages); one-fourth of the day is spent on "The Physical Environment" (which focuses on science and math); and the rest of the day is given to "Developing Creative Interests and Abilities" (which allows students freedom to develop their own interests in art, music, home economics, and industrial arts). Each pod has a team of teachers, assistants, student teachers, and interns, and the instructional program is not predetermined but is planned on a day-to-day, week-to-week basis by the instructional team and the students. The part of the day devoted to creative interests is totally controlled by the students and subject to change as they see fit.

"The teachers don't push you into learning," a diminutive sixth-grader explains. "They let you come in by yourself and do it the way you want. We learn more because we want to—and it's so great because after you've done your work nobody cares if you visit with your friends."

"You can't help but learn more, there are so many things to do—and in the afternoon (during the time allotted to creative interests) you can do anything you want."[30]

A final point: as a result of student demand, the school is open seven days a week!

Discussion questions

1   Is the deprivation of David Krech's rats comparable to that of disadvantaged children? Why or why not?
2   Krech found that rats learn best when they live in a cage with other rats; Jackson found that schoolchildren experience continual frustration and distraction as a result of their proximity to many other people in the classroom. How do you reconcile these findings?

[30] Cass, p. 75.

What is life in schools like?

3 William Glasser says that the school alone must bear responsibility for children's failure to learn. What does his statement imply about the causes of failure? In order to eliminate such failure, do you think the school should draw more heavily on the culture of the neighborhood, or should it try to counteract the neighborhood's influence? Why?

4 Talcott Parsons found that children who identify with the role of the teacher, rather than with peers, tend to go on to college. Taking into account the findings we report in this chapter about teachers' behavior and about peer relationships, what do you think would be the effect on a child's personality of identification with the teacher? with peers? How do you think Parsons' finding would be affected if teachers taught more indirectly, asked more divergent questions, and performed fewer "gatekeeping" functions?

5 Did you identify with teachers more than with peers when you were in elementary school? If so, are the behaviors you developed as a result useful to you in college? If not, how do you reconcile your presence in college with Parsons' finding?

6 Which of the hypothetical explanations for the discrepancies between elementary and secondary students in Neugarten's study seems most convincing to you? Why? What are the implications of this discrepancy and of your explanation for it?

7 Do you agree with James Coleman that an adolescent subculture exists and that its values are different than those of the adult culture? of the school? What effect did peer pressure have on your behavior in high school? Is its effect different now? If so, how? And how do you explain this difference?

8 What additional incidental learnings might result from the teacher behaviors described on pages 222–223? How do school rituals relate to incidental learnings?

9 Many people maintain that the school should develop disciplined minds, and should therefore emphasize high academic standards and mastery of subject matter. Do you agree? If so, how would you reconcile your views with the findings about teacher behavior in this chapter? If not, what findings would you draw on to support your views?

For further reading

• Adams, Raymond S., and Biddle, Bruce. *Realities of Teaching: Explorations with Video Tape.* New York: Holt, Rinehart & Winston, 1970. An examination and analysis of classroom life using videotape recordings. It provides a number of concepts that can be used in classroom observation and is very useful for gaining insight into teaching practices.

• Barker, Roger G., and Wright, Herbert F. *One Boy's Day.* New York: Harper and Brothers, 1951. A minute-by-minute account of the events and activities of an elementary-school boy during one school day. The reader is struck by the boredom that characterizes much of the day.

• Bellack, Arno, *et al. The Language of the Classroom.* New York: Teachers College Press, 1966. An attempt to describe the linguistic behavior of teachers and pupils in selected high-school social studies classes. Classroom discourse is viewed as a language game, and the characteristic verbal moves of pupils and teachers are classified and analyzed.

• Blishen, Edward, ed. *The School That I'd Like.* Harmondsworth, England: Penguin Books, 1969. A compilation of British secondary-school children's descriptions of the kinds of schools they would like. The book is fascinating reading and amounts to a passionate and sustained attack upon the British educational system, which might appropriately be applied to our own schools.

- Coleman, James S. *The Adolescent Society.* New York: Free Press, 1961. A sociological study of the high school as an adolescent social system. Coleman's major thesis is that, due to peer influence and the reward system of the high school, academically talented students seek to become not scholars but athletes and social leaders.
- Cuban, Larry. *To Make a Difference.* New York: Free Press, 1970. A candid view of the problems faced by teachers in inner-city schools. The book's major thesis is that the individual teacher must match the methods and materials of instruction to the student. The author discusses different learning styles, the teacher as liaison with the community and as curriculum developer, and specific problems such as race, discipline and expectations.
- Dennison, George. *The Lives of Children.* New York: Random House, 1969. The story of the First Street School in New York City, an alternative school which saw itself as an environment for growth and treated relations between the children and the teachers as the very heart of the school. A fascinating account of an alternative school based on freedom for children and teachers alike.
- Galloway, Charles. "Nonverbal Communication." *Theory Into Practice* 7 (December 1968): 172–175. This article describes a system for observing nonverbal communication in the classroom.
- Glasser, William. *Schools Without Failure.* New York: Harper & Row, 1969. A psychiatrist details the shortcomings of current education, contending that it is failure-oriented. Glasser advocates the use of the class as a counseling group which spends time daily developing the social responsibility necessary to solve behavioral and educational problems within the class.
- Goldhammer, Robert. *Clinical Supervision.* New York: Holt, Rinehart & Winston, 1969. This book on supervision is also most appropriate for beginning teachers, particularly Chapter I. Goldhammer's major thesis is that teaching tends to follow patterns, from which students may learn lessons not intended by the teacher.
- Grannis, Joseph. "The School as a Model of Society" in *Kaleidoscope: Readings in Education,* Kevin Ryan and James M. Cooper, eds. Boston: Houghton Mifflin, 1975, pp. 100–112. Grannis argues that every school presents its students a model of society. He believes that it is not subject-matter content but the structure of the school that instructs most systematically. Grannis describes three models of school which he has observed: the family, the factory, and the corporation.
- Havighurst, Robert J.; Neugarten, Bernice L.; and Falk, Jacqueline M., eds. *Society and Education.* Boston: Allyn and Bacon, 1967. A collection of readings on the sociology of education, which treats such issues as: the school in the social status structure; the school as a socializing agent; the school in the local community; the school in the wider society; and the teacher. The number and variety of articles is vast.
- Jackson, Philip W. *Life in Classrooms.* New York: Holt, Rinehart & Winston, 1968. Using anthropological methods, Jackson analyzes and categorizes everyday occurrences in classrooms. To understand life in elementary-school classrooms, Jackson believes we have to appreciate the cultural significance of its humdrum elements, such as repetition, waiting, interruptions, frustration, and constant rapid-fire interchanges between teacher and students.
- Kaufman, Bel. *Up the Down Staircase.* Englewood Cliffs, N.J.: Prentice-Hall, 1965.

What is life in schools like?

An easy-to-read, humorous, and poignant semi-fictionalized account of a beginning teacher's experience in a New York City high school. A thoroughly enjoyable book.

- Kohl, Herbert. *36 Children*. New York: New American Library, 1968. A popular account of a Harvard graduate teacher's first year in a ghetto school in Harlem. Describes the students' initial hostility and the ways Kohl overcame it. The book also describes vividly the difficult conditions under which teaching is practiced in some sections of New York City.
- Kozol, Jonathan. *Death at an Early Age*. Boston: Houghton Mifflin, 1967. A first-year teacher's account of life in a Boston ghetto school. Tyrannization of the children, cynicism, condescension, racism, and anti-intellectualism are dominant themes in Kozol's account. The book has become a rallying-point for critics and educational reformers.
- Leonard, George. *Education and Ecstasy*. New York: Dell, 1968. Based upon the work of advanced innovative schools, brain-research laboratories, and experimental communities, this book urges that education become an ecstatic unity of learning and living.
- Postman, Neil, and Weingartner, Charles. *Teaching as a Subversive Activity*. New York: Dell, 1969. A direct, no-nonsense book which urges teachers to adopt the inquiry approach to teaching in their classrooms. Provocative, to say the least.
- Sarason, Seymour B. *The Culture of the School and the Problem of Change*. Boston: Allyn and Bacon, 1971. An examination of school cultures and the problems inherent in attempting to bring about change. The author highlights the importance of the role of the principal in any change process.
- Schrag, Peter. *Voices in the Classroom*. Boston: Beacon Press, 1965. A description of schools in various areas of the United States. Schrag attempts to look at the culture of the schools and how they differ from one another.
- Silberman, Charles E. *Crisis in the Classroom*. New York: Random House, 1970. Sponsored by the Carnegie Foundation, Silberman's book argues that American schools are grim, joyless places—oppressive, intellectually sterile, and aesthetically barren. This condition, Silberman argues, is due primarily to the mindlessness of American education. However, he finds hope in the implementation of concepts borrowed from British primary schools.
- Smith, Louis M., and Geoffrey, William. *The Complexities of an Urban Classroom*. New York: Holt, Rinehart & Winston, 1968. An intensive analysis of a single seventh-grade classroom with a middle class teacher in a slum school. Beginning with a description of the behavior of the teacher and pupil as the school term starts, the authors use these data to develop a framework of initial social structure and process in the classroom.
- Spindler, George, ed. *Education and Culture*. New York: Holt, Rinehart & Winston, 1963. A collection of readings by anthropologists whose studies relate to education. The tools and techniques used by anthropologists offer the reader a number of fascinating insights into education in America.

Films

- *Anything You Want To Be* (Liane Brandon, 16mm, b&w, 8 min.). A tragicomedy about a high-school girl who finds that her life has been too well defined by others' expectations: she should be class secretary, not president; a nurse and not a doctor; a housewife and not an intellectual. She is primed by her guidance counselor, her parents, her boyfriend, and others for the roles she must fulfill as a "successful woman."

- *Asking Questions* (EDC, color, 7 min., 1966). This film looks at the types of questions teachers can ask to stimulate children's activities and science learning. It was shot in an upper primary school in Tanzania as part of the African Primary Science Program.
- *End of a Morning* (EDC Film Library, 16mm, b&w, 16 min.). Documents a classroom of four-year-olds at the Hilltop Head Start Center in Roxbury, Massachusetts. Attention is focused on the completion of their morning's activities.
- *Football* (Time-Life Films, 16mm, b&w, 1 hour). Documents the ritualism surrounding the annual football game between two high schools in Miami.
- *Four Students Series* (Indiana University, b&w, 1966). Four students were filmed in their normal school activities in a strict documentary approach. Settings vary with each subject and extracurricular activity in which the student participated. There is no narration and no conscious attempt to organize the experiences depicted according to any psychological theory. There are four individual titles in the series: *Keith — A Second Grader* (23 min.); *Dick — A Fifth Grader* (21 min.); *Greg — An Eighth Grader* (22 min.); and *Alice — A High School Junior* (22 min.).
- *Give Us the Children* (NBC, color, 78 min., 1970). Beginning with a look at the crisis in inner-city schools, the film then considers some encouraging alternatives. It focuses on two experimental school plans, the Parkway Program in Philadelphia and the 49th Street School in Los Angeles.
- *Gum* (Liane Brandon, 16mm, b&w, 6 min., 1968). A film by the Theatre Arts and Filmmaking class at Quincy High School (Quincy, Massachusetts). They describe it as "a tragicomic student view of the double standard, a wicked teacher, a role-reversing fantasy, and an ironic conclusion."
- *High School* (Zipporah Films, 16mm or 35mm, b&w, 74 min.). Frederick Wiseman's *High School,* filmed at an upper-middle-class public high school in Philadelphia, depicts episodes in student life, with particular attention to acts of repression on the part of faculty and administrators.
- *High School Rising* (Boston Newsreel, 16mm, 15 min.). High-school students analyze how the schools exploit, oppress, and manipulate them through the tracking system, reinforcement of sex roles, and lies in the classroom.
- *Inside Out* (Jack Robertson, color, 56 min., 1971). A viable educational system can be built, says this film, if we use the community to provide experiences for high-school students in urban areas and use the school to create meaning, order, and value from those experiences. The film contrasts the disaster of urban education in New York's Bedford-Stuyvesant section with the promise of the School Without Walls in Philadelphia.
- *Interaction in Learning* (Indiana University, b&w, 29 min., 1969). The different types of social interaction that arise in school and the effect of these contacts on the shaping of individual identity are presented. Students in the Cincinnati Public Schools are seen in informal class discussions and presentations, as well as in formal classes with their teachers.
- *The Kindergarten Child, Part II* (Massachusetts Department of Education, 16mm, b&w, 48 min., 1968–70). This film was produced to stimulate interest in early childhood education and to help school systems and schools of education prepare kindergarten staff and curricula. Although this film depicts a single morning in a kindergarten classroom, it has been divided into six separate episodes, with blank film inserted between sections, for convenience in stopping the projector for discussion.
- *Le Sujet C'est Nous* (Liane Brandon, 16mm, b&w, 13 min., French dialogue, 1969). An extremely interesting film made by members of a fourth-year French

class at Quincy High School (Quincy, Massachusetts) for "cultural exchange." By depicting a variety of lifestyles in their high school, and narrating in French, the group hoped to communicate their ideas about school and "life in general."

- *Nobody Waved Goodbye* (Macmillan Audio Brandon, b&w, 80 min., 1964). This National Film Board of Canada feature has been widely recognized as one of the few valid fictional expressions of young people's problems. Two teenagers in love are forced to confront their parents over the girl's pregnancy and the boy ends up stealing a car for their escape. The style is cinéma vérité, which gives a successful sense of immediacy and simplicity.

- *No Reason to Stay* (National Film Board of Canada, b&w, 28 min., 1967). Why do some intelligent, sensitive students drop out of school? This film presents the case study of high-school student Christopher Wood, who feels that what he has to memorize has no relationship to important social issues or to his own personal development. Imaginative editing and several fantasy sequences add to the crisp reality of this film.

- *Portrait of the Inner City School* (Pennsylvania State University, b&w, 19 min., 1965). This film illustrates unconscious discrimination against the disadvantaged child, through textbooks, teaching techniques, and visual materials. It presents positive techniques used by successful teachers to emphasize learning and individual maturity.

- *The Reality of Success* (Media Five, color, 28 min., 1971). A lecture by Dr. William Glasser to the faculty of the Palo Alto Unified School District, this film summarizes the seven steps to success in teaching and counselling that Dr. Glasser discusses in *Schools Without Failure*. Numerous examples of reality therapy at work are given.

- *Summerhill* (National Film Board of Canada, color, 28 min., 1967). The most outstanding film record of a visit to A. S. Neill's "free" school. In the film Neill explains his objectives, which are basically to make school a preparation for a life of learning, and the effectiveness of his methods can be seen in activities of the children at work and play.

- *They Can Do It* (EDC Film Library, 16mm, b&w, 35 min.). This film, made in the Pastorius Public School in Philadelphia, documents the school experiences of 26 six-year-old first-graders who have never been in school before. Starting with the second day of school, the film records the class on six separate occasions throughout the school year.

- *Vignette Series* (EDC, b&w, 1968–   ). These films are continuous observations at close range of a child or a small group of children in classroom situations. They are especially useful for posing a given behavioral question and for planning the use of space in a classroom. The vignettes include: *Chairs* (9 min.); *Injections* (10 min.); *Marble Games* (12 min.); *Seven-Day Itch* (7 min.); *Waterplay* (12 min.); and *Wall Washing* (12 min.).

- *The Way It Is* (NET, b&w, 60 min., 1967). A vivid documentary which takes the viewer into the chaos of the ghetto school and reports on what is being done in one particular school as an example of moderate success. The focus is on Junior High School 57 in Bedford-Stuyvesant, where members of a New York University special learning project are shown in classrooms, teachers' meetings, and visits with parents.

Filmstrip

- *School Building* (American Association of School Administrators, 167 frames, b&w, 1973). Based on the Exhibition of School Architecture held at the AASA convention in San Francisco, this filmstrip contains interior and exterior views and plans for 32 selected elementary, middle, and high schools. It is accompanied by a discussion manual describing each frame.

Videotapes

- *Catalog of Video Tapes for Teacher Education* (Carleton College, b&w, 1971). Available in various formats, this collection of video protocol materials is virtually unequalled as a source of observations of "the classroom as it is." They were recorded in actual classrooms to provide bases for discussing many types of teaching styles. The catalog describes hundreds of tapes in different grade levels and curriculum areas.
- *A Day at Pacific High School* (Raindance, 1/2" videotape, Sony, 30 min.). A "youth rap" with students from Pacific High School in Los Gatos, California.
- *Dynamics of Classroom Behavior* (Great Plains National ITV Library, videotape and videocassette, b&w, 1969). This series of twelve 30-minute programs features Dr. Rudolf Dreikurs, who uses discussions and demonstrations to reveal student motivation in the classroom. Illustrated problems include the slow learner, the underachiever, the acting-out and the passive resistant pupil, and the exceptional and the handicapped child.
- *Hanging Out in the School Playground* (Raindance, 1/2" videotape, Sony, 30 min.). An edited videotape of kids hanging out in the school playground in Berkeley, California, and the West Village, New York City.

Refer to Appendix for addresses of distributors.

What is life in schools like?

7   What is taught ?

The curriculum of the schools is examined constantly by teachers, professors, textbook publishers, and parents. What should be taught in the schools? What is taught? What freedom and/or constraints are or should be placed upon the teacher regarding what he can teach? The 1960s was a decade of much new curriculum development in the sciences, mathematics, social studies, English, and foreign languages. In the 1970s many educators are questioning the impact and relevance of these curricula for today's needs. We have some definite biases regarding what should be taught, which we express in this chapter. Whether or not you agree with them, we hope that you will be stimulated enough to give serious consideration to the important issues raised.

Chapter contents

The current curriculum
Where does the existing curriculum come from?
What is the current curriculum?
Is the existing curriculum relevant to today's society?
How is a new curriculum developed?
Needed: a survival curriculum

Baseball, debating, reading, science. . . . Yes, along with love, tolerance, and independence. Frustration as well as mathematics and dramatics. Values and ceramics, woodshop and poise, history and boredom, auto mechanics and lead-ership — all are learned in school, some intentionally, and others in reaction to or in spite of the teacher's intentions.

We define the curriculum as all of the organized and intended experiences of the child for which the school accepts responsibility. In other words, the curriculum is not just the intellectual content of the subjects taught, but also the methods used to teach it, the interactions that occur between people, and the school-sponsored activities that contribute to "life experience."

The current curriculum

During your high-school years, many daily activities organized under the aus-pices of the school were probably considered "extracurricular." The formal courses of study — history, science, mathematics, English — were curricular, while participation on the football team, cheerleading, Future Teachers club, or the band belonged to another, lesser, category. But, we ask, shouldn't all activities that are school sponsored and contribute to the growth and development of the students be considered part of the curriculum? We strongly suspect that informal learning experiences are at least as important to intellectual and social develop-ment as are the formal courses of study. Consider, for example, the following list of goals.[1] Choose the three or four you consider most important and decide whether each is best achieved in a context of formal courses, informal school experiences, or a combination of the two:

1 develop skills in reading, writing, speaking, and listening
2 develop pride in work and a feeling of self-worth
3 develop good character and self-respect
4 develop a desire for learning now and in the future
5 learn to respect and get along with people with whom we work and live
6 learn how to examine and use information
7 gain a general education
8 learn how to be a good citizen
9 learn about and try to understand the changes that take place in the world
10 understand and practice democratic ideas and ideals
11 learn how to respect and get along with people who think, dress, and act differently
12 understand and practice the skills of family living
13 gain information needed to make job selections
14 learn how to be a good manager of money, property, and resources
15 practice and understand the ideas of health and safety
16 develop skills to enter a specific field of work
17 learn how to use leisure time
18 appreciate culture and beauty in the world

A strong argument could be made that each of these goals is best attained by a combination of formal and informal learning experiences. Some, certainly, cannot be achieved through formal educational channels alone. Nevertheless, most of the efforts that go into curriculum development are still concentrated on traditional subject matter. The typical elementary or high school is organized according to subject-matter divisions, despite the efforts of some educators to replace them with an experience-based curriculum. Some historical background may help to explain the current strong emphasis on traditional subject-matter areas.

Where does the existing curriculum come from?

Curricula are always changing in one way or another. Nevertheless, we can distinguish between sweeping changes that represent new philosophies of learning and teaching and minor adjustments that leave the overall curriculum relatively intact. What follows is not a thorough history of American curriculum revision, but a brief overview of the educational philosophies that have prompted major curriculum change, to help you better understand the motives that molded today's curriculum.

Shifting motives

Two curriculum writers have identified five major motives that have held sway more or less consecutively and have dominated the development of the curriculum in American schools: 1) religious, 2) political, 3) utilitarian, 4) the movement for mass education, and 5) the movement for excellence in education.[2]

---

[1] These 18 goals were part of a questionnaire given to a sample of Phi Delta Kappans. The results of the questionnaire can be found in the September 1973 issue of *Phi Delta Kappan*, pp. 29–32.
[2] J. Minor Gwynn and John Chase , Jr., eds., *Curriculum Principles and Social Trends* (New York: Macmillan, 1969), pp. 1–29.

The religious motive held sway from approximately 1635 to 1770, when the schools were expected to promulgate the religious beliefs of the community. The period 1770–1860 was characterized by a politically motivated desire to produce a literate populace in order to ensure the preservation of liberty and the new democratic form of government. Utilitarian goals from 1860–1920 resulted from the pressure of a rapidly expanding economy for educated people to fill the new jobs that were being created. The mass education motive (1920 to the present) is a product of the belief that all children are entitled to equal educational opportunities. Although this principle is widely espoused, it has yet to be achieved. The movement for excellence in education (1957 to the mid-1960s) was prepared for by the discovery during World War II that many high-school graduates were virtually illiterate in mathematics and science, but concern and action lagged until 1957, when Sputnik focused upon the public schools the most critical attention they had received in decades.

Sputnik and the reaction to progressivism

When the Russians launched Sputnik, the American public—which had complacently believed American schools to be far superior to any other country's—reacted against what they considered the "softness" of the curriculum and demanded a return to the "meat and potatoes" of learning—the academic disciplines, with particular emphasis on science and mathematics. More students were competing for college entrance, middle class parents wanted to make sure their children were prepared for the increased competition. During the so-called "progressive education" era of the twenties, thirties, and forties, the schools had emphasized citizenship and self-adjustment. If the progressive curriculum can be seen as child-centered or society-centered, curriculum development during the fifties and sixties must be considered discipline-centered; this approach was characterized at the time as a return to excellence in education, though many critics today question the superiority of such a disciplinary approach.

Prosperity was a major factor in the extensive curricular change of the fifties and sixties. The middle class saw education as the path to a good life for their children. The more education one received, the more likely one was to earn a good income and enjoy the comforts of life. As a result, the public was willing to spend increasing amounts of money for education. As is so often the case, however, action lagged behind intentions until Sputnik's launching triggered intense awareness of the public-school curriculum. Because of its concern for national defense and worldwide prestige, the federal government poured huge amounts

PEANUTS

DON'T TELL ME YOU TOOK THAT BLANKET TO SCHOOL TODAY?!

SURE, WHY NOT? IT CALMS ME DOWN, AND HELPS ME TO GET BETTER GRADES

BUT DON'T THE OTHER KIDS LAUGH AT YOU?

NOBODY LAUGHS AT A STRAIGHT "A" AVERAGE!

of money into curriculum development projects, teacher training workshops, and research. The influence of the federal government on the development of new curricula cannot be underestimated. Prior to this period the federal government had played a limited role in education, which was considered the exclusive responsibility of the individual states. During the 1950s the role of the federal government in public education was a hotly debated issue; the outcome is obvious in the fact that federal involvement in education is taken for granted today.

Another contributory factor was the tremendous postwar knowledge explosion, which was forcing new approaches to curriculum planning by making many areas of the existing curricula obsolete. In addition, a combination of social and political factors encouraged a new approach to the educational needs of the country; the 1954 Supreme Court decision outlawing "separate but equal" education meant that schools and educators had to rethink their approaches to time-honored traditions.

Jerome Bruner (1915–   )

Jerome Bruner has achieved a certain fame among Harvard psychology students for his imitations of babies, baboons, and slow lorises, and his sparkling enthusiasm for knowledge and discovery. Outside the Harvard community, however, he is better known for his studies of child development and his important work in educational psychology and curricular reform.

Bruner grew up in Lawrence, Long Island, where he spent his childhood fishing, sailing, and reading voraciously. He remembers that school was no challenge—it was too easy—and that he was always looking for something new to read. His father, a German-Jewish watch manufacturer, died when Bruner was 12. After high school, Bruner went to Duke University for his B.A., and received a Ph.D. in psychology from Harvard in 1941. He served in the Office of War Information and then returned to Harvard, where he remained until moving to Oxford University in England in 1972 to be the Watts Professor of Psychology.

Bruner joined the critics of American education fifteen years ago, when he served as secretary of a conference of scientists, scholars, and educators at Woods Hole, Massachusetts, on the teaching of science. For years there had been a gulf between "serious" psychology and such mundane matters as pedagogy; scholars looked down their noses at what they considered the province of teachers' colleges. The only exception was B. F. Skinner, the renowned behaviorist, who has done pioneering work on teaching machines and programmed instruction. Bruner's report on the Woods Hole conference. *The Process of Education,* was hailed as a major contribution to curriculum reform and won him instant fame. It has since been translated into twenty-two languages and is studied by teachers all over the world. The most memorable statement in the report, and the gist of Bruner's argument, is quoted widely: "Any subject can be taught effectively in some intellectually honest form to any child at any stage of development." According to Bruner, a school subject is not something one "knows about," but something one "knows how to do." It is a way of thinking and doing, rather than a collection of facts.

In keeping with his famous statement of a decade ago, Bruner has developed a fifth-grade social studies curriculum called *Man: A Course of Study,* which provides ten-year-olds with materials like those social scientists use and encourages them to investigate what is human about human beings. The course, which includes units on the life cycle of the salmon, on baboons, and on the Netsilik Eskimos, has been adopted by more than 1500 schools.

In 1960 Bruner and psychologist George Miller organized Harvard's Center for Cognitive Studies, where they investigated the sensorimotor acts of the infant—sucking, looking, reaching, grasping—as if they were observing the behavior of an unknown species. From these simple, innate activities the baby develops four crucial abilities: voluntary control of his behavior; internal control of his attention; the power to carry out several actions simultaneously; and the use of reciprocal codes that pave the way for speech. By studying infants long before they learn to talk, Bruner and others have concluded that language competence is just one aspect of the infant's ability to systematize learning. They suggest that the human mind is equipped with programs for the development of finer and more adaptable skills, not only for language but also for the use of hands, eyes, and tools. If Bruner and his co-workers succeed in decoding these mysteries of the mind, the implications for education will be profound.

Bruner advocates more problem seeking and problem solving for all learners, from infants to college students. He has proposed a dual curriculum for colleges that could satisfy both traditionalists and innovators. On Mondays, Wednesdays, and Fridays, students would continue to take traditional courses; on Tuesdays and Thursdays they would be free to govern their learning in experimental ways. This experimentation might include taking part in university budget decisions and teacher evaluation and, most important, learning to deal rationally with their own problems.

One way to implement such a dual curriculum is to make basic changes in student living arrangements. Bruner acted on his interest in extracurricular learning by becoming Master of Currier House, a new Harvard-Radcliffe coed residence. He helped solicit private funds for a day care center at the House, and invited people from many spheres of life to dine with students. He and his students wanted Currier House to serve an an example of how a community can encourage and make use of its members' initiative to deal with its own problems, both simple ones like the care of babies and large ones like drug abuse. Rather than limiting the curriculum to course work, Bruner sees the dual curriculum as an opportunity for students to put knowledge to work in their own lives.

In 1971 Bruner left Harvard to continue his research at Oxford University.

The discovery method

The curriculum reform movement was crystallized by the publication in 1960 of *The Process of Education,*[3] a short book by Jerome Bruner, a Harvard psychologist. Bruner's ideas, though by no means entirely original with him, were the most profound and elegant expression of the spirit and convictions behind the movement for curriculum change. Bruner's basic thesis was that any discipline could

[3] Jerome S. Bruner, *The Process of Education* (New York: Random House, 1960).

be and should be studied, at any level of complexity, in terms of its "structure." Bruner defined the structure of a discipline as the concepts and methods of inquiry that are its most basic components. Instead of studying random facts or incidental phenomena, students should learn the principles that constitute the heart of a discipline. A knowledge of fundamentals would enable the student to inquire into and solve problems in the discipline independently. Learning the structure of a discipline would equip the student to transfer useful concepts from one situation to another, or, in other words, to learn how to learn. This Bruner considered crucial, because the totality of knowledge in any discipline is too massive for anyone to acquire, and because knowledge changes so rapidly that what is current one year might be out-of-date the next. Bruner urged that students be provided opportunities to become problem solvers through direct and prolonged experience with objects or raw data, in the same way that a historian studies history or a biologist biology. Teachers were encouraged to let students discover meanings for themselves. This "discovery" or "inquiry" method, Bruner asserted, would make it possible to teach young children complex concepts in language they could understand. Having learned a concept on a simplified level, they could later return to it at a somewhat more advanced level. Thus, the concepts fundamental to the discipline's structure would be studied over and over throughout the school years, but each time from an increasingly complex point of view. The curriculum of the discipline would resemble a spiral; as the student moved along the spiral, he would re-encounter familiar concepts in more complex forms.

Bruner's ideas alone did not cause the tremendous curriculum reforms of the 1950s and 1960s; many forces for change were already in motion prior to the publication of *The Process of Education.* However, Bruner's concept of the structure of disciplines catalyzed the already widespread reaction to the fusion of disciplines that had occurred in the schools, and it was implemented in numerous curriculum development projects. These projects have had considerable impact on the public schools' curricula, particularly in the areas of mathematics, biology, chemistry, physics, and foreign languages. Their influence on social studies and English has not been as great, because there have been so many different social studies projects that their impact has been diffused, and because little agreement has been reached regarding objectives and methods for teaching English.

The new projects have generally had less impact at the elementary level than at the secondary level, with the notable exception of mathematics and, possibly, science. Many elementary educators considered the study of distinct disciplines inappropriate to the elementary school. They felt that the significant problems of mankind could not be studied through the disciplinary approach, and called instead for an integrating curriculum that would treat life as something whole rather than piecemeal. They also were concerned that emphasis on underlying concepts, abstractions, and intuitive behavior would lead to neglect of practical operations and applications. Since the new curricula were designed to reform disciplines already well established in the schools, it appeared to many that they would leave no room for emerging fields. But probably more than anything else, the elementary educators objected to planning from the top down, from the secondary to the elementary, which failed to take into account sufficiently the developmental processes of young children as learners—their interests, their individual differences, and the irregularity of their growth. To them, curriculum reform seemed to be putting the discipline before the child.

Not surprisingly, the feeling that the curriculum unwisely stresses the subject above the learner is shared by many secondary educators as well; they question the relevance of such a curriculum. So do we.

What is the current curriculum?

Looking at the courses of study prescribed by the fifty states, one discovers that the similarities far outweigh the differences. We will discuss some of the reasons for this phenomenon later, but in the meantime let's examine what is presently taught in elementary and secondary schools across the country.

At both levels the curriculum is organized into subject-matter areas, which ordinarily are science, mathematics, social studies, foreign languages, English, reading and language arts, the fine arts, and physical education; the latter three areas tend to emphasize developing skills rather than mastery of a particular body of knowledge.

In some elementary schools all subjects are taught by one teacher; other schools bring in specialists to teach the fine arts and physical education, and still others hire specialists to teach reading, science, and mathematics.

Science

Science instruction in elementary schools is in, to put it simply, a state of flux. Many schools still base their science programs on the notion of social utility; what is taught must be of practical use in solving problems that people face every day. This approach is out of favor with leaders in science education because the knowledge explosion may make presently "practical" information quickly obsolete. Science educators are proposing that students learn the conceptual schemes upon which each branch of science is based, and the processes by which scientists acquire new knowledge, in order to keep pace with the rapid expansion of knowledge.

In an effort to "catch up with the Russians," a number of science curriculum revision projects were funded by the National Science Foundation and other federal agencies after the launching of Sputnik in 1957. These projects—which were developed by people of diverse backgrounds, including leading scientists, science educators, teachers, psychologists, educational evaluators, and artists—differed in format and intention, but each called for new teaching roles. The teacher can no longer be considered the fount of knowledge. Instead of dominating the learner, the teacher must create an open, nonthreatening atmosphere which offers the child numerous opportunities to manipulate scientific objects and materials. In addition, the teacher is discouraged from simply *telling* the students answers and encouraged to allow them to ask questions, face problems, and pose tentative solutions; she should foster an environment that encourages an inquiry approach. Since these teacher skills differ fundamentally from those demanded by more traditional programs in science, a number of workshops have been funded by the National Science Foundation to train teachers in the new approaches.

Among the most widely adopted elementary science curriculum projects are the Science Curriculum Improvement Study (SCIS), a project developed at the University of California, Berkeley; *Science—A Process Approach,* a project developed by the American Association for the Advancement of Science (AAAS), Washington, D.C.; the Elementary Science Study (ESS), a project developed by

Education Development Center, Inc., Newton, Massachusetts; and the Minnesota Mathematics and Science Teaching Project (MINNEMAST), a project developed at the University of Minnesota, Minneapolis.

Similar projects were developed for secondary schools in the biological and physical sciences, particularly biology, chemistry, and physics. Most notable of these efforts are the Biological Sciences Curriculum Study (BSCS), the Chemical Bond Approach Project (CBA), the Chemical Education Material Study (CHEM Study), and the Physical Science Study Committee (PSSC).

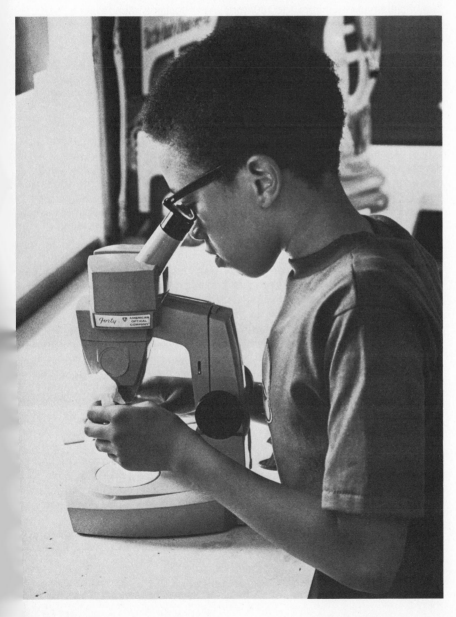

What is taught?

Mathematics	Mathematics education was equally affected by Sputnik. As a matter of fact, mathematics was the first area in which curriculum builders undertook the revision process. Since math is taught on a K-12 basis, most of the new projects incorporated all grade levels to ensure continuity.

Mathematics today is viewed as a language which both communicates ideas about numbers and describes the quantitative aspects of ideas, objects. At the elementary-school level, mathematics instruction attempts to help children assign meaning to numbers. A distinction is made between *number,* which is a mental concept, and *numeral,* the physical symbol that represents that concept. That a child can count from 1 to 100 does not necessarily mean that he possesses an understanding of number concepts. As a result, mathematics today stresses *structure* rather than drill and computational skills.

Among the foremost mathematics projects are the School Mathematics Study Group (SMSG), the Greater Cleveland Mathematics Program, the Madison Project of Syracuse University and Webster College, the University of Illinois Committee on School Mathematics (UICSM), and the University of Maryland Mathematics Project; the most widely adopted of these is the SMSG project.

While the major thrust of the 1960s in mathematics was the development of curriculum materials that stressed the structure of the discipline, it is likely that future efforts will de-emphasize the formalism of the new math of the 1950s and 1960s. One new area that is almost certain to play an important role in mathematics instruction is the conversion to the metric system. Extensive retraining will be necessary for both teachers and teacher educators as the United States moves toward implementing the metric system.

Social studies

Social studies—the study of man, his ideas, actions, and relationships—is not a discipline in the same sense as are mathematics or science, although it draws on the various social science disciplines for its content and methods of inquiry. (A discipline has been defined as an area of inquiry containing a distinctive body of concepts and principles, with techniques for exploring the area and for correcting and expanding the body of knowledge.)[4] In contrast to the sciences and mathematics, fundamental concepts and processes have not been identified and agreed upon by curriculum builders in social studies. History has traditionally been the king of the social studies, at both the elementary and secondary levels, and, although some inroads have been made by other disciplines, it still remains dominant.

The pattern of courses taken in high school has also remained relatively standard for the past twenty-five years. Civics and world history are traditionally taken in the ninth and tenth grades, although many students take no social studies courses then. American history is usually taken in the eleventh grade. Problems of democracy and elective courses such as economics, American government, and sociology are taken in the twelfth grade.

The most common approach to social studies at the elementary level focuses on the "widening horizons" of a child's environment. In the primary grades, childre

---

[4] Arthur W. Foshay, "Knowledge and the Structure of the Disciplines," in *The Nature of Knowledge: Implications for the Education of Teachers,* ed. William A. Jenkins (Milwaukee: University of Wisconsin, 1961).

study the family, the home, and the school; as their scope of attention expands, they study the neighborhood, the local community and other types of communities, the state, the nation, and other parts of the world. Thus, the social curriculum is conceptualized as a series of concentric circles, with the child at the center, and each grade level focusing on a particular ring of the circle. History and geography dominate the social studies in the elementary school, as does the use of a single textbook. There is heavy emphasis on learning to interpret graphs, charts, and maps and on the development of communication skills.

Some of the new curriculum projects take an interdisciplinary approach, while others focus on individual disciplines, such as anthropology, geography, economics, political science, and sociology. No single social studies project has gained the general acceptance and wide distribution that SMSG has in mathematics and BSCS in biology. However, over fifty new social studies projects have been developed since 1960, making it highly unlikely that any one of them could dominate the field.

While the numerous social studies curriculum projects have had varying degrees of success, there is no doubt that they have affected the way social studies are being taught in many schools. Increased attention is being given to making social studies programs more meaningful, more individualized, and more personally relevant to the student. More emphasis is being placed on inquiry, personal values, reflective thinking, and active social participation by students. Additionally, innovative use of different teaching procedures, including simulation and gaming, and the use of multimedia are growing.[5] The commercial publishers have responded with a wide variety of books and supplementary materials that enliven the classroom. We are hopeful that social studies instruction will continue to change in these directions.

Language arts

The language arts program seeks to develop in children the skills of reading, writing, speaking, and listening. The importance of language arts cannot be overemphasized, since no subject can be successfully studied without language skills. Most elementary language arts programs share the common goal of developing in the student the following capacities:

1 intelligent use of common modes of communication
2 the ability to talk formally and informally with and to a group and individuals, and to listen effectively and courteously

[5] John Jarolimek, "In Pursuit of the Elusive New Social Studies," *Educational Leadership* 30 (April 1973): 599.

© 1970 United Feature Syndicate, Inc.

What is taught?

3   the ability to read analytically and critically for information
4   enthusiasm for continued learning through communication
5   facility with the English language through awareness of language patterns and structure, and effective skills in writing including spelling and handwriting
6   ability to use the tools of the language arts, particularly the dictionary, encyclopedias, and other reference and resource materials[6]

Language arts curricula must be organized to foster continuous growth and increasing sophistication in the four major skill areas during the elementary years, and graded elementary schools ordinarily employ sequential curricula.

A number of curriculum reform projects in language arts on the secondary level have been developed in recent years, supported by the federal government. In 1961 the U.S. Office of Education launched Project English — now known as the English Program of the U.S. Office of Education — in an attempt to improve instruction at all levels in English literature, reading, and writing; to coordinate the efforts of teachers, school administrators, and university professors in improving the quality of English teaching; to sponsor research, experimentation, and dissemination; and to assist universities to establish centers for the development of new curriculum materials and teaching methods.

An investigation of the various projects that have emerged from these new curriculum centers reveals that they have several characteristics in common.[7] 1) Student activities involve listening and speaking to one another in natural settings. The stress is on informal discussion rather than platform presentations. 2) Traditionally, the schools have tried to standardize the language of the students and to purify it of ungrammatical patterns. Rather than attempting to extinguish "bad" language patterns, the new projects concentrate on exploring acceptable alternative possibilities and testing their effects. In other words, the new language instruction explores grammatical structures and linguistic units to see how they work, without prescribing proper and improper usage. 3) At one time literature was regarded as a means to teach reading skills and as an instrument for moral education. More recently it has been used to portray our cultural heritage and to illustrate style, technique, and character development. The use of contemporary literature, paperbacks, and individualized reading programs is growing in popularity, and increasing effort is being made to find literature that involves students, elicits intense personal response, and motivates the students to further reading. 4) English classes are taking advantage of the increasing interest in new media, particularly by studying and discussing serious films. Some schools offer film-making and multimedia presentations as part of the English program. 5) The new curricula are emphasizing interdisciplinary study, in conjunction with other areas of the humanities such as music, art, and occasionally history.

A second major influence on the English curriculum was the Anglo-American Seminar on the Teaching of English held at Dartmouth, England in 1966. The participants in the seminar — leading scholars, teachers of English and English education — came to the conclusion that the traditional content-centered curricu-

---

[6] William Vernon Hicks, W. Robert Houston, Bruce Cheney and Richard Marguard, *The New Elementary School Curriculum* (New York: Van Nostrand, 1970), p. 158.
[7] Robert Hogan, "What's New in Curriculum — English," *Nation's Schools* 84 (July 1969): 37–38.

lum is sterile and that treating English as a "discipline" is restrictive as well as unworkable. The participants agreed that English is more than the structural "tripod" of literature, language study, and composition it had been considered for more than a decade.

One new approach to English is outlined in James Moffett's *A Student-Centered Language Arts Curriculum, Grades K–13*.[8] Taking human discourse as the central unifying concept, Moffett offers a series of activities intended to develop logically and cumulatively the student's own language powers. In effect, each student produces his own language texts by experimenting with narrative, dialogue, improvisation, and biography, and recording the results. This approach rejects explicit instruction in rhetoric or literary data and instead emphasizes the validity of oral language as a basis for all other activities in English.

However, such new approaches have met strong resistance, partially because of widespread philosophical controversy about the nature of English itself. Despite the work of the curriculum centers and of individual spokesmen, the majority of teachers and scholars of English maintain that the "discipline" approach to English is the only viable one; they acknowledge that its implementation needs revision, but find no fault with the concept itself. They regard only written literature as valid, to the exclusion of oral composition, and insist that some form of grammar study be maintained. Thus, as in social studies, change is slow to come to the English classroom. One survey indicates that few of the curricular innovations advocated by the new curriculum centers are being implemented in the classroom.[9]

Foreign languages

The foreign language programs of our public schools have changed considerably over the last twenty years. Prior to World War II, most foreign language instruction stressed reading and writing, to the virtual exclusion of listening and speaking. Furthermore, foreign language instruction was almost exclusively the domain of the secondary schools. With the 1950s came the introduction of a new kind of foreign language instruction to elementary as well as high schools. The new audiolingual approach is designed to develop competence in speaking and listening to others speak a foreign language. As evidence of this dramatic change, the number of language laboratories—rooms equipped with listening tapes, headsets, and machines that can monitor the pace of the student and allow him to respond to the tapes—in public schools nationwide has grown from several dozen in 1957 to at least 8,000 by 1966. There is, however, some evidence that their use is not as widespread as was once believed.

The adoption of the audiolingual approach necessitated the retraining of many foreign language teachers and, with support from the National Defense Education Act and the U.S. Office of Education, hundreds of summer workshops have been held. In addition to French, German, Spanish, Italian, and Russian, new materials have been developed for the study of Arabic, Chinese, Japanese, Portuguese, Greek, and Hebrew.

[8] James Moffett, *A Student-Centered Language Arts Curriculum, Grades K–13: A Handbook for Teachers* (Boston: Houghton Mifflin, 1968).
[9] Fred I. Godshalk, "A Survey of the Teaching of English in Secondary Schools," *School and Society* 98 (April 1970): 249–250.

Many foreign language instructors have concluded, however, that the radical audiolingual approach of the early 1960s was not very successful.[10] Instruction today seems to be combining the more traditional methods with some practice in the audiolingual approach. The present consensus is that a combination of the two will produce better foreign language instruction.

The arts

Teachers of the fine and applied arts have been fighting an uphill battle to maintain a secure position in the regular school curriculum. During the post-Sputnik era, budgetary cutbacks were made in the arts to finance enriched programs in mathematics and the sciences. Recently, however, many public-school art programs have become sources of pride.

Art and music in the elementary school are ordinarily taught by regular classroom teachers, although some schools hire specialist teachers in one or both areas. Dance and drama are largely ignored in the elementary school, though children of this age are less inhibited and seem to enjoy these activities more than do students in the secondary schools. The small amount of instruction in the arts provided for elementary students is replaced in high school by drama clubs, orchestras, bands, and dance groups. In most instances, instruction in music or dance during a child's elementary-school years takes the form of private instruction outside the public school.

In recent years a few schools have been trying to stimulate interest in the arts by actually bringing various types of artists — musicians, painters, and poets — into the schools to teach children. The overall results of these programs have been good, with many children discovering that they have talents that had never been exposed before.[11]

Elective and vocational courses

Most high schools today offer their students a number of options regarding the courses they take. While the average high-school student graduates with 16 to 20 units — a year-long course representing one unit — large high schools may offer as many as 100 courses. The average student, then, will probably choose among optional courses according to his interests or academic ambitions.

Although college preparation has been the major goal of many high schools, increased effort has been made recently to provide well-balanced programs for students not planning to attend college. This trend is especially evident in rural areas where small local high schools are being replaced by comprehensive regional high schools. Some of the new courses, such as industrial education, distributive education, home economics, business education, and agriculture, are specifically vocational in nature. Others, such as driver education, consumer education, and conservation, have been added to the curriculum because of an obvious societal need or in response to student interest.

A new curriculum thrust that is receiving much attention these days is that of career education — an attempt to reform and refocus education so that what is taught in the classroom has a clear relationship to the student's future plans. Career education also stresses that students must understand the range of

[10] Gerald A. Hayn, "High School Language Instruction in the 1970's." *Hispania* 56 (March 1973): 98.
[11] Diane Divoky, "Art Is a Many Splendored Thing." *Learning* 2 (December 1973): 10–16.

career options available to them, starting at an early age. Career education would not be a subject in and of itself, but would permeate the entire curriculum. This topic will be discussed in greater detail in Chapter 11, "What's New in Education?"

Activities and other aspects of the curriculum

At the beginning of this chapter we defined curriculum as all the experiences for which the school accepts responsibility, including activities pursued outside the formal course of study. Such organized noncredit activities are the primary vehicle by which the schools promote one of their main stated objectives, individual growth and development. For example, most high schools offer a program of varsity and intramural sports, as well as civic, social, and hobby clubs. Many schools have active student government organizations (which are more often regarded as a means to promote cooperation among students than as real decision-making bodies with the power to affect life in the schools).

What is taught?

Is the existing curriculum relevant to today's society?

Perhaps the most basic function of all education is to increase the survival chances of the group. When educational systems have not fulfilled this function, whole civilizations have been known to disappear. What happened in those civilizations is that environmental conditions changed, requiring the development of new skills, new ideas, and new concepts to survive, but the more conservative elements of society insisted on maintaining the traditional educational forms. As long as the environment remained stable or changed very slowly, the skills necessary for survival also remained constant. In such times, when a culture is proven able to ensure the survival of the group, education can be content to transmit that culture. If, however, the dominant characteristic of the environment is change, concepts and skills useful for survival must be separated from what is useless or outmoded, the former retained and the latter discarded. In addition, new concepts and skills appropriate to the new demands of the environment have to be developed to replace those that are discarded.

Our society and our environment are presently undergoing change at a rate unprecedented in mankind's history. The population of the world is expanding at an almost geometric rate, and exerting severe pressure on the environment. We are consuming natural resources at such a rate that it is only a matter of time before many will be depleted. We are polluting the air we breathe and, at the same time, destroying huge tracts of plants which provide us with oxygen. We are fouling the water we drink and, as a consequence, must spend billions of dollars to try (not very successfully) to purify it. Racial and ethnic prejudices, which have gone unchallenged for decades, are no longer being endured by their victims. Nations now possess the power to annihilate one another at the push of a button. In short, we have reached a point at which many leading thinkers are questioning man's (note: not the United States' or the U.S.S.R.'s, but *man's*) ability to survive another century on this planet.

If we are to rely on education to increase our chances of survival, education must turn its attention to the concepts and skills—that is, survival strategies—necessary to cope with or control such environmental change. Our ability to recognize and to discard concepts and approaches that have been rendered irrelevant, and to substitute new ones in their places, may indeed determine our survival. We must question the relevance of our curriculum.

The Saber-Tooth Curriculum

In his classic satire on curriculum irrelevance, *The Saber-Tooth Curriculum,*[12] Harold Benjamin—using the pseudonym J. Abner Peddiwell—describes how the first school curriculum was developed in the Stone Age. The earliest educational theorist, according to Benjamin's book, was a man named New Fist, who hit upon the idea of deliberate, systematic education.

Watching children at play, New Fist wondered how he could get them to do the things that would gain them more and better food, shelter, clothing, and security. He analyzed the activities that adults engaged in to maintain life and came up with three subjects for his curriculum: 1) fish-grabbing-with-the-bare-hands, 2) woolly-horse-clubbing, and 3) saber-tooth-tiger-scaring-with-fire. Although the children trained in these subjects enjoyed obvious material benefits as a result

[12] J. Abner Peddiwell [Harold Benjamin], *The Saber-Tooth Curriculum* (New York: McGraw-Hill, 1939). One chapter of this book is reproduced in *Kaleidoscope: Readings in Education,* the companion volume to this text.

some conservative members of the tribe resisted the introduction of these new subjects on religious grounds. But, in due time, many people began to train their children in New Fist's curriculum and the tribe grew increasingly prosperous and secure.

Then conditions changed. An ice age began, and a glacier crept down over the land. The glacier brought with it dirt and gravel which muddied the creeks, and the waters became so dirty that no one could see the fish well enough to grab them. The melting waters from the approaching ice sheet also made the country wetter, and the little woolly horses migrated to drier land. They were replaced by antelopes who were so shy and speedy that no one could get close enough to club them. Finally, the new dampness in the air caused the saber-tooth tigers to catch pneumonia and die. And the ferocious glacial bears who came down with the advancing ice sheet were not afraid of fire.

The thinkers of the tribe, descendants of New Fist, found a way out of the dilemma. One figured out how to catch fish with a net made from vines. Another invented traps for the antelopes and a third discovered how to dig pits to catch the bears.

Some thoughtful men began to wonder why these new activities couldn't be taught in the schools. But the wise old men who controlled the schools claimed that the new skills did not qualify as *education*—they were merely a matter of *training*. Besides, the curriculum was too full of fish-grabbing, horse-clubbing, and tiger-scaring, the standard cultural subjects, to admit new ones. When some radicals argued that the traditional subjects were foolish, the wise old men said that they taught fish-grabbing not to catch fish but to develop agility; horse-clubbing to develop strength; and tiger-scaring to develop courage. "The essence of true education is timelessness," they announced. "It is something that endures through changing conditions like a solid rock standing squarely and firmly in the middle of a raging torrent. You must know that there are some eternal verities and the saber-tooth curriculum is one of them!"[13]

The Saber-Tooth Curriculum was written in 1939, but its continuing applicability seems to be one of the true "eternal verities."

What's relevance?

Before one can determine whether a particular curriculum is relevant, some difficult questions must be asked: relevant to what? To life in society as it is now, as it probably will be in the future, or as it ideally should be? Relevant for whom? For the intellectual elite or for the common man? For the individual

[13] Peddiwell, pp. 43–44.

learner, or for society and its needs? And who determines social needs—the
adults who represent the "establishment," or some other group? The question of
curriculum relevance is very complicated, for it draws upon one's entire philosophy of education. Is education's primary purpose to help students develop their
minds by exploring ideas of the past that have proven to have enduring
meaning? Or is education's primary purpose to help students experience growth
through interaction with their environment? Is there a particular body of knowledge or repertoire of skills that all members of our society should possess? Or
should students be free to explore many different areas in accordance with their
own needs, curiosities, and interests? Should education give priority to the study
of immediate problems and to developing the processes, understandings, and
skills necessary for their solution? Or should education concentrate on guiding
behavior according to agreed-upon standards, and on study of the past as a way
of preparing for the future?

In a society as large and pluralistic as the United States, all of these philosophical positions, and more, have committed supporters. How can the schools
incorporate in their curricula such diverse philosophies? Obviously, they cannot.
If a certain philosophy is dominant within a given community, the curriculum of
its schools is likely to reflect that set of beliefs, and those who don't agree will
remain dissatisfied. More often than not inertia keeps traditional programs
ensconced in the schools until a catalytic event, such as Sputnik's launching or
rioting in white neighborhoods, or an intellectual force, such as the progressive
education movement, arouses enough momentum to bring about change. It is
only reasonable to expect that the philosophies that have molded the present
school curriculum will dominate until an opposing point of view gains enough
support to supplant them.

Mortimer Smith argues that all educational philosophies, however diverse, fall
into two basic categories and characterizes them as follows:

*On this matter of priorities in education, the picture seems clear: One group
believes that the school must maintain its historic role as the chief institution in
charge of intellectual training; another group—and perhaps the dominant one in
public education—maintains that intellectual training is only a part of the
school's total program, and not necessarily the most important part.*[14]

If one considers the school's primary objective to be the intellectual training of
students, any curriculum that does not emphasize scholarship will be judged

---

[14] Mortimer Smith, "Fundamental Differences Do Exist," *American Education Today,* ed. Paul Woodring
and John Scanlon (New York: McGraw-Hill, 1964), p. 29.

irrelevant. Conversely, if one believes that the school should emphasize the development of the "whole child"—his emotional and social, as well as intellectual, growth—a curriculum devoted exclusively to English, history, the sciences, mathematics, and foreign languages will be considered inappropriate for many students and thus irrelevant.

The main charge of the public schools' critics is that the curriculum is irrelevant to the needs of many children and of society. They accuse it of emphasizing knowledge and skills for which many students have no use. They argue that unless a student is preparing for college, teaching him to bisect an angle or to recite facts about the ancient Egyptians is a poor use of his time (and perhaps of the college-bound students' time too). They charge that the traditional subject-matter approach to the curriculum ignores the learner's needs and interests.

A corollary criticism is that studying unrelated subjects, each by a different method and according to a unique logic, makes the integration of knowledge quite difficult. The problems we encounter in life do not come neatly organized according to subject matter; such distinctions are arbitrarily imposed on them by people.

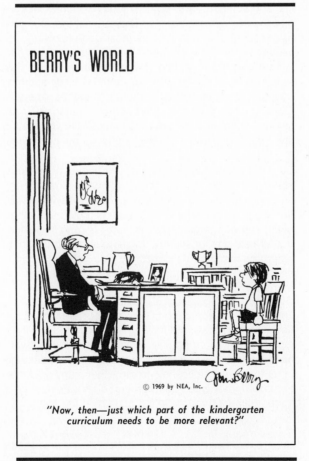

BERRY'S WORLD

© 1969 by NEA, Inc.

"Now, then—just which part of the kindergarten curriculum needs to be more relevant?"

What is taught?

The arbitrariness of the boundaries between disciplines is evident in the emergence of fields of study with names such as biochemistry, psycholinguistics, operations research, biophysics, and ecology—to name only a few. These fields have come into being in response to problems that could not be solved within the limits of any one discipline; they demanded a multidisciplinary approach. If problems do not come prepackaged in distinct disciplines, why does the public school impose on students a curriculum made up of discrete subjects, each of which must be studied at an assigned time? If high-school students apply in one class ideas learned in another, it is more a matter of chance than of planning. To the extent that we allow the school curriculum to be dominated by the disciplines, we deny students the opportunity to become more than superficially acquainted with profound public problems. The fascinating story of the discovery of DNA, the heredity molecule, by James D. Watson and Francis Crick, is a beautiful example of the arbitrariness of the disciplines. Watson, a biologist, recounts in *The Double Helix*[15] that, though untrained in chemistry, he brought to the project something more valuable, a different perspective and a fresh viewpoint; the solution won him and Crick the Nobel Prize.

The arbitrary selection of disciplines is another serious weakness of the curriculum. Most of the subjects offered—history, English, foreign languages, mathematics, and science—are required today because they were required yesterday, and the day before and. . . . They are not the sole survivors of a careful appraisal of what subjects are most worth knowing. They can, in fact, be seen as vestiges of an era when man's knowledge was much more limited; these subjects encompassed much of what was then known. But that is hardly the case today—what about cybernetics, anthropology, sociology, psycholinguistics, ecology, and psychology? Or computer sciences, operations research, statistics, black studies, aesthetics, and human relations? Or philosophy, theology, semantics, logic, and group dynamics? Do you think any of these subjects should be represented in the public-school curriculum?

But even if new subjects replace traditional ones, our prime objection would still stand: subject-matter fields should not be studied simply because someone says they should be. The importance of studying ecology, for example, does not lie in its inherent value as a system of thought, but in the use that can be made of the knowledge gained in its study. By and large, the more importance a particular field has for society, the more relevance it will have for the student as an emerging member of that society. Education will be irrelevant to students' development, or even undermine it, if it does not address itself to crucial social issues and the problems of growing up.

The discipline approach is very appropriate for some students, but many others find it so restrictive and limiting that they are literally "turned off." If the discipline-oriented curriculum cannot respond effectively to the criticisms that have been leveled against it by students and educators, protest is likely to take other forms. Arthur Foshay predicts that many students will simply refuse to enroll in discipline-oriented courses, and cites as evidence a 10 percent drop in physics enrollment throughout the country in the last ten years.[16]

[15] James D. Watson, *The Double Helix* (New York: Atheneum, 1968).
[16] Arthur Foshay, "How Fare the Disciplines?" *Phi Delta Kappan* 51 (March 1970): 349–352.

Many students are currently insisting that their education become more personally involving. Nevertheless, most disciplines continue to emphasize objectivity and logic, which students who lack prior interest in a subject tend to interpret as impersonality. We are not arguing against logic; we are observing that an exclusively objective approach may permanently discourage a student from ever developing an interest in a subject. It makes more sense to us to start with the students' interests, concerns, and needs, and then demonstrate the value of objectivity in situations that demand it. Many school dropouts, when asked why they left school, offer as a primary reason the meaninglessness and irrelevance of what they were taught. Consider, for instance, this statement by a young black high-school dropout:

Now, from almost the beginning in school all they've been teaching was math, science, social study, history and English. Ever since I have been in school, that's all I heard.

Then they repeated it the next year and over and over.

What do you want to hear about the Romans for? They're dead. Like history—you get the same thing over and over.[17]

We don't need to sacrifice the intellectual quality of the best of the new curricula in order to find ways of allowing real problems a place in the curriculum. We must develop new syntheses of the actual and the conceptual suitable for students to study. Now that you know our position on the issue of curriculum irrelevance, how do you feel about it?

How is a new curriculum developed?

When you begin to teach, it is likely that the curriculum you use will already have been formulated. It may have been developed by a large national curriculum project such as SMSG or BSCS, or it may be the work of teachers within the school district. Your school may provide a curriculum guide—a compilation of objectives and activities for a particular course—whose purpose is to aid the teacher in planning and organizing the course for the year. These curriculum guides range in quality from being nearly worthless to acting as a source of helpful ideas, particularly for beginning teachers. When you begin to immerse yourself in the curriculum, you are likely to ask such questions as, "How does one develop a curriculum? Are there any guidelines? How do you choose what should be included and what should be omitted? Is it purely a matter of choice on the part of the developers? Is the curriculum based on any particular philosophical position? Will people with different philosophies of education develop different curricula, or will they be basically the same?"

---

[17] Quoted in George H. Weber and Annabelle B. Motz, "School as Perceived by the Dropout," *Journal of Negro Education* 37 (Spring 1968): 131.

These kinds of questions have been posed for years by curriculum developers, and the result has been a number of curriculum development models.[18] However, the unembellished facts of life about curriculum development are that very few curricula are developed according to clearly articulated principles. Much of what is taught in the schools today is developed by teachers, either individually or in groups, and tends inevitably to be influenced by such factors as what's available in texts, what other teachers are doing, guidelines established by the school district or the state, what the department has done in the past, the teachers' own preferences, seat-of-the-pants intuition, how former students have responded to certain topics and learning experiences, what's happening in the media, and what college courses the teachers have taken—the proportion differing for each teacher according to the phase of the moon and the number of days until Christmas.

We do not mean to put down teacher-developed curricula. The important thing to remember is that *the curriculum is what happens to the kids, not what is in the curriculum guides or the resource units.* Any number of factors influence this "final" or "received" curriculum. It is also not our purpose to describe in detail how to go about developing curriculum in a systematic and orderly way. We do want to discuss, however, a number of principles or guidelines that we believe to be basic to the development of a relevant and meaningful curriculum.[19]

First, *a curriculum should not be prepackaged, rigidly scheduled, or uniform throughout a school system. Instead, it should be flexible and geared to the unique needs of the students.* A prepackaged curriculum says, in effect, "Whether you're black, white, brown, or yellow, whether your parents earn $30,000 or $1,500 per year, whether you can read well or just barely, whether you're secure and have developed a good self-concept or not, here is what you need to learn!"

A flexible curriculum geared to the unique needs of the students says, in effect, "This curriculum is designed to help you deal in personal terms with the problems of human conduct, rather than with the requirements of various subject disciplines. We start with you, the learner, not with the content, because you are more important than the subject matter."

Second, *a curriculum should start from an "experience" base, rather than a "symbol" base.* Because symbols are abstract, they are not appropriate starting points for instruction. It is not that symbols and abstractions are unimportant—in fact, they are crucial in our society—but abstraction must be grounded in the concrete reality of the individual student's life if it is to have meaning for him. As the "Cone of Experience" on page 257 illustrates, the kinds of experiences that can be provided the student vary on a continuum from the most direct to the highly abstract. When direct experience is impossible, contrived or dramatized experiences are often good substitutes. For example, a study of government might be initiated by having the students role-play individuals on a desert island

[18] Two of the most recognized books on curriculum development are Ralph W. Tyler, *Basic Principles of Curriculum and Instruction* (Chicago: University of Chicago Press, 1950) and Hilda Taba, *Curriculum Development: Theory and Practice* (New York: Harcourt, Brace & World, 1962).
[19] The authors are indebted to Mario Fantini and Gerald Weinstein for elucidating these principles in their pamphlet, *Toward a Contact Curriculum* (New York: Anti-Defamation League of B'nai B'rith, 1969).

with an ample supply of food, clothing, and shelter. The only rule is that they are not permitted to make up *any* rules! In one classroom, the students concluded after about three sessions that they could not function without rules to protect individuals' rights. They then proceeded to develop basic rules and a village government. After that, they were eager to compare their village rules with an actual small community's laws. As Fantini and Weinstein put it, the cardinal rule of this approach is, "Experience first, we'll talk later!"

Third, *a curriculum should be present-oriented rather than past-and-future-oriented.* "You need to study this because it will help you get a good job." "Studying the Romans will help us understand and appreciate our lives today." "When you get to college you will be glad you studied this." While middle class children may be better able to accept long-range goals (and even this is a dubious assumption), lower class children have difficulty understanding time as a continuum.[20] As a result, justifications of past-oriented study alluding to its future value seem phony to many students.

[20] Basil Bernstein, "Social Class and Linguistic Development: A Theory of Social Learning," in *Education, Economy, and Society,* ed. Halsey, Floud, and Anderson (New York: Free Press, 1961), p. 297.

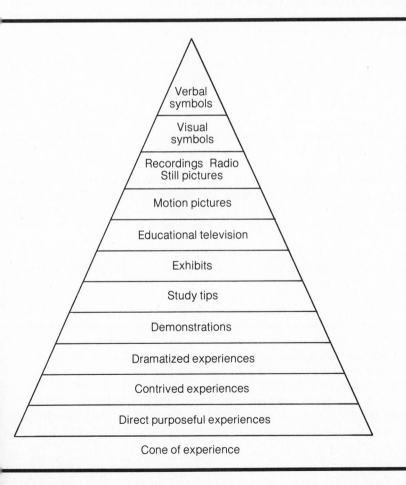

From *Audiovisual Methods in Teaching,* Third Edition, by Edgar Dale. Copyright © 1946, 1954, 1969, by The Dryden Press. Reprinted by permission of The Dryden Press.

Verbal symbols

Visual symbols

Recordings Radio Still pictures

Motion pictures

Educational television

Exhibits

Study tips

Demonstrations

Dramatized experiences

Contrived experiences

Direct purposeful experiences

Cone of experience

What is taught?

Because most of what we currently teach is either future- or past-oriented, it lacks relevance for present-oriented students. Or, as Fantini and Weinstein argue, "To a child who has not been socialized in such a way as to make specific connections between present events or activities and future goals a process which emphasizes long-term goals becomes discriminatory. The disadvantaged child is a kind of existentialist—to him, the present moment is absolute and relevant, all else is meaningless verbiage."[21] A curriculum, to be truly meaningful, must use the present as a starting point for learning. This is not to say that the study of past- or future-oriented material should be discarded, but that it must follow upon and be integrated with present-oriented material and experiences.

Fourth, *a curriculum should emphasize* why *rather than* what.

"On what date did Columbus discover America?" "What's the specific gravity of iron?" "What are the major exports of Japan?" "What were the major causes of the Civil War?"

If you were to conduct a systematic study, or even a random sampling, the chances are that you would find the majority of curriculum guides, examination questions, and classroom discussions to be *what*-oriented rather than *why*-oriented.

"What" questions can be useful, but they have limited transferability. Compare the potential usefulness of these two pieces of information:

Alaska is the largest of the fifty states.

If two persons have had different experiences with words, or if they view the communication situation differently, the meaning of what is said will differ for them.

The first statement can be looked up in a reference book; it is an isolated piece of information which has limited value. The second statement cannot be derived from any convenient source, but its meaning can be applied to many situations and can help an individual understand why failures of communication occur.

Since students cannot be taught everything that is known, the curriculum must incorporate concepts and ideas that can be widely applied, both within and outside the classroom.

Fifth, *a curriculum must be based on reality rather than fantasy or sterility.* Dick, Jane, and Spot live in a white house in the country; a smiling Mexican boy sits atop a burro; Mr. Adams, the butcher shop owner, is always smiling; and the clean, well dressed, middle class children are always alert and responsive to the teacher—and the whole thing is as unreal and antiseptic as a cartoon. It would be surprising if any child recognized himself in Dick or Jane, but children who live in urban areas and have never been to the country cannot possibly identify with them. And if the smiling Mexican boy is an accurate representation of his country, why is there so much poverty and hunger in Mexico?

[21] Fantini and Weinstein, *Toward a Contact Curriculum,* p. 22.

Phony Curriculum

Imagine a unit of study, somewhere in the primary grades, on "The Family. . . ." How is "family" generally represented in the early grades?

The houses in which families live never, as far as we are told, include toilets. Members of the family never scratch themselves, utter obscenities, cheat on their wives, fix traffic tickets, drink beer, play the horses, falsify their tax returns, strike one another, make love, use deodorants, gossip on the telephone, buy on credit, have ulcers, or manifest a million other signs of life that even the most culturally deprived child knows about in the most intimate detail. . . .

Certainly, at their dinner tables, no textbook fathers talk about having out-bargained that New York Jew, about the niggers who are trying to take over the neighborhood, the cops, the Birchers, the hippies, the war, and so on. On the contrary, one may safely expect the textbook family to be disembodied, apolitical, generally without a specific ethnic identity or religious affiliation, free of social prejudice, innocent of grief, economically secure, vocationally stable, antiseptic and law-abiding straight down the middle. It occupies a universe from which disaffection, divorce, cynicism, loneliness, neurosis, bastardy, atheism, tension, self-doubt, wrecked cars, and cockroaches are inevitably absent.

Unless he is downright dull, it is impossible to imagine that at some level of experience the child is not aware of the thundering disparity between the real world and the school's priggish, distorted, emasculated representations of that world. It seems reasonable to suspect that the child's knowledge almost certainly includes the realization that, in plain language, the curriculum is phony, at least in relation to the example we have considered.

From *Clinical Supervision: Special Methods for the Supervision of Teachers* by Robert Goldhammer. Copyright © 1969 by Holt, Rinehart and Winston, Inc. Reprinted by permission of Holt, Rinehart and Winston, Inc.

One of the most serious deficiencies of our present curriculum is its stereotyped, middle class, all's-right-with-the-world approach. When junior high-school students study other countries, accurate glimpses of the lifestyles are conspicuously absent from their textbooks. As Jean Grambs states, "The school demands of children that they deny what their own sense experiences tell them and accept instead the school's version of reality."[22] It is almost as if many schools are afraid to deal with real life problems and prefer to whitewash them. The school must not only acknowledge reality in the curriculum, but also must help the student to interpret it and his relationship to it. Merely to expose the child to the harshness of reality without equipping him to interpret it is potentially harmful. But if children are to relate to the curriculum, they must perceive it as real and personally meaningful instead of artificial and unrelated to their experience.

[22] Jean Grambs, *Schools, Scholars, and Society* (Englewood Cliffs, N.J.: Prentice-Hall, 1965), p. 80.

Sixth, *a curriculum must give equal emphasis to affective and cognitive content.* For years the school's role has been primarily to dispense knowledge, packaged according to subject matter. If you ask a high-school instructor what he does for a living, he is likely to reply, "I'm an English (social studies, science, French) teacher." Accordingly, we tend to view the role of the teacher in terms of the subject matter dispensed. Questions such as "Why do I feel the way I do?" "What do others think of me?" "Do I care?" "Why do I want to do that?" "Who am I?" and "What can I do about things I don't like?" are legitimate in a curriculum concerned with the whole child. But rarely has the curriculum formally recognized the importance of the learner's feelings, concerns, or fears. Yet there is considerable psychological evidence that unless feelings are acknowledged they may impede learning.

We would argue, however, that an affective curriculum is legitimate in its own right, irrespective of its tie to cognitions. Unless a person has learned to recognize his fears, wants, anxieties, concerns, needs, and pleasures, and has either accepted them or learned to cope with them, he will be incomplete as a human being. One of the major reasons for the current popularity of the "human potential" movement is that our schools have virtually ignored this area of life. As a result, many college students and adults are attempting to compensate for a need that should have been fulfilled many years earlier.

Needed: a survival curriculum

In a paper entitled "Education for Survival,"[23] philosophy professor Michael Scriven submits that our educational system is severely mismatched with our current needs. Education today prepares the child to survive in society *as long as it remains stable,* and even this it accomplishes rather inefficiently. Students, he argues, must be educated to create and adjust to revolutionary change. "The survival of a society whose citizens are not *directly* educated to instigate and handle radical change, and in particular a society whose citizens are educated in a way that depends on the absence of radical change, is simply a temporary accident of evolution."[24] Since the one thing that we can be sure of is change, the intermediate aims of Scriven's survival curriculum are to create in people the capacities to a) produce, and b) rationally evaluate and relate to socially and intellectually revolutionary *suggestions, candidates, threats,* and *actions.*

The curriculum of any high school can be examined to determine whether it is educating students for survival. Scriven asserts that students should derive from the curriculum a general familiarity with the arguments for and against abortion, censorship, incest taboos, the graduated income tax, dependents' exemptions, contraception, the Fifth Amendment, local control of schools, liberal education, police review boards, pacifism, charity, states' rights, the United Nations, the need for police, euthanasia, nationalization of foreign-owned industry, jury trials, excise taxes, war, automation, unionism, *de facto* school segregation, sumptuary laws (especially those regulating the use of drugs, alcohol, and nicotine), equal time rules for TV, "mental illness," violent revolution, monasticism, legalized prostitution, a guaranteed income, the death penalty, segregated private clubs,

[23] Michael Scriven, "Education for Survival" (paper prepared for the Ideal School Conference Series, Elk Grove Training and Development Center, April 9, 1968). Reproduced in *Kaleidoscope: Readings in Education,* the companion book to this text.
[24] Scriven, p. 2.

premarital chastity, egocentric hedonism, suicide, subsidized art, environmental contamination and conservation, compulsory schooling, voting, labor arbitration, blood tests, and military service. How many of these topics received attention when you were in high school?

Each of these topics impinges on several academic disciplines, but Scriven argues against spending a single moment of class time studying disciplines for their own sake. This he considers an academic luxury. "[Although] some points from game-theory, welfare economics, and functional anthropology need to be made and discussed in explaining the role of an ethical system, it is mere professional conceit to suppose they cannot be appreciated without a *course* in each subject."[25] What is needed is to extract relevant concepts and data from many subjects. "Education is giving us cake today when we need bread."[26]

Scriven defines the Survival Curriculum in terms of three areas of learning: *knowledge, skills,* and *motivation.* The *knowledge* necessary to survival has several sources. We need, first, knowledge of man as an individual, including information on sex, drugs, insanity, neuroses, birth defects, and diseases.

We need basic familiarity with the nonhuman world, including information on food production potentialities, radioactive and industrial waste contamination, the magnitude of the pest and parasite problem in food production and storage, the size of our coal and oil reserves, the knowledge explosion and the data storage problem it creates. Scriven urges that we structure the curriculum around real problems, introducing theoretical concepts whenever necessary, rather than starting with academic fundamentals and working gradually toward practical application.

Survival education also requires knowledge of the government, economics, anthropology, and sociology of major current and past cultures and of deviant civilizations. This area of the Survival Curriculum would emphasize the problems, failures, and mistakes, as well as the achievements, of our culture. Theories of the nature and foundations of government, law, economics, and ethics would be studied, not at an academic level of abstraction but for awareness of the practical and easily comprehensible issues involved.

[25] Scriven, p. 16.
[26] Scriven, p. 17.

© 1970 United Feature Syndicate, Inc.

What is taught?

The Survival Curriculum would enhance sensitivity without making value judgments. "Instead of legislating the course of aesthetic education, for example, education should modify itself to develop the appreciations that children naturally discover. The high school and college male finds cars and girls beautiful, *Mad* funny, rock music, science-fiction and some television serials exciting—a marvelous basis for providing the facts and contrasts that refine such appreciations and increase the enjoyment they produce."[27]

Scriven lists the following cognitive and social skills as necessary to the curriculum:

1   the super-Rs: speed reading, shorthand/typing, calculating/programming, memory training
2   analytical reasoning
3   interpretive skills
4   scientific method
5   people study
6   skills of appreciation: art appreciation, sensory awareness training courses

The *motivational* aspect of the Survival Curriculum is designed to reinforce motives that Scriven believes necessary to survival. These include physical motives such as the desire to exercise, cognitive motives such as the desire to solve problems, and moral motives such as the desire to help others.

Proposals such as Scriven's make sense to the authors. The world is changing at a fantastic rate—physically, psychologically, and socially. Because the discipline approach fails to meet the needs and concerns of students in specific and of society in general, and because the transfer of knowledge from study to the solution of real problems is not made explicit, we submit that the discipline approach is no longer fruitful. The curriculum of the public schools cannot continue to deal with reality obliquely. It must concern itself directly with mankind's problems. It *is* a matter of survival.

Epilogue

Though the public-school curriculum is never entirely static, most changes are of a low order of magnitude. The subject-matter approach introduced in the nineteenth century to teach science, mathematics, English, or language arts, history, and foreign languages is still intact. We have obviously argued in this chapter that the discipline approach to the curriculum is outmoded. Though the content itself is not necessarily obsolete, studying subjects separately, unrelated to the pupils' lives and interests or to mankind's problems, is an organizational arrangement subject to charges of "irrelevancy."

An even more serious issue is the schools' responsibility to contribute to man's ability to survive. How are the schools educating students to eliminate air pollution, purify polluted waters, control the population explosion, increase food production without the use of harmful pesticides, or dispose of our waste products without fouling our environment? Most don't even acknowledge that such problems exist! Lest you think we exaggerate, let us quote from Dr. Paul Ehrlich, author of *The Population Bomb,* and a professor of biology at Stanford University

[27] Scriven, p. 29.

Many of the creatures of the earth have seniority over us. They made it this far by remaining compatible with their environment, by adapting and adjusting to the natural circumstances of their existence. There are many species that have vanished because they could not adapt. It's not at all inconceivable that man will follow these creatures into extinction. If he continues to reproduce at the present soaring rate, continues to tamper with the biosphere, continues to toy around with apocalyptic weapons, he will probably share the fate of the dinosaur. If he learns to adapt to the finitude of the planet, to the changed character of his existence, he may survive. If not, nothing like him is likely to evolve ever again. The world will be inherited by a creature more adaptable and tenacious than he.[28]

Who is that creature? The cockroach.

In the face of the potential holocaust predicted by Ehrlich and many other frightened scientists, it is almost inconceivable that our public schools can continue to teach mathematics and science and social studies without relating them to the real problems of the human race.

The children of today cannot afford to grow up ignorant of these problems and unequipped to cope with them, but well versed in quadratic equations and the problems of the Jamestown colony in 1607. It is time that our teachers began educating students to face the issues of today rather than yesterday. The world has changed. We must rid ourselves of our own saber-tooth curriculum.

Discussion questions

1 Which of the five motives identified by Gwynn and Chase as influencing curriculum development since 1635 do you think are still operative? What evidence can you marshal to support your views?
2 How well do you think the public schools are increasing the survival chances of Americans? What parallels, if any, do you see between the Saber-Tooth Curriculum and the curriculum you were offered in high school? With which of the two basic philosophical stands summarized on page 252 are you most in sympathy? What evidence can you muster to support your position?
3 "To the extent that we allow the school curriculum to be dominated by the disciplines, we deny students the opportunity to become more than superficially acquainted with profound public problems" (page 254). If you do not agree with our assessment of the relevance of current curricula (and many people do not), what arguments can you advance to support your view? If you agree, what arguments can you add?
4 Should a teacher be allowed to teach a curriculum of her own design? Where does professional autonomy and the teacher's freedom of choice come in? What should be its limits?
5 Do you believe every discipline has an inherent structure? What might be a convincing argument against this view?
6 How do you react to Scriven's Survival Curriculum? Do you agree with his basic premises? Would you like to teach such a curriculum? If you were to teach such a curriculum, how would you prepare yourself to be competent in the areas he suggests?

[28] Interview with Dr. Paul Ehrlich, *Playboy* 17 (August 1970): 154.

What is taught?

For further reading

- Birnbaum, Norman. "The Arbitrary Disciplines." *Change* 1 (July–August 1969): 10–21. This article raises some fundamental questions regarding the arbitrariness of the scholarly disciplines. Birnbaum asserts that recent changes in society necessitate the creation of new systems for codifying knowledge.
- Bruner, Jerome. *The Process of Education.* New York: Random House, 1960. In this influential volume, Bruner advocates studying the structure of each discipline in order to develop learners with a true understanding of the discipline. Many of the concepts explicated in this volume undergirded the curriculum reform movement of the late 1950s and early 1960s.
- Divoky, Diane. "Art Is a Many Splendored Thing." *Learning* 2 (December 1973): 10–16. Describes the efforts of a number of organizations to give children exposure to musicians, painters, and poets in classroom contexts. The article also lists some resources for the individual teacher interested in moving ahead on her own arts program.
- Eisner, Elliot W., ed. *Confronting Curriculum Reform.* Boston: Little, Brown, 1971. An excellent series of articles by major thinkers in curriculum development regarding issues to be faced in curriculum reform.
- Fantini, Mario, and Weinstein, Gerald. *The Disadvantaged: Challenge to Education.* New York: Harper & Row, 1968. While focusing on the disadvantaged, this book addresses the education of all children by re-examining and re-evaluating traditional modes of education, and proposing the beginnings of a new, more adequate process of education. Current educational processes are described, analyzed, and diagnosed with respect to the cultural norms of several subcultures. Both theoretical and practical.
- Glennon, Vincent J. "Current Status of the New Math." *Educational Leadership,* 30 (April 1973): 604–608. A brief review of the major thrusts of the "new" math of the 1950s–1960s and some projections about where mathematics instruction will be going in the future.
- Goodlad, John. *The Changing School Curriculum.* New York: Fund for the Advancement of Education, 1966. An easy-to-read account of the major curriculum development projects of the fifties and sixties and their outstanding characteristics.
- Gwynn, Minor J., and Chase, John. *Curriculum Principles and Social Trends,* 4th ed. New York: Macmillan, 1969. A major curriculum source book which treats the history of curriculum development in both elementary and secondary schools, as well as major influences in curriculum development. The modern curriculum movement of the sixties, influences on curriculum change, and models for curriculum revision are discussed.
- Haven, Elizabeth W., *et al.* "High School Curriculum Survey." *School and Society* 98 (April 1970): 239–254. A report by the Educational Testing Service which attempted to assess the impact of the major curriculum projects on the public schools. A brief but very enlightening survey of what is actually being taught in the public schools.
- Hayn, Gerald A. "High School Language Instruction in the 1970's." *Hispania* 56 (March 1973): 94–99. Identifies the weaknesses of the audiolingual approach employed in the 1960s and predicts what foreign language instruction will be like during the 1970s.
- Hicks, William Vernon; Houston, W. Robert; Cheney, Bruce; and Marquard, Richard. *The New Elementary School Curriculum.* Princeton: D. Van Nostrand, 1970. A description of the major curriculum areas currently being taught in the elementary schools.

- Jarolimek, John. "In Pursuit of the Elusive New Social Studies." *Educational Leadership* 30 (April 1973): 596–599. A brief review of the contributions the new social studies projects have made and some speculations on the major concerns of social studies in the 1970s.
- Peddiwell, J. Abner [Harold Benjamin]. *The Saber-Tooth Curriculum.* New York: McGraw-Hill, 1939. A satirical spoof on the origins of schools, the inadequacies of the curriculum, and the reluctance of educators to keep the curriculum relevant to societal needs. Humorous and entertaining reading.
- Rutledge, James A. "What Has Happened to the 'New' Science Curricula?" *Educational Leadership* 30 (April 1973): 600–603. A current review of the impact the "new" science curricula have had on science teaching in the schools.
- Saylor, J. Galen, and Alexander, William M. *Curriculum Planning for Modern Schools.* New York: Holt, Rinehart & Winston, 1966. Attempts to analyze the process of curriculum planning, to define the basic elements that should constitute the determinants of an educational program, and to describe the principles and procedures that should guide curriculum change.
- *Social Education* 36 (November 1972). The entire issue is devoted to an analysis of twenty-six social studies projects, including rationale and objectives, content, methodology, and conditions for implementation for each of the projects.
- Tyler, Ralph W. *Basic Principles of Curriculum and Instruction.* Chicago: University of Chicago Press, 1950. This little booklet is the classic rationale for curriculum development. Tyler stresses the need to use several data sources, including the learners' needs, in order to develop an adequate curriculum. Although developed in the fifties, Tyler's principles for curriculum development are still held to be valid.
- Van Til, William, ed. *Curriculum: Quest for Relevance.* 2nd ed. Boston: Houghton Mifflin, 1974. Focuses on curriculum development for the 1970s. Contains a series of widely diversified positions, including the entire contents of an issue of the *Phi Delta Kappan* (March 1970) edited by Dr. Van Til and devoted to elementary- and secondary-school curriculum.

Films

- *Another Way to Learn* (EDC, b&w, 12 min., 1969). This film documents an early attempt to introduce the English "integrated day" in an American primary classroom. It was filmed in a Wellesley, Mass., first grade, and the materials in use were drawn from the Elementary Science Study (ESS) program.
- *Build Yourself a City* (Philadelphia Board of Education, 16mm, b&w, 15 min., 1967). The Philadelphia Cooperative Schools Program was a six-week summer project in which 100 junior and senior high-school students, representing diverse educational backgrounds, contributed their own points of view to the study of communications, urban affairs, and drama. This film documents the urban affairs course, which "presented an alternative to crises becoming the form of change." The narration is from three perspectives: that of a curriculum developer, a social studies teacher, and a city resident who helped to teach the course.
- *Classrooms in Transition* (EDC, b&w, 31 min., 1969). This film is an overview of the change in classroom appearance and function when ESS materials were introduced into the Cardozo Model School District, Washington, D.C. It surveys classrooms from preschool through junior high school, and the sound track includes commentary by teachers and the ESS staff.
- *Eastern District High School Students View the World* (The Moving Image, 16mm [kinescope made from a television program], b&w). Several students appear

What is taught?

with their film teacher, Linda Bastian, to discuss the way films are made in their school. The films shown cover many different themes and use various film techniques.

- *Hello Darwin* (University-at-Large, 16mm, color, 48 min.). A fifth-grade Boston public-school class studies Darwin's theories of evolution by means of *Man: A Course of Study*. The film attempts to show what Bruner means by "Education is a process, not a product."
- *Hi, School!* (IDEA, color, 28 min., 1970). Consciously designed to counter the "negative reports" on American high schools, this film examines the concept of the relevant curriculum whereby a traditional high school becomes a "learning headquarters" for community involvement by students. Settings vary from a mini-course in television production to an apprenticeship in skeletal reconstruction at a museum of natural history.
- *Instructional Development* (Indiana University, b&w, 17 min., 1971). Instructional development is a systematic approach to instruction based on decisions about the learner, learning, evaluation, and the learning environment. Sub-tasks are identified and sequenced, standards are devised, and the environment is structured. In this film teaching of music and tennis are treated as examples.
- *It's Between the Lines: Drama for the Classroom* (Philadelphia Board of Education, 16mm, b&w, 15 min., 1967). This film also documents a portion of the 1967 Philadelphia Cooperative Schools Program: a course in which both improvisational and formal drama are explored with students of middle-school age.
- *The Kindergarten Child, Part II* (Massachusetts Department of Education, 16mm, b&w, 48 min., 1968–70). This series of short episodes ("Did you forget I'm five?") presents various teaching methods, materials, and curricula which can be used effectively in the kindergarten classroom.
- *Making Sense: Inside and Out There* (Philadelphia Board of Education, 16mm, b&w, 10 min., 1967). This film is also about the 1967 Philadelphia Cooperative Schools Program. It shows how the communications course combined a multimedia approach with a series of metaphors to teach basic communications skills and understanding.
- *My Name Is Children* (NET, b&w, 60 min., 1967). Using scenes of children and teachers in the Nova Elementary School in Fort Lauderdale, this film depicts the inquiry approach to motivating students. Children are shown in small groups and in individual work, while teachers coordinate their plans and discuss individual student problems at daily meetings.
- *Objects and Activities in Learning* (Indiana University, b&w, 29 min., 1969). In the Cincinnati Public Schools, real objects and activities are used to give learning a concrete basis. This film emphasizes the use of tangible objects both in early education and in high-school courses.
- *A Time for Learning* (University-at-Large, color, 38 min., 1969). Jerome Bruner and colleagues discuss their innovative fifth-grade social studies curriculum. The film intercuts this discussion with footage of actual classroom interaction and presents Bruner analyzing examples of classroom experience with the program.
- *What's New at School?* (Carousel and CBS, b&w, 45 min., 1972). The first half of this CBS News documentary examines a traditional New York State elementary school that makes children restless, apathetic, resentful, and unsuccessful. This is contrasted with an "open" classroom in North Dakota where sixth-graders are encouraged to develop according to their own interests and needs. Informality, a variety of resources, and self-reliance are stressed in place of teacher

direction and the search for the "right" answer. An incisive narration and better than average color photography of actual classrooms make this an effective, although overly generalized, film.

- *With Such As These* (Center for Curriculum Design, b&w, 18 min., 1972). This film presents insights into the negative feelings many students derive from dehumanizing classroom practices. It is an interesting example of dramatized attitudes if used in conjunction with some of the documentary materials available on classroom techniques.

Videotape

- *System of Teaching Reading by Color Coding Words* (Electric Eye, ½" videotape, several hours). This tape, produced by a group whose motto is "Tell a vision, not sell a vision," presents the work of Dr. Caleb Gattegno at San Jose State.

Audiotapes

- *The Curriculum* (National Education Association, 57 min., 1971). This audiotape is divided into seven short sections, each designed to serve as the basis for a discussion session. Three sections discuss the Philadelphia Parkway Program, and another concerns a suburban experiment in free-form education. The tapes are intended to lay out options for education change in the 1970s.
- *Jonathan Kozol: Political Indoctrination in the Public Schools* (Pacifica, 73 min., 1973). Through a very personal account of his own career and vivid examples of inhuman teaching, Mr. Kozol explains why he feels that our educational system is essentially worthless. Fired from one system for "curriculum deviation," and hired ten days later at another school for "curriculum development," Kozol has seen many aspects of the misuse of the curriculum.
- *The Parkway Program: The Curriculum* (National Education Association, 7" reel, 3.75 ips, 8:40 min.) This sound segment is part of a longer tape on *The Curriculum,* intended to serve as a discussion starter. Demonstrates how the entire Philadelphia community has become the school's campus.
- *What Did You Learn in School Today?* (Pacifica, 30 min., 1969). Several fifth- and sixth-graders were interviewed in New York City schools about what they were learning by WBAI radio station. The questions covered such topics as China, George Washington, and slavery. Some good insights into children's views on controversial subjects, but the tape's main value is to illustrate how early political and social issues enter children's minds.

Multimedia

- *Designing Effective Instruction* (General Programmed Teaching, workshop kit, 1973). This kit of workshop materials provides the basis for a seminar on the planning of effective instruction. It emphasizes behavioral objectives, validation, and the practicing and perfecting of specific skills. Designed especially for group use, the workshop kit includes fifteen audiotapes and twelve color filmstrips as well as workbooks.

Refer to Appendix for addresses of distributors.

The real world

8 How are schools governed and controlled?

Very few beginning teachers are concerned about issues related to school governance and control. The topic seems remote to them; it is something administrators and teacher organization representatives care about but is not particularly vital for beginning teachers concerned with learning how to survive. We feel differently; we believe that beginning teachers must have some understanding of the way schools and school systems operate since they will be affected personally by control and governance decisions. If you do not understand how these decisions are made and how they might affect you as a classroom teacher, your effectiveness as a professional will certainly be diminished.

Chapter contents

How governance differs from control
Who legally governs public education?
The state board of education
The local school district
Who actually controls American public education?
Professional educators
Informal group power
Parents and teachers
Control by business
Control by the federal government

How do you explain the fact that:

- your favorite high-school teacher was not given tenure?
- superintendents have a job expectancy of no more than three years?
- the black studies curricula which everyone was talking about a couple of years ago never got off the ground?
- in some schools teachers are expected to police bathrooms and lunch yards?
- two years after the new elementary school opened it needed major repairs?
- the last school bond issue in your town was decisively defeated?
- a textbook with a fresh approach to some aspects of "the system" was removed from circulation after a year, even though the teachers favored its use?
- your high-school student newspaper was heavily censored?
- purchasing or construction contracts don't always go to the lowest bidder or the most qualified firm?
- in many school districts teachers have little or no voice in the selection of textbooks or supplementary materials?

How do you explain the school's image of resistance to change?

It is quite likely that at least one of these questions applies to your local school district; their answers all reflect the disparity between governance and real control of the public schools. The purpose of this chapter is to explore how schools

270 The real world

are officially organized and governed and how they are actually controlled. While there is a legal authority for the schools and an organization established to exercise this authority, the school system is controlled in large part by informal forces which do not appear on any organizational chart. We will first examine the legal governing authority that exists in most school districts, and then discuss the influence of informal groups.

We have tried to draw from literature and experience to describe how things really are, not how they're supposed to be. The result will, we hope, give you insight into school control which will help you be a better professional teacher.

How governance differs from control

How is controlling different from governing? The right to govern is delegated legally, but domination or command that results in "control" of people or of a situation is not necessarily officially sanctioned. Often, however, the governing person or group also exercises control, as in the case of a strong president or a king whose powers are not constitutionally restricted. In other instances, those who govern exercise little real control, as in the case of a figurehead king who is manipulated by someone else behind the scenes.[1] Such situations have occurred from time to time in monarchies when young boys have succeeded to the throne and the real power and control have been wielded by advisors and guardians. Between these two extremes is the situation in which those who legally govern share power with persons or groups possessing no legal authority. This state of affairs is prevalent in public education. Considerable control over the operation of our schools is exercised by persons without legal authority, largely through personal connections and the exertion of pressure on legal officeholders.

The experience of a group of women PTA leaders who decided to collect money for UNICEF illustrates the workings of the system.[2] The women prepared and submitted what they thought was a routine permit request to the city council. To their amazement, the council refused the permit. Outraged, the PTA group made plans to attend the next council meeting *en masse*. At this point some interesting developments began. In the words of one of the leaders:

I received a call from a lady down at the city offices and she said, "I hear you are getting up a group." I replied that we sure were, following which she asked, "Just what do you want, a permit or a public display?" I said, we want a permit, of course. Then she said for me to call three persons in town and tell them what we wanted. I called the three persons and we had a permit the next day.[3]

[1] This situation reminds us of the governing husband who insisted that he made all the big decisions in his family while his wife made the small ones. He decided what the nation should do about the energy crisis, inflation, and foreign policy, while his wife made the decisions concerning their family budget, where they lived, and where he worked.

[2] This example is cited by Ralph B. Kimbrough, "An Informal Arrangement for Influence Over Basic Policy," in *Governing Education: A Reader on Politics, Power, and Public School Policy,* ed. Alan Rosenthal (New York: Doubleday, 1969), p. 111

[3] *Ibid.*

The next time members of this PTA want something done at the city council, they will undoubtedly work through the same informal channels that secured their permit so effortlessly. They have learned that the legally elected city council is influenced and controlled by unofficial outside forces.

Another example of extralegal control might be the teacher who is a life-long community resident and has taught at least two generations of townspeople. If she disagrees with a position taken by the new principal, who has come from another state, she might command more influence outside the school than he could. Thus, even though he legally governs, she exercises more real control.

Who legally governs public education?

In most countries, the public schools are a branch of the central government, federally financed and administered and highly uniform in curricula and procedures. In the United States, however, responsibility for the public schools has evolved as a state function. Each of the fifty states has legal responsibility for the operation and administration of public schools within its own boundaries. In most aspects of public education (we will discuss certain exceptions later) the authority of federal, county, and city education agencies is subject to the will of the state authorities.

♩ Horace Mann (1796–1859)

Horace Mann was the radical educational reformer of his day. Though trained as a lawyer, he became eminently successful as an educator and politician. Asked why he had exchanged the practice of law for education, he answered that "the interests of a client are small compared with the interests of the next generation."

Born in Franklin, Massachusetts, not long after the Revolutionary War, Mann received only the most rudimentary schooling until he was fifteen. Most of his education was self-acquired, a circumstance that profoundly influenced his philosophy of education. He studied diligently in order to be admitted to Brown University, where he became a brilliant student. In 1827, Mann was elected to the Massachusetts House of Representatives, and a luminous political career lay ahead of him, but he became committed, instead, to education and to the use of political methods to bring about educational reform.

Mann made it his aim to abolish the cruel floggings that were then routine in the public schools. Schoolmasters believed it their duty to drive the devil out of their students, and many schools administered from ten to twenty floggings a day. Most school-keepers believed flogging to be an aid to learning. Not only were students treated cruelly; attendance at school was itself a punishment. Schools were often little better than hovels: the lighting was poor and many buildings were unsanitary and unsafe. Mann criticized corporal punishment and inadequate facilities in public speeches, lectures, and letters, and lobbied for reform in the state legislature and in Congress. He was not always well received. Once, when he and the Governor of Massachusetts were to address an audience, they arrived to find the hall dark and its floors unswept. Mann promptly took off his coat, lit the lamps, and took to the hall with a broom.

Horace Mann saw education as a tool of liberation by which the poor could raise themselves, blacks could become emancipated, and handicapped children could adjust to their disabilities. After all, Mann reasoned, education had brought him fame and position. It was over 100 years ago, then, that the idea of social mobility through education was born in America.

In order for education to be as powerful a force as he envisioned it, Mann thought it imperative to lengthen the school term and to raise teachers' salaries. To make learning more relevant and enjoyable, he helped introduce new textbooks designed to illustrate the relationship between knowledge and the practical problems of society. Mann organized libraries in many schools, making books readily available to students. He believed less in the formal curriculum than in individual learning—undoubtedly because of his own self-education.

Mann was responsible for the establishment of the Massachusetts Board of Education, and for the founding in 1839 of the first normal school, in Lexington, Massachusetts. Although it opened with only three students, the concept spread and was widely imitated throughout the country. Mann was intensely interested in teacher training, and believed that teachers should be intellectual, moral, and cultural models for their communities.

Many of Mann's ideas were controversial, but he was most violently denounced for his position on religion in the schools. Though a religious man, he believed that religious training belonged outside the schools, which should be run by the state. As a result of his views, Mann was attacked from many Boston pulpits.

Mann did not limit his reformist zeal to educational issues. When he was elected to Congress in 1849, he denounced slavery and attacked the industrial system, urging that workers be better paid, child labor be abolished, factories be made safer, and slums eliminated. No educator, he said, could remain neutral about social injustice. Theories and ideals must be put into practice in society; otherwise, he argued, education is mere empty words.

Mann was regarded as a dreamer and a visionary by many of his colleagues. When he took over the presidency of Antioch College in 1852, opened its doors to all races and religious sects, and admitted women on an equal basis with men, some educators predicted that these measures would promote the collapse of higher education. Mann aroused further annoyance by remarking that many Antioch students were more brilliant than their professors. Were he alive today, Mann might still be fighting for ideas he espoused more than a century ago. Many people have not accepted them yet.

How are schools governed and controlled?

Although legal responsibility for school governance belongs to the state, policy decisions and administration are ordinarily delegated to local boards of education, which exist because Americans have come to insist on control of schools at the local level. However, the state does not relinquish all its responsibilities, and retains the power to revoke or countermand decisions made by the local units. One result of this delegation of authority to local units is that the efficiency and achievements of school systems vary widely across the nation, and even within individual states.

The state board of education

The state's legal responsibility for public education requires it to establish an organizational framework within which the local units can function. The result is the establishment of state boards of education to exercise general control and supervision of schools within the state. It is the state's policy-making body.

The chief state school officer

The executive officer of the state board of education—whose title may be, depending on the state, "chief state school officer," "superintendent of education," "commissioner of education," "secretary of the state board of education," or others—generally has responsibility for teacher and administrator certification, organization of the program of studies, curriculum revision, application of the state finance law, approval of school sites and buildings, collection of statistical data, and direct supervision of elementary and secondary educational programs. He exercises little direct administrative authority over local educational officers, but his indirect influence is widely felt on the local level. In some states he is elected by the voters, while in others he is appointed by the state board of education.

The local school district

To facilitate local control of education, the state creates local school districts for the purpose of carrying out the educational program in conformity with state educational policy. The school district is thus a unit of the state government and is usually distinct from the local municipal government.

The school board

The policy-making body of the school district is the local school board of education, which represents the citizens of the district in setting up a school program, hiring school personnel to operate the schools, determining organizational and administrative policy, and evaluating the results of the program and the performance of personnel. Although school board members are elected by the citizens of the local district, they are state officers and not, as many people think, simply local representatives. Thus board members must operate the schools in conformity with the guidelines and policies established by the state board of education, and not on a strictly local perspective.

The superintendent of schools

The superintendent, who is selected by the local school board to act as its executive officer and as the educational leader and administrator of the school district, is undeniably the most powerful officer in the local school organization. Theoretically, the superintendent's role is administrative and executive—he keeps the schools functioning—while the board of education retains legislative and policy-making responsibilities. In practice, however, the superintendent has become the major policy maker in the public schools. Consider the following description of his powers:

. . . the administrator is in a position either to promote broad participation in decision-making and creativity on the part of individuals in the organization or to

run a tight ship and discourage the efforts of any of the participants to rock the boat. The administrator does more than set the climate for the participants of the organization. He establishes certain goals; he allocates resources; he develops the criteria for the selection of personnel; he is the bridge between the organization and the broader society from which he derives the resources with which it has to operate. He controls the use of sanctions, both positive and negative, within the organization, and by his use of them, he establishes the determinants for the behavior of subordinates.[4]

Who actually controls American public education?

There is no easy answer to this question. It is like asking who controls America. The President does — but so does Congress. The Supreme Court does — but so do the local police. The giant corporations do — but so does a small but influential group of political activists. Similarly, the formal, legally constituted bodies control or influence certain aspects of public education as a consequence of the authority invested in them. The federal government exerts influence on public education through the passage and enforcement of legislation. Professional educators, including superintendents, principals, university professors, and leaders of organizations, possess a major portion of the control and decision-making power over public education by virtue of the offices they hold and the organizations to which they belong. These professional organizations, though they lack legal authority, have considerable influence.

It is not the intention of this chapter to examine the authority and power possessed by each of these groups that enable them to control certain aspects of public education. However, a brief look at the roles of the professional educator, informal group power, and the federal government yields some fascinating insights into how decisions about public education are actually made.

Professional educators

One observer of American education, James D. Koerner, has charged that important decisions in education emerge from a "labyrinthine structure of forces and countervailing forces, but that the interests of professional educators tend to be dominant."[5] When Koerner refers to "professional educators," he does not, unfortunately, mean classroom teachers. He is speaking of several organizations he considers to have disproportionate influence on the administration of the schools — the National Education Association (particularly its administrative branches), state departments of education, departments and schools of education in colleges and universities, educational accrediting organizations, and other groups such as school administrators. A more detailed discussion of the NEA and the American Federation of Teachers follows in Chapter Nine.

Koerner argues that the people most directly involved — classroom teachers, parents and other laymen, and academic specialists in departments other than education — have for too long been dominated by the professional education "fraternity." For instance, the state board of education is entitled to do nearly anything it chooses, within the limit of the law, affecting education in the state. However, Koerner asserts, it rarely governs in any but the most general way. The

---

[4] Keith Goldhammer, *et al., Issues and Problems in Contemporary Educational Administration* (Eugene: University of Oregon Center for the Advanced Study of Educational Administration, 1967), pp. 3–4.
[5] James D. Koerner, *Who Controls American Education?* (Boston: Beacon Press, 1968), p. 155.

How are schools governed and controlled?

Would you believe that each of these incidents actually happened?

- *A local builder took ten minutes of a board meeting to present a proposal that local residents build the three million dollar high school with their own labors—"the old church raising type of idea."*
- *Hundreds of residents claimed vociferously that a two-story school building was cheaper than a one-story building, despite public testimony to the contrary by architects, and evidence from studies made by building experts throughout the nation.*
- *The editor of a local newspaper editorialized for months in opposition to home economics before he discovered that it was required by State law. It was the superintendent who finally told him.*
- *A local builder attacked the school board for securing property at exorbitant prices, and had to be informed in detail about the requirements of terrain for school buildings, and of the real estate practice of marking-up the property which was being considered by the board.*
- *Several residents confessed that they did not know what a bond issue was, although a community-wide campaign had been conducted for a number of weeks, which included daily coverage on the front pages of most local papers.*
- *A woman threatened to go straight to the* board of education *if she could not get satisfaction from the* school board. Norman D. Kerr

board of education usually allows the state department of education to make policy, or yields its power to local school authorities. State departments of education and the superintendencies of local school districts are staffed by professional educators, and as a result the influence and power wielded by this group is much greater than Koerner believes it should be.

Looking at the local scene, Koerner argues that the power of local school boards is greatly overestimated, and that local control is largely a myth. He attributes the school board's weakness to three sources: its preoccupation with housekeeping details, its failure to assert authority, and external controls forced on it by other bodies. The board's preoccupation with trivia instead of policy making and its failure to assert its authority is seen by Koerner as the result of the superintendent's increased power. Although in theory the superintendent is the servant of the board, in recent years he has increasingly become its leader.[6] Because local school boards often lack adequate staff to do their own research, they must rely on professional educators (primarily the superintendent and his staff) for such services. As a result the superintendent has become the major policy maker in the public schools.

In many school districts, for example, the school board agenda is prepared by the superintendent, with occasional suggestions from the board members. Matters relevant to the educational program are often conspicuously absent from the agenda. When someone remarked that the school board in one particular district seemed to devote very little time to education, the superintendent replied,

[6] Roscoe C. Martin, "School Government," in Rosenthal, *Governing Education,* p. 279.

The real world

"They don't know anything about it; but the things they know they talk about, like sidewalks, sites, and so forth. I let them go on sometimes because I don't want them to talk about curriculum."[7]

The outside controls exerted on the local board are numerous and strong. Koerner cites a hypothetical example of a board that wishes to make changes in the vocational training curriculum. Realizing that vocational training no longer serves the needs of the students, the board decides to cut back on its programs. This is, theoretically, one of the local school board's sovereign rights, but a number of events are likely to occur to change the board's mind. First, the vocational education lobby might exert pressure on other members of the local government and on the state legislature or state department of education to protect the interests of vocational education teachers. Second, the regional accrediting association might come to the aid of the status quo, threatening possible disaccreditation of the schools involved if the board does not rescind its decision.[8] Third, the National Education Association state affiliate might "investigate," and through its power "persuade," the board to a different view. Does the board, then, in fact have the power to control the curriculum?

It should be noted that Koerner's views are but one interpretation of how school systems and education in general are controlled. There are many in education who do not support his view that education is overly dominated by the professional education "fraternity," or that the superintendent is so all-powerful. In fact, the high turnover of superintendents may be indicative that school boards are more influential than Koerner gives them credit for being.

Koerner's hypothetical example illustrates how various educational groups and associations protect vested interests in the continuation of, or opposition to, certain programs or practices, and can exert pressure on the legally constituted body responsible for making such decisions. It is appropriate at this point to discuss the role of superintendent, since he is quite often the direct recipient of these pressures.

Informal group power
Outside pressures on the superintendent

In a 1965 study sponsored by the New York Board of Regents, Ralph B. Kimbrough interviewed a large number of school board members and superintendents in the state of New York. Among other questions, he asked: "In actual practice, whose views carry the greatest weight in the important decisions in each of these areas (such as the curriculum and staff selection)?" The responses indicated that the superintendent was allowed to make all such decisions.[9]

The superintendent thus has almost complete control over the internal operations of the school district, an area in which the informal power structure takes little interest. However, Kimbrough's findings indicate that decisions pertaining to

---

[7] Norman D. Kerr, "The School Board as an Agency of Legitimation," in Rosenthal, *Governing Education,* p. 159.
[8] While accreditation does not bring distinction to a school, the lack of it is a stigma. Its graduates will have trouble gaining entrance to certain colleges and universities, and teacher organizations may discourage their members from teaching there.
[9] *School Boards and School Board Membership; Report of the New York State Regents Advisory Committee on Educational Leadership,* 1965, pp. 58–59, as cited in Koerner, *Who Controls American Education?,* p. 141.

How are schools governed and controlled?

Are school boards representative?

In a nationwide survey conducted by Girard D. Hottleman, director of educational services for *The Massachusetts Teacher,* it was verified that school boards are not representative of the public in terms of many characteristics.

"American schools whose constituencies are primarily the poor," Hottleman says, "are governed primarily by upper-middle-class, propertied, moneyed, white, middle-aged Republican men. . . . If we assume that school board members pursue the ordinary amount of self-interest behavior, then the actions of typical school board members are not apt to be harmonious with the needs of public school children." Some of the survey's findings:

- *51.2 per cent of the general population are women; 20 per cent of school board members are women*
- *37 per cent of registered voters in the communities surveyed are Republican; 63 per cent of school board members are Republican*
- *The average income in communities surveyed is $11,694; the income of board members is $22,682*

Reported in the *Saturday Review of Education* 1 (April 1973): 51.

economics, which might have great impact on the community, are not made by the superintendent but by the informal power structure in the community.

The superintendent is subjected to pressure by a number of different groups and individuals, which impinges on his decision-making power. Table 8.1 identifies the pressures to which superintendents and school board members say they are exposed and the percentage of superintendents and school board members who report being subjected to each form of pressure. Table 8.2 identifies the various interest groups that superintendents and school board members think are responsible for attempts to pressure them.[10] As might be expected, parents and PTAs are the most frequent source of pressure on superintendents and school board members. As you examine both tables, think about these questions: Who applies what pressures? Who wants more money for the schools? Who wants less? Are politicians more interested in getting their friends hired or in reducing the tax rate? What interest groups object to the use of particular textbooks? What kinds of pressure do members of the press apply? And does the most frequent source of pressure have the most clout?

Gross's survey indicates that parents, followed by teachers and school board members, are most likely to demand money for the schools, and that the town finance committee or city council is most likely to apply pressure to reduce expenditures. Because local and municipal officials fear that the voters will consider them responsible for all local taxes, including school levies, they use whatever means they can to reduce taxes, including pressuring the superintendent and the school board to limit school expenditures.

[10] Tables 8.1 and 8.2 represent the results of a study conducted among over 100 superintendents and 500 school board members in Massachusetts. Neal Gross, *Who Runs Our Schools?* (New York: John Wiley & Sons, 1958), pp. 49–50.

Superintendents reveal that school board members and parents often apply pressure to have friends hired by the school district or to have teachers they dislike fired. Interestingly, although newspapers are not normally a source of pressure, they do at times try to promote greater emphasis on school athletics. Local businessmen are likewise interested in promoting athletic competitions.[11]

[11] Neal Gross, "Who Applies What Kind of Pressures," in Rosenthal, *Governing Education*, pp. 91–99.

Table 8.1 Percentage of superintendents and school board members exposed to specified pressures

Pressure	Superintendents (N = 105) %	School board members (N = 508) %
Demands that the schools should place more emphasis on the three R's.	59	53
Demands that the schools should teach more courses and subjects.	64	47
Protests about the use of particular textbooks.	19	19
Protests about the views expressed by teachers.	49	41
Demands that teachers should express certain views.	13	12
Protesting school tax increases or bond proposals.	73	70
Demanding more money for the general school program	66	52
Protesting the introduction of new services (in addition to academic instruction) for pupils.	39	36
Demanding the introduction of new services (in addition to academic instruction) for pupils.	63	49
Demands that school contracts be given to certain firms.	46	24
Demands that teachers be appointed or dismissed for reasons other than competence.	46	24
Demanding the introduction of new teaching methods.	29	35
Protesting the introduction of new teaching methods.	43	28
Demanding that greater emphasis be placed on the athletic program.	58	52
Demanding that less emphasis be placed on the athletic program.	40	38

Source: Neal Gross, *Who Runs Our Schools?* (New York: John Wiley & Sons, 1958), p. 49. Reprinted by permission of the publisher.

How are schools governed and controlled?

Table 8.2 Percentage of superintendents and school board members who said they were exposed to pressures from the specified individuals and groups

Individuals or groups who exert pressure	Superintendents (N = 105) %	School board members (N = 508) %
1 Parents or PTA	92	74
2 Individual school board members	75	51
3 Teachers	65	44
4 Taxpayers' association	49	31
5 Town finance committee or city council	48	38
6 Politicians	46	29
7 Business or commercial organizations	45	19
8 Individuals influential for economic reasons	44	25
9 Personal friends	37	37
10 The press	36	19
11 Old-line families	30	26
12 Church or religious groups	28	18
13 Veterans organizations	27	10
14 Labor unions	27	5
15 Chamber of commerce	23	5
16 Service clubs	20	11
17 Fraternal organizations	13	9
18 Farm organizations	12	4
19 Welfare organizations	3	1

Source: Neal Gross, *Who Runs Our Schools?* (New York: John Wiley & Sons, 1958), p. 50. Reprinted by permission of the publisher.

One superintendent related an incident about the chairman of the school board who called to inquire about the bus contract. The usual complaints had been received about the bus service, and the chairman argued that a friend of his, the owner of a local taxi service, could do a better job. The superintendent replied that the company that presently held the contract cost less than would the chairman's friend's company, and also provided better equipment and more experienced drivers than could be obtained locally. "That's all very well and good," the chairman responded, "but you've got to learn to support the local community if you're going to stick around."

One hour later the superintendent received a telephone call from another school board member, who usually supported him on crucial issues. The school board member explained that he knew what he was about to ask was against the rules, but that he thought he would ask anyway. His niece had applied for a teaching job—was there anything the superintendent could do to help her? He knew that she didn't have as much experience as some of the other applicants, but he felt sure she would make a pretty good teacher. After all, he had known her all her life. The conversation ended with the board member asking the superintendent to do what he could.

The pressures brought to bear on both superintendents and school boards are tremendous. The superintendent's job is particularly vulnerable to pressure, since his livelihood depends on community support, and inability to reconcile the conflicting pressures of different groups is a major reason for the short job span of the average superintendent. These pressures may also influence how he administers the public schools. As Gross says, "If he must spend much of his time placating certain pressure groups, anticipating threats, and developing strategies to deal with them, he will not have much time left to administer the schools efficiently and work with his staff to develop and carry out an effective educational program. He may not have time to do these things at all."[12] Thus, while the superintendent possesses considerable power, he maintains it only so long as he is effectively able to handle outside pressures.

How is such pressure exercised?

The influence of informal groups on decision making in school districts has only recently been explored, but data from a number of case studies indicate that an informal power structure exists in many, and probably most, school districts.[13] These data further indicate that the pressure of informal groups of power elites, such as middle class businessmen or key influentials, has a telling influence upon decisions; this important power is exercised in most local school districts by a relatively few persons who hold top positions of influence in the informal power structure of the school district. In fact, these informal groups tend to exert far more influence than do formal organizations on basic decisions affecting the public schools.

Evidence from case studies of many school districts reveals that the composition of these power-wielding informal groups varies; however, businessmen are the largest single occupational group represented. Kimbrough states that, "as a consequence of their superior status, businessmen exercise the greatest effect upon, and often dominate, educational policies in the nation."[14] In contrast to Koerner's assertions, Kimbrough found that educators are poorly represented at the top levels of the power structure, with the occasional exception of the superintendent. Kimbrough agrees with Koerner that most school board members are not part of the informal power structure.

How do these influential members of informal groups actually exercise their power? Kimbrough cites an example from a medium-sized district. First, let us assume that an educational project costing several million dollars is proposed for the local school system and that there exists an informal group of community leaders who will be positively affected by the project if it is approved. The project may have been proposed by one of the leaders of this group, by an organization or public official, or it may have evolved through some combination of circumstances. Kimbrough's studies indicate that the following activities may be expected:

[12] Gross, pp. 103–104.
[13] Kimbrough, "An Informal Arrangement," pp. 105–136.
[14] Kimbrough, p. 119.

How are schools governed and controlled?

There will be an increase in interactions among the leaders of the power group. These interactions to discuss the proposal may occur at civic occasions, on the telephone, or at social gatherings. Small groups of leaders may get together for personal discussions. Thus, definite action is preceded by considerable informal talk.

Because of the project's importance, a meeting of the top power-wielders in the group is held to resolve differences of opinion and to make a decision, for which the preliminary informal interaction has provided a framework. A decision is reached, and plans for action are drawn up.

A fanning-out process then occurs — key persons not at the meeting are drawn into the group and numerous others are alerted about the decision. This process involves the use of persuasion and reasoning to convince others of the logic of the decision. The public officials who will formalize the decision may, at this point, experience some form of subtle anticipatory coercion. The "Big Men" rarely make direct threats but will, if necessary, later resort to threats, bribes, coercion, and political deals.

If for some reason formal action on the project does not proceed according to the wishes of the power brokers, key supporting personnel are induced to resort to parliamentary roadblocks, such as appointing a study committee or referring the issue to a standing committee established for such emergencies. This maneuver allows time to exert heavier pressure for a favorable decision.

Power or control is exercised on a different level by other individuals and groups outside the formal decision-making structure, including the Parent-Teachers Association, taxpayers' associations, and teachers' organizations. Some individuals who influence decisions informally through group membership also occupy positions within the formal organization; teachers are a notable example.

Informal interpersonal relationships are often used to achieve desired objectives, as in the case of a certain principal who managed to get for his school materials and privileges denied other principals.[15] A casual observer might

[15] Kimbrough, "An Informal Arrangement," pp. 128–129.

What gift are YOU laying at the feet of EDUCATION this Christmas, O Politician?

Eight trillion bucks worth of POOLS, AUDITORIUMS and AUDIO-VISUAL EQUIPMENT! I got a few BUSINESS FAVOURS to get rid of, you know?

What's YOUR gift, O Trustee?

The real world

have attributed his success to his aggressive personality. However, the real explanation was that he usually sat by the assistant superintendent in charge of administration at Rotary Club meetings. Whenever he wanted something he simply told the assistant superintendent at the meeting. Try to trace that decision-making process on a formal organizational chart!

In many school districts there exist two administrative networks: one formal and legally recognized; the other informal, friendly, and, in many instances, far more efficient than the official one. Consider the situation that permits the following kinds of occurrences in one large school district. A university professor, speaking at an inservice workshop for teachers, utters some uncomplimentary remarks about the school board's attitude toward segregation. While the professor is still talking, the remark is reported to a member of the school board, who calls the professor at the end of his speech to tell him that the city will no longer participate in the workshop. A teacher who has received good reports from her superiors is not rehired because she does not believe in filing lesson plans. When the dismissal is announced, there is no dissent; the favorable reports have been forgotten. A principal who has refused to let a child transfer into his school under the open-enrollment regulation, because there is no more space, receives a call from a legislator or school board member and suddenly discovers that he does have an empty seat and will be glad to accommodate the child.

'arents and eachers

The local parent-teacher organization serves as a communications link between parents and the formal school organization, with teachers usually acting as representatives of the schools. The formal school system ordinarily operates by means of down-the-line communications. When the formal hierarchy does not respond to up-the-line communications from parents or teachers in a manner satisfactory to them, the informal system can be resorted to in an attempt to get a more favorable response.

An in-depth study of modern DANCE BAND STAGING which I researched PERSONALLY in ACAPULCO and LAS VEGAS and TAHITI! What's YOURS O Principal?

Some new BARBER SHEARS, a revised HEM LINE CODE and a system of BELLS, WHISTLES and LIGHTS that'll REVOLUTIONIZE BETWEEN PERIOD TRAFFIC FLOW in the HALLS!

Good! Anyone see the STAR we're supposed to be following?

There's a GLOW up ahead but I think it's just a BONFIRE at a STUDENT RIOT!

Cartoon by Barry Base

An instance of this occurred when the energetic principal of a New Haven, Connecticut, school in a low-income neighborhood organized the PTA in an attempt to improve the school's facilities. He began by going to an important neighborhood leader and persuading her that the children in the school needed help. Convinced, the woman and the principal went to work on the PTA. In order to arouse parent involvement, they convinced the PTA to endorse a hot lunch program; this required the PTA to raise funds and hire kitchen help. As the PTA became more active, the principal began a campaign for a new school to replace the old one. When the city administration raised obstacles, the principal called together the PTA members and other neighborhood leaders to ask their support for a new school. Within twenty-four hours they were exerting pressure on the administration. Needless to say, the problem was solved.

However, teachers have become increasingly frustrated by the impotence of most parent-teacher organizations and their ineffectiveness as a means of implementing teachers' educational aims. Consequently, the role of teachers' organizations in determining educational policy is ever increasing. Largely as a result of collective bargaining techniques, including strikes and the threat of strikes, teacher organizations are winning more and more power over educational policy.

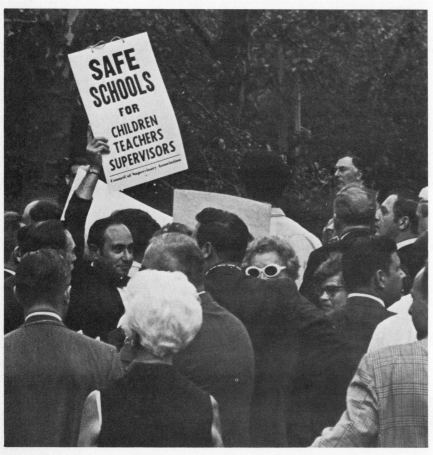

The real world

Dialogue

Jim   We haven't given much attention in this chapter to one of the key fig-
       ures in the business of governing and controlling schools.

Kevin Who's that?

Jim   The principal. He's the one whose influence the teacher feels most.
       No other person influences school environment, faculty and student
       morale, curriculum, and instruction as much as the principal.

Kevin I tend to agree, but one study I know of found that in the primary
       grades 63 percent of the students didn't know the principal's name,
       and 86 percent had never spoken to him. And the 14 percent who
       had spoken to him had done so in a negative situation. That study
       doesn't indicate much impact.

Jim   Oh, but it does! I would say that the principal was influencing the
       students tremendously. His absence from their daily life was having
       an impact on them.

Kevin Well, in that sense, yes.

Jim   The critical factor, as far as I'm concerned, is that the principal see
       himself as the school's leader rather than its administrator. If he is
       skillful and adept at human relations, decision making, and facili-
       tating staff wishes, he can enhance the conditions in which he, his
       staff, and the students work.

Kevin I think that his attitude toward children is the single most significant
       factor in determining or changing the school's climate. He can set
       the tone of the entire school through his actions.

Jim   My advice to young teachers who are looking for their first jobs is to
       find out as much as they can about their prospective principal's
       beliefs about children and about how learning should occur. I'd also
       talk to other teachers in the school about his leadership ability. Does
       the school reflect his beliefs about children and learning? If the
       teachers can't tell what his beliefs are, he can't be much of a leader.

As recently as 1956 one expert succinctly characterized teacher influence thus: "Teachers as a group have little or no say in the formulation of school policy."[16] Today, however, many teacher organizations have won recognition as the official bargaining representatives of their members, while in the past, boards of education insisted on dealing with teachers as individuals. Teacher organizations are also demanding that issues previously considered the prerogatives of school boards and superintendents be subject to collective bargaining. Among these issues are teacher and paraprofessional salaries, clerical and secretarial assistance, curriculum development, fringe benefits, inservice training, class size determination, textbook selection, and even the appointment of department heads and other school administrators. As one commentator has put it, "They want to negotiate everything." In an increasing number of school districts, teacher organizations are winning the right to negotiate these issues with school

[16] Daniel Griffiths, *Human Relations in School Administration* (New York: Appleton-Century-Crofts, 1956), p. 106.

How are schools governed and controlled?

boards. As another observer has remarked, "It is not at all difficult to foresee a time when virtually all American teachers will be employed under collective bargaining contracts that cover not only salaries but a long list of other items."[17]

Control by business

Collective bargaining is one of many procedures that educators are borrowing from the business world. But the impact of business on education is not a new phenomenon. Industrial growth in the United States was paralleled historically by the application of industrial principles in the schools. At the height of an industrially inspired "efficiency movement" in the 1920s, a number of business techniques of dubious educational merit were introduced into the schools. Schools were compared to factories whose products were students; dollar values were assigned to parts of the curriculum; the size of classes and teacher loads were increased for the sake of efficiency, and detailed clerical records were kept. Education was, in effect, confined to cost-saving and mechanical functions to reduce "overhead." The public then demanded a profitable return on money "invested" in schools. Some teachers and educators fought the trend, but so powerful and far-reaching was the movement that their voices were not heard. It was later recognized that educators had gone overboard in applying commercial principles, unscientifically, to a social institution. But the damage had been done, and many such practices of questionable educational value are still used in countless schools across the country.

Increasing attention has been given in recent years to the amount of control business exercises over education. In one recent study, Grace Graham shows that the great prestige of the business world has enabled it to have significant influence on American education.[18] Today's schools by and large endorse and teach the values of business. The dominant theme of the "business creed" consciously and unconsciously disseminated by businessmen is praise for the achievements of American capitalism; the fundamentals of this creed are being absorbed by most students throughout the school day.

In general, teachers seemingly stress many of the values that businessmen praise highly. For example, teachers struggle to inculcate respect for hard work, punctuality, neatness, a sense of duty, and acceptance of the sanctity of private property.[19]

Teachers usually grade their pupils at least partly on the basis of how hard they try. They emphasize the importance of education as preparation to get a job. "This emphasis by educators on the economic rather than on the intellectual and aesthetic contributions of education to a full life indicates the extent to which teachers themselves accept the businessmen's creed."[20]

Charles Reich argues in *The Greening of America* that the young are rejecting the values of business. He asserts that a new consciousness is emerging which will impel the young to try to humanize the institutions of the corporate state and to transform their goals from profits to the public good. If Reich's controversial thesis proves correct, we should expect the business values that currently prevail in American education to give way to humanitarian principles.

[17] Koerner, *Who Controls American Education?*, p. 42. A more detailed discussion of teacher organizations follows in Chapter Nine.
[18] Grace Graham, *The Public Schools in the New Society* (New York: Harper & Row, 1969), Chs. 2, 6, and
[19] Graham, p. 27.
[20] Graham, p. 28.

The real world

The public knows more about potato prices, the number of hogs slaughtered, and the status of bank loans than it knows about its schools. Davereux Josephs, chairman of President Eisenhower's Committee on Education Beyond High School.

Just as war is too important to be left to the generals, education is too important to be left to the educators. Paul Woodring, *A Fourth of a Nation.*

Both the school board and the superintendent are vulnerable to influence from the business community. In most school districts, the superintendent resembles an executive or business manager more then he does an educational philosopher. Knowledge of budgeting and finance is essential for hiring and success as a superintendent. Most school boards are also likely to have a business orientation, since businessmen have continually been well represented on local boards. As a result, school boards tend to be economy minded and to stress the elimination of frills and the reduction of overhead—approaches that may be sound in business but are unlikely to encourage educational experimentation.

The National Association of Manufacturers, the public-relations arm of the business community, runs a comprehensive and far-reaching public relations program directed at the schools, which consciously disseminates the "business creed."[21] The NAM exerts influence to try to eliminate from the curriculum and from textbooks any tendency toward "creeping collectivism," and promotes "pro-American" doctrines. Local manufacturers are urged to investigate what is being taught their own children and to find out how much money is being spent by taxpayers to spread doctrines abhorrent to the business community.[22] Another NAM public-relations project is Business Education Day, when teachers and local business leaders exchange roles. Its purpose is to show educators how our economic system functions, and the exchanges provide a channel of communication between schools and the community. However, the project also tends to promote a pro-management slant on business issues, and the American Federation of Teachers, a union organization, has taken a strong stand against closing the schools at taxpayers' expense for the advantage of a particular interest group. Business corporations also give the schools free products, such as films, pamphlets, records, graphs, and slides, to promote their images. It is estimated that the cost of free instructional material entering the nation's schools from private sources is greater even than the cost of textbooks.[23]

During the 1960s, the relationship of business to education underwent a change. While business had always courted and asserted its influence on education, the lines between the two remained distinct; during the last decade, however, the boundaries between public education and private industry have become blurred. People now speak of the "partnership" of business and education. A number of

[21] Graham, p. 18.
[22] S. A. Rippa, *Education in a Free Society, An American History* (New York: David McKay, 1967), p. 156.
[23] William O. Stanley, *Education and Social Integration* (New York: Columbia University Press, 1953), pp. 6–9.

How are schools governed and controlled?

mergers between manufacturers of educational hardware and the communications media reflect the ever-increasing scope of the "education industry": big business has entered the educational market. During the sixties many people were predicting that as companies such as Westinghouse, General Electric, Time-Life, and Xerox merged with publishing companies that the impact on education would be great. This has not proven to be the case, however. The educational offspring companies of these large corporations have not even approached the kinds of successes that were once predicted for them.

Businesses have offered direct assistance to schools, particularly in the large cities; in some instances businesses have even "adopted" particular schools, offering technical, managerial, and financial aid. Performance contracting, an arrangement long employed in industry whereby the contracting business guarantees to produce certain results or not be paid, is becoming more common in education. Business firms are contracting with school districts on this basis to raise the reading and mathematical skills of students. School management and budgeting processes are being revitalized by the "systems" approach, borrowed from private industry.

The concept of "accountability," or responsibility for producing certain growth outcomes on the part of students, will have significant implications for education. It is probable that teachers' functions and roles will be redefined in terms of accountability. Private companies will offer schooling in competition with local school boards, and contracts will be drawn on a performance basis. The involvement of big business could bring about far-reaching changes in school finance. It is one thing for the PTA to lobby for state or federal legislation; it is quite another when the combined forces of, say, IBM and GE support a bill.

Big business is directly challenging educators for control of education. Many educators feel threatened by big business in general, and by the computer in particular. But any discussion of control of education, now or in the future, would be incomplete without a review of the federal government's role, to which we now turn.

Control by the federal government

It could be argued that the most powerful educational decision-making body in the United States is the Supreme Court, several of whose decisions in recent years have had a profound effect on education. A prime example is *Brown* v. *Board of Education of Topeka,* the 1954 desegregation decision that struck down the doctrine of separate but equal educational facilities. Because some of the Court's decisions have reduced the power of state and local educational authorities, deep resentment has been generated among those who abhor this "federal intrusion" into state rights. Many people, of course, applaud the Court's decisions as steps to make American education more responsive to democratic principles.

The federal government also exerts powerful influence on education through legislation providing monetary aid to local and state authorities and through the administration of these monies by federal offices and departments. Congressional acts apportioning federal funds to education have increased in number and scope in recent years. They have provided funds to selected schools, colleges, cities, states, school boards, and agencies to finance a wide variety of projects, including construction of buildings and other educational facilities; improvement of instruction or administration; development of educational personnel, including teachers and paraprofessionals, particularly for poverty areas; loans for prospective teachers, and educational research. Today the federal government provides for almost 8 percent of the total cost of public elementary and secondary education.[24]

Because most federal aid is categorical—that is, the money must be spent for purposes that are specified generally in the legislation and more precisely by the federal agency administering the funds—the federal government is able to exert influence on school districts and institutions that accept or seek this aid. For example, in order to qualify for federal funds to improve its reading program, a school district must conform to the guidelines and restrictions that accompany the money. Many financially stricken school districts are grateful for funds regardless of the restrictions on their use.

There is a danger inherent in this situation that a school district might be tempted to divert its own resources from a much-needed program to a less important project which the federal government would be willing to help finance. Thus, the prospect of federal money may encourage neglect of a local district's particular needs. Despite these potential dangers, the majority of educators support the federal government's role in education.

[24] National Education Association Research Report 1973–74, "Financial Status of the Public Schools, 1973," p. 35.

How are schools governed and controlled?

During the early 1970s President Nixon attempted to institute a revenue-sharing plan, whereby a number of federal programs would be discontinued and the monies redistributed to state and local education agencies to spend as they best determined. Congress rejected the proposed plan in 1973 but the President proposed it anew in 1974. It is not known at the time of this writing whether Congress will approve such a plan.

While some educators favor the proposed revenue-sharing plan, others oppose it, believing that the federal programs have served as agents of change. If revenue-sharing becomes a reality it will mean that the federal government's direct influence on education in the country will be considerably reduced.

Discussion questions

1 Can you offer any examples from your experience of the distinction between governance and control? How do you suppose the persons in control obtained their power? What were the advantages and disadvantages of this state of affairs in the situations you are familiar with?
2 What do you see as the advantages and disadvantages of the public schools being a branch of the federal government? Are you familiar with any country where this is the case? What is its school system like? How does it compare to the system you are a product of?
3 How were the interests and values of business reflected in your education? Were you aware of the influence of commercial values and methods on your schooling at the time? What is your opinion of this state of affairs?
4 Do you think the PTA is a potentially effective means of influencing school policy? Where do you think the interests of teachers and parents coincide? Where do they diverge? In what areas do you think informal influence might be more effective than collective bargaining?
5 What do you see as the advantages and disadvantages of collective bargaining? of accreditation? of accountability? Would you teach in an unaccredited school? Would you be willing to be held accountable for the learning of your students?
6 In the light of what you have learned from this chapter, what do you think of Paul Woodring's statement that "education is too important to be left to the educators"?

For further reading

- Broudy, Harry S. *The Real World of the Public Schools*. New York: Harcourt Brace Jovanovich, 1972. The book deals with the role of special interest groups, professionalism, the problems of standards and accountability, among other topics.
- Koerner, James D. *Who Controls American Education?* Boston: Beacon Press, 1968. Koerner's major thesis is that professional educators and their organizations exert major control over American education. Koerner deplores this, and urges that changes be made to reduce the power of superintendents, professors of education, state departments of education, and the professional organizations.
- Lurie, Ellen. *How to Change the Schools*. New York: Vintage Books, 1970. A parents' handbook on how to fight the large, bureaucratic school system in order to bring about the changes desired. An excellent example of using the informal control system to bring about changes in the formal system.

- Rogers, David. *110 Livingston Street.* New York: Random House, 1969. 110 Livingston Street is the address of the New York City school district administration offices. The author examines the operation of the city schools, with particular emphasis on the bureaucratic structure. His is not a book favorable to the school system.
- Rosenthal, Alan, ed. *Governing Education.* New York: Doubleday, 1969. A compilation of readings on the politics of education. Case studies, as well as expository articles, demonstrate how educational decisions are made and who makes them. Chapters by Kimbrough and Gross are particularly interesting.
- Saxe, Richard W. "Toward a Feary of Administration." *The National Elementary Principal* 49 (April 1970): 26–30. A humorous article that attempts to explain administrative behavior as a function of fear. Saxe believes that bizarre administrative behavior results from a corruption of the ideal form of bureaucracy, and that this corruption is based on fear. Fun to read.
- Schrag, Peter. *Village School Downtown: Politics and Education — A Boston Report.* Boston: Beacon Press, 1967. A case study report on the politics of Boston as related to educational issues.
- Strahan, Richard Dobbs. *The Courts and the Schools.* Lincoln, Neb.: Professional Educators Publications, 1973. Chapters 1–5 are excellent brief reviews of school governance and administrative responsibility.
- Summerfield, Harry L. *The Neighborhood-based Politics of Education.* Columbus, O.: Charles E. Merrill, 1971. An investigation of various neighborhoods in a city and how the neighborhood politics influence education in those neighborhoods.
- Wirt, Frederick M., and Kirst, Michael W. *The Political Web of American Schools.* Boston: Little, Brown, 1972. An analysis of the formal and informal power systems that control schools in America.

Films

- *A Chance to Learn* (NBC, color, 17 min., 1968). This film comments on some of the issues underlying the confrontations taking place in schools. It finds many people in agreement that the public-school system in the inner-city is breaking down and that antagonisms are growing between children, parents, and educators. Disagreements arise over the questions of who will control the schools, who will decide who teaches in them, and who will decide what is taught.
- *Community Control* (Boston Newsreel, 16mm, 50 min.). Documents the struggle of the black and Puerto Rican communities to control their own schools. The forces they are working against include the police, who enforce the political decisions of the municipal bureaucracy, and the teachers' union, which is striking against the demands of the community.
- *Educational Planning in North Dakota* (North Dakota Department of Public Instruction, color, 30 min., 1969). A report on the needs and plans of a specific state as determined by its Department of Public Instruction. Researched and narrated by Dr. Kent Alm, who presents the viewpoint of an unusually innovative state education administration. This film includes an interesting section on population trends and their relationship to school building plans.
- *I Ain't Playin' No More* (EDC, b&w, 61 min., 1970). This film records the educational process being followed in the Morgan Community School, a public elementary school in Washington, D.C. with a community school board. Under the dynamic leadership of Principal Kenneth Haskins, an aggressive effort was

made to bring parents of students into an intense and continuing involvement in the life of the school. The film examines the effects of this kind of community control on the school experience, focusing on such problems as teacher-student respect, freedom of expression, and appreciation of differences.

- *No Little Hope* (Center for Urban Education, 16mm, color, 28 min.). Documents the meaning of education to various people in New York City. Through the words of the people interviewed, many of them parents, it becomes clear that "the process of education" cannot be fully understood without taking into account parents, the community, mass media—and, of course, the schools.

- *On Strike* (Newsreel, b&w, 25 min., 1969). Students and community groups at San Francisco State College were unable to convince the college's governing boards to stop racist practices, tracking, and miseducation, according to the demands raised in this film. They were forced to resort to a militant strike with the central purpose of turning the school away from corporate interests and toward serving the people of the local community. Perhaps the best of the Newsreel school documentaries, this film illustrates the way in which crisis of control can become a key issue if students and community groups ally.

- *Quiet Too Long* (National Education Association, b&w, 29 min., 1967). Two representatives of the new militancy among teachers were filmed in scenes in classrooms, on the streets, in budget meetings, and in public gatherings. Bill Adams, a black elementary teacher, and John Uram, a white guidance counselor, try to rally their community to realize the harmful effects of poor school facilities. They work with citizens' groups and local politicians to press for an adequate school budget. This film is an unusual instance of a professional teachers' organization advocating independent action by teachers who want to lobby for better school conditions.

- *School Boards in Crisis—Five Facing Ten* (IDEA, color, 26 min., 1970). Designed to promote understanding of the role of local boards of education, this film concentrates on the pressures and counterpressures exerted on elected school officials. Dramatized conflicts over desegregation, new teaching patterns and curricula, and teacher militancy point out that school boards have many constituencies and are forced to resolve problems along political lines.

- *The Teacher Gap* (Indiana University Audio-Visual Center, 16mm, b&w, 60 min., 1965, NET). Compares the efforts of two communities to provide quality education to large numbers of students. The less successful approach of Bay City, Michigan, in relation to the success of Newton, Massachusetts, is attributed to a difference in the community's attitude toward education.

Audiotapes

- *Public Education as a Business Enterprise* (Center for the Study of Democratic Institutions, 21 min., 1969). An education colloquium debates the proposition that private corporations should replace, or at least supplement, public schools. Although generally denounced, some conditional support emerges for this reorientation of school control in a highly charged discussion.

- *Religion in the Schools* (Center for the Study of Democratic Institutions, 3.75 ips, reel, $\frac{1}{2}$ track, 59:10 min.). John Cogley, editor of *The Center* magazine, leads a staff discussion of the Supreme Court decision on prayers in public schools.

- *"The Learning Tree" Incident* (Pacifica, 30 min., 1970). Gordon Parks' bestselling novel was removed from the public-school libraries in Richmond, California, on the grounds that it was obscene, profane, and unsuitable for use in schools. Schoolteachers in Richmond instituted grievance proceedings to contest this censorship, and at the same time they began to investigate other instances of the violation of academic freedom. Four teachers involved in this controversy within the educational system are interviewed in this audiotape.

- *The System* (National Education Association, 3.75 ips, reel or cassette, 55:45 min. total). This hour-long audiotape is divided into seven short sections, each intended to serve as the basis for a complete discussion. The topics are: A Call to Action (3:20 min.); Toward Cooperative Governance (17:10 min.); Public Schools of Choice (7:10 min.); The Teacher as Decision Maker (6:40 min.); Parent Power (5:20 min.); The North Dakota Story: System Reform Through Teacher Education (8:20 min.); The North Dakota Story: Parents as Partners (8:25 min.).

Refer to Appendix for addresses of distributors.

How are schools governed and controlled?

9

Where have teachers been and where are they going?

This chapter focuses on teaching as a profession or occupational group. An attempt is made to show how this rather abstract concept, "professionalism," affects the daily life of the classroom teacher. The occupation of teaching is placed in an historical perspective so that the recent energetic drive for power and professional status by teachers may be more properly evaluated. The two major professional organizations representing teachers are described and critically evaluated.

The essence of a career in teaching is work and involvement with the young. When someone is thinking about becoming a teacher, his thoughts and daydreams usually revolve around interaction with students. Rarely does he bother with hypothetical issues beyond the scope of the classroom. This is both natural and appropriate, since the teacher's success or failure depends on his effectiveness with children. Nevertheless, there is more to being a teacher than this. Teachers work within a system that exposes them to pressures from many quarters. Frequently the prospective teacher is somewhat naïve about the pressures and forces that will impinge upon him, and naïveté can be dangerous, in terms both of making a career decision and of making a successful career.

To help you see this point, we would like you to indulge in a set of daydreams for a few moments. We will offer you a series of brief scenarios and, after reading each one, you should reflect on how you might react. As you read each one, imagine yourself teaching in that ideal classroom you carry around in your head. Assume that all indications are that you are doing a fine job. You are really enjoying it. Your students are making nice progress. They seem to be interested in their work. A few parents have indicated that although they were initially worried that their precious child was to have a new (read "untested") teacher, they are thrilled with his progress in your class. Okay. Things are going very well . . . and

1 Two mothers ask for a conference with you. You haven't met them, and know only that they are parents of two girls who act very quiet and cliquish in class. At the conference, the mothers come right to the point. They claim you favor the boys in your class and systematically ignore the girls—not just their girls, but all the girls. They say you teach only to the boys. The mothers become quite emotional and suggest that since you are a young unmarried woman you are working out your preoccupation with boys on the class. [If you are a male, reverse the situation. The mothers are parents of boys and are accusing you of excessive interest in little girls. Fiend!!] They say they have talked to some of the other mothers of girls in the class and claim that these mothers agree. They came to warn you that they "intend to take action!" On that note, they raise eyebrows, pick up purses, and huff out.

2 Four days in a row representatives of the Yearbook Committee burst into your classroom unannounced and literally take over. They claim they are signing up subscribers for the Yearbook, but they take a good ten minutes each time, most of which is devoted to wisecracking, showing off, and subtly putting you down in various ways. Their attitude is something on the order of, "Look, teach. You're new in this school and you've got a lot to learn. We've been here four years and we know our way around. Don't try to pull rank on us." When they finally leave, it takes a long time to get your students back in a mood to do some serious work. You complain to the principal (who happens to be a former Yearbook advisor) and he tells you, "Yearbook is one of the biggest things in this school. It is a student-run activity in which everyone takes great pride. Last year the Yearbook won Honorable Mention in the South-Southwestern Regional Yearbook Conference for high schools with over 2,000 and under 2,500 students with a lower middle class socioeconomic population. All of us who were here last year were very proud of the kids and what they did for the school. I know once you're here with us a little longer, you'll get into the swing of things. I'll send you a few copies of past Yearbooks. I know you're going to help this year's Yearbook staff in every way you can. They're really great, live-wire kids and come from some of our best families."

You ask around and find out that you should expect visits from the Yearbook staff three or four times a week for the next two months. They have pictures to take, workers to enlist, advertisements to sell . . . and new teachers to break in.

3 You get a special-delivery letter from a group called PAP (Patriotic American Parents). You have heard that they are very active in your area and are especially interested in schools. Their letter informs you that their lawyer is preparing a case against you for using books that are on their disapproved list. (You didn't know there was such a list but, sure enough, there is and you have.) They claim they have evidence that you are waging a subtle but nevertheless vicious war against the cause of justice and liberty and have succeeded in temporarily deflecting the minds of some of your students from the truth. Furthermore, they want to know why you display the UN flag. Finally, you are said to recite the Pledge of Allegiance in a much too hasty fashion, which is clearly a sign of your disrespect for country. This is the first you have heard of these charges or even of the Patriots' interest in you. They have requested that you respond in writing by next week or they will begin legal proceedings.

Jim	Reciting the Pledge of Allegiance too fast!!? Aren't we going a bit overboard here?
Kevin	Maybe so. But . . .
Jim	But what?
Kevin	But not too many years ago Gordon Lish, an English teacher at Mills High School in Burlingame, California, was fired. Although he was a distinguished scholar and edited an important literary quarterly, he was found guilty of reciting the pledge too rapidly and of telling his students that they didn't have to crouch under their desks during nuclear attack drills!
Jim	Hard to believe!

4 In late January, the superintendent—who holds a conference with each new teacher—told you he thought you were doing a fine job and that he wanted you to return next year. In passing, he remarked that he would be getting a contract to you in the spring. Toward the end of April, you got a little nervous and called him. You spoke to his executive secretary, who said not to worry, that you were on the list and that a contract would be coming before long. You stopped worrying. Today is the last day of school, and you find a very nice personal note from the principal in your school mailbox. He thanks you for your fine work during the year and says he is sorry you will not be back next year. You call the superintendent's office. He is in conference, and his executive secretary says that they are not renewing your contract. She cannot remember speaking to you in April. She knows nothing about the case. She does know, however, that the Board of Education has put on a lot of pressure for cuts in next year's personnel budget. She ends by telling you, "You must be very disappointed, dear. I know how you feel."

5 You noticed something peculiar when you sat down at the faculty dining table one lunch hour. Conversations stopped, and you had the distinct impression your colleagues had been talking about you. A few days later, an older teacher stopped you in the hall after school and said, "I don't want to butt in, but you really are upsetting Mrs. Hilary and Mrs. Alexandra." Mrs. H. and Mrs. A. have the classrooms on either side of yours. Apparently, they claim your class makes so much noise that they can't get anything done. Both are very conservative teachers in the tradition of the school. You believe in a more open approach to education. Although your class is somewhat noisy occasionally, it is never chaotic and its noise is usually a by-product of involvement and concentration. Twice Mrs. Alexandra has sent messengers with notes asking that your class be a bit more quiet. You have always complied. You hardly know either teacher. You have never really talked to Mrs. Alexandra except to say hello. Mrs. Hilary, with whom you've chatted, prides herself on being a disciplinarian. What she means, you have inferred, is that she is able to keep the children quiet. You know Mrs. Alexandra is chummy with Mrs. Hilary. You go to the vice-principal for advice. He seems to know all about the case, but only from the Hilary-Alexandra angle. Inexplicably, he gets quite angry and claims that until you came along the faculty got along beautifully. Further, you are being very unprofessional to make complaints against experienced teachers. You feel as if you are trapped in a Kafka novel.

6 You had been teaching Industrial Arts for two months when you met another new teacher at a faculty meeting. A few weeks later you chaperoned a dance together. Then you began going out on "real dates." By Christmas you knew you were over the edge. On New Year's Eve you proposed. Forty-eight sleepless hours later she accepted. On Valentine's Day you both announced it to your students (none of whom were surprised) and to your faculty colleagues (who didn't have a clue). You have both been doing well and want to stay on at your jobs next year. On Washington's Birthday, you get a notice from the personnel director calling your attention to the Board ruling against hiring couples. You know that there are no openings in any nearby schools. You plan to get married on the first Saturday in June after school ends. Your fiancée is crying.

These little horror stories are designed to provoke the realization that you can be an effective teacher and still have trouble keeping your job. What is the common theme running through each of these anecdotes? You, the teacher, were succeeding in your work with children, but forces outside the classroom began to impinge on you. A parents' vigilante group accused you of prejudice. The Patriots wanted to make a target case of you. When the Yearbook wise-guys start playing havoc with your class, the principal failed to back you up. On two occasions the school system bureaucracy was ready to put you on the unemployed rolls. Two of your colleagues damaged your reputation with the faculty and administration. Other than that, it's been a super year.

While you may feel confident that you could handle some of these situations, it is doubtful you could cope with all of them. In some cases you would be powerless to respond effectively to your adversaries, and might end up a helpless victim of circumstances. Fortunately, a teacher is not alone. Like many other occupational groups, teachers have organizations that protect them from such indignities and injustices. These organizations function on several levels, from the local to the national, and their very existence can keep situations like those described above from occurring, except in rare instances. But when they do occur, these organizations are committed to supporting the teacher.

In becoming a teacher, you are doing more than committing yourself to work with children. You are joining an occupational group composed of other individuals with similar responsibilities, concerns, and pressures, whose help you need and who in turn will need your help.

Teachers as a powerless group

Having confronted the individual teacher's potential powerlessness against impinging pressures, let us turn to the occupational group or profession of teaching. Just as individuals can have different degrees of power, so it is with groups of people. A great deal has been written lately about the power of the military-industrial complex to shape the policy of our government both at home and abroad. Charles Reich's *The Greening of America* and John Kenneth Galbraith's *The New Industrial State* describe the power of the giant corporations to affect the texture of our lives. We are becoming increasingly aware of the power of labor unions to affect the nation's economic health, and the power of the American Medical Association to influence the quality and nature of health service. Although the public is beginning to change its earlier view of teachers as faithful and docile public servants, teachers are generally not considered to be in the same league as the power groups mentioned above. There is a good deal of rhetoric about teachers having the future of the country—its youth—in their hands, but they are rarely given the commensurate power. Nor have teachers as a group strongly influenced the conditions of their own employment. Though in recent years teachers have struck (or, more euphemistically, "withheld their services"), by and large we have been a quiet, unmilitant profession.[1] Think back for a moment to Chapter Eight. Teacher power did not loom particularly large in the discussion of who controls the schools. The important decisions about a community's educational programs have not been made by teachers, either individually or in a group.

[1] The issue of teacher power is discussed more fully in Chapter Ten.

To the faculty:

The following teachers are to be commended on achieving 100% attendance yesterday: NONE.

There will be a fire drill at the end of the fourth period today: please do not give any tests.

Circulars on open school day have been placed in your letter-boxes. Please read them carefully and follow instructions.

Teachers who line up in front of the time clock waiting to punch out in the afternoon create a crowded condition in the doorway. Please wait until dismissal bell rings before coming down.

The office telephone is not to be used for personal calls. Please use the pay-telephone in the basement.

Teachers' interest committee meeting today during lunch period in room 404. Please come promptly with your lunch: last month no one showed up!

Memos from the main office. From the book *Up the Down Staircase* by Bel Kaufman. © 1964 by Bel Kaufman. Published by Prentice-Hall, Inc., Englewood Cliffs, New Jersey. Pp. 197–198.

You've come a long way, teach!
The Colonial Period

In 1647 a law was passed in New England which required towns of fifty or more families to establish elementary schools and towns of 100 or more families to establish Latin grammar schools at the secondary level. Religious instruction was the mainstay of these Colonial schools, but the character of many of the teachers was hardly exemplary. Many were drunkards. Some were sadists and swindlers. Some ran up debts and then skipped town, occasionally with the school's meager funds. This behavior is at least partially explained by the fact that teachers were held in very low esteem and paid pitifully meager salaries. The Colonial teacher received wages equivalent to those of a farmhand.

Teaching was hardly a profession in Colonial America. Schools were poorly equipped, and students attended irregularly. The school term was short, making teaching in many cases a part-time occupation. And along with his teaching and janitorial responsibilities, the teacher had a number of "extracurricular duties." Take the example of a New York schoolmaster, Johannes von Edkellen, who contracted to teach in the town of Flatbush, Long Island, in 1682.

He had to agree to clean the church, ring the assembly bell, read portions of the Bible, hear the children recite questions and answers out of the catechism, give them religious instruction, provide a basin of water for baptismal purposes, furnish bread and wine for the communion, act as a messenger for the consistory, give funeral invitations, ring the funeral bell and dig graves. (Reprinted by permission of Coward-McCann, Inc., from *What's Happened to Teacher?* by Myron Brenton [p. 67]. Copyright © 1970 by Myron Brenton. Much of the information in this chapter about the history of teaching in America has been adapted from Brenton's very lively account.)

To keep the teacher in an itinerant status, he was "boarded round," living with a different family each week in order to stretch out meager school funds. These and other indignities kept the turnover rate high and contributed to keeping the status of teachers low.

While teacher groups are becoming increasingly aggressive about salaries and welfare benefits, they have no firm place in the formal governance of the schools and little impact on educational decision making. In the previous chapter, a distinction was made between governance and control of the schools. It seems logical that teachers, because they outnumber administrators and work full-time in the schools, should have gained a good deal of control of what actually goes on there, but this does not appear to be the case. Of course, they have control over a good deal of what happens in their own classrooms. In fact, however, what happens in a teacher's classroom is severely limited by forces outside the classroom over which she and teachers' organizations have very little control. The major curriculum decisions—what should be taught—are not made by teachers. Hiring and tenure decisions are neither made by nor, in fact, much influenced by teachers or teacher groups. If a new school is to be built, the

Where have teachers been and where are they going?

teachers who will work in the new building are rarely, if ever, consulted about the kind of environment they would consider most suitable and conducive to learning. When a new principal is chosen, the teachers are not asked to participate in the decision making. Rarely are they even asked what they think the new principal's qualifications should be. As one Arkansas teacher stated, "I've been teaching in this same school and living in this same community for twenty-six years. I've had all sorts of commendations and good teaching awards. But in twenty-six years not once has anyone on the school board or any of the administrators asked my advice on an educational matter. I haven't been asked about one darned thing."

Discouraging as this picture may seem to some of you, not all teachers are dissatisfied with the existing state of affairs. Some are quite content to simply teach and leave all the squabbling to what they call "the militants." They think teachers have come a long way in recent years and that they should be satisfied with what they have gained. They would agree with the statement, "Education is too important to be left in the hands of educators." The more militant teachers, however, feel that this attitude is itself the problem, and that this kind of passivity has kept teachers oppressed and the quality of their service low. They assert that teaching will not truly become a profession until their colleagues take a more vigorous, independent position. And this leads us directly to the question, "Is teaching a profession?"

Teaching: a profession or a trade?

A profession is more than a group of individuals all engaged in the same line of work. Professions have a more-or-less recognizable set of characteristics that distinguish them from nonprofessions.[2] As you read the list of characteristics of a profession, check whether or not you think teaching qualifies on each premise.

Does teaching qualify?

Yes ☐   No ☐

First, a profession renders a unique, definite, and essential social service. Only the people in the particular profession render the service. For instance, only lawyers practice law. The service rendered must be considered so important that it is available to all the people in a society.

Yes ☐   No ☐

Second, a profession relies upon intellectual skills in the performance of its service. This does not mean that physical actions and skills are not needed, but rather that the emphasis in carrying on the work is on intellectual skills and techniques.

Third, a profession has a long period of specialized training. Because professional work requires special intellectual skills, specialized intellectual training is needed. General education, such as that represented by a bachelor's degree, is

[2] We have drawn heavily on an excellent book by Myron Lieberman entitled *Education as a Profession* (Englewood Cliffs, N.J.: Prentice-Hall, 1956). For a fuller discussion of whether or not teaching is a profession, we recommend this book to you.

valued, but not considered adequate. The specialized training must cover a substantial period of time and not be obtained in cram courses or correspondence schools.

Yes ☐ No ☐

Fourth, both individual members of the profession and the professional group enjoy a considerable degree of autonomy and decision-making authority. Whereas factory workers have very limited decision-making powers and are closely supervised in the performance of their work, professionals are expected to make most of their own decisions and be free of close supervision by superiors. Also, professional groups regulate their own activities rather than having outsiders set policies and enforce adherence to standards.

Yes ☐ No ☐

Fifth, a profession requires its members to accept personal responsibility for their actions and decisions. Along with having a high degree of freedom and autonomy, the professional must shoulder a large measure of responsibility for his performance. Since the professional's service is usually related to the human welfare of individuals, this responsibility is an especially serious one.

Yes ☐ No ☐

Sixth, a profession emphasizes the services rendered by its practitioners more than their financial rewards. While the personal motives of any individual professional are not necessarily any higher than any other worker's, the professional group's public emphasis is on service.

Yes ☐ No ☐

Seventh, a profession is self-governing and responsible for policing its own ranks. This means there are professional groups who perform a number of activities aimed at keeping the quality of their services high and looking out for the social and economic well-being of the professional members. Also, these self-governing organizations set standards of admission and exclusion to the profession.

Yes ☐ No ☐

Eighth, a profession has a code of ethics which sets out the acceptable standards of conduct of its members. In order for a professional group to regulate the quality and standards of service, it needs a code of ethics to aid it in enforcing these high standards.

Yes ☐ No ☐

These, then, are the major requirements of a profession. Few professions satisfy all of them fully. However, the list does serve as a benchmark by which occupational groups can measure themselves and direct their development if they wish to enjoy professional status.

The question "Is teaching a profession?" probably arouses little interest in many of you. Most people thinking about a career in teaching are more interested in whether it will be a personally rewarding way to spend their time than in whether or not it is a profession. Will teaching bring me personal satisfactions? Will it provide an outlet for my talents and energies? Will I be effective with kids? These questions are, we suspect, closer to your skin. Whether or not teaching fits the specifications of a profession appears to have very little bearing on these issues. Nevertheless, the professionalism of the teacher and the related issues are

```
CIRCULAR #59

Please keep all circulars on file, in their order.

TOPIC: TEACHERS' WELFARE

The president of the United Federation of Teachers has asked the

Board of Education to support legislation for higher death benefits and

pensions for teachers who die or are hurt in the line of duty.  Your

support of this measure is needed.

                    ─────────────────────

FROM:    James J. McHabe, Adm. Asst.

TO:      All teachers

Since school aides have relieved teachers of many non-teaching

assignments, teachers are requested to report to the office for

further assignments.

                              JJMcH
```

important to teachers and have an effect on the quality of education. While the issues raised may not seem particularly close to your skin right now, they will when you teach. Trust us!

Two sides of the issue

The case FOR teaching as a profession

The very nobility of the teacher's work is evidence in favor of its status as a profession. Society has entrusted teachers with its most important responsibility—the education of the young. Although teachers have never received the respect that is their due, through the course of history great minds have acknowledged their worth. Martin Luther asserted that the teacher's vocation was second only to that of the ministry. Thomas Carlyle in *Sartor Resartus* calls teachers "fashioners of souls," who ought to be "world-honored dignitaries" like generals and field marshals. As more and more people recognize how crucial education is to the fulfillment of our personal and national goals, the opportunities and rewards of the teacher will improve.

Although children learn from many people—from mothers to television entertainers—teachers are the specialists who pass on to the young the key skills necessary to participate effectively in the culture. They aid the young in acquiring the most difficult, if not the most important, skills: those that involve thinking and manipulating ideas. Neither reading nor geometry is often learned on the street. Although teachers do not undergo a particularly lengthy period of specialized training, they are in a sense continually training. Teachers are expected (and, in some states, required by law) to continuously upgrade their teaching skills.

The autonomy of the teacher, like that of every professional, is somewhat limited. Unlike lawyers and doctors, who can reject clients, a teacher's students are assigned to him. He also has a supervisor, his principal or department chairman. He teaches a curriculum that has been chosen or developed largely by others. However, within these limits, the teacher has an immense area of personal control. He normally determines the method of instruction. He decides which aspects of the curriculum he will highlight and which he will cover quickly. The limits on his creativity are few or nonexistent. After the initial few years of teaching, he is seldom, if ever, supervised. The teacher's classroom is his castle. And if a teacher feels that he does not have enough autonomy or does not agree with his administrator, he is free to move to another school. However, a teacher's autonomy is accompanied by a responsibility to teach effectively. Like any professional, he must be able to justify the manner in which he renders his social services. He must be able to justify his grading policy and his evaluations of student work. The teacher is expected to claim responsibility for his actions and to be open to criticisms of his teaching performance.

Teachers are represented by organizations, such as the National Education Association and the American Federation of Teachers, whose major function is improving education by improving the teaching profession. They provide information and aid to the classroom teacher; they support him against unjust pressures from members of the public or the school board; they set standards and censor teachers who violate these standards; finally, they attempt to influence legislation and public opinion about education and teaching. Also, they have established codes of ethics to guide teachers' professional activities.

Some argue that teaching is not a profession because teachers lack the autonomy of, say, a small-town lawyer, or because they have not achieved the economic status of dentists and doctors. These arguments are superficial. So, too, is the assertion that teaching is not a profession because many teachers do not act like professionals. Neither do many ministers, architects, and lawyers. Certainly the crucial nature of the teacher's work and the selfless spirit of service of the best teachers raises teaching to the level of a profession.

The case AGAINST teaching as a profession

The roots of the teaching "profession" go back to ancient Greece, where slaves called *paidagogos,* or pedagogues, taught children to read and write and helped them memorize passages of poetic history. Recently teachers, along with such other occupational groups as barbers, beauticians, and taxidermists, and according to a recent commercial—even dishwashers, have latched on to the term "professional" in an attempt to raise their salaries and their status. But a careful look reveals that teaching does not qualify as a profession. If education is a teacher's unique function, he has a great deal of competition. Ignoring for a moment the mounting criticism of compulsory miseducation (i.e., forcing children to attend school even when education is inferior), let us admit that teachers have no monopoly on education. Children today learn a tremendous amount from the media: *Sesame Street,* public-affairs specials, talk shows, Walter Cronkite, *Time,* films, novels, Bob Dylan, George Carlin, Rod McKuen, *Seventeen, Popular Mechanics.* Then there are the nonteacher educators: parents, ministers, older friends, neighbors, employers, close friends, coaches, scout leaders, playground and camp counselors, grandparents. The world is bursting with teachers and those who hold forth in school buildings have only a small piece of the action.

Where have teachers been and where are they going?

You've come a long way, teach!

II The Nineteenth Century

The nineteenth century was a period of immense growth and development for the country as a whole and for education. Schooling gradually became compulsory, and new and better schools were established, with improved curriculum and equipment. Normal schools for the training of teachers came into being in many states. Special journals for teachers were published and professional associations formed. Conventions were even held for teachers, usually to deal with "practical" classroom concerns. Myron Brenton reports on a teacher institute held in Jamestown, Pennsylvania, on January 14, 1858:

. . . teachers gather to discuss these questions: Is it better for teachers to board around? Should the teachers encourage pupils to chew tobacco? Should teachers open their schools in the morning by reading a portion of the Scripture? Should the door be closed against pupils who are not present at 9 o'clock in the morning? Should the rod be used in school? Should the wages of females be equal to those of male teachers?
Brenton, *What's Happened to Teacher?*, p. 69.

The place of females in teaching was a major issue in the nineteenth century. Industrialization and urban migration created new and attractive work opportunities, and schools could no longer compete for men's services. As a result, teaching became tagged as a "feminine" occupation by mid-century. A forerunner of the women's liberation movement, suffragette Susan B. Anthony, told a group of disgruntled male teachers why people held them in such low esteem:

It seems to me that you fail to comprehend the cause of the disrespect of which you complain. Do you not see that so long as society says that woman has not brains enough to be a doctor, lawyer or minister, but has plenty to be a teacher, every one of you who condescends to teach tacitly admits before Israel and the sun that he has no more brains than a woman?
Brenton, *What's Happened to Teacher?* p. 69.

The nation's general prosperity during the nineteenth century had no effect on the teaching profession. Teachers' salaries were wretchedly low. Teachers were among the worst trained, lowest paid, and most shabbily treated of professional workers. They were continually subjected to verbal and even physical abuse from hostile parents and, occasionally, students themselves. They were constantly being evaluated and examined by capricious laymen who knew nothing about education and cared less.

Pay remained abysmally low and, on top of this, women were discriminated against in pay scales. In Massachusetts in 1874, men teachers received a monthly salary of $24.51; women were paid $8.07. In Connecticut, during the same period, men earned $16.00 and women earned $6.50 a month. Shoemakers, harnessmakers, blacksmiths and other skilled workers often earned twice the wage of men teachers. As for the image of the teacher, a bitter teacher described him in the August 1864 issue of *Illinois Teacher* as "someone who can parse and cypher; has little brains and less money; is feeble minded, unable to grapple with real men and women in the stirring employments of life, but on that account admirably fitted to associate with childish intellects. . . ."

Amidst major educational reform and the expansion of education, the teacher's personal life was still seriously restricted. In a typical New England school system, men were allowed one evening a week for courting; two evenings if they were regular churchgoers. Teachers were expected to vote in accordance with the sentiments of the majority of the community. Loyalty oaths of a political nature were common to insure "right thinking" in the teacher. This practice continued until after the Civil War. In fact, it has never quite died away.

While teaching has intellectual and theoretical foundations, and requires a rather short period of specialized training (considerably less than some of the skilled trades), entrance into the profession is not particularly competitive, particularly on intellectual grounds. If it is a profession, it is one composed of a large percentage of average folks.

Although there is a good deal of talk about teachers' autonomy and decision-making power, both exist at a very low level. Teachers are the second rung from the bottom (superior only to students) of the hierarchy commanded by the Board of Education. They teach whom they are told, what they are told, and when they are told. If their supervisors do not like the results, teachers are only rarely protected by their professional group from being fired (or, more gently, "not re-hired") by the Board of Education. Most of the important decisions that affect teachers' daily lives, even those that bear directly on the standards of their own profession, are made by nonteachers. Teachers do not evaluate other teachers. Administrators do that. Teachers do not have much to do with (and very little say in) the preservice training of teachers. By and large, university professors do that. Teachers do not control licensing and certification of teachers. Laymen and bureaucrats do that. Some teachers, like factory workers, even have to punch a timeclock (more genteelly, they "sign in and sign out" . . . to the same effect). In sum, they have very little to say about what goes on.

The same is true of the teacher's responsibility. Teachers are rarely fired because Johnnie can't read or Samantha failed calculus. After a teacher achieves tenure, it takes something like a serious sexual offense for him to lose his job. As for the professional organizations policing their own ranks, there is much rhetoric but next to no action. The professional organizations exist primarily to protect teachers, increase their salaries, and expand their welfare benefits. Most teachers are minimally involved and interested in professional organizations and their activities, except when they call a strike—an odd activity for a "profession." Most teachers claim they are too busy to take an active role in professional affairs. This lack of real involvement in professional activities might stem from the fact that so many teachers have second jobs, either as housewives or in the labor market. They are unenthusiastic about working for higher standards because one of the first sacrifices to professionalism would be their second jobs. In actual fact, teachers work in circumstances very different from those of other professionals. They are hired, like other public servants, rather than operating as independent agents. They are on a fixed salary schedule and protected by

Where have teachers been and where are they going?

tenure laws, rather than having independently to find a market for their services. Teaching is a low-pay, high-security job, rather than a high-pay, low-security profession. Seniority as a teacher is more important than competence. Talk about professionalism may be personally satisfying to teachers, but it does not conform to the facts of the teacher's occupational life.

A third possibility

Like most important questions, "Is teaching a profession?" cannot be answered satisfactorily with simple pro and con arguments like those offered above. Also, teachers vary so much in knowledge, commitment, and expertise that it is difficult to come up with a definitive answer. However, our view is that teaching is a semi-profession. In certain ways teaching is clearly eligible for professional status and in certain others it deviates sharply from accepted canons of professionalism. On the one hand, teachers provide an intellectual service to the community. They undergo specialized training to master the theoretical basis of their work. Ethical standards guide their work with students. On the other hand, they function like many other lower-level white collar workers and civil servants. Seniority and security are the rule, rather than excellence and independence. Like many other occupational groups that are called professional, teaching, at this moment in history, only partially qualifies.

Another way to look at the issue is to think of teaching as in the *process of becoming a profession*. As the historical descriptions of the work and living conditions of teachers that accompany this chapter show, things are improving at a dramatic rate. Nevertheless, "you've got a long way to go, Teach!" Whether teaching becomes a profession in your career lifetime will depend on some of the following factors. First, teachers must take on a larger role in the governing of their career affairs. While the direction of education and the schools should be in the hands of many groups (parents, community leaders, students, and teachers), control over the teaching profession *per se* should be in the hands of teachers. Up to now, the great mass of teachers has taken the attitude "Let George do it."

Ten forty-three.
In exactly TWO MINUTES
I'll ring the
FIRST BELL and
they'll all
stand still!

All, that is, except
your potential DEVIATE!
Your fledgling REBEL!
Your incipient BOAT-
ROCKER! THEY'LL try
to move alright!
THEY'LL have to
learn the HARD
way not to move!

So I'll SCREAM at 'em
and take their NAMES
and give them FIVE
DETENTIONS and EXTRA
HOMEWORK! NEXT time
they won't move
after the first
bell!

The real world

As a result, outsiders make the major decisions about who should teach, how they should be trained, and under what conditions they should render their services. In this sense, teachers are an oppressed minority group. While teachers are eating better these days, we still lack self-determination.

Second, teachers must demand better training. As long as the public feels that any reasonably intelligent person can walk in off the street and do a teacher's job, people will not treat teachers as professionals. We do not for a moment mean to imply that teachers should adopt artificial trappings, like a doctor's smock or a general's uniform, to seem more distinctive and impressive. Rather, we must *appear* better because we *are* better. Like architects and surgeons, we must know our craft, and our work must be imbued by a sense of high purpose. When that happens, the public will be able to tell the difference.

Third, we may have simply to recognize that all of the two-and-a-half million people working in the American schools are not interested in and, in some cases, not capable of measuring up to the standards of professionalism. At present, what we, the authors, are calling (and, incidentally, will continue to call) the teaching profession is a mixed bag, with large numbers of transients "just passing through," large numbers of rather uncommitted teachers, and large numbers of truly excellent, dedicated career teachers.

Let us define a career teacher as one who plans to, and actually does, make a life occupation of teaching; one who is philosophically, emotionally, and spiritually committed, that is, never satisfied with what he does and how well he's doing it, and who fully intends to keep on growing for the rest of his life.[3]

[3] Quoted at the 1963–64 convention of the National Commission on Teacher Education and Professional Standards (NEA), in Myron Brenton, *What's Happened to Teacher?* (New York: Coward-McCann, 1970), p. 242.

Because when they've learned not to question the FIRST BELL, they'll learn not to question their TEXTS! Their TEACHERS! Their COURSES! EXAMINATIONS!

They'll grow up to accept TAXES! HOUSING DEVELOPMENTS! INSURANCE! WAR! MEN ON THE MOON! LIQUOR LAWS! POLITICAL SPEECHES! PARKING METERS! TELEVISION! FUNERALS!

Non-movement after the first bell is the backbone of Western Civilization!

Cartoon by Barry Base.

Where have teachers been and where are they going?

You've come a long way, teach!

III The Early Twentieth Century

With the dawn of the twentieth century, America came into her own as a nation and as an international power. This new maturity brought about a broadened outlook and a general loosening of mores. Not so, however, for the teacher. Teachers remained more-or-less enslaved to Victorian decorum. As late as 1920, teachers who smoked cigarettes had a difficult time getting jobs in California, Tennessee, and Illinois. In Mississippi and Kansas, teachers were not allowed to attend dances; if they did, it meant instant dismissal. A town in Louisiana required its teachers to stay around over weekends and be in bed by 10:00 p.m. In one Ohio county, teachers who dated other teachers faced the threat of immediate dismissal. School boards generally frowned on bobbed hair. Many contracts stipulated a long list of no-no's: no dates, no petting, no dancing, no smoking, no short skirts. We have all heard a great deal about the Roaring Twenties. If teachers took part in the fun, it was strictly on the quiet. What follows is an excerpt from the teacher's contract of one North Carolina town:

I promise to take a vital interest in all phases of Sunday school work, donating of my time, service and money without stint for the benefit and uplift of the community.

I promise to abstain from dancing, immodest dressing, and any other conduct unbecoming a teacher and lady.

I promise not to go out with any young man except as it may be necessary to stimulate Sunday-school work.

I promise not to fall in love, to become engaged or secretly married.

I promise to remain in the dormitory or on the school grounds when not actively engaged in school or church work elsewhere.

I promise not to encourage or tolerate the least familiarity on the part of any of my boy pupils.

I promise to sleep eight hours a night, eat carefully, etc., etc.
Brenton, *What's Happened to Teacher?*, p. 74.

The nation enjoyed increased prosperity but, again, teachers did not share in it. In the early decades of the century teachers were barely paid a subsistence wage. One way that teachers could save money (and nosy school boards could keep an eye on them) was by living in community-owned boardinghouses, called "teacherages." While these houses were generally well-kept and inexpensive and provided the teacher with companionship, it was quite difficult for a teacher to have a private life.

A society's image of a group is mirrored in its popular culture. One researcher read sixty-two novels published since 1900 to discover fiction's image of the teacher. The male teacher, he found, was portrayed as solitary, effeminate, and

· impractical. The female teacher was either young, single, and frustrated or a tired sexless old maid. Another researcher looked at portraits of teachers in movies and books before 1950 and saw passive lives—monotonous, pedestrian, colorless—worthy of pity, but scarcely worthy of the respect granted to those who provide leadership and inspiration to the young.

In this description of the "career teacher," Walter Beggs of the University of Nebraska captures the essence of the professional teacher. He goes on to estimate that only about one out of four teachers presently practicing fit his definition. And herein lies the difficulty. Until the great majority of teachers qualifies by Beggs's definition, or until there is a qualitative regrouping of those presently identified as "teachers," teaching will not be called a profession.

The professional associations

The protection of teachers' freedom and the improvement of their working conditions and rewards will not just happen. In the words of Ernie Lundquist, "Nobody gives you nothing for nothing." Whatever advance teachers make will occur as a result of their hard work and readiness to fight for what they believe.

Our country has many troublesome problems and there is great competition for resources. For instance, it was clear during the sixties that the space program and the war in Southeast Asia enjoyed a higher priority than did civil rights, pollution, and education. In the rough-and-tumble of a democracy, teachers need someone or something to look out for their interests and the interests of the recipients of their services, children. This is the function of the teachers' associations. At present, there are two national organizations, the National Education Association and the American Federation of Teachers, which claim to speak for teachers. They represent teachers to the federal, state, and local governments, to educational authorities at the state and local level, and, finally, to the general public. It is important to know something about them, because if you become a teacher they will claim to be speaking for you.

WEREN'T YOU HEAD OF THE ENGLISH DEPARTMENT AT THE HIGH SCHOOL?

I USED TO BE BUT I COULDN'T RESIST THE LURE OF BIG MONEY—

9-24

BRICKMAN

Washington Star Syndicate, Inc.

Where have teachers been and where are they going?

Two views of the big city teacher

The status of the teacher as a professional is particularly precarious. New York City recruiting brochures paint a glowing picture of the teacher's professionalism, of the opportunities for professional development, and of the personal relationship between administrative staff and teachers:

The administrative staff is composed of men and women with a modern outlook. They realize the value of creativity in teaching, encourage innovation and new approaches, and understand the need for academic freedom within a professional atmosphere. But even more important, they know that the most effective teaching will result where the teacher is recognized as an individual and is given the opportunity to make full use of his abilities and specialties. The personal relationship established between the administration and the teachers has promoted the progress of education both in the schoolroom and at the level of professional development.

The picture painted by the report of the Mayor's Advisory Panel on Decentralization in the New York City Schools, commonly called the Bundy Report, is altogether different:

New York City teachers are isolated at the end of a long chain of command. They are not consulted regularly, if at all, about curriculum, or classroom surroundings, or the criteria on which colleagues, to say nothing of supervisors, are chosen. Initiative and innovation, if not discouraged, are administratively difficult because of the uniformity imposed perforce by a highly centralized system. Furthermore, the Panel has it on the word of teachers who appear to be dedicated to their profession that in too many schools teachers are fearful. They are said to be subject to overt and subtle reprisals (including, ironically, assignment to difficult classes) for any criticism of the school. The way to avoid reprisals, as one teacher put it, "is to take all directives from the supervisors at face value and never question, criticize, suggest, or file grievances."

Anthony G. Oettinger, *Run, Computer, Run: The Mythology of Educational Innovation* (Cambridge: Harvard University Press, 1969), pp. 112–113.

Before discussing the two major organizations, we should point out that there are many different teacher organizations operating at a multiplicity of levels. Normally, each school district has professional associations that are linked to county, regional, and state organizations. Of perhaps greater importance to the beginning teacher are organizations of teachers in particular specialties at these different levels. There are active organizations for teachers of reading, English, mathematics, home economics, and all the established curricular areas. They play an important part in keeping the teacher informed about his field through journals, inservice training institutes, and conferences and conventions. Because there are so many of these organizations and their activities are so varied, we will restrict our attention to the large umbrella organizations, the National Education Association and the American Federation of Teachers.

Johann Pestalozzi (1746–1827)

Well into middle age, Johann Pestalozzi gave every sign of being a bungling failure. As a youth in Zurich he hated school, and afterward pursued a long series of abortive occupational ventures. Nor was he a success as a personality. Raised by his widowed mother and a maid, he developed great sensitivity but remained overly dependent on women and slightly effeminate. In later life, the fame he achieved reportedly went to his head. But despite all his personal failings, Pestalozzi is both a hero and a model for educators.

After attending the University of Switzerland, where he finally learned to enjoy studying and became active in social and political reform, Pestalozzi established an orphanage in his own home, where he taught neglected children the rudiments of agriculture and simple trades. But the orphanage failed in 1780 and Pestalozzi, in despair, went into seclusion to write *The Evening Hour of a Hermit,* a moving compendium of aphorisms and reflections.

Much later, at the age of fifty-two, he began a new career. When Napoleon's armies massacred the citizens of the town of Stans, he collected several dozen destitute children and cared for them under extremely difficult conditions. Pestalozzi made the Institute for the Poor an educational experiment, teaching the children to spin, weave, and do farm work, as well as to study. But because he had accepted more students than he could accommodate, including retarded children, he was forced to close the school for lack of funds. This was one more failure in an uninterrupted series, but Pestalozzi was undaunted. He had found his vocation in teaching and his happiness among children.

In 1805 Pestalozzi founded a boarding school in an abandoned castle at Yverdon, which flourished for twenty years. It quickly became famous and attracted students from all over Europe. Its curriculum, which emphasized drawing, writing, singing, physical exercise, group recitations, map-making, and field trips, was based on the principle of "sense impression"—the idea that we understand only what we observe clearly, and that words and ideas have meaning only when they are related to concrete objects. Pestalozzi thus put considerable stress on the importance of concrete situations in the child's learning. The study of geography involved field trips and the construction of elaborate models of whole territories. Pestalozzi anticipated modern methods of math instruction by using concrete objects to develop number competence. Four students or four chairs, for instance, illustrated the concept "four." Students learned to read and write with slates, pencils, and alphabet cards. Pestalozzi also emphasized the importance of art in the curriculum, not only as an emotional outlet for the children but also to encourage creativity and develop intellectual discipline.

Pestalozzi's educational theory was built on the assumption that human beings are motivated by three drives: primitive impulses, social needs, and ethical yearnings. He conceived of education as the process by which ethics triumphed over animal impulses. His model of learning was the family, with the teacher acting like a father and serving as a model to be imitated. The ideal of love governed Pestalozzi's philosophy of education—love that should not be modified or withdrawn even if the student misbehaved. The teacher, he was convinced, should never punish or show disapproval, a very novel attitude in the early nineteenth century. The Yverdon curriculum offered carefully graded instruction, allowance for individual differences, and ability grouping; in general, Pestalozzi was less concerned with "meeting standards" than with the integrity of the student and his work.

Misunderstood by his contemporaries, who considered him too radical and emotional and accused him of taking children too seriously, Pestalozzi nevertheless achieved fame and international influence within his lifetime. He came to be called the Christopher Columbus of elementary education because he opened up so much new territory in that field. Several foreign governments sent teachers to Yverdon for instruction—Pestalozzi's teacher-training department was unique at the time—and he was made an honorary citizen of the French Republic and knighted by the Czar. Such fame might make any man dizzy.

Advocates of love and acceptance in the educational process owe and acknowledge a heavy debt to Johann Pestalozzi.

The National Education Association

The National Education Association, or NEA, is a complex institution difficult to describe briefly. Perhaps a metaphor might help. Think of the NEA as a huge department store which sells many kinds of goods and services to a very diverse clientele. Think of it, too, as an old established firm with deep traditions and a large, loyal clientele. In fact, the NEA has over one million and a half members and directly affects almost as many more. To serve special interest groups within the Association there are twenty-nine different departments, national affiliates, and associated organizations (such as The Department of Vocational Education, Public School Adult Education, and School Librarians), numerous Headquarters Divisions (Research, Human Relations Council, International Relations), and approximately twenty-five Commissions (NEA and American Textbook Publishers Institute, NEA and American Legion, Teacher Education and Professional Standards). It operates on the national, state, and local school district levels. It provides a variety of services to its more than 8,000 local level affiliates. It has an annual operating budget of over thirty million dollars.

The NEA was founded in 1857 as, significantly, the National Teachers Association. Shortly after the Civil War, its name was changed to the National Education Association and it became, generally speaking, the professional organization for school administrators. Up until World War I, the NEA had a small and relatively constant membership of about 10,000. The American Federation of Teachers had been founded in 1916, with the primary purpose of organizing classroom teachers, rather than anybody who could claim the label "educator." This competition was a strong incentive to the NEA to broaden its membership and its concerns. In the next fifty years the NEA grew tremendously, not only in membership but also in services and national influence.

The goals of the NEA, as declared in its Charter, are "to elevate the character and advance the interests of the profession of teaching and to promote the cause of education in the United States." In recent years it has been influential in improving the preservice training of teachers and raising the entrance qualifications for teaching, largely through the establishment and activities of the National

Commission on Teacher Education and Professional Standards. Much of the NEA's energies, however, are expended on services for its membership. The NEA conducts studies on practical issues of instruction in various teaching fields and with various types of children. It has an active research department which supplies data on teacher supply and demand, working conditions and salaries, and a great variety of issues related to schooling and the professional status of teachers. It makes these data and studies available to local and state associations for their efforts to improve conditions at their level. It engages in lobbying efforts at the national, state, and local levels to influence legislation in accord with its vision of how public education should be conducted. Because of its lobbying efforts, the NEA can take a major share of the credit for various federal aid to education programs. Also, the NEA aids teachers whose legal rights are being violated or who are being treated unethically. In sum, it is attempting to move education and the profession of teaching forward on a very broad front.

The NEA has made mistakes, and it is frequently criticized for its slowness to take action on important issues and problems. It avoided taking a stand on the Supreme Court's important school desegregation decision of 1954. Recently, however, it has championed the black teachers in some southern states who have lost their jobs as a result of the consolidation of black and white schools. Only within the last ten years has it begun to respond to the deteriorating state of education in the nation's urban centers. Critics claim that its size and broad representation—rural and urban, north and south, administrators and teachers—make it slow to respond to pressing social and educational problems. A more persistent criticism, particularly in the sixties, came from classroom teachers, who make up the bulk of the dues-paying membership. They complained that the NEA was too busy with "broad front" educational issues to give adequate attention to the problems of teachers.

During the same period, by contrast, the American Federation of Teachers was acting quite militantly on behalf of teachers. Furthermore, teachers argued, the NEA was dominated by school administrators, who do not always have teachers' interests at heart. (A school administrator who can keep teachers' salaries and benefits at a low level is highly valued by some Boards of Education.)

More recently, the NEA has begun to move again. A transferral of power from the school administration groups to the Classroom Teachers' Association has taken place. The Association is becoming more aggressive. It has dropped its former objections to strikes and now looks on the strike as a last-resort but legitimate weapon to attain its ends. It is taking a more vigorous role in elections from local school board to the Presidency, and politicians are paying serious attention to teachers. What was once "the great big happy educational family" of NEA is beginning to show cracks and rifts. This is frequently the price of movement. The cause of its power shift and increasing militance is said to be the rise of the American Federation of Teachers.

The American Federation of Teachers

If the NEA can be compared to a large department store, then the American Federation of Teachers, or AFT, more closely resembles a small specialty store that aggressively promotes a few items. In contrast to the NEA, the AFT has traditionally been interested exclusively in representing teachers and other nonsupervisory school personnel.

John Dewey, the great American philosopher and educator, took out the first AFT membership card in 1916 and remained an active member throughout his entire life. Dewey thought there ought to be an organization exclusively for teachers. As we have indicated, this "teachers only" emphasis has been a major instrument in the AFT's struggle with the NEA for the allegiance of teachers. The AFT contends that in the NEA's broad efforts to improve education little has been done to improve the lot of the classroom teacher.

In the structure and successful operation of schools, the teacher is central. Good teachers make good schools. The professional teacher not only knows how to direct the educational and personal development of children in the classroom, he also joins with his colleagues in an effective organization to advance the interest of teachers, pupils, and the schools through collective bargaining.[4]

The AFT has a membership of over 400,000, making it approximately one-fourth the size of the NEA. Although the AFT has less than 2,000 local affiliates throughout the country, in recent years it has built up great strength in major urban centers. The AFT won a major victory in 1960, when its affiliate, the United Federation of Teachers (UFT), became the sole bargaining agent for all New York City teachers. At present, the AFT represents teachers in New York City, Chicago, Philadelphia, Washington, D.C., Cleveland, Pittsburgh, Kansas City, St. Louis, Detroit, and Boston.

The leadership of the American Federation of Teachers thinks of their organization as a part of the labor movement. The AFT itself is affiliated with the AFL-CIO, which in turn has a membership of over fourteen million. Much of the AFT's recent growth has been due to success in introducing the collective bargaining process into the annual salary negotiations of teachers. Through the use of the strike, and the threat of strikes, it has been responsible for raising starting salaries of beginning teachers to over $10,000 in some major cities. In New York City, a teacher with seven years' experience and a master's degree now receives just under $20,000 a year. Although the AFT is noted for hard bargaining on bread-and-butter issues, such as salaries, benefits, and retirement after twenty-five years of service, it has also been a defender of academic freedom and of greater participation in decision making by teachers. Recently it has formed a group within the AFT to continually study questions of educational policy. The organization is called QuEST, standing for Quality Education Standards in Teaching. QuEST operates as an ongoing study group, investigating such questions as teacher education and certification, the use of paraprofessionals, and the effect of federal money on local education.

Although the AFT has been considered the more liberal of the two major teachers' organizations, it has recently been criticized for growing protectionism. It has appeared to be the foe of the attempts of urban communities to put the control of the schools into the hands of neighborhood people. Also, AFT's strong commitment to win more autonomy for classroom teachers in dismissing and disciplining "disruptive" children has been interpreted by some poor and minority group people as against the interests of their children.

[4] *Goals of the American Federation of Teachers AFL-CIO* (Washington, D.C.: The Federation), p. 3.

NEA Code of Ethics

Preamble
The educator believes in the worth and dignity of man. He recognizes the supreme importance of the pursuit of truth, devotion to excellence, and the nurture of democratic citizenship. He regards as essential to these goals the protection of freedom to learn and to teach and the guarantee of equal educational opportunity for all. The educator accepts his responsibility to practice his profession according to the highest ethical standards.

The educator recognizes the magnitude of the responsibility he has accepted in choosing a career in education, and engages himself, individually and collectively with other educators, to judge his colleagues, and to be judged by them, in accordance with the provisions of this code.

Principle I—Commitment to the Student
In fulfilling his obligation to the student, the educator—
1 Shall not without just cause restrain the student from independent action in his pursuit of learning, and shall not without just cause deny the student access to varying points of view.
2 Shall not deliberately suppress or distort subject matter for which he bears responsibility.
3 Shall make reasonable effort to protect the student from conditions harmful to learning or to health and safety.
4 Shall conduct professional business in such a way that he does not expose the student to unnecessary embarrassment or disparagement.
5 Shall not on the ground of race, color, creed, or national origin exclude any student from participation in or deny him benefits under any program, nor grant any discriminatory consideration or advantage.
6 Shall not use professional relationships with students for private advantage.
7 Shall keep in confidence information that has been obtained in the course of professional service, unless disclosure serves professional purposes or is required by law.
Shall not tutor for remuneration students assigned to his classes, unless no other qualified teacher is reasonably available.

Principle II—Commitment to the Public
In fulfilling his obligation to the public, the educator—
Shall not misrepresent an institution or organization with which he is affiliated, and shall take adequate precautions to distinguish between his personal and institutional or organizational views.
Shall not knowingly distort or misrepresent the facts concerning educational matters in direct and indirect public expressions.
Shall not interfere with a colleague's exercise of political and citizenship rights and responsibilities.
Shall not use institutional privileges for private gain or to promote political candidates or partisan political activities.
Shall accept no gratuities, gifts, or favors that might impair or appear to impair professional judgment, nor offer any favor, service, or thing of value to obtain special advantage.

Where have teachers been and where are they going?

Principle III—Commitment to the Profession
In fulfilling his obligation to the profession, the educator—
1   Shall not discriminate on the ground of race, color, creed, or national origin for membership in professional organizations, nor interfere with the free participation of colleagues in the affairs of their association.
2   Shall accord just and equitable treatment to all members of the profession in the exercise of their professional rights and responsibilities.
3   Shall not use coercive means or promise special treatment in order to influence professional decisions of colleagues.
4   Shall withhold and safeguard information acquired about colleagues in the course of employment, unless disclosure serves professional purposes.
5   Shall not refuse to participate in a professional inquiry when requested by an appropriate professional association.
6   Shall provide upon the request of the aggrieved party a written statement of specific reason for recommendations that lead to the denial of increments, significant changes in employment, or termination of employment.
7   Shall not misrepresent his professional qualifications.
8   Shall not knowingly distort evaluations of colleagues.

Principle IV—Commitment to Professional Employment Practices
In fulfilling his obligation to professional employment practices, the educator—
1   Shall apply for, accept, offer, or assign a position or responsibility on the basis of professional preparation and legal qualifications.
2   Shall apply for a specific position only when it is known to be vacant, and shall refrain from underbidding or commenting adversely about other candidates.
3   Shall not knowingly withhold information regarding a position from an applicant or misrepresent an assignment or conditions of employment.
4   Shall give prompt notice to the employing agency of any change in availability of service, and the employing agent shall give prompt notice of change in availability or nature of a position.
5   Shall adhere to the terms of a contract or appointment, unless these terms have been legally terminated, falsely represented, or substantially altered by unilateral action of the employing agency.
6   Shall conduct professional business through channels, when available, that have been jointly approved by the professional organization and the employing agency.
7   Shall not delegate assigned tasks to unqualified personnel.
8   Shall permit no commercial exploitation of his professional position.
9   Shall use time granted for the purpose for which it is intended.

National Education Association, *Code of Ethics of the Education Profession,* adopted by the NEA Representative Assembly, July, 1968; amended July, 1970. Reprinted by permission of the Association.

The two professional organizations appear to be at the edge of merger. Already, the New York state affiliates of the NEA and AFT have merged. The national representatives of the two groups are said to be very close to agreement on merger plans. During the last several years, both organizations have spent a great deal of time, money, and talent competing with one another. A merger would eliminate that waste and create one giant organization which could speak authoritatively for all the nation's teachers. In fact, teachers would represent the largest group within organized labor, with the exception of the teamsters. Political power of teachers in national elections and the ability to call a nationwide school shutdown would give teachers, for better or for worse, immense power. Whether or not such a merger will serve the general good of the people, we'll have to wait to see.

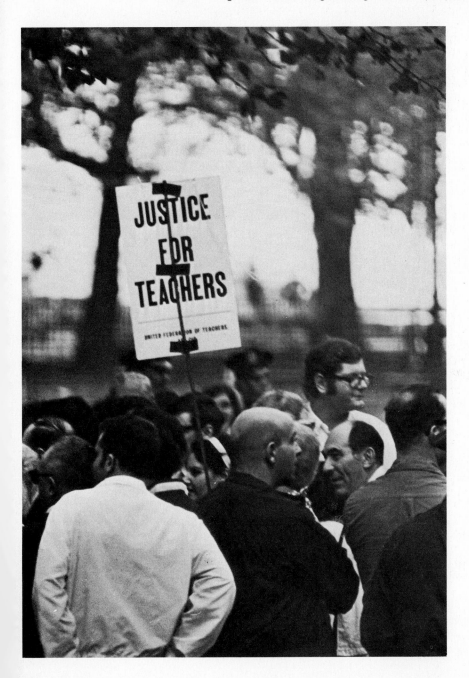

Where have teachers been and where are they going?

AFT Bill of Rights

The teacher is entitled to a life of dignity equal to the high standard of service that is justly demanded of that profession. Therefore, we hold these truths to be self-evident:

I   Teachers have the right to think freely and to express themselves openly and without fear. This includes the right to hold views contrary to the majority.

II They shall be entitled to the free exercise of their religion. No restraint shall be put upon them in the manner, time or place of their worship.

III They shall have the right to take part in social, civil, and political affairs. They shall have the right, outside the classroom, to participate in political campaigns and to hold office. They may assemble peaceably and may petition any government agency, including their employers, for a redress of grievances. They shall have the same freedom in all things as other citizens.

IV The right of teachers to live in places of their own choosing, to be free of restraints in their mode of living and the use of their leisure time shall not be abridged.

V   Teaching is a profession, the right to practice which is not subject to the surrender of other human rights. No one shall be deprived of professional status, or the right to practice it, or the practice thereof in any particular position, without due process of law.

VI The right of teachers to be secure in their jobs, free from political influence or public clamor, shall be established by law. The right to teach after qualification in the manner prescribed by law is a property right, based upon the inalienable rights to life, liberty, and the pursuit of happiness.

VII In all cases affecting the teacher's employment or professional status a full hearing by an impartial tribunal shall be afforded with the right to full judicial review. No teacher shall be deprived of employment or professional status but for specific causes established by law having a clear relation to the competence or qualification to teach, proved by the weight of the evidence. In all such cases the teacher shall enjoy the right to a speedy and public trial, to be informed of the nature and cause of the accusation, to be confronted with the accusing witnesses, to subpoena witnesses and papers, and to the assistance of counsel. No teacher shall be called upon to answer any charge affecting his employment or professional status but upon probable cause, supported by oath or affirmation.

VIII It shall be the duty of the employer to provide culturally adequate salaries, security in illness and adequate retirement income. The teacher has the right to such a salary as will: a) Afford a family standard of living comparable to that enjoyed by other professional people in the community; b) To make possible freely chosen professional study; c) Afford the opportunity for leisure and recreation common to our heritage.

IX Teachers shall not be required under penalty of reduction of salary to pursue studies beyond those required to obtain professional status. After serving a reasonable probationary period a teacher shall be entitled to permanent tenure terminable only for just cause. They shall be free as in other professions in the use of their own time. They shall not be required to perform extracurricular work against their will or without added compensation.

X   To equip people for modern life requires the most advanced educational methods. Therefore, the teacher is entitled to good classrooms, adequate

teaching materials, teachable class size and administrative protection and assistance in maintaining discipline.

XI These rights are based upon the proposition that the culture of a people can rise
only as its teachers improve. A teaching force accorded the highest possible
professional dignity is the surest guarantee that blessings of liberty will be
preserved. Therefore, the possession of these rights imposes the challenge to be
worthy of their enjoyment.

II Since teachers must be free in order to teach freedom, the right to be members
of organizations of their own choosing must be guaranteed. In all matters pertaining to their salaries and working conditions they shall be entitled to bargain
collectively through representatives of their own choosing. They are entitled to
have the schools administered by superintendents, boards or committees which
function in a democratic manner.

American Federation of Teachers, *Bill of Rights*. Reprinted by permission.

Professionalism at the crossroads

Myron Lieberman, a long-time student of teacher professionalism, has said that
the history of education shows very clearly that strong teacher organizations are
required to prevent arbitrary, irresponsible action by school boards and
officials.[5] The accounts in this chapter of the historical treatment of teachers
underline the need for teachers to assert themselves. In dollars and purchasing
power, the salaries of teachers have almost doubled since 1940. In school districts where teachers and boards of education have engaged in collective
bargaining, or where teachers have engaged in militant actions, teachers have
received more money than in districts where teachers have been less active. On
the other hand, teachers still play a negligible role in determining educational
policies and have made only marginal improvements in their working conditions.
As mentioned earlier, though, teachers are about to merge their two professional
organizations. Once these presently antagonistic groups merge, "teacher power"
will become a potentially revolutionary force in American education.

The basis for this new power of teachers will be twofold: politics and work stoppage. At present, teachers' organizations (both NEA and AFT) are vigorously
developing local and state level political organizations. Organizational leaders
are hoping to achieve their purposes through the election of friendly candidates
and the support of favorable legislation. An organization with approximately two
million dues-paying members, many of whom are willing to actively involve
themselves in political campaigns, would be a major new force in the American
political scene. Second, teachers will wield power through the potential for state
and even national work stoppages. At present, over half the married women in
America are working. When the schools close, many of them must stay home to
tend to their children. Besides the educational consequences, a national work
stoppage would have a severe economic impact on the nation. Therefore,
between politics and work stoppages, a new teacher's professional organization
will wield a great deal of power.

[5] Lieberman, p. 13.

Where have teachers been and where are they going?

This new power could be used, of course, to the direct benefit of children. It could be used to improve teacher education, to give teachers a greater say in their own professional affairs, to divert more funds to educational research and innovative projects and, in general, to improve the professional services available to the public.

The new power and autonomy of teachers is not necessarily good, however. Nor is professionalism in itself desirable. Professionalism may, indeed, work against the highest goals of education. When all the rhetoric is pruned away, professional groups, whether they be the American Medical Association, the American Bar Association, or the National Education Association, appear to exist primarily for the benefit of their members. In the interest of protecting and expanding the rights of its members, a professional group may ride roughshod over the needs and rights of the client group. For instance, insisting on tenure rights for all teachers who have taught for three years or more, makes it difficult to get rid of incompetents. In the big cities, basing eligibility for transfer to more congenial schools on seniority may be robbing the most difficult schools of exactly the experienced teacher talent those schools need. Behind the never-never-land jargon of professionalism, one often finds naked self-interest. Occasionally, teachers use their "professional status" as a barrier to protect themselves from criticism by children and parents. "How dare you question what I have done. *I am a professional!*" The question of professionalism is a tricky one. It seems that it ultimately reduces to a need for balance. The teachers' right to be rewarded and safeguarded against unfair practices must be carefully balanced against the students' and the taxpayers' right to be served justly and well by the teacher. It is a constant struggle to strike an even balance. As Myron Brenton has said,

Every professional group closes ranks to protect its own; teachers are no exception. But teachers are the exception in that they seem to want—at this juncture, at least—the best of both worlds: the security of the civil servant and the prestige and rewards of the professional. More than that, they want a major say in matters of educational policy while getting tenure protection. In other words, they want power without accountability, which is basically an antidemocratic stance.[6]

At this moment in history, the direction the teaching profession will take is unclear. The struggle between the NEA and the AFT appears to be resolving, but a struggle between organized teachers and the public seems to be gathering momentum. The course of these events will definitely be affected by the energies and ideals that the next generation of teachers brings with them into the profession.

Discussion questions

1 Do you think that teachers should devote themselves to becoming professionals? If so, what must they do? Are you willing to do it? How do you feel about Walter Beggs's description of the "career teacher" on page 307?
2 Do teachers need a professional organization? What are the essential functions performed by such a group?

[6] Brenton, p. 255.

3　Compare the NEA Code of Ethics and the AFT Bill of Rights. How do the assumptions and attitudes about teaching represented by the two documents differ? What seem to be the overriding concerns of the two organizations? How do the images of teachers they project differ? To what extent do you think a merger of the NEA and the AFT would solve the problems of each and end the competition between them? What new problems might such a merger create?

4　Do you think that discrimination or prejudice against women is still a factor in the working conditions or image of teachers today?

5　Our capsule reports on teaching in past centuries illustrate the immense amount of attention that was paid to teachers' conduct and personal lives. On what assumptions about the role of the teacher was this practice based? Do you think any such concern is justified? Do you think there is any kind of behavior outside the classroom that should be forbidden to teachers, or that should be cause for dismissal? To what extent is the teacher's personal life still subject to scrutiny by school officials?

6　For you, right now, what seem the most important issues for teachers to concern themselves with—increased power? higher salaries? better training? something else? Be prepared to defend your choice. What can you do to work for the changes you consider most important?

7　What dangers or weaknesses seem to be endemic to professional organizations? Would you be willing to sacrifice security for professionalism? Will you be a professional? Why?

8　What is your opinion of tenure for teachers? What arguments for or against it can you suggest? Would you be willing to work in a school system that did not offer tenure?

9　How do people react when you tell them you are thinking of becoming a teacher? Why?

For further reading

- American Federation of Teachers. *Goals of the American Federation of Teachers.* Washington, D.C.: The Federation, n.d. A statement of philosophy and priorities by the major labor-related professional association of teachers.
- Brenton, Myron. *What's Happened to Teacher?* New York: Coward-McCann, 1970. A professional writer's view of the new mood among teachers, and their reasons for moving from passivity to militance. Highly readable journalistic account of the teaching profession.
- Corwin, Ronald, G. *Militant Professionalism: A Study of Organizational Conflict in High Schools.* New York: Appleton-Century-Crofts, 1970. This book examines the question of teacher militancy from the point of view of a sociologist. The organizational forces affecting the individual high-school teacher's professional behavior are explored.
- Darland, David. "Preparation in the Governance of the Profession." In *Teachers for the Real World,* ed. B. Othaniel Smith, *et al.,* pp. 135–150. Washington, D.C.: American Association of Colleges for Teacher Education, 1969. The former editor of the *Journal of Teacher Education* outlines how and why teachers must take over the governance of their own profession.
- Dreeben, Robert. *The Nature of Teaching: Schools and the Work of Teachers.* Glenview, Ill.: Scott-Foresman, 1970. This book presents a sociologist's view of who teachers are and what kind of work they do. The book provides a corrective to the often romanticized view of teaching.

- Fischer, Louis, and David Schimmel. *The Civil Rights of Teachers*. New York: Harper & Row, 1973. This book by two lawyer-educators provides an up-to-date view of the teacher's relationship to the law. It covers such topics as freedom of speech, loyalty oaths, political activity, and the teacher's private life.
- Kaufman, Bel. *Up the Down Staircase*. Englewood Cliffs, N.J.: Prentice-Hall, 1964. This uniquely written novel conveys in realistic fashion the web of relationships and forces that impinge upon a teacher's life. It contains a particularly humorous description of the beginning teacher's relationship with her administrators.
- Lieberman, Myron. *Education as a Profession*. Englewood Cliffs, N.J.: Prentice-Hall, 1956. The occupation of teaching is carefully analyzed to determine how it "fits" the standard qualifications of a profession and how it does not.
- Lindsay, Margaret, ed. *New Horizons for the Teaching Profession*. Washington, D.C.: National Education Association, 1961. Highly readable report of the "New Horizons" project, which examined the status of teaching and charted new goals for the profession.
- National Education Association. *The NEA Handbook*. Washington, D.C.: The Association, 1973–1974. A yearly directory of the NEA and its component organizations. Outlines the Association's purpose, status, recent activities, and achievements.
- Rosenthal, Alan. *Pedagogues and Power: Teacher Groups in School Politics*. Syracuse, N.Y.: Syracuse University Press, 1969. This book discusses the whole question of teacher militancy and demands for decision-making authority.
- Stinnett, Timothy M., and Huggett, Albert J. *Professional Problems of Teachers*. New York: Macmillan, 1963. A study of the professional needs of teachers and the ways in which school systems normally try to meet them. A good introduction for people planning to teach.
- Stuart, Jesse. *The Thread That Runs So True*. New York: Charles Scribner's Sons, 1948. An autobiographical account of the famous writer's experience as a teacher in a one-room school. Interesting description of the problems and successes of a beginning teacher, and also of life in rural America.
- Vollmer, Howard M., and Mills, Donald L., eds. *Professionalization*. Englewood Cliffs, N.J.: Prentice-Hall, 1966. This collection of essays deals with several professions (including teaching) and the professionalization process. Highly specialized but interesting volume.
- Waller, Willard. *The Sociology of Teaching*. New York: John Wiley & Sons, 1965. Originally written in 1932, this survey of what students and citizens thought of teachers and education thirty years ago still contains much of value. It is rich in incisive analyses of the teacher's role and suggestions for prospective teachers.
- Woodring, Paul. *A Fourth of a Nation*. New York: McGraw-Hill, 1957. Presents a major program to improve American education. Although somewhat dated, it was influential in changing the direction of the American schools in the 1950s and 1960s.

Films

- *The Dynamics of Negotiations* (Educational Service Bureau, color, 45 min., 1969). Nationally recognized specialists detail the process of educational negotiations from the opening sessions to the finalizing of agreements. This film is designed to teach techniques of collective bargaining for application by local teacher negotiating teams.

- *New York City Teachers' Strike* (AFL-CIO, b&w, 27 min., 1962). The first large New York City teachers' strike, not the more recent one, is documented in this film produced by CBS News. Members of AFT Local 2 are interviewed about their protest against wages and working conditions. PTA leaders carrying coffee to the picket lines comment on the necessity for parents to join teachers in calling attention to the failures of the city and state educational administrations. Union President Cogan replies to an injunction, and Board of Education officials explain why they feel the strike is illegal. Until a more current film is made, this film will help to raise discussion issues of teachers' right to strike and the relationship of teacher grievances to parent concerns.
- *Quiet Too Long* (Guggenheim Productions, 16mm, b&w, 29 min.). Presents scenes in the classroom, on the streets, in budget meetings, and at a space center, reflecting the new militancy among teachers determined to persuade citizens and local politicians of the need for improved school facilities, better teaching conditions, and adequate school budgets.
- *Solving Impasses in Negotiations* (Educational Service Bureau, color, 35 min., 1970). When collective bargaining runs into trouble, says this film, teachers and their negotiations team need to reorganize their plans and restate their needs more effectively. This film is a good example of the complex view that teachers function both as public servants and as employed and unionized workers.
- *A Whisper of Dissent* (IDEA, color, 35 min., 1969). Chet Huntley, former NBC news anchorman, leads this tour through a number of the issues in collective negotiations. Teachers, principals, and government figures present both their points of view and their emotions about collective bargaining. The film is addressed to the community at large for use in school systems that make contracts with organized groups of teachers.

Audiotapes

- *On Education* (Center for the Study of Democratic Institutions, 39 min., 1970). Beginning with an excerpt from retiring President Robert Hutchins's farewell address to students at the University of Chicago, this tape goes on to pursue in remarks and answers to questions Mr. Hutchins's views on American education. He speaks from the perspective of a teacher about the state of educational institutions.
- *The Organized Profession* (National Education Association, 54 min. total, 1970). This tape presents a discussion by NEA members of collective negotiations and the political role of teachers. It is divided into six short segments, each of which is intended to stimulate a discussion session. The individual topics are as follows: *A Call to Action* (3 min.); *The New York State Teachers Association Tackles Professionalism* (15 min.); *Instructional Councils: One Way to Begin* (7 min.); *Negotiation: More Than Bread and Butter* (11 min.); *The Teacher as Politician* (10 min.); *Wanted: A Secretary of Education* (8 min.).

Refer to Appendix for addresses of distributors.

10   What are the tension points in American education?

Rarely does a day go by when educational issues fail to make headlines in newspapers across the country. Sex education, teacher strikes, inequality of educational opportunity, decentralization, local control of schools, and drug usage are only a few of the issues that we read about daily. This chapter will explore some of the most sensitive and controversial issues in American education. Naturally, in such a short space we will be able to treat each topic only briefly. You are urged to pursue additional reading on any of the issues that particularly interest you by consulting the section entitled "For Further Reading" at the end of the chapter.

Chapter contents	**Inequality of educational opportunity**
	Compensatory education
	Desegregation
	Model subsystems
	Parallel systems
	Total system reform
	School finance reform
	Student rights
	Teacher power
	Sex education
	Student drug use
	Sexism and sex role stereotyping
	Religion and the schools
	Accountability

Before you launch into the rest of the chapter, take a few moments to answer the following questions about the most controversial topics in American education in order to assess your own position. Compare your responses with those of your classmates.

1   Should school officials have the right to regulate student freedom of speech in school newspapers? student use of profanity? student wearing of armbands to protest some political action?
2   Is drug usage a serious problem in your local community? Are the schools doing a good job of teaching about the effects of drug use? Are they treating the subject honestly? Should this topic be taught in the schools?
3   Do you favor or oppose a system that would hold teachers and administrators accountable for the progress of students?
4   Should teachers be paid on a standardized salary scale, or should each teacher be paid on the basis of the quality of his work?
5   Do teacher organizations have too much power? Should they have the right to strike for higher salaries and better working conditions?

6   Do schools perpetuate sexism, thereby limiting the human potential of both boys and girls, but primarily girls?
7   Do you believe that local control and financing of schools is desirable?
8   Should each public-school student within a state have an approximately equal amount of money spent on his education per year, or should the amount vary depending on each community's financial ability to support its schools?
9   Do you approve or disapprove of public schools offering courses in sex education? What if these courses discussed topics such as birth control?
10 Do you support or oppose giving public tax money to parochial schools?

Opinion on these issues is extremely diverse. Whatever your views, however, you and your classmates are probably short on data to support your opinions. This is not unusual, since even people who feel strongly about these topics have often not really investigated the arguments for the other side and weighed the issues in order to arrive at a reasoned, logical position. Because these topics touch on our religious, political, or philosophical convictions, we usually respond to them emotionally rather than rationally.

The goal of this chapter is simple: to explore opposing positions on some of the most controversial topics in American education today in order to equip you, as a teacher, with understanding of, and sensitivity to, the exposed nerve endings of American education. Keep in mind the significance of these tension points: they are the result of an attempt to educate children in a pluralistic society. That is, our society is made up of diverse individuals and groups, each with different axes to grind and different ideas about what a school should be, what it should teach, and what life in school should be like. Tension points are inevitable when diverse groups and individuals with different objectives for the schools attempt to achieve their objectives. As a teacher, you will certainly be involved. Since teachers have a deep responsibility to the schools, it is important that they provide leadership in seeking enlightened solutions to these complex and touchy issues.

One warning: our coverage of these tension points is like an iceberg, one-ninth of which is visible, while the other eight-ninths is submerged. We only skim the surface of these issues; you should not be satisfied to stop here. It is your responsibility to don the diving suit if you want to find out what those icebergs really look like.

Inequality of educational opportunity

There is probably no issue in education today more important or more emotionally loaded than the charge that children of the poor, and of blacks, Chicanos, Puerto Ricans, and Indians are educationally discriminated against by the public schools. Statistics reveal, for example, that twelfth-grade Negroes in the urban Northeast read at the ninth-grade level and do mathematics at the seventh-grade level, while southern Negroes, Mexican-Americans, Puerto Ricans, and Indian Americans achieve at even lower levels. Dropout statistics attest to an even greater inequality between white middle class children's education and that received by children of the poor and minority groups. There is ample evidence, notably the Coleman Report and the report on racial isolation prepared

Dialogue

Kevin   *I think it's a little unfair to ask the reader to respond to our questions without giving him a chance to see how we would respond to them.*

Jim   *All right, let's pick a few and respond. What about question 3 on accountability?*

Kevin   *In theory, I'm in favor of more accountability on the part of teachers and administrators, but I don't see how they can be held accountable for student progress when so many factors like class size, instructional materials, and the like are beyond their control. Right now we're pretty unsophisticated about the whole question, but I suspect that procedures will be developed in the future that will make teacher accountability a reasonable process.*

Jim   *Questions 7 and 8 are interesting for me. I would like to see school districts organized so that gross inequalities in per pupil expenditures from district to district are remedied. Unless poor districts can pay salaries and obtain materials comparable to those of richer districts, we'll continue to perpetuate inequalities. Local control does allow for more experimentation than do the centralized systems typical of European countries. I guess I would like to see finances more centralized to even out per pupil expenditures, but I'd like local control over curriculum. How do you feel about public tax money going to help parochial schools?*

Kevin   *Thanks a lot for the hot potato. This is a terribly complex issue. A few things are clear, though. With the costs of education soaring every month, many parochial schools are going out of business and will continue to. A related point is that few parents who would like to send their children to parochial schools can afford to pay taxes for the public schools and pay tuition to a parochial school. Unless public tax money is used to support parochial schools—for instance, to support the nonreligious teaching and curriculum expenses—this question will just be academic because there will be only a handful of parochial schools left. Also, taxes would have to be increased to accommodate former parochial-school students in the public schools. However, it appears that the Supreme Court has already taken a firm stand on this issue, voting against all plans to support parochial schools with tax dollars.*

---

by the Commission on Civil Rights, that massive inequality exists in public-school educational achievement along social class and racial lines.[1] In other words, students of low socioeconomic status and minority group background score much lower than white middle class students on a variety of verbal and numerical tests.

Whatever the reasons, large numbers of poor and minority-group students are leaving school without the verbal and computational skills necessary to function effectively in American society. Who, if anyone, is to blame for this situation? the

---

[1] James S. Coleman *et al., Equality of Educational Opportunity* (Washington: U.S. Government Printing Office, 1966); and U.S. Commission on Civil Rights, *Racial Isolation in the Public Schools* (Washington: U.S. Government Printing Office, 1967).

schools? teachers and administrators? Or is the responsibility that of society as a whole, and are the schools merely a scapegoat? Talk to five different people and you will probably hear five different opinions about where blame should be affixed. But assessing blame is not a particularly fruitful exercise. Better questions can be asked, such as: What is meant by equality of educational opportunity? How is it measured? What are the responsibilities of the school system for providing equal educational opportunity? How can the achievement of poor and minority-group students be improved? Simple enough questions, but their answers are guaranteed to be controversial.

Equality of educational opportunity is hardly a new concept in American education, but its components have changed dramatically in the last two decades. For a long period in our history, the idea of equal educational opportunity involved the following elements:

1 providing a *free education* up to the time when the majority of students entered the labor force
2 providing a *common curriculum* for all children, regardless of background
3 providing that children from diverse backgrounds attend the *same school*
4 providing equality within a given *locality,* since local taxes supported the school system[2]

As a result of *Brown* v. *Board of Education,* the 1954 Supreme Court decision that held that segregated schools are inherently unequal because the *effects* of such separate schools are likely to be different, a new component was introduced into the concept of educational opportunity: that equality of educational opportunity is defined in terms of the effect, rather than the provisions, of schooling. In the *Brown* decision, the Supreme Court found that even when facilities and teacher salaries were identical, "equality of educational opportunity" did not exist.

Prior to *Brown,* the community and educational institution were expected only to provide equal resources—teachers, facilities, materials—and responsibility for advantageous use of those resources lay with the child and his family. Today many people have come to consider it the responsibility of the educational institution, not the child, to create achievement. As James Coleman states:

The difference in achievement at grade 12 between the average Negro and the average white is, in effect, the degree of inequality of opportunity, and the reduction of the inequality is a responsibility of the school. This shift in responsibility follows logically from the change in the concept of equality of educational opportunity from school resource inputs to effects of schooling.[3]

Others do not accept Coleman's assertion, arguing that the school should do its best to provide equal educational resources to all its students, but that it cannot be held accountable for differences in student learning. Although it is agreed that many poor minority children are not learning at a rate comparable to white

[2] James Coleman, "The Concept of Equality of Educational Opportunity," *Harvard Educational Review* 38 (Winter 1968): 11.
[3] Coleman, p. 22.

What are the tension points in American education?

Anselmo Garza (1944–   )

When Anselmo Garza resigned his position as a Spanish teacher in a Texas high school after two-and-a-half months, his superintendent called him a "complete failure." As a sixth-grade teacher in the same school system the year before, he had been a hero.

The oldest of seven Mexican-American children, Anselmo was born and went to school in Harlingen, Texas, a town about twenty miles from the Mexican border. The Garza family lives in the Mexican section, called the *barrio,* and is supported by Anselmo's father, who works as a migrant farm laborer. The children joined their father in the cotton fields each summer until picking machines took their jobs away. Since then Mr. Garza has migrated to Michigan in the summer to harvest strawberries and cucumbers.

Anselmo made the highest marks in his class at Harlingen High School and went on to Pan American College, a small state liberal arts school in Edinburg, Texas, on scholarship. Although trained as a secondary-school teacher, on returning to his hometown Anselmo was offered a position teaching in the all-Chicano elementary school he had attended. Before he began his first day at the school, the principal told him, "These sixth-graders are three years behind in reading. Don't feel bad if you don't last a whole year with them. These kids will probably drop out next year. Oh, by the way, make sure they don't speak Spanish anywhere, and don't check out any books to them because they can't read."

On the first day of school Anselmo spoke to his pupils in Spanish and told them that the principal had said they couldn't read. "I know better," he told them. "I was in this same room and I graduated from college with honors." The rapport was instantaneous. Anselmo knew enough about self-fulfilling prophecies to understand that children won't learn if they're expected not to learn. He threw out the workbooks and taught spontaneously. He filled the classroom with books and told the children they could read whenever they wanted to. Dusty, unused film strips were retrieved from the stockroom and the pupils learned to read from the scripts. The principal stopped in one day and left in amazement. "I wouldn't have believed it if I hadn't seen it," he remarked. "Those kids were asking thoughtful questions and were really engaged in learning!"

After a successful first year of teaching, Anselmo was assigned to teach high-school Spanish, which was more in keeping with his preparation. Ironically, he replaced his own former Spanish teacher. As a result of segregation by tracking, Anselmo's classes were either all-Chicano or all-Anglo. While all the Chicanos did well on a standardized test, scoring in the 80's and 90's, and while most of the Anglo students failed, the Chicano class was labeled as a lower track. But Anselmo's real problem was with his second-year class of Anglos. Their motivation and achievement were low. For weeks he adhered to the grammar and drills in the syllabus. Realizing that the students were not making progress, he attempted to motivate them by asking why they were taking Spanish. This quickly led to broader discussions about education and its relation to life. "Some started to see that there is something wrong with a system that makes them work only for a grade and prevents Chicanos from getting into high average classes. They had believed that theirs was the best of all possible educational systems, but I was questioning and getting a few others to question the whole structure."

In 1968 the Chicano movement was just beginning to gain momentum and support. The Chicanos wanted the schools to stop spanking children for speaking Spanish on the playground, and they wanted their place in history respectfully taught. The school's textbooks were full of stories about American heroes killing Mexicans. The Anglo students were upset by the Chicano protests, but Anselmo told them he supported the demands. He later explained: "I'm going to get in trouble with my views on education, politics, the Vietnam war, racism, and bigotry." He felt he had to make them see that they had only one point of view — one that begged for elaboration.

The parents of some Anglo students complained about Anselmo's unorthodox ideas. He was asking the students to open their minds and to think about their educations and their lives — subjects ordinarily not mentioned in school. The principal called Anselmo into his office five times in response to parents' complaints. Each time the principal told him he was in trouble. Finally, on the fifth visit, both the principal and the superintendent told Anselmo that he was in deep trouble and that they would not support him. Anselmo resigned. On the day he submitted his resignation, the bilingual newspaper put out by the high-school Spanish classes was dedicated "to Anselmo Garza, the greatest teacher we have ever had."

In Harlingen some say it is un-American to speak Spanish; children who speak it on the school grounds have had tissues stuffed in their mouths. The widely repeated slogan of this viewpoint is: "Be smart. Be right. Speak English." Anselmo was called a Communist for advocating a bilingual policy for the school and for quietly encouraging Chicanos to support protests. He says, "I think the only way to change the dominant Anglo culture is to reach the high-school students and get them thinking."

Anselmo is currently a student at the Harvard Graduate School of Education. He came to Harvard to tell people concerned about education what is happening "off the beaten path" in American schools. When he completes his work for an advanced degree he plans to return to Harlingen to work with and educate Chicanos.

---

middle class children in our schools, opinions vary considerably as to the locus of the problem. At one extreme it is assumed that failure to learn is a result of the student's own deficiencies — physical, economic, mental, cultural, or environmental. At the other extreme is the idea that if pupils are failing it is the school system that needs rehabilitation. This position assumes it is the school's obligation to diagnose the learner's needs, concerns, and cognitive and affective style, and to adjust its program accordingly. As with most issues, the answer probably lies somewhere in between — the students do have certain deficiencies but the school needs to learn how to overcome them.

What are the tension points in American education?

Schooling is conducted within a framework of power and struggle for power. It is no more protected from the abuse of power than are political enterprises. John Goodlad

It is undeniable that the achievement of white middle class children and poor lower class minority children is unequal—the important question is how the achievement of poor and minority group children can be improved. As you are probably already aware, solutions to this problem are proposed from many quarters, and considerable friction exists between groups who advocate different approaches. The five most widely advocated approaches to the reform of public education are compensatory education, desegregation, model subsystems, parallel systems, and total system reform.[4]

Compensatory education

Compensatory education is an attempt to overcome deficiencies in the learner by grafting extra education onto the regular school program, or to avert potential learning problems through preschool programs such as Project Head Start. Programs such as the Ford Foundation-supported Great Cities School Improvement Programs, Title I of the Elementary and Secondary Education Act, New York City's early Higher Horizons Program, and the recent More Effective Schools Program were all aimed at remedying specific learner defects, such as verbal retardation, lack of motivation, and experiential and sensory deprivation, which prevent the student from participating effectively in the learning process.

A tremendous amount of money and energy has been spent attempting to develop special programs to improve the academic achievement of poor children. Unfortunately, evidence indicates that little headway has been made in most of the programs. The parents of children enrolled in these compensatory programs, whose expectations were initially very high, became increasingly dissatisfied with their results.

Some observers of compensatory education programs criticize them for simply offering massive doses of methods that have not worked previously. They see little point in strengthening programs that have failed in the past. Proponents of this approach argue that expenditures thus far are a mere drop in the bucket, considering the enormity of the problem. They also argue that a simultaneous attack must be made on external factors that contribute to low achievement, such as poor housing, family instability, and low income. Furthermore, they argue that while many compensatory programs did not achieve results, others did succeed. What we need, they say, is to pattern our future compensatory programs after those that were successful, such as the Follow Through program.[5] Despite these arguments, the compensatory education route to achieve equal educational opportunity is not nearly as popular among educators, parents, and politicians as it was in the 1960s.

[4] The authors wish to acknowledge Mario Fantini's identification and elaboration of these five approaches in his discussion of implementing equal educational opportunity, *Harvard Educational Review* 38 (Winter 1968): 160–175.
[5] Harold H. Webb, "Compensatory Education? Yes!" *Educational Leadership* 30 (December 1972): 206–212.

The real world

Desegregation

Since 1954, one of the prime motivating forces in school integration efforts has been the assumption that Negro students' achievement will improve in an integrated school environment. Notably, the findings of the Coleman Report and the U.S. Commission on Civil Rights support this assumption. The latter asserts:

Negro children suffer serious harm when their education takes place in public schools which are racially segregated, whatever the source of such segregation may be. Negro children who attend predominantly Negro schools do not achieve as well as other children, Negro and white.[6]

From the late 1950s to the mid-1960s, efforts were made to desegregate schools, particularly in the South. Despite the time, energy, and money expended, the nationwide results have been rather poor. One estimate indicates that only 23 percent of the more than six million Negro students in the United States attend integrated public schools.[7] In urban settings, integration has proven almost impossible to achieve, primarily because of the growing concentration of black and other nonwhite minorities in the inner cities. While in the fifties and sixties many blacks fought and demonstrated for integration, today many blacks and other minority group members are resisting integration at the option of the white majority. They are focusing instead on gaining control over the schools their children presently attend.

At least two other factors have contributed to integration's poor track record. First, blacks are resentful that the present power structure makes integration an option of the white community. Second, minority groups feel a strong need for racial identity and pride. Many parents fear that this sense of identity will be lost if integration takes place, and that the best way of insuring racial pride is to operate the schools under the control of the Negro community with a curriculum especially designed to foster a sense of identity among the children.

Decentralization and community control

Community control over the schools is not perceived by blacks as a throwback to the old "separate but equal" situation which the 1954 Supreme Court decision overruled. They argue that when blacks achieve quality education under their own jurisdiction, they will be prepared to enter a society on a basis of parity rather than deficiency. Thus, they argue, equality of educational opportunity will best be achieved by concentrating more power and control over the schools in the hands of the parents and the community, and allowing them to hire teachers, develop curricula, and govern their children's education.

Attempts to decentralize large city school districts are a direct outgrowth of inner-city minorities' dissatisfaction with unequal education and with the lack of response to their demands for change. Many large school districts have administratively decentralized their school systems by breaking down the bureaucracy of the central office and distributing more decision-making power to smaller field-oriented administrative units. Although the central school board retains power, this type of decentralization aims toward making the field administrators more sensitive to the community residents within their boundaries.

[6] U.S. Commission on Civil Rights, *Racial Isolation*, p. 1.
[7] Alexander M. Bickel, "Desegregation: Where Do We Go From Here?" *Phi Delta Kappan* 51 (June 1970): 518–522.

What are the tension points in American education?

At this time only two major cities, New York and Detroit, have attempted a type of
decentralization that is more than administratively oriented, i.e., one that creates
a number of community school boards with the usual decision-making responsibilities that school boards normally have. The overriding notion of this type of
decentralization is to provide local communities within large urban areas more of
an opportunity to play an active decision-making role in the schools that their
children attend. Under this type of decentralization the educational system becomes more accountable to parents for both the results and resources of education.

Opponents of community control argue that decisions are made without consulting professional educators, that staff are chosen along racial lines, and that
professional competence is judged by unqualified people. Advocates of community control insist that teachers should be chosen for their positive attitudes
toward students, rather than on the basis of longevity. They also argue that local
control allows mothers and other community personnel to assist the teacher in
the instructional process. Most of all, local community control allows for a re-
sponsiveness to the children's needs which, they insist, never existed under a
centralized school system.

One educator who has been involved in evaluating educational programs in
eight of the thirty-two decentralized school districts in New York City asserts that
the community control system is not functioning well.[8] The system has not succeeded in any substantial way in reversing the trend of failure among large
numbers of ghetto children. In the May 1973 elections of local school board
members in New York City, only 12 percent of the eligible voters turned out.[9] This
show of voter apathy is not what one would expect if the local control system
were working well. The local systems have also become a patronage base for
local politicians who, when elected to local school boards, appoint many unqualified persons to school positions.

Whether integration or decentralized community control offers the best hope for
equal educational opportunities for minority groups is a moot point. It does not
appear at this time, however, that most major urban cities are moving toward
community control decentralization. With the exception of New York City and Detroit, most large cities are maintaining decision-making power in a central school
board while decentralizing the administrative operations. We will probably continue to see a great deal of experimentation in an effort to solve the complex
problems of large school systems.

Busing

Look at the picture on page 333. This photo was taken in the fall of 1974 in
Boston, Massachusetts. What feelings do you have when you look at the picture?
Busing to achieve integrated schools is one of the most controversial and
inflamatory issues in education today. Emotions on the topic run very high; so

[8] R.O. Washington, "The Politicalization of School Decentralization in New York City," *Urban Education* 8
(October 1973): 223–230.
[9] Washington, p. 229.

high, in fact, that white parents have slashed bus tires, burned buses, and physically prevented buses from running in order to avoid having their children bused to other schools to achieve integration.

The federal court system has been the prime mover in ordering school districts to employ busing in the desegregation process. The United States Supreme Court in the *Swan* v. *Charlotte-Mecklenburg* (1971) case, for example, found that the school authorities had an obligation to prepare students for a pluralistic world by having a ratio of black and white students in each school reflecting the ratio for the district as a whole. The Court concluded that the need to hasten desegregation was great and busing was deemed an appropriate measure, providing that the distance of travel was not so great as to either risk the health of the children or impinge significantly on the educational process.

Busing to achieve desegregation has had mixed success. One of the most successful busing plans was that initiated in Berkeley, California in 1968. Berkeley desegregated its elementary schools by two-way, cross-town busing. A later survey found that the whites did not leave the community, that there was no high

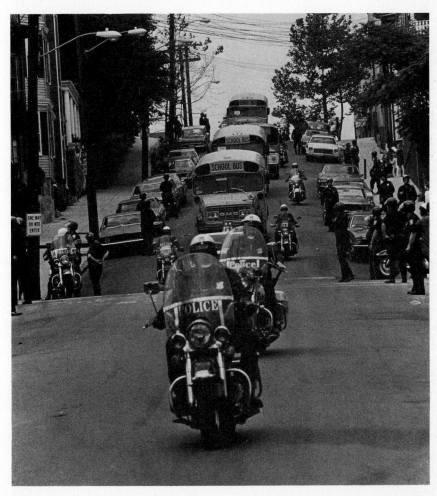

What are the tension points in American education?

teacher turnover rate, and that the SAT reading scores indicated that white, black, and Asian students all made better progress after desegregation.[10] On the other hand, in many other communities attempts to desegregate the schools by busing have met with tremendous community resistance.

Busing, of course, is not the real issue. Busing is only one means to achieve an integrated society. Polls indicate that even those who are opposed to busing agree that our society needs to be integrated. The real problem is that existing housing patterns function to segregate our society and our schools. As long as existing housing patterns continue, busing must be considered as one method to achieve integregated schools. The following quotation succinctly captures what we believe to be the heart of the busing issue. Examining the drawbacks to busing, the authors state:

In some cases disruptions will occur, some schools will lose enthusiastic parental support and child participation in extra-curricular activities, additional safety hazards may be encountered, and extra time may be needed. The problem with this position is that these drawbacks are not certain to happen. When weighed against the results of not *busing, such drawbacks may appear to be the lesser of two evils. Not busing assures that some children are spared inconvenience, but it may equally assure that the profound social and racial divisions we face today are maintained and aggravated. It does not seem likely that separation of races and social classes, whether* de facto *or* de jure, *will ever promote good human relations and social cohesiveness, not to mention equality of opportunity. Exclusiveness on the part of one group and submission on the part of the other may provide social order, but it will almost certainly create rankling suspicions and resentments, a debt that will sooner or later have to be paid.*[11]

Model subsystems

A model subsystem is an experimental program created within the existing school system to explore new improved teacher training methods, curriculum development, and community participation. If these experimental programs prove effective, their methods may be disseminated and adopted throughout the entire school system. A number of these experimental programs have been developed in cities such as Washington, New York, Boston, and Syracuse.

Because these programs are experimental, they are frequently able to attract the participation of institutions and persons outside the educational establishment. For example, Howard University, Antioch College, and Trinity College assisted an experimental subsystem in Washington, D.C., called the Cardozo Project in Urban Teaching. This project was one of the chief models for the legislation and operation of the national Teacher Corps. Other sources of talent and ideas for model subsystems are community agencies, U.S. Office of Education research and development centers, Peace Corps and Vista veterans, private industry, and the professions.

It does not appear likely, however, that model subsystems will be able to exert enough influence to change bureaucracy-hardened school systems in more than a token way. For the most part, they receive only short-term funding, and tend to focus on isolated ways of improving learning rather than on system-wide reform.

[10] Howard Ozmon and Sam Craver, *Busing: A Moral Issue* (Bloomington, Ind.: Phi Delta Kappa Educational Foundation, 1972): 33–34.
[11] Ozmon and Craver, p. 36.

Parallel systems

There have always been alternatives to public education for those who could afford to send their children to private schools. For the children of the poor, there are no alternatives. Imagine the frustration of parents who see their children falling further and further behind in academic achievement, but cannot afford to send them to private schools, and who are convinced that the system is unresponsive to their children's needs but lack the power to bring about change. In response to these frustrations, educational critics such as Christopher Jencks and Kenneth Clark propose that the poor should be offered options to the current public education systems. They propose a voucher system under which the government would grant vouchers to parents equal to the amount of public money spent each year for the child's education. The parents would be free to use the voucher to pay for their child's education at any school they chose.

Proponents of the parallel school system concept argue that the public schools have a monopoly on educational services, at least for poor children. If competing schools were created, they argue, the public schools would be forced to develop ways to deal effectively with poor children or suffer the consequences of diminishing financial support. The voucher system is discussed in more detail in Chapter Eleven.

The parallel system deserves experimental implementation, which it is receiving under a federal government grant. It is unlikely, however, that it could ever endanger the actual existence of the public schools, and doubtful that the public would support a private system of publicly supported schools.

Total system reform

We can see deficiencies in each of the four basic approaches to equal educational opportunities. Compensatory education has thus far done little to raise the academic achievement level of children of the poor and minority groups. Desegregation has stalled in urban areas, where blacks and other minority groups inhabit the inner-city while the whites flee to the suburbs. Besides, many black people are demanding local community control which would, in effect, postpone integration efforts until parity in educational achievement is reached. Model subsystems have achieved only limited success in isolated situations and show little promise of initiating change of the magnitude necessary to deal with the problem effectively. The parallel system promises to create alternatives to the public schools, but avoids the challenge of reforming the schools where most children receive their education and probably will continue to do so.

It appears, at least to our eyes, that reform of total school systems—structure, decision-making power, teacher training, curriculum, and organization—offers the most promise of creating equal educational opportunity for poor children. Admittedly, the task is enormous, but some encouraging examples do exist. In Louisville, Kentucky, for instance, efforts have been made to use a systems approach to the renewal of the school district.[12] The school leaders recognized that partial change is rarely successful because the rest of the system tends to reject or isolate the innovations. In Louisville an effort was made to concentrate resources at first in a limited number of schools, rather than dissipating the resources. As success was achieved in these schools, other schools would then receive the new resources, until the entire system had been overhauled.

[12] Russell C. Doll, Barbara J. Love, and Daniel U. Levine, "Systems Renewal in a Big-City School District: The Lessons of Louisville," *Phi Delta Kappan* 54 (April 1973): 524–534.

What are the tension points in American education?

The organizational framework for instruction was dramatically changed, along with changes in teaching and administrative personnel. The community was involved through the creation of neighborhood school boards. Instructional materials, objectives, and methods were systematically examined and revised. The administrative structure was dramatically changed to improve decision making.

It would appear that only when the educational problems of a district become intolerable does dramatic total system reform occur. In addition to Louisville, the Detroit school system is currently involved in similar total school reform as a result of tremendous financial and educational problems. While it is too early to evaluate the results of both efforts, it does appear that more large school districts will recognize that the band-aid approach to creating equal educational opportunity does not work.

Arguing for a total system approach to change, Mario Fantini summarizes our position very succinctly when he says:

In the subsystems, models of excellence must swim against the tide of the status quo system. The total approach has no such constraint; there is no boring from within, for everyone starts at the reform gate at the same time. In a federation of autonomous subsystems, each with an equitable share of resources, instructional practices would operate in an open, competitive market. The most successful models would be on display as a challenge to other school systems to adopt their approaches or surpass them in performance.[13]

[13] Fantini, p. 170.

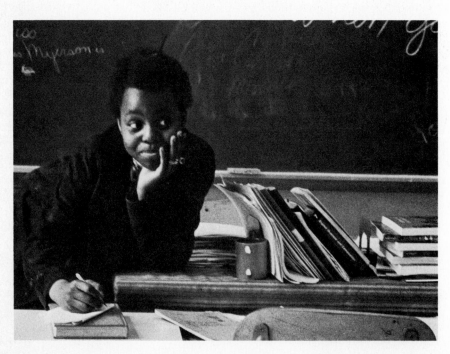

The real world

School finance reform

Many knowledgable educators and politicians argue that one of the greatest causes of unequal educational opportunity is the method used to finance school systems. As we noted in Chapter Eight, education is a responsibility of each state, but only 41 percent of the revenue used to finance public elementary and secondary schools comes from the states. The federal government contributes less than 8 percent, while local sources account for 51 percent.[14] The primary means used by local agencies to obtain money for the schools is the property tax. School districts whose property values are high generate much more money to finance their schools than districts whose property values are low. Within the same state, for example, the average amount of money spent per child in one district may be more than twice the amount spent in a nearby district.

In 1971 a class action suit, *Serrano* v. *Priest,* was filed by pupils and their parents against California state and county officials concerned with financing public schools. The suit charged that the school financing scheme was unconstitutional. The Supreme Court of California supported the parents' claim that the quality of a child's education may not be a function of wealth other than the wealth of the state as a whole. The court also held that the California system of financing the schools primarily on the basis of local property taxes violates the 14th Amendment to the U.S. Constitution.

In 1973 the Supreme Court of the United States reversed a similar decision (known as the *Rodriguez* case) involving the school finance system of the state of Texas by a 5-4 vote. The Court found that the Constitution was not violated because the right to an education is not guaranteed explicitly or implicitly by the Constitution. The Court did state that their finding should not be interpreted as a victory for the *status quo* but urged the states to solve obvious inequalities.

Many state constitutions contain equal protection clauses, unlike the U.S. Constitution, and education has been interpreted as a protected right in many states. Thus, the precedent established by the *Serrano* case has led other state courts to rule that their school financing systems violate their state constitutions.

State governments continue to wrestle with the problems of equalizing educational opportunity and financial responsibility. Educators, parents, and public officials are greatly concerned that the quality of a child's education not be dependent on whether he lives in a school district with high property values. Many of these concerned citizens are urging that the state government become responsible for raising educational revenue and for distributing the full costs of local schools to school districts. The school districts would continue to be in charge of the operation of the local schools, but they would no longer have to sponsor school bond elections to raise money.

Many different schemes for financing public schools will probably be tried in the different states. There is no doubt that the issue is complex and difficult to solve. The courts have provided the impetus for school financial reform, but it will be the primary responsibility of state legislative bodies to develop school finance systems that may be expected to produce equal educational opportunities.

[14] National Education Association Research Report 1973–74, "Financial Status of the Public Schools, 1973" (Washington, D.C.), p. 35.

What are the tension points in American education?

Student rights

In the late 1960s and early 1970s, American high schools experienced great student unrest and many student strikes. The underlying issue in the majority of student strikes and disruptions was adult control over all decision making, and the absence of democratic procedures in the high schools. It is easy to build a case that student unrest in the high schools is a result of the way students are treated. If questioned, a majority of students would probably describe their high schools as basically undemocratic. Students are barred from taking part in decisions that affect them as individuals and citizens. When their proposed innovations or complaints produce conflict, it is usually met with arbitrary action by teachers and administrators. Students are often not extended the rights of individuals in a democratic society. They usually have no say in what they are to learn or in how they are expected to dress. The typical student government has little or no real power in the governance of the school, and is readily recognized by the students as a sham. The student newspaper usually has a faculty advisor who censors articles that might offend certain elements of the community, but about which the students themselves may feel strongly. In short, there is little reason to expect high-school students to form an allegiance to the democratic political system, because they do not experience democracy in their daily lives in school.

In recent years many students and their parents have questioned whether schools or school officials have the power to infringe upon the rights of students, who as citizens of the United States possess certain Constitutional rights.

A number of court cases aimed at determining what rights children maintain while they are students and what rights the schools possess, have been recently tested. While the total parameters of student rights have yet to be completely defined, the courts have generally indicated that students must be accorded basic Constitutional and statutory rights and freedoms, thereby forcing school officials to show some compelling reason for establishing rules or taking actions that infringe upon these basic rights.

In a study conducted in three southern states, a questionnaire was administered to 815 high-school students in three schools — one rural, one urban, and one suburban.[15] The questionnaire was designed to identify student perceptions of ways in which their human rights had been violated in their respective school environments. Table 10.1 summarizes the results of the questionnaire. While all of the human rights described in the questionnaire are not legally protected, the findings certainly indicate that these students believe many of their rights are violated by school officials. One of the students phrased his thoughts rather eloquently:

One feeling seems to dominate the administration's policy toward students — fear The attitude seems to be "nip it in the bud," but there's no attempt to discover if it is a weed or a rose.[16]

---

[15] Thomas H. Buxton and Keith W. Prichard, "Student Perceptions of Teacher Violations of Human Rights, *Phi Delta Kappan* 55 (September 1973): 66–69.
[16] Buxton and Prichard, p. 67.

Table 10.1 Ranking of most frequently violated rights by percentage (N = 815)

Question	Frequently	Sometimes	Combined Percentage
Have you been made to feel that the opinion of the teacher is the only one and yours doesn't count?	24%	57%	81%
Have you been denied the use of the restroom when necessary?	30%	48%	78%
How often does your school principal veto reasonable ideas presented by the student government association?	21%	55%	76%
Have you been prohibited from dressing as you like?	25%	43%	68%
How often have you not been allowed enough time to properly prepare for a school project?	10%	53%	63%
How often have you been *un*involved in helping plan some aspect of your classes or your work?	15%	45%	60%
Have you been denied the right to question your punishment?	16%	41%	57%
Have you ever been degraded or treated with disrespect by a teacher?	10%	45%	55%
How often has the student government association been denied a voice or student representation in the policy making of your school?	12%	38%	50%
Because you may not be a "top student," do you feel that teachers ignore you or discriminate against you?	10%	40%	50%

Source: Thomas H. Buxton and Keith W. Prichard, "Student Perceptions of Teacher Violations of Human Rights," *Phi Delta Kappan* 55 (September, 1973): 67.

Court decisions have clearly said that schools can no longer act as though a student's rights as a citizen were shed upon entering the school. Capricious and unreasonable regulations and practices that infringe on students' rights as citizens will no longer be tolerated by students, parents, or the courts.

What are the tension points in American education?

It is interesting to note that, at the same time students are demanding more freedom and less authoritarian dominance by school administrators and teachers, a Gallup Poll indicates that the American public sees discipline as the greatest problem of the local schools.[17]

If student decision making in school affairs that concern and affect students is thought to be desirable, then it is obvious that the communication gap between schools and the American public must be bridged. Teachers and administrators must take the lead in this process. Students must be treated as citizens in a democracy if they are in fact to act like citizens in their schools and, later, on the college campus and in the community. Warning public-school personnel of the consequences of excluding students from decision making, Charles Silberman states, "In a war between faculty and students, the students are bound to win; there are more of them, and put to the test, they can be defiant in the most ingenious ways."[18] Forewarned is forearmed.

[17] George H. Gallup, "Fifth Annual Gallup Poll of Public Attitudes Toward Education," *Phi Delta Kappan* 55 (September 1973): 45.
[18] Charles E. Silberman, *Crisis in the Classroom* (New York: Random House, 1970), p. 340.

Teacher power

Smaller classes, duty-free lunch periods, more planning time, more clerical and technical assistance, a clearly defined grievance procedure with binding arbitration, clearly described seniority rights, an improved transfer policy, more realistic teaching loads, more adequate counseling for students, curriculum provisions for potential dropouts, a more direct role in curriculum change, cultural enrichment programs for students, a larger school role in the development of values and morality, greater diversity of teaching materials, more teaching aids, a greater say in instructional budgets, provisions for usable curriculum guides—these are only some of the demands made by teacher organizations in contract negotiations with public-school districts.

The day of meek Miss Dove is over. Teachers, through their professional organizations, are demanding both improved benefits for themselves and revised and updated instructional policies for the schools. Teachers are calling for administrators and school boards to relinquish some of their decision-making power to those whom they believe are most qualified to make instructional and curricular decisions.

Demands, of course, arouse conflict. As teachers demand higher salaries, more clerical assistance, and improved personal benefits, all of which require additional funds, legislators must propose and the public must accept increased taxes. And as teachers demand greater decision-making power, those who now hold such power must be willing to relinquish it.

If such conflict does occur, and the teachers feel strongly about the issues in question, they increasingly resort to strikes or the threat of strikes to pressure the opposition into capitulating to their demands. In 1969–70, for example, there were 171 teacher strikes in the United States, involving 117,000 teachers. The comparable figures for 1968–69 were 131 strikes and 129,000 teachers.[19] Two of the largest walkouts were in 1968—one in New York City involving over 50,000 teachers for 36 school days, and one in Florida involving 25,000 teachers. In the Florida case, many of the striking teachers were not re-employed by their school districts when the strike ended. In the fall of 1973 there were over 100 teacher strikes in the United States, including more than two dozen in Michigan.[20]

Teacher strikes generate much ill will. As long as the actions of teacher associations or unions do not disrupt the education of their children, most parents are indifferent to the arrangements teachers make for dealing with their employers. Many parents support teachers' demands for salary increases and improved instructional programs but do not sanction strikes as a means of obtaining desired results because such tactics disrupt their children's schooling. Parents also resent strikes because they undermine the climate of friendliness and cooperation in which children work best. Strikes often result in divisiveness between teachers, parents, pupils, school administrators, and school board members. Parents and children are frequently pressured to take sides in the dispute.

[19] "Teacher Strikes Increase," *Phi Delta Kappan* 52 (October 1970): 132.
[20] *NEA Reporter* 12 (December 1973): 6.

What are the tension points in American education?

It is almost always with great reluctance that teachers strike. Strikes can mean loss of pay, fines, loss of jobs and, possibly, jail terms in states where teacher strikes are illegal. Teachers usually do not resort to a strike unless they feel very strongly about the issues and are convinced they have exhausted all other alternatives.

"Perhaps the best way to avoid this whole problem," says Joseph W. Cassidy, Commissioner of the Education Commission of the States, "is to remove the causes of [teachers'] unrest. . . . This solution, however, may be as distasteful to the legislator and the school board member as a strike itself. It seems to me that we have these two choices: (1) strikes or sanctions, or (2) removal of the cause for strikes or sanctions."[21] The second option is, of course, the more desirable, but it is not always possible. As Cassidy indicates, some legislators and school board members see a teacher strike as a lesser evil than an increase in taxes, even if the additional tax funds are for improved instruction for children. When this is the case, teachers believe they must point out the school system's weaknesses as strongly as they can. As one striking teacher organization has stated:

We sincerely — and most firmly — believe that our efforts to become first-class citizens, under the law, will provide a better school system in Warren, for Warren school district children. Somehow, sometime, someone must call out the shortcomings of this school system and its operations and make it the kind of leading educational system that Warren citizens have long indicated they prefer. If not now, when? If not teachers, who?[22]

Teacher power is also being manifested in other ways besides strikes. Teacher organizations have come to realize that many of their goals can best be achieved by legislation. Accordingly, many state and local teacher organizations have formed political action committees whose major purpose is to elect candidates to state and federal offices who are known to be favorable to educational interests. Besides contributing money to the candidates' campaigns, teachers are volunteering for campaign work to ensure that their candidates are elected. Teacher organizations are realizing the tremendous power they can wield through the ballot box. United States Senator Claiborne Pell of Rhode Island attests to the power of teachers:

Before the teachers began to help me, I was a 2-to-1 underdog. Now, thanks to an army of teachers who knocked on thousands of doors and made thousands of

[21] Elizabeth S. Hendryson, "Parent Reaction to Teacher Power," *The National Elementary Principal* 48 (January 1969): 18.
[22] Robert Kowalczyk, "The Teachers' Advocate," *NEA Journal* (January 1969): 53.

phone calls, I have won by more than 33,000 votes. My election is a victory for teacher power. This victory is a victory for education, and you can be sure that I will continue to fight in Washington for a better deal for education.[23]

If teacher organizations can succeed in helping to place substantial numbers of their candidates in state and federal legislatures, then the financial and overall picture for education is likely to brighten considerably.

Sex education

"What schools need to do is treat sex as they would digestion—no more, no less."

"Sex education is more than just knowledge of the mechanics of the sex act, and the development and birth of a baby. The physical aspect should not be emphasized at the expense of its psychological and social aspects."

"Sex education is a Communist conspiracy to corrupt youth."

"Sex, love, birth, and family life are all one package and should be discussed in the reassuring warmth of the parents' presence."

Sex education is a headline-grabber in newspapers throughout the country, especially in smaller communities. The statements above represent four different positions on sex education, and give evidence of the controversy surrounding it. According to a Gallup Poll taken in April, 1970, 72 percent of the parents interviewed expressed their approval of sex education in the public schools, while 22 percent were opposed.[24] But the minority is often very vocal in its opposition.

Most people agree that children should be given information about sex; the controversy centers around two subsidiary issues: 1) is the school the appropriate institution to offer such instruction? and 2) if so, should it limit instruction to strictly factual information, or should the psychological, social, and ethical aspects of sex also be included in the curriculum?

With respect to the first issue, some people argue that because sex is such an intimate topic, and is closely related to religious and moral beliefs, sex education is the responsibility of the home and/or the church.

Advocates of sex education in the schools respond that they would agree with the above position if parents did, in fact, provide adequate sex information for their children. Unfortunately, they argue, this simply is not the case. The majority of parents fail to assume the responsibility to teach their children about sex because: 1) they don't know how to respond to their children's questions; 2) they

---

[23] Claiborne Pell, "A Victory for Teacher Power," *Today's Education* 63 (January-February 1974): 69.
[24] George Gallup, "Second Annual Survey of Public's Attitudes Toward Public Schools," *Phi Delta Kappan* 52 (October 1970): 107.

Mutilated Books

The school authorities of the Mepham Central High School District on Long Island who cut forty pages on human sexuality out of four hundred copies of a textbook on health had in mind the protection of seventh-graders' morals. A little pedagogical sophistication might have told them that every pupil whose normal sense of curiosity has not yet been dulled by pedantry will rush to the nearest library to read the missing chapters. This is probably more than ordinary teaching could have accomplished. But such unintended increases in readership cannot offset the consequences of the barbaric example of book mutilation. A school that puts scissors to books slashes civilization and leaves it bleeding.

cannot bridge the "conversation gap" between their own viewpoint and that of their children; 3) they overestimate the age at which sex information is most appropriate; and 4) they are inhibited and uncomfortable discussing sex. Many students complain that their parents either waited too long to give them information about sex, failed to give them any information at all, or provided more misinformation than reliable facts. Advocates assert that the public school is the only institution that has access to most children over an extended period of time, and that the responsibility must fall to the school because of the demonstrated failure

Cartoon by Sidney Harris

The real world

of the home, church, library, and medical profession to provide effective sex education. The courts seem to concur with this opinion since in virtually every case where the school board's right to offer sex education in the curriculum was tested, the courts have supported the school board.[25]

Argument among advocates over the kind of sex education the schools should offer is equally heated. One position can be succinctly summarized as: Sex Education, No! Sex Information, Yes! People who adhere to this position do not believe the school should impart attitudes or moral and ethical value judgments in relation to sex. They argue that it is not the schools' place to take stands on masturbation, petting, and premarital sexual intercourse. Others agree that issues such as these should not be discussed from an ethical or moral standpoint, but are in favor of a curriculum that promotes respect for one's own body and acceptance of sex as a normal and basic aspect of human relationships.

While very few people want the schools to preach a particular ethical stance toward sexual issues, many people believe that the distribution of sexual knowledge alone is not enough. The role they propose for the schools is to teach students to analyze the range of value systems relating to sex, leaving decisions about sexual standards and behavior up to the students. They envision a sex education program that would help the student develop a moral code based on knowledge, responsibility, and belief in the worth of individual fulfillment on a moral basis. This, they believe, can best be accomplished not by avoiding value issues, but by exploring them without favoritism or prejudice.

Student drug use

Student drug use is a serious problem in our nation. Recognizing that ignorance and misinformation are major complicating factors surrounding drug usage, many communities and states—and even the federal government—have initiated drug education programs. These programs are designed to teach students, teachers, administrators, and parents the abuse potential of specific drugs, their pharmacological properties, the meaning of drugs to the individual, and the legal ramifications of drug usage. The federal government appropriated $12.4 million—a sixfold increase— for drug education during fiscal year 1971, including a training program for 150,000 teachers and 75,000 students and community leaders. Evidence of the need for such a program is the tendency of many adults to lump all drugs into the same category. To equate the risks of pot with those of LSD or heroin—as many adults do—is akin to ignoring the differences between beer, hard liquor, and straight wood alcohol. Many of the programs also attempt to explore the question of *why*. Why would kids of all ages and backgrounds be tempted to try drugs in the first place? Attempting to answer this kind of question helps adults and adolescents cope with the underlying problems rather than limiting their attention to the symptom—drug usage.

Although the need for drug education is widely recognized, what is taught, how it is taught, and official approaches to student drug use vary markedly. In New York

[25] M. Chester Nolte, "Why Boards Are Winning Sex Education Battles," *American School Board Journal* 160 (June 1973): 23.

City, policemen pose as students in order to gather evidence against drug users, while in San Francisco four high schools have no-questions-asked crash pads staffed by nurses, psychiatrists, technicians, and student aides.

How does all this affect you? Particularly if you teach in a secondary school, it is quite possible that some of your students may be using drugs. If you suspect this to be the case, what should you do? Talk to them? If so, what would you say? Seek advice from an older teacher or the principal? Report them to the police? Call the parents? Mind your own business? Obviously, we cannot answer these questions for you. We can, however, urge several approaches.

First, become familiar with the signs of drug use. Know the differences between various types of drugs and the signs of their use. Second, avoid sermonizing; try instead to present objective facts about drugs and their known effects. Third, if a student indicates that he wants to talk to you about a drug problem, talk to him and ask him what you can do to help. His answer may range from just providing him a listening outlet to arranging for him to see a specialist in a drug clinic. However, if you do not know anything about drugs, don't pretend you do. Fourth, know and understand the legal implications of drug usage. Fifth, don't just ignore obviously heavy users with the rationale that it is none of your business. The course of action you choose to take is up to you, but you can't just hide your head in the sand and expect the problem to disappear.

Sexism and sex role stereotyping

A strong social force in today's society is the feminist movement. Women are asserting, and rightfully so, that societal values and mores have discriminated against women as a class and have significantly limited the development of their human potential. The evidence cited to support the contention that women in our society have been denied educational and employment opportunities that have been extended to men is irrefutable to anyone possessing some degree of objectivity.

One assertion that has been made by many persons who support the feminist movement is that schools are a primary institution where sexism abounds and is even taught informally in the curriculum.[26] These feminists argue that along with the home environment, the schools are where girls learn that a certain set of interests and behaviors are expected of them and that very little deviance is encouraged or even tolerated. Similarly, boys learn what interests and behaviors are expected of both them and the girls. It is the active encouragement in schools of such sex-role stereotyping that feminists find so objectionable. While sex-role stereotyping is damaging to both sexes, it is particularly so for females since the roles and characteristics assigned to females are less desirable than those assigned to males.

How do schools contribute to and perpetuate sex-role stereotyping? Certainly one way is through the books and other reading materials that are used in instruction. One study, conducted by a group called the Women on Words and Images, examined 134 books used in New Jersey schools.[27] The books represented 18 major textbook companies. Boys and men are present in the books overwhelmingly more often than girls and women, with a 6 to 1 discrepancy between male and female biographies. Women appear in 25 different occupations, men in 147. The men's jobs represent a wide range of possibilities, while the women's are limited to traditionally female pursuits such as telephone operator, secretary, nurse, and teacher. A content analysis of the "active mastery" stories, where the main character exhibited cleverness, problem-solving ability, bravery, acquisition of skills, and adventurousness, indicated males were portrayed four times as often as females. In contrast, girls were more often portrayed as passive and dependent, restricting their goals, practicing domesticity, being incompetent, and being victimized or humiliated by the opposite sex. Other similar studies tend to support these findings.

Feminists are concerned not only with how the curricular materials transmit sex-role stereotypes but also with the fact that many teachers and counselors do the same thing in their interactions with students. For example, female high-school students are often advised that certain professions are "appropriate" for men, while others are "appropriate" for women. One study discovered that, in fact, counselors respond more positively to female clients who hold traditionally feminine career goals than to those who wish to prepare for professions usually reserved for men.[28] One woman reports:

Women have frequently told me that their high school counselors had advised them to become legal secretaries when they wanted to become lawyers, nurses when they wanted to become doctors.[29]

[26] Sexism has been defined by the authors of a pamphlet called *Guidelines for Improving the Image of Women in Textbooks* (Scott, Foresman) as referring to " . . . all attitudes and actions which relegate women to a secondary and inferior status in society."

[27] Betty Levy and Judith Stacey, "Sexism in the Elementary School: A Backward and Forward Look," *Phi Delta Kappan* 55 (October 1973): 106.

[28] Nancy Frazier and Myra Sadker, *Sexism in School and Society* (New York: Harper & Row, 1973), p. 138.

[29] Frazier and Sadker, p. 138.

What are the tension points in American education?

The following letter was written by an elementary-school girl and appeared in a book called *Children's Letters to God*. Eric Marshall and Stuart Hample, compilers (New York: Simon and Schuster [Pocket Books], 1966).

Do you think this little girl has been the victim of sexist practices or attitudes?

Dear god,
    Are boys better than girls? I know you are one but please try to be fair.
                    LOVE
                    Silvia

School systems are also charged with being sexist regarding adults who work in the systems. In 1971 one source reported that 88 percent of elementary-school teachers were women, but only 22 percent were elementary-school principals.[30] The same source also reports that in 1971 there were only 2 women among the 13,000 district superintendents in the United States.

The elimination of sexism and sex-role stereotyping in schools will be a complex procedure that will require the cooperation of teachers, administrators, school boards, counselors, educational publishers, and parents. Your role as a teacher will be especially important. As you interact with your pupils and as you select and use instructional materials, your sensitivity to this problem will help determine the attitudes of our future generations. Hopefully, educators will lead in efforts to evaluate school policies, curriculum, and practices with regard to sex bias and will eliminate sexist discrimination (along with racial and ethnic discrimination) in our schools. Remember, if you're not part of the solution, you're part of the problem.

[30] Frazier and Sadker, pp. 97–98.

Religion and the schools

May public tax money be spent for the support of parochial schools?
What religious observances, if any, are permitted in public-school classrooms?
May religious holidays be observed in public schools, and if so, which ones?
From what public-school activities may an individual be excused for religious reasons?
May public-school authorities rent or lease space to or from religious institutions for school purposes?

"Congress shall make no law respecting an establishment of religion, or prohibiting the free exercise thereof. . . ." During the past two centuries, the American judicial system has interpreted the First Amendment to the Constitution inconsistently with respect to religion and the public schools. The controversy surrounding this issue is not new; it has been a bone of contention since the beginning of public education in the United States. Where do we stand today?

Until the middle of the twentieth century, religious observances, including Bible reading and prayers, were common in the public schools. In fact, Bible reading and the recitation of the Lord's Prayer were required by the constitutions or by statutes in a number of states. In a 1963 decision, however, the Supreme Court ruled both unconstitutional. In an earlier decision, the Court had ruled against the recitation of a nondenominational prayer, holding that Bible reading and prayer violate both clauses of the First Amendment. The Court recognized that the schools did not compel a child to join in religious activities if his parents objected, but held that the social pressures exerted on pupils to participate were excessive. In essence, no distinction was felt to exist between voluntary and compulsory participation in religious activities.

The Court did note in its decision that the study of comparative religion, the history of religion, and the relationship of religion to civilization were not prohibited by this decision. It would also appear that, although the Bible may not be used to teach religion, it may, if objectively presented, be used in such areas of study as history, civics, and literature.

In another recent case, the Supreme Court approved the right of public-school pupils who so desire to say prayers and read scriptures of their choice in the morning before school starts or after the regular school day has terminated. If prayers are said during lunch period they must be silent. Needless to say, the Court has also ruled that direct religious instruction is not permitted in the public schools. Nor may public-school teachers place religious pamphlets in schoolrooms.

A related issue is "released time." In a series of decisions, the Court ruled that a state could not allow teachers employed by specific denominations to conduct religion classes in public-school buildings during the regular school day. However, the Court did rule constitutional a New York City program that permitted students to leave the school grounds during the school day to receive religious instruction elsewhere. Its reasoning was that the state must be neutral in regard to religion and, since no public funds were involved, the schools should cooperate with religious institutions by adjusting students' schedules.

What are the tension points in American education?

The real controversy, however, centers around the use of public tax revenues to aid private and parochial schools. The Supreme Court has already ruled that public money can be used to provide textbooks to private-school students; but what other kinds of aid can, or should, the public provide? This question is currently generating considerable heat, smoke, and even fire.

The major breakthrough for private and religious schools was the passage of the Elementary-Secondary Education Act of 1965, which funneled millions of dollars into parochial schools through federal programs. In addition, parochial schools in many states have been receiving assistance ranging from pupil transportation, textbooks, health services, and general auxiliary services, to salary supplements for teachers. In general, state assistance in areas other than transportation, milk, school lunch programs, and textbooks is attacked in the courts. People oppose the use of tax money to support nonpublic or parochial schools for reasons ranging from outright prejudice to fear that such assistance will undermine the public-school system. The National Education Association and the American Federation of Teachers have consistently opposed the allocation of public money to private schools on the grounds that the public schools are not adequately funded now and that the situation would worsen if tax money went to private schools.

The other side of the argument is that the private schools, which provide education for approximately six million students a year, are lightening the burden of the public schools. For financial reasons, many of these schools are being forced to close. If, for example, the Catholic school system should collapse, five million new students would enroll in the public schools, creating a massive shortage of space, teachers, and money. Advocates of private-school aid argue that, by partially subsidizing private schools to keep them in operation, the public schools can avoid a deluge of students whom they would be unable to assimilate readily. Some sources estimate that if the Catholic schools were shut down the public-school system would cost an additional $4 billion a year to operate.

In his 1970 education message, President Nixon revealed that private schools are closing at the rate of one a day. He added: "This government cannot be indifferent to the potential collapse of such private-parochial schools." None of the supporters of private-school aid urges support for religious instruction; they do advocate state and federal aid for school lunches, buses, secular textbooks, and the purchase of secular services.

Accountability

Earlier in this chapter, we discussed the way in which the legal definition of equality changed from an emphasis on resources to a focus on *results*. A related development is the growing insistence by parents and other concerned adults that if children fail to learn in school how to read, write, and perform computations, the school must be held accountable for their failures.

The accountability movement is insisting that the public schools can no longer measure success in terms of the number of dollars spent on each child's education, the teacher-pupil ratio, or the educational level of the teachers. Advocates of accountability argue that these measures are at best indirect, and that the only real test of a school is its students' achievement of knowledge, skills, and attitudes the school is attempting to teach. Only by looking at the results of students' schooling, they argue, can we ascertain the worth of the schools.

Another source of support for accountability is primarily financial. As schools become increasingly expensive to operate, inflation erodes the buying power of the dollar, and property taxes—which support much of public education—reach their tolerable limits, the public is demanding that the schools demonstrate what they are accomplishing. The public is no longer willing to vote for increased taxes until they see what they are getting for their money.

Few would deny that the schools should be held accountable for their performance, but the definition and nature of accountability are matters of controversy. Should the schools be held accountable only for improvement in reading and arithmetic, skills which are easily measured? Or are the schools also responsible for the personal and humane outcomes of education, which are not so easily measured? If school personnel are held accountable only for improving easily measurable skills, might they not neglect other equally important educational outcomes? In any given year, is the student's improvement in reading more important than strengthening his self-concept and his ability to work and play with other children? Clearly, there are no pat answers to these questions. Many public-school personnel who support accountability in theory are concerned about how it might work in practice.

Who is to be held accountable for any given child's progress? the superintendent? the principal? the teacher? How reasonable is it, for example, to hold a given teacher accountable for the progress of her students if she is teaching in a dilapidated building, using books that are fifteen years out of date, and trying to cope with 50 percent more children than should be there? How democratic would it be to allow teachers no control over the standards to which they are expected to perform?

While the notion of accountability is appealing to many people, several fundamental questions must be answered before it can be put into practice:

- To what extent should teachers, principals, superintendents, and the community itself be held responsible for results?
- If school personnel are to be held accountable, to whom should they be answerable? the school board? the community? And how are results to be defined and measured?
- How will each participant's contribution to a child's learning be determined and distinguished from that of other participants?

The issue of accountability is one of the most complicated problems facing education in the near future. One thing appears certain: even if specific accountability proposals are not adopted, the debate over its merits and drawbacks is bound to help school personnel think more precisely about their goals, methods, and measures of achievement.

Discussion questions

1 Do you agree that equality of educational opportunity should be defined by its effects rather than its provisions? Can you think of an analogy to support your case for or against this position?

2 In view of compensatory education's lack of success at combating the problems of inequality in educational opportunity, why do you suppose it is so popular?

3 Why do you believe it so difficult to integrate public schools?

4 How do you feel about our statement that total system reform alone will solve the problem of unequal educational opportunity? Do you envision yourself as active in that kind of reform movement?

5 Do you agree with our analysis of the causes of student unrest or with the solution we propose? Why or why not?

6 What do you see as the advantages and disadvantages of teachers' strikes, from the point of view of teachers and from that of parents and students? Over what issues would you be willing to strike? Would you jeopardize your job? Would you go to jail?

7 Where do you stand in the controversy over sex education in the schools? On what assumptions do you base your stand? Is the issue important enough to you to cause you to make your stance public, at the risk of community criticism?

8 What kind of drug education program do you think would have been most appropriate in the high school you attended? (Pretend you are an outside consultant hired to make recommendations concerning drug use and drug education in your high school.)

9 Can you recall any sexist behavior that you have observed in schools? Do you think sexism and sex-role stereotyping is a problem in our schools?

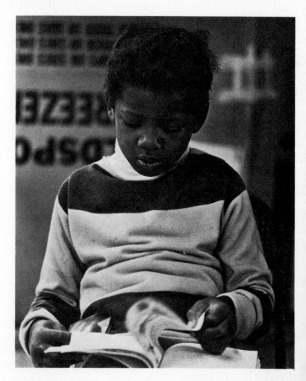

The real world

10 Where do you stand on the issue of public support for parochial schools? If your view prevails, what will be the effects on private education—and on society as a whole?

11 What do you, as a prospective teacher, feel is your responsibility concerning your students' performance? For what are you willing to be held accountable? skills acquired? facts remembered? personal growth? What factors would you insist on controlling before you accept responsibility? What dangers do you foresee?

For further reading

Accountability

- Combs, Arthur W. *Educational Accountability: Beyond Behavioral Objectives.* Washington, D.C.: Association for Supervision and Curriculum Development, 1972. A noted humanist's treatment of the topic.
- Dyer, Henry. *How To Achieve Accountability in the Public Schools.* Bloomington, Ind.: Phi Delta Kappa Educational Foundation, 1973. A short, thoughtful treatment.
- Ornstein, Allan C., and Talmage, Harriet. "The Rhetoric and the Realities of Accountability." *Today's Education* 62 (September-October 1973): 70–80. A view of accountability that represents many teachers' opinions.

Decentralization and Community Control

- Fantini, Mario, and Gittell, Marilyn. *Decentralization: Achieving Reform.* New York: Frederick A. Praeger, 1973. Authors advocate decentralization and community control. Book suggests tactics and strategies for making urban institutions, services, and political processes more accessible to the people.
- Green, Robert L. "Community Control and Desegregation." *School Review* 81 (May 1973): 347–356. An article advocating community control in order to create quality metropolitan educational systems.
- Ornstein, Allan C. "Administrative/Community Organization of Metropolitan Schools." *Phi Delta Kappan* 54 (June 1973): 668–674. An excellent analysis of the different kinds of decentralization plans in operation.
- Washington, R.O. "The Politicalization of School Decentralization in New York City." *Urban Education* 8 (October 1973): 223–230. An evaluation of the New York City decentralization plan.

Drug Abuse

- de Lone, Richard H. "The Ups and Downs of Drug-Abuse Education." *Saturday Review of Education* (November 11, 1972): 27–32. An article that views the drug issue as a lever to school reform.
- Eddy, John. *The Teacher and the Drug Scene.* Bloomington, Ind.: Phi Delta Kappa Educational Foundation, 1973. A short booklet covering many relevant aspects of drug usage.
- *Teaching About Drug Abuse.* Springfield, Ill.: Illinois Interagency Drug Abuse Education Development Committee, Office of the Governor, 1971. This book contains an overview of drug abuse, teacher prevention approaches, and other useful information. Endorsed for use by teachers in Illinois schools.

Inequality of Educational Opportunity

- Bowles, Samuel. "Towards Equality of Educational Opportunity?" *Harvard Educational Review* 38 (Winter 1968): 89–99. The author argues that a number of changes are necessary if equality of educational opportunity is to be achieved, including reallocation of funds for educating poor children and a redistribution of political power within our society.

- Coleman, James S., *et al. Equality of Educational Opportunity.* Washington, D.C.: U.S. Department of Health, Education, and Welfare, 1966. The major sociological study of the 1960s examining the inequalities that exist in our educational system.
- Jencks, Christopher, *et al. Inequality.* New York: Harper & Row, 1972. A controversial, major piece of work whose thesis is that schools can contribute little to help their students achieve economic success and occupational prestige.

Religion

- Duker, Sam. *The Public Schools and Religion: The Legal Context.* New York: Harper & Row, 1966. Examines the major controversies over the relationship of public schools and religion.
- Peterson, LeRoy; Rossmiller, Richard A.; and Volz, Marlin M. "The Law, Religion, and Public Education." *School and Society* 96 (December 7–21, 1968): 466–471. Examines the major court decisions regarding religious issues and the public schools.
- Pollak, Stephen J. "Parochiaid: End of the Line?" *Today's Education* 63 (November-December 1973): 77–79, 96. An up-to-date review of the recent Supreme Court rulings on religion and the schools, particularly regarding financial aid.
- Sizer, Theodore, ed. *Religion and Public Schools.* Boston: Houghton Mifflin, 1967. A book of readings on religion and the public schools, presenting different perspectives from a broad ideological spectrum.

School finance reform

- Benson, Charles, and Shannon, Thomas A. *Schools Without Property Taxes: Hope or Illusion?* Bloomington, Ind.: Phi Delta Kappa Educational Foundation, 1972. A brief paperback that explores the background for school financial reform and suggests some solutions to the problems.
- Berke, Joel S., and Kirst, Michael W. "How the Federal Government Can Encourage State School Finance Reform." *Phi Delta Kappan* 55 (December 1973): 241–244. Two well-known school finance experts base this article on their testimony to a congressional committee. They urge the federal government to spur the states on in financial reform by offering incentives.
- Hornbostel, Victor O. "School Finance Reform." *Today's Education* 62 (November-December 1973): 71–76. A brief, easy-to-read overview of the major issues in school finance reform.

Sex Education

- Flatter, John, and Pietrofesa, John J. "Human Sexuality: What Is the School's Role? *Clearing House* 47 (October 1972): 71–74. A strong position that schools must deal with human sexuality and help students develop suitable lifestyles based upon rational attitudes and values.
- Nolte, M. Chester. "Why Boards Are Winning Sex Education Battles." *American School Board Journal* 160 (June 1973): 22–23, 26. A review of how the courts are responding to efforts to stop sex education in the schools.
- Weinstock, H. R. "Issues in Sex Education." *Educational Forum* 34 (January 1970): 189–196. The author states that the schools are the most qualified institution to teach sex education since the home, church, library, and medical profession have demonstrated their inability to do so.

Sexism and Sex Role Stereotyping

- Frazier, Nancy, and Sadker, Myra. *Sexism in School and Society.* New York:

Harper & Row, 1973. An excellent treatment of the topic, including many examples of sexism in the schools.
- *Phi Delta Kappan* 55 (October 1973). The theme of this issue is education and the feminist movement. Contains many good articles on the topic.
- Saario, Terry N.; Jacklin, Carol Nagy; and Tittle, Carol Kehr. "Sex Role Stereotyping in the Public Schools." *Harvard Educational Review* 43 (August 1973): 386–416.

Student Rights

- Buxton, Thomas H., and Prichard, Keith W. "Student Perceptions of Teacher Violations of Human Rights." *Phi Delta Kappan* 55 (September 1973): 66–69. Article reports results of a survey conducted in three southern states.
- Haberman, Martin. *Student Rights: A Guide to the Right of Children, Youth, and Future Teachers.* Washington, D.C.: U.S. Office of Education, 1973. Listed in ERIC, number ED 070 752. The paper summarizes the right of students in elementary and secondary schools by examining case histories.
- Strahan, Richard Dobbs. *The Courts and the Schools.* Lincoln, Neb.: Professional Educators Publications, 1973. Chapter 7, "Students' Rights on Campus," provides an excellent review of court interpretations concerning student rights.

Teacher Power

- Guthrie, James W. and Craig, Patricia A. *Teachers and Politics.* Bloomington, Ind.: Phi Delta Kappa Educational Foundation, 1973. This short booklet explores teachers' emerging political roles.
- Meyers, Donald A. *Teacher Power: Professionalism and Collective Bargaining.* Lexington, Mass.: D.C. Heath, 1973. A recent statement on issues related to teacher power.
- Reeves, Richard. "Teachers, Politics and Power." *Learning* 2 (November 1973): 10–14. An excellent article that describes how teacher organizations are becoming more involved in political actions.

Films

- *A Chance for Change* (Contemporary/McGraw-Hill, b&w, 39 min., 1965). Preschool-age youngsters in a poor black community in Mississippi learn to work out their own ideas without fear of adults in a Head Start Center. Documenting everyday activity in the playground, classroom, cafeteria, and on nature walks, this film is an outstanding example of the optimism and dedication that marked the Head Start program at its inception. It was produced for the Child Development Group of Mississippi and stresses the possibilities for genuine change through preschool learning situations.
- *A Chance to Learn* (NBC Educational Enterprises Code #006C1, 16mm, color, 17 min.). Daniel Moynihan and Charles Hamilton discuss some of the basic issues underlying the confrontations taking place in schools across the country: Who shall control the schools? Who shall decide who teaches in them? Who shall decide what is taught? The public-school system in Rochester, New York, is used as an example.
- *The Child Experts* (Time-Life, b&w, 40 min., 1968). This study, made in Britain by the BBC, maintains that the way a child is brought up depends on the social class of his parents. Class effects begin to take hold as early as six months, and by the age of five a middle class child is substantially ahead of the working class child. Little evidence is available to show that schooling can help redress this

imbalance. In conclusion, five experts give their views on bringing up normal children from birth to age five.

- *Cloud 9* (EDC Film Library, 16mm, 25 min.). Documents the reactions of fifth-graders in the Cardozo Model School District in Washington, D.C., to the death of Martin Luther King.
- *The Coleman Report: Equality of Educational Opportunity* (Anti-Defamation League, b&w, 55 min., 1969). The Coleman Report, released by the Office of Education in 1966, revised conceptions of ways to achieve equality in education for disadvantaged children. The film supports Coleman's recommendation of school integration along economic class lines. It presents a discussion by Daniel Moynihan and Thomas Pettigrew on the ramifications of the report as discussed in their joint Harvard-MIT seminar on its findings. They range over such topics as the value of compensatory education, the role of the school in eliminating discrimination, the effect of class integration on the advantaged child, and the ways of initiating changes in the public schools called for by the Coleman Report.
- *Community Control* (Boston Newsreel, 16mm, 50 min.). Documents the struggle of the black and Puerto Rican communities to control their own schools. The forces they are working against: the police who enforce the political decisions of the municipal bureaucracy and the teachers' union, which is striking against the demands of the community.
- *Confronted* (NET, b&w, 60 min., 1965). This film records the confrontation of several northern communities with the issue of integration in schools, jobs, and housing. Of particular interest to education students is the segment describing a campaign in Malverne, Long Island, by white citizens who opposed the state commissioner's effort to maintain a racial balance in public schools. The film also contains comments from whites in Chicago opposed to "open occupancy" laws and to affirmative action hiring programs. This is an interesting document of people's reactions before the power of the camera via television was widely understood.
- *Education* (American Educational Films, color, 25 min., 1972). Deals with the new techniques educational institutions will have to devise to meet the needs of students who are more self-aware. The film predicts an emphasis on tailor-made courses rather than prepackaged materials, on students' direction of their own learning progress, and on the use of the computer for mass educational purposes.
- *From Cradle to Classroom* (Contemporary/McGraw-Hill, color, 51 min., 1968). This film describes new programs that are attempting to make an impact on the formative years from ages one to four. Special teaching machines and instructional techniques are used to increase not only physical skills but also motivational, verbal, and conceptual abilities. Controversial educational drills and toys for younger children, and reading and logic exercises for the older half of the group, are explained and demonstrated.
- *The Frustrated Campus* (Indiana University Audio-Visual Center, 16mm, b&w, 47 min.). This film, produced for NET, presents students, faculty, and administrators of several universities as they debate some of the issues confronting higher education, i.e., infringement of others' rights by student militants and the university's role in solving social problems such as racism and war.
- *The Game* (Mass Media Ministries, 16mm, b&w, 28 min., 1967). Explores the emotional conflicts that arise in sexual relations, from the viewpoint of a teenage boy. Few adults are seen or heard from and no moralizing mars the impact of viewing this personal event.

- *Grooving* (Benchmark Films, 16mm, color, 31 min., 1970). Produced for the New York State Narcotics Addiction Commission, this film is remarkably honest and reasonable. Although the message is clearly antidrug, it is presented through unscripted rap sessions about drugs among kids ranging in age from fourteen to eighteen.
- *Hear Us O Lord* (NET, color, 51 min., 1968). This film examines the responses of families in Cook County, Illinois, to a school desegregation order. It also looks at the Dan Lang family and their neighbors in South Holland, Illinois, which was the first incorporated suburb in the country ordered to desegregate its schools by busing. The filmmakers were able to record very frank reactions by white parents to the issue of sending their children to school with black children.
- *High School Rising* (Newsreel, b&w, 15 min., 1969). Stills, live footage, and rock music are combined in an artful but technically flawed way to make a statement about high schools today. The film criticizes the use of police and narcotics agents to patrol school corridors, the effects of the tracking system, and the distortion of the history of black, brown, and poor white people offered in school courses.
- *Hooked* (Churchill Films, 16mm, b&w, 1966). A film that assumes that you have already read the statistics and heard the "lectures." There is no narration, no charts, no interviews with doctors or other professionals, no newsreels of arrests — just honest conversation with former drug addicts as they look back on their addiction.
- *It Happens* (Pyramid, color, 25 min., 1973). An open-ended film, intended for discussion, on teenage pregnancy. A young girl, unmarried, must find where to go for tests and counseling without her parents' knowledge. She wrestles with the questions of marriage, abortion, adoption, and motherhood. This film has much the same format as *Phoebe* (Contemporary/McGraw-Hill, b&w, 28 min., 1968). *Phoebe* is more interestingly produced, with unusual editing and musical effects, but it has a slightly dated feeling, primarily because of changes in fashions and hair styles, which can be avoided by using *It Happens.*
- *Kenneth Keniston: This Student Generation: Conflict and Commitment Part II* (APGA Film Sales, 16mm, b&w, 35 min., 1968) An Associate Professor of Psychology at Yale and author of *Young Radicals* and *The Uncommitted,* Kenneth Keniston discusses "alienated" students, radicals, black militancy, violence, and drug use on campus.
- *Marked for Failure* (NET, b&w, 60 min., 1965). Harlem street life and schools are the subject of this film, which examines the learning handicaps that affect children from depressed areas. The discussion of efforts being made to overcome these disadvantages is dated, but the film remains valuable as a document on the conditions of schools and the street-corner society of a densely populated inner-city neighborhood.
- *Not Me* (Contemporary/McGraw-Hill, color, 54 min., 1971). This is a chillingly authentic chronicle of the history of a 13-year-old drug addict — from the forces that compel him to "give it a try" to his ultimate addiction and fatal overdose. Without preaching and without offering facile solutions, the film shows how the elements of home, neighborhood, friends, and school combine to bring about the needless end of a young life. The film was produced by the New Jersey Community Action Training Institute and was selected for showing at an exhibit on the "Drug Scene" at the Museum of the City of New York.
- *One Step at a Time* (Infomatics, color, 25 min., 1972). This film records the Michigan Department of Education's effort to achieve educational accountability

What are the tension points in American education?

in its school system. It details the six logical steps of an accountability model: common goals, performance objectives, needs assessment testing, instructional improvement, evaluation, and recommendations for improvements. Educators are shown working with community groups to bring about the changes required to achieve accountability.

- *The Three R's . . . and Sex Education* (NET, b&w, 60 min., 1971). This documentary explores several opposing responses to the teaching of sex education in schools. Germantown Friends School in Pennsylvania teaches about sex in order to help students make moral decisions. Dr. Billy James Hargis, head of the Christian Crusade, believes sex education to be the leading edge of a Communist conspiracy in schools, and he is joined by the John Birch Society. Confrontations between the PTA and the Board of Schools in Cedar Rapids, Iowa, illustrate the degree of community feeling this issue can arouse. The film also shows teachers being trained to teach sex education.

Audiotapes

- *The Berkeley Schools Desegregate* (Pacifica, 30 min., 1967). A documentary for radio on the Berkeley schools, which became the first in California to achieve balanced integration.
- *Campus Unrest — What is it About?* (Center for the Study of Democratic Institutions, 3.75 ips, reel, $\frac{1}{4}$ track, 44:25 min.). This tape was made at a three-day conference on Students and Society attended by twenty-two students from eighteen schools and colleges. The discussion revolves around the question, "Is reform of the university any longer possible?" There is no consensus among the students.
- *The Drug Scene Series* (BFA Educational Media, 30 min. each, 1971). Each tape in this series deals with a specific drug or class of drugs. They are intended to be information resources for teachers and other professional people who want unbiased information on the symptoms and effects of drug abuse. The series consists of eight tapes, which discuss (after an introductory presentation) marijuana, marijuana laws, heroin, methadone, hallucinogens, pills, and alcohol.
- *The End of Schooling: A Strategy for Revolt* (Noumedia #7005, 3.75 ips, reel, $\frac{1}{4}$ track, mono or stereo, 1.5 hours, 1970). In the third of three lectures given at Yale University, Ivan Illich discusses possible solutions to the destructiveness and illusory goals of institutionalized schooling.
- *Intelligence Tests and the Black Child* (Pacifica, 45 min., 1970). Gerald West, speaking to an NAACP meeting at San Francisco State College, questions whether standard IQ tests actually measure the intelligence and potential abilities of the ghetto child. An interesting early challenge to the doctrine of Arthur Jensen and followers that intelligence tests *do* reveal differences in intellectual ability along class and racial lines.
- *A Matter of Genes* (Center for the Study of Democratic Institutions, 29 min., 1971). Arthur Jensen defends his hypothesis that "genetic factors are strongly implicated in the average black-white intelligence difference." Jensen also comments on his ideas about methodology in education and in sociological research.
- *Programming Behavior* (Big Sur, 4 hours, 1966). Dr. B. F. Skinner, the psychologist who developed operant conditioning and various learning machines, participates in a dialogue on humanism. He discusses methods of operant conditioning that can be applied to discovery and exploration of the inner self. The program also includes a presentation by Dr. Joe Kamiya, a researcher in alpha wave conditioning.

- *Reading, Writing, . . . and Race* (Center for the Study of Democratic Institutions, 40 min., 1967). Participants examine integration and compensation as two models for making public schooling more effective. This varied and vociferous discussion features the late Senator Robert Kennedy; Oscar Lewis, anthropologist; Kenneth Clark, black sociologist; Neil Sullivan, Superintendent of Schools in Berkeley; and Robert Hutchins, former President of the University of Chicago.
- *The 1970 Spring Crisis of Violence* (Noumedia, 3.75 ips, reel, $\frac{1}{4}$ track, mono or stereo, 1.3 hours, 1970). A public talk by Margaret Mead at Mountain High School, in West Orange, New Jersey, on the roots of the 1970 spring crisis of violence, the peculiar conditions of our time, an historical review of crisis, education, and the need to listen. A dialogue evolves between Dr. Mead and the parents and students in the audience.

Videotapes

- *Political* (Videofreex, $\frac{1}{2}$", Sony, Old and New Generation tapes). A videotape on political issues in high schools called "High School Confidential."

Filmographies

- *Films Suitable for Head Start Child Development Programs* (Department of Health, Education, and Welfare, 1973). This government publication lists films available on a free-loan basis from Modern Talking Picture Service. The catalogue deals primarily with the subject of early childhood education and development, but it also includes films addressed to teachers and aides in day care centers who need advice on activities planning. A small selection of infant development films are also indexed.
- *99+ Films on Drugs* (Educational Film Library Association, 1970). Originally published by the Extension Media Center of the University of California, this is a valuable guide to films on the abuse of mind-affecting drugs. A good selection procedure, outlined in the beginning of the book, was used to review the rapidly increasing number of film treatments of drug abuse. Many good films did not find their way into this volume, but it remains the best single source of titles on this subject, and it is frank about the shortcomings of the films it does list.

Refer to Appendix for addresses of distributors.

What are the tension points in American education?

Where are schools going?

11

What's new in education?

This chapter examines some innovations that are currently in use and seem to have promise. The chapter is organized around two sections: one on curricular and instructional innovations, and the other on organizational innovations.

We have chosen to end our book by looking at what's new in education. This is an optimistic chapter, based on our belief that we can and will improve our participation in the unfinished work of the schools.

Chapter contents

Curricular and instructional innovations
Individualized instructional systems
Open education
Career education
Moral education
Bilingual education
Computer-assisted instruction (CAI)
Organizational innovations
Nongraded schools
Competitive education and accountability
Middle schools
Year-round schools
School design

Change, innovate, reform. . . . James Cass of *Saturday Review* has said that the most notable aspect of American education for the last twenty years has been the preoccupation with change. The large majority of educational innovations have had little lasting impact on the schools of our nation. Despite these poor results, educators are continually examining and experimenting in an effort to improve the quality of education for our children.

Education, as we have seen, is a fairly stable institution. How will it prepare people to face an unstable world—one that sometimes seems to be spinning apart or falling apart, or even blowing itself apart? Will we become victims of "future shock," unable to cope with rapid change and information overload?

Can existing educational institutions prepare youngsters for this new world? Does education itself offer sufficient diversity in response to this changing world? And if educators don't meet this challenge, what will be the result? Some would agree with Peter Drucker, who considers education too important to be left to educators who " . . . still talk of minor changes, or adjustments and improvements. Few of them see much reason for radical changes. Yet education will in all likelihood be transformed within the next decade *by giant forces from without.*"[1] Others predict that if education doesn't change sufficiently, people will

[1] Peter Drucker, *The Age of Discontinuity* (New York: Harper & Row, 1969), p. 334.

seek alternatives outside the system; they will either create their own schools or entirely reject the validity of schools. In a sense, the institution of education is like a car. Despite frequent lubrication and constant maintenance, worn-out parts must be replaced; eventually it might become necessary to abandon the model entirely and shop for a new set of wheels.

Educators are now working on replacing the worn-out parts, and better communications systems are spreading new ideas more rapidly than ever before. But none of these new ideas represents *the* answer. The only adequate response to diversity is continuously to reflect it in action. We need to guard against letting our innovations become as inflexible and embedded in tradition as the methods they have replaced.

Innovations are rarely isolated in their effect. A new educational movement that deals principally with a reorganization of school staffing is sure to affect curriculum and instruction as well. It is very rare that a new procedure is simply "tacked on" to one area of a system without affecting its other parts or the system as a whole. Considering nongraded schools without simultaneously examining curriculum and teacher instruction is futile. In a sense, then, any innovation is as "instructional" as it is "organizational," or vice versa.

Curricular and instructional innovations are generally attempts to bring school practices into line with individual and societal needs. They attempt to cope with

What's new in education?

the individual student's needs to progress at his own rate, follow a curriculum that interests him, learn more about the world of work, and develop moral standards for a better society.

Organizational innovations tend to operate on the principle that in order to change people's ways of behaving, it is necessary to change the structures in which people operate. If this is not done, then the old structure prevents people from changing.

New ideas in education reflect a growing concern with individualization of instruction; students themselves are diverse, and attempts to reach them must involve a recognition that they learn at different rates and through different modes of instruction. When you read or hear about a specific proposal or innovations—or if you have the opportunity to implement change in the classroom—ask yourself how it can improve the quality of the individual student's learning situation.

Curricular and instructional innovations

Individualized instructional systems

Individualizing instruction means different things to different people. Some people use the term to suggest that all of the students proceed through the same curriculum but at different rates. To others, it means that the same curriculum is presented to all students but by different instructional methods, depending on the learning style of the students. For still others, it means that different curricula are offered to meet individual needs, allowing each student to choose the instructional objectives that best fit his unique interests and needs.

Individually Prescribed Instruction (IPI), originally developed at the University of Pittsburgh's Learning and Research Center, is a systematic approach to individualization for elementary-school children. The essential characteristics of the IPI system are: the student's freedom to move through the curriculum at his own rate of progress; behavioral objectives—that is, objectives stated in terms of what the learner should be able to *do* when he has mastered the lesson, arranged sequentially in order of complexity (see pages 365–366 for further explanation of behavioral objectives); the intention that the student work on objectives until he achieves them, thus emphasizing accomplishment rather than failure; emphasis on self-direction, self-initiation, and self-evaluation on the part of the learner; individualized techniques and materials providing a variety of instructional alternatives; the organization and management of the total school environment to facilitate individual instruction; provision for continuous feedback on the effectiveness of the program.

IPI is currently available in four areas: language arts, mathematics, social studies, and science. Because its objectives are so clearly stated, teacher direction is at a minimum. Instead, diagnosis is a crucial aspect of IPI; placement tests are administered to students to determine the instructional program appropriate for each child. Before each unit, a pretest is administered to the child to determine the point within the unit where he should begin, or whether he has already mastered the material. At the end of the unit, a posttest is administered to see if the child has in fact achieved the behavioral objectives. If the student has not done so, the teacher notes where he has fallen short and prescribes additional instruction. There are also curriculum-embedded tests, taken while the student is progressing through the curriculum, designed to provide data on the mastery of each behavioral objective and to determine whether he needs additional work.

Behavioral objectives

"Behavioral objectives identify goals and describe outcomes or performances learners should have as a result of participation in an activity." (H. H. McAshan, *Writing Behavioral Objectives* [New York: Harper & Row, 1970], p. 8.) The behavioral objective specifies not only the goal but also the behavior the learner will have to manifest as a means of determining his success in achieving the goal.

Objectives are often stated so ambiguously that they are subject to different interpretations. Consider the following general objective: "The students should know the difference between a revenue tariff and a protective tariff." Does the teacher who chose this objective want the student to be able to write definitions of the two terms? Or does he want the student to identify correctly written descriptions of the two terms? Or, given a description of a specific tariff, does the teacher want the student to identify orally what kind of tariff it is?

You can see that the objective as stated above is too vague for a student to determine exactly what he is supposed to know about tariffs. Here is the same objective written behaviorally: "Given written definitions of both revenue and protective tariffs, the student will be able to correctly identify orally to the instructor the name of each type of tariff on his first attempt." The clarity and specificity of this objective are the advantages of behavioral objectives. Programmed instruction, computer-assisted instruction, and systems for individualizing instruction are dependent on the translation of their goals into behavioral objectives.

The following fable is an eloquent argument for the need for behavioral objectives in the instructional process:

Once upon a time a Sea Horse gathered up his seven pieces of eight and cantered out to find his fortune. Before he had traveled very far he met an Eel, who said,

"Psst. Hey, bud. Where 'ya goin'?"

"I'm going out to find my fortune," replied the Sea Horse, proudly.

"You're in luck," said the Eel. "For four pieces of eight you can have this speedy flipper, and then you'll be able to get there a lot faster."

"Gee, that's swell," said the Sea Horse, and paid the money and put on the flipper and slithered off at twice the speed. Soon he came upon a Sponge, who said,

"Psst. Hey, bud. Where 'ya goin'?"

"I'm going out to find my fortune," replied the Sea Horse.

"You're in luck," said the Sponge. "For a small fee I will let you have this jet-propelled scooter so that you will be able to travel a lot faster."

So the Sea Horse bought the scooter with his remaining money and went zooming through the sea five times as fast. Soon he came upon a Shark, who said,

"Psst. Hey, bud. Where 'ya goin'?"

"I'm going to find my fortune," replied the Sea Horse.

"You're in luck. If you'll take this short cut," said the Shark, pointing to his open mouth, "you'll save yourself a lot of time."

"Gee, thanks," said the Sea Horse, and zoomed off into the interior of the Shark, there to be devoured.

The moral of this fable is that if you're not sure where you're going, you're liable to end up someplace else — and not even know it.

Robert F. Mager, *Preparing Instructional Objectives* (Palo Alto: Fearon, 1962), p. vii. Reprinted by permission of the publisher.

The instructional materials used in IPI programs include worksheets, tape and disc recordings, programmed materials, individual readers, manipulative devices, and computer-assisted instruction. Since no two students learn in quite the same way, IPI attempts to present a variety of instructional materials.

Another individualized program, with characteristics similar to those of IPI, is Individually Guided Education (IGE). However, IGE differs from IPI on several counts. First, IGE utilizes a multi-unit school organization within which the instruction of groups of different-aged children becomes the responsibility of units or teams of teachers. Second, IGE addresses itself to improving home/school communication to ensure that the school's efforts are supported and reinforced by the parents. Third, IGE leaves most instructional decisions in the hands of the teachers, whereas the IPI materials are more prescriptive. Fourth, IGE has developed its system at the secondary- as well as the elementary-school level.

The evidence gathered thus far on these two systems indicates that teachers, students, and parents are enthusiastic about them. Furthermore, the students' cognitive achievement level indicates that they do as well as or better than non-IPI or non-IGE students on standard tests.[2] By 1973 IPI was serving 100,000 schoolchildren across the country, and IGE was being used in over 1,000 schools in 18 different states.[3]

Public schools in the next two decades will increasingly assume characteristics similar to those of the IPI and IGE programs. Behaviorally stated objectives, self-pacing, self-direction, self-evaluation, and alternative modes of instruction will

[2] Ronald E. Hull, "Selecting An Approach to Individualized Education," *Phi Delta Kappan* 55 (November 1973): 170–171.
[3] Hull, p. 169.

become commonplace in our schools. Students will no longer be considered in groups, but individually. This does not mean that students will no longer participate in instructional groups, but that they will do so only as part of their own individually prescribed learning. Peer interaction is an important part of the instructional process, and care must be taken not to isolate students from one another in an attempt to individualize instruction.

Open Education

One of the most exciting recent imports from Great Britain is a new approach to teaching in primary schools. Known by a variety of names—"the open classroom," "the integrated day," "the Leicestershire model," "the British infant school"—it represents less a new teaching style than it does a set of shared attitudes and beliefs about learning, schooling, and the nature of childhood. The traditional elementary-school classroom situation and the usual roles of teacher and student are rejected. It is a highly individualized, child-centered learning experience based on the assumption that learning will be more effective if it develops from what interests the learner, rather than what interests the teacher. The teacher does not adbicate her position and authority in the classroom; instead, she facilitates learning by structuring the environment to respond optimally to each child's needs and interests. The child, rather than the teacher, is the source of learning.

There are four basic principles operating in an open classroom. First, the classroom is decentralized; open space is divided into flexible "interest areas" according to function. The room does not look like a classroom. Second, the children are free to explore the room and choose their own activities. Third, the environment is rich in learning resources—books, rulers, measuring tape, tinkertoys, tape recorders, and dozens of other instructional materials. And, finally, the teacher and the aides spend most of their time with individual children or small groups, and rarely present the material to the class as a whole.[4]

Respect for and trust in the child are perhaps the most basic underlying principles of open education. An American visiting an open classroom for the first time is usually surprised by what he sees—the room has no identifiable front or back, the children are all doing different things at different times, and the teacher may be working with an individual child or observing. There is a beehive of activity, yet discipline problems are almost nonexistent. When it is no longer the teacher's responsibility to maintain order and control and the children are not required to sit still and be quiet, discipline problems seem to disappear.

The theoretical rationale for the open classroom stems mainly from the work of the Swiss child psychologist, Jean Piaget. Much of Piaget's lifetime has been spent studying children and their developmental stages. He believes that it is a waste of time to tell a child things that he can't experience through his senses. The child must be allowed to manipulate objects, try different experiments, pose questions, and test his findings against other children's perceptions. Communication among peers is an essential part of a child's learning. Only after a child has had a great deal of sensory experience is he ready to comprehend abstract concepts. Piaget is critical of the traditional classroom approach for emphasizing conceptualization without offering the child the opportunity to experience through his senses.

[4] Ronald and Beatrice Gross, "A Little Bit of Chaos," *Saturday Review* (May 16, 1970): 71–73, 84–85.

What's new in education?

The open classroom approach received widespread publicity in Great Britain in 1967 when a Parliamentary Commission, now referred to as the Plowden Committee, urged its adoption by all English primary schools. American schools are also increasingly adopting this approach. The state of North Dakota, for instance, is remodeling its elementary schools along the lines of the open classroom, in conjunction with the University of North Dakota's New School for Behavioral Studies in Education. Although the results of tests evaluating the students' progress in reading and mathematics are not conclusive at this time, there are indications that the children are enjoying this new approach. Charles E. Silberman reports the following anecdotal accounts of interviews conducted in North Dakota:

"Last year we had to work all the time. Now we can play all the time," one little *boy volunteers to the visitor, as he "plays" with a complicated mathematical game.*

"The children won't stay home even when they're sick," a Minot teacher reports.

And a woman teaching in a wooden two-room schoolhouse wrote, in her self-evaluation, "I have had several mothers tell me that this is the first year they haven't had to fight every morning to get their youngsters to school. I think this is perhaps my greatest accomplishment."

From a father's letter to an elementary school principal: "May my son come to school earlier? There's so much he wants to do and he can't seem to fit it all in during the regular hours."

The science area in a second- and third-grade room in Starkweather. A small group of eight-year-olds guide their visitor through a display of seashells and rocks, talking knowledgeably as they go. Next they come to a section containing a snakeskin, jars of pickled frogs, pickled deer brains, pickled pig brains, and the pride of their display, a pair of pig's eyes rolling wildly in a jar of formaldehyde. Oblivious to the visitor's queasy stomach, the boy who had performed the surgery on the pig calmly discusses the procedure he used. He goes on to point out the toughness of the white of the eye: how he discovered the toughness while trying to pierce it, why the white of the eye has to be tough, and how it compares to the toughness of the white of the human eye. The visitor is relieved when the group moves on to a display of brilliantly colored photographs of dinosaurs, fossils, even insects, and then to a map of the moon, a microscope, slides, and other more familiar material.[5]

Some educators are concerned that essential skills such as reading and mathematics may be left up to chance in an open classroom. Teachers who have worked in open classrooms dismiss their concern on the grounds that their experience indicates children want to learn to read and solve mathematical problems, but do not want to be governed by a set timetable ("All right, children, put away the reading books—it's time to do math."). These teachers believe the children will learn to read when they are ready to do so.

[5] Charles E. Silberman, *Crisis in the Classroom* (New York: Random House, 1970), pp. 289, 294. Copyright © 1970 by Charles E. Silberman.

An open classroom does not require an exceptional teacher. But the teacher does need alertness and readiness to respond to and help individual students in their various activities. Since the curriculum is not restricted to the teacher's lesson plans but is literally everything that is going on in the room, it can be as unpredictable and as broad as the children's interests. However, the teacher need not be afraid to admit ignorance in certain areas. In fact, the teacher can seize such opportunities to help the student by designing experiments or research problems himself. In this way, the teacher functions as a model and demonstrates to the child that ignorance is a problem to be solved, rather than a source of shame.

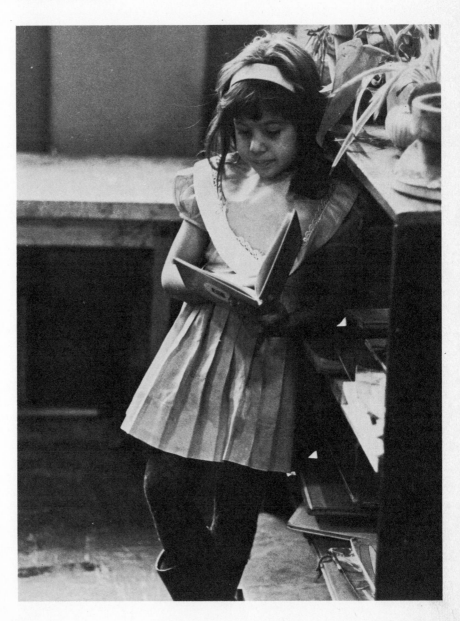

What's new in education?

Jim   It's becoming clear to me that one of the most significant movements in education today, and one that's particularly attractive to today's youth, is the movement toward informal education.

Kevin   The term "informal education" is being kicked around a good deal these days. What exactly do you mean by it?

Jim   I mean the rejection of the notion that learning occurs only as a result of formal teaching. I think today's students believe that the most significant learning occurs as a result of self-discovery and that truth can be acquired only through personal involvement and experience that is self-directed. Since most formal instruction is definitely not self-directed, many people are seeking alternatives outside the formal educational establishment.

Kevin   Do you mean such things as the free schools and the alternative schools movement?

Jim   Yes. Usually these movements allow individuals to shape their own learning based on what is meaningful to them and are, it seems to me, what kids are seeking. They want education to help them answer such questions as, "Who am I?" "What do I want to do with my life?" "How can people relate more honestly to one another?" "How can prejudice, dishonesty, and injustice be overcome in our society?"

Kevin   Do you really think formal educational institutions are incapable of allowing this type of human exploration to occur? Or do you think this can be accomplished only through the informal education movement because of the restrictions placed on conventional schools?

Jim   I think there's enough discontent now within the educational establishment that we are seeing many more public schools revise their curricula to deal with questions like "Who am I?" If we don't change in this direction, I think we're in trouble.

There is no doubt that the open education approach will become increasingly popular in the years ahead. Although similar to IPI and IGE in its emphasis on individualized instruction, it differs in its openness and in the child's almost total responsibility for what and when he wants to learn. IPI's and IGE's behavioral objectives largely predetermine the scope of the curriculum, leaving the child free to move through it at his own rate. Whereas IPI and IGE gradually allow the student more responsibility for designing his own curriculum, the open classroom gives the child that responsibility at the outset. Both approaches promise tremendous improvement over current practices in most schools, and both deserve to be tried on a large scale. We are at a stage in education when alternatives are needed, not final answers. The answers will come only after extensive testing of the alternatives, and IPI, IGE, and the open classroom promise significant results.

Career education   Educational writings and discussions in the late 1960s and early 1970s displayed a great concern over the issue of "relevance" in education. Critics charged that the education received by children in elementary and secondary schools was not relevant to their needs as individuals or to society's need for creative, productive citizens. The schools particularly came under attack on the question of how well they were preparing students to function in the world of

work. The schools were perceived by many to be overly academic for a majority
of students so that when students finished their education they were poorly informed about what career opportunities existed and poorly prepared to function
in those jobs.

Responding to these criticisms, the U.S. Office of Education initiated conferences, curriculum development projects, and teacher training programs designed to infuse elementary and secondary schools with more concern and
attention toward career education. Briefly stated, the goals of career education
are to permit students to select a career based on an understanding of the many
available options, and to provide training in the broad area of career choice so
that they will have usable skills whether they drop out of high school, graduate
and go to work, or continue in higher education toward a professional career.

In order to accomplish these goals, the advocates of career education envision
starting early in elementary school and continuing through high school or college. Career education would not be taught as a separate subject, but would infuse the entire curriculum and be attended to by virtually all teachers. Students
would become aware of the various kinds of career opportunities that exist, see

adults working in these various career areas, and be able to structure their school curriculum choices in order to receive training in the career area that interests them.

There are, of course, many ways that the goals of career education can be achieved. Some programs are designed to be school-based, while others may be employer-based, home- or community-based, or centrally located for rural populations. Multimedia materials are being developed to help children learn about career opportunities. At one school, for example, first-graders view slides of an electrician at work, listen to tapes on the work of an electrician, and wire up light bulbs and switches to get the feel of what an electrician does.

At another school district in New York, fifth- and sixth-graders have opportunities to visit persons in occupations that interest the children. More than 100 community businesses and services are cooperating in this venture.

While there are many enthusiastic advocates of career education, some educators express concern over the way some of the programs are being developed and operated. These critics are worried that career education will: push children into making career choices prematurely, track students into certain career areas based on their socioeconomic status, train students in skills that are or soon will be obsolete in their chosen career area, or reinforce sex-role stereotyping by pushing girls into occupational areas that have been traditionally open to women.[6]

What is the future of career education? Is it likely to become a permanent concern of the schools, or is it just another passing fancy? As of 1973, 750,000 children were participating in over 100 career education pilot projects in every state in the union.[7] Evaluations of these projects by educators, parents, students, and citizens will certainly help to determine career education's future. As with most curricular innovations, a large measure of its success will be determined by the teachers. Extensive inservice training will certainly be necessary to provide new skills and understandings to experienced teachers. Preservice teacher education will also have to change in order to prepare new teachers with these same skills and understandings. Unless this extensive rethinking of preservice and inservice teacher education takes place, career education is not likely to survive.

Moral education

The United States is going through a tumultuous period in its history. In the last ten years we've been confronted by one social problem after another. We went through a long, ugly, and unpopular war. The citizenry has been shaken by crimes in the street and crimes in the White House. Leaders of industry and business have defrauded the people, and sabotage by workers has reached epic proportions in some industries. Religious observance has declined. The sexual mores have changed sharply. The old feel alienated from the young, and the young from the old. Not only have our values changed, but the former value consensus in the society seems to have been fragmented. In this atmosphere of moral confusion and doubt, many people are turning to the schools to assume a more vigorous role.

[6] Lee Sproull, "Career Education Boondoggles," *Learning* 2 (October 1973): 38–41.
[7] John R. Ottina, "Career Education Is Alive and Well," *The Journal of Teacher Education* 24 (Summer 1973): 86.

The idea of the public schools teaching values is not new. For many years in this country the schools explicitly taught children how to behave under a particular set of values and moral precepts. This teaching reflected the views of the dominant group, white, Anglo-Saxon Protestants. The explicit teaching of morals and values, and occasionally religious doctrine, was a major cause for the rise of the parochial schools in this country. In the nineteenth century, newly arrived immigrants to these shores felt threatened by the values their children were being exposed to in schools. Religious groups, like the Roman Catholics, felt impelled to establish their own schools to ensure the transmission of their values and religious traditions to their young. Other religious groups followed.

During the twentieth century, we have seen a gradual, steady moving away from this explicit teaching of morality in the public schools. First, all traces of direct religious teaching were removed from the schools. Second, the moral implications of behavior became a taboo subject for classroom discussion because of the widely held view that one's moral choices in behavior were undergirded by one's religious beliefs. Public schools, then, made a concerted effort to avoid the areas of moral or ethical behavior and of individual values.

This is not to say, however, that schools were or are not affecting the values of students, or that moral training is not going on in the schools. Certain behavior is consistently rewarded by teachers and comes to be valued by the student. Coming to school every day and on time is rewarded behavior. Regularity and punctuality become valued. Working hard and getting answers are rewarded, and industriousness and certain kinds of achievement become valued. Competitiveness is rewarded and aggressive interpersonal behavior becomes valued. Students learn that certain kinds of behavior, like punching each other, is "bad," while other kinds of behavior, like beating every one in the class on a test, is very good. Students are quite quick to pick up these school values. They learn what a teacher wants from them, both in terms of their intellectual and social behavior. They usually can tell whom the teacher likes and whom she does not like. All of this provides a climate for moral education. It is not part of the formal curriculum of the school, but a major part of the invisible or hidden curriculum. Some of this is surely helpful, and some dangerous, but all is unsystematic and rather accidental.

What's new in education?

What we have then is a situation where on the one hand the older generation is deeply concerned by its inability to effectively transmit to the young its morals and values, and on the other hand the schools, which have the capacity to do this but are formally giving the area a wide berth.

For years research told us that attempts at character education and morality training were ineffective. Recently, however, there has been a renewed interest in this area by educational researchers and practitioners. Two approaches to moral education seem particularly promising: the values clarification work developed by Sidney Simon and his associates,[8] and the moral thinking research being conducted by Lawrence Kohlberg and his associates.[9]

Values clarification skills refer to a group of techniques that can be used by a teacher in order to help students gain a clearer understanding of the ideas and things that they personally value. Many of these techniques have a game-like quality and are capable of stimulating great interest among students. Also, the skills are relatively easy to learn. Another advantage is that they can be adapted to various subject matters and to various time constraints. They can be the focus of a long unit or they can be squeezed into a few moments before a bell. Underlying values clarification is the belief that children should know their own values and be able to relate them to decision making. Also, the child becomes aware of the fact that other students may have very different values and, in the process, he should become more tolerant of these differing values.

Lawrence Kohlberg's work deals with moral thinking, or how people engage in thought about moral issues. His work is based on the developmental psychology of Jean Piaget, which sees the child as taking an active, spontaneous part in his own mental growth rather than being a passive receiver of external messages and influences. Kohlberg has shown that in the same way that people go through distinct stages of cognitive growth, they go through distinct stages of moral thinking. He has found six separate stages of moral thinking, ranging from a pre-conventional level where the child makes moral choices based on the direct physical consequences of an action (stage 1) to the post-conventional level where the individual makes choices on the basis of principles of justice and human brotherhood (stage 6). It should be clear, however, that these stages refer to structures or ways of thinking rather than particular answers to particular moral questions. This is important since the teacher is able to focus on moral thinking, rather than dictating what an individual should think.

Research in this area is beginning to yield some principles of teaching. First, people go through the various stages sequentially, and all do not get to the higher levels. Further, principles of moral reasoning can not be taught directly, but the teacher can facilitate transition from stage to stage by structuring certain kinds of situations. For instance, a student is aided in progressing from one level to the next by encountering moral reasoning at one level higher than his present stage. Students are able to recognize the inadequacy of moral reasoning at levels below their own but are incapable of appreciating moral reasoning more

[8] L. Raths, M. Harmon, and S. Simon, *Values and Teaching* (Charles E. Merrill, 1966).
[9] Lawrence Kohlberg, "The Child as a Moral Philosopher," *Psychology Today* 7 (1968): 25–30.

than one level above their own. The latter finding explains much of the ineffectiveness of traditional preaching about moral issues. In brief, Kohlberg sees the student as a moral philosopher, going through stages of development that demand increasingly sophisticated moral thinking. The teacher, on the other hand, is both a moral philosopher and a moral psychologist. In addition to considering the moral implications of his actions and values, he must understand the child's way of thinking and be able to adapt his teaching to it.

While the beginnings in this area are both promising and provocative, much more research needs to be done. There is a danger that moral education could degenerate into indoctrination. Also, moral education could transgress into the family's area of responsibility. As in any other area, moral education can be perverted by poor teaching. Such a prospect presents a special danger here, since an individual's moral reasoning and values are of such fundamental importance.

Bilingual education   In the southwestern part of the United States, 40 percent of the Mexican-American students do not finish high school. In Boston in 1972, out of a school-age Puerto Rican population of about 10,000, only 63 graduated from high school. Between 1965 and 1969 only 4 Puerto Ricans graduated from high school in Boston.[10]

Students whose native language is not English constitute one of the most conspicuous failure groups in the American educational system. Because of their

[10] Lawrence Wright, "The Bilingual Education Movement at the Crossroads," *Phi Delta Kappan* 55 (November 1973): 183–186.

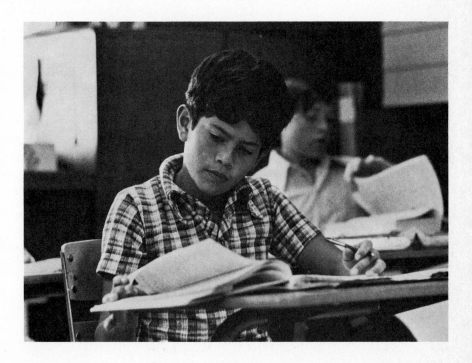

What's new in education?

difficulty in speaking, writing, and understanding English, these students fall farther and farther behind in school, with overwhelming numbers of them dropping out before finishing high school.

In order to cope with this problem, Congress passed the Bilingual Education Act in 1968. Under that act, $400 million was authorized for a six-year period to establish adequate bilingual education programs. Since that time, however, only $35 million has been allocated to support 213 projects in 32 states and territories and involving 19 languages other than English. Obviously this amount is totally inadequate to even begin to cope with the five million school-age children whose native language is not English. State support of bilingual programs, with a couple of exceptions, is practically nonexistent at the present time.

Bilingual programs ideally include equal numbers of non-English-speaking children and children proficient in English; in actuality, few programs have many English-speakers. The teachers, of course, are supposed to be bilingual, but because of the scarcity of bilingual teachers many of them speak only English and are supported by ethnic aides. There is also a tremendous need for textbooks, and testing and supplementary materials in the native language of the child.

In January 1974 the U.S. Supreme Court issued a far-reaching decision in the case of *Lau* v. *Nichols*. The case involved a class action suit on the behalf of Chinese-speaking students in San Francisco, but it has implications for all of the nation's non-English-speaking children. The Court found that, "There is no equality of treatment merely by providing students with the same facilities, textbooks, teachers, and curriculum; for students who do not understand English are effectively foreclosed from any meaningful education." Basing its ruling on the Civil Rights Act of 1964, the Court held that the San Francisco school system unlawfully discriminates on the basis of national origin when it fails to cope with these children's language problems. Although the Court gave the school district free rein on how to teach the children English as a second language, the ruling means that bilingual education in our schools will dramatically increase in an effort to comply with the Court's ruling.

In these days when the teacher supply is greater than the demand, bilingual teachers, particularly those who speak Spanish, will be very much in demand. If you possess this competency, or still have time to build it into your college program, you could help solve a serious educational problem, while at the same time greatly enhancing your employment opportunities.

Computer-assisted instruction (CAI)

A number of prominent educators and computer technologists predict that within the next two decades the direct use of the computer for instructional purposes will become widespread in both elementary and secondary schools. Already today the rudiments of CAI are operating successfully in thousands of secondary schools in the form of a timesharing terminal located in the school.

CAI both frightens and excites many teachers. They have read where CAI would help relieve them of many burdensome tasks, but they don't really understand how it works and what it can do. As will be seen from our discussion the most important aspect of CAI is its potential for individualizing instruction. Presently the computer is able to facilitate instruction in several major areas including: 1) drills and practice, 2) simple games, 3) inquiry mode, and 4) individualized testing.[11]

Drill and practice exercises are used to supplement the regular curriculum taught by the teacher. The student sits at a keyboard much like that of a typewriter and is furnished with repetition in specific skill areas such as mathematics, reading, spelling, or foreign languages. The student proceeds at his own pace working on skills that he particularly needs.

Many types of simple games with educational value are available on computers today. They provide the student with opportunities to develop strategies for solving problems. In addition, games for amusement, such as tic-tac-toe, are also available.

Many of the lessons that are now available on computers are predetermined and controlled by the program. The idea behind the inquiry system is to establish a learner-controlled, responsive learning system. In this system, after a student is presented with information he can ask the computer any question he wishes. He can continue to do this, receiving answers from the computer, until he wishes to proceed to the next part of the learning program. Of course, sometimes the computer must inform him that it is unable to answer a specific question. While this capability does now exist, there are relatively few good programs in existence at this time.

The computer can also be used to evaluate students going through individualized programs. When the student feels he is ready to be evaluated, he can go to the computer and take the test; his record is then updated and made available to the teacher.

As computer technology costs are reduced and educational institutions and industries start producing computer programs, the computer will become a standard form of instruction in the public schools. Some educators fear that CAI will impose a rigid system of impersonalized teaching and lead to excessive standardization of education, but CAI proponents believe the opposite. They argue that CAI will make teaching even more personalized by increasing individualized instruction and freeing the teacher from routine tasks. They also believe that the wide use of computers will permit the introduction of an almost unlimited diversity of curriculum.

One thing is clear, though: if the computer does become commonplace in schools, the role of the teacher will change drastically. The computer, not the teacher, will impart facts and concepts to the students. The teacher will diagnose student learning difficulties and prescribe appropriate instruction. Many students will be working by themselves while the teacher works with small groups or individuals. It is also likely that many of the routine tasks the teacher now performs will be assumed by paraprofessional assistants.

[11] William D. Hedges, "The Principal, the Computer, and Emerging Applications to Instruction," *Phi Delta Kappan* 55 (November 1973): 174.

Jim	*Here we are more than halfway through this chapter and the reader is probably wondering about the significance of all these innovations in education.*
Kevin	*It's really hard to say. Some, like individualized instructional systems and open education, have been tried out in many schools and have helped create a new spirit and excitement in some of them.*
Jim	*Sometimes I wonder whether all or most of these innovations aren't just fluff that occupies people's attention and energy while the real problems are ignored. In other words, how much effect are these new developments actually having, and how many of them are just being tried because the school district wants to tell the taxpayers that they are hip and up-to-date?*
Kevin	*I know what you mean, and I think that the "bandwagon effect" does motivate some school districts. But some schools try them because they really believe they will improve learning and instruction. Whether they do or not is difficult to prove.*
Jim	*I have another theory. I think many school districts try them because they are manageable, might make a difference, and provide a sense of direction and accomplishment for those involved. The larger problems—like racial prejudice, equality of educational opportunity, and survival in a changing society—are so huge and amorphous that many educators label them insoluble, and concentrate instead on problems of a lower order of magnitude.*
Kevin	*You may be right. Certainly the purposes of new developments must be questioned and fitted into a larger picture based on one's own philosophy of education and what learning and schooling are, and should be, all about. What worries me, though, is that innovations in education may just be minor variations on a bad theme—at a time when we need thorough reform in education.*

Organizational innovations

Nongraded schools

Do you remember descriptions of the old one-room country schoolhouse? Students ranging in age from five to fourteen or fifteen were all taught by the same teacher in the same room, each studying material appropriate to his own learning level? We normally think of this scene as pretty old-fashioned. In many respects it is, but one aspect of it is extremely modern: the nongraded character of the school. Grade levels made no sense in a one-room schoolhouse because there was no way to separate the students accordingly. In effect, the teacher was forced to treat each student differently; each was at a different level of achievement in reading, 'riting and 'rithmetic. Grouping of the students made sense only when several were at the same level of achievement for a particular learning task.

Schools in America were ordinarily ungraded until 1848, when the Quincy Grammar School in Boston introduced graded levels. By 1860 the graded system had been widely adopted, especially in the cities, and was rapidly becoming standard practice in elementary schools.

Although graded classes were originally advocated as a means of individualizing instruction, it eventually became apparent that in practice this was not true.

The graded school did not markedly alter the lock-step teaching of the monitorial school which preceded it. Instead, by specifying precisely what was to be covered each day in each subject area and by rigidly adhering to the textbook presentation a program resulted which was sterile, uninteresting and forbidding for all of the pupils. Moreover, those who could not attain the predetermined levels of mastery were doomed to failure and the unhappy prospects of retardation and non-promotion. Lock-step teaching can best be described as everyone doing the same thing, in the same way, at the same time. Soon this regimen became the model style for elementary teachers.[12]

One of the characteristics of the grade-level system is that for each level and subject there is a standard curriculum that is taught to each child. This practice assumes that there is such a thing as "fifth-grade social studies," or "third-grade science." In other words, the grade-level system operates on the premise that all children within a certain age group should have mastered a certain body of knowledge and set of skills by the end of a school year. If a student is able to exceed these institutional expectations, he is said to be working "above grade-level"; if he cannot meet official expectations he is said to be "below grade-level" in that particular skill.

[12] Joseph Shea, "Organizational Patterns for the Elementary School," in *The Elementary School—Principles and Problems,* ed. Joe Frost and G. Thomas Rowland (Boston: Houghton Mifflin, 1969), p. 310.

Cartoon by Short and Weaver

"I'M IN THE NON-GRADED THIRD GRADE."

What's new in education?

The grade-level system is an organizational convenience that allows the biological, psychological, and physiological differences among children to be ignored. That students at any given age level possess individual differences that influence both their ability to learn and their rate of learning has been common knowledge for many years. But teachers and administrators have persisted in organizing the public schools according to age level and a lock-step curriculum.

A number of educators have recently advocated the establishment (or re-establishment) of nongraded schools as a way of forcing schools and teachers to treat students as individuals. John I. Goodlad and Robert H. Anderson point out that the nongraded school is designed to allow continuous pupil progress. By abolishing grade barriers, each child, whatever his ability, is enabled to move forward in his learning as rapidly and smoothly as possible.[13] Thus, in a nongraded school some pupils will require a longer period of time than others to achieve certain kinds of understanding or attain certain developmental levels.

Goodlad and Anderson note that the realities of child development defy the rigorous ordering of children's abilities into a conventionally graded structure. Children entering first grade, for example, may differ in mental age by as much as four full years. Thus, to reach most children, work levels must be aimed for two years below grade expectancies as well as for two years above. This spread of mental age increases as the children advance through the various grade levels. Grouping by grade level, which in essence amounts to grouping by age level, thus makes little sense educationally. Teachers are asked, first, to ignore the emotional and intellectual differences that exist among children at any given age level, and, second, to act as if there were objectively such a thing as fifth-grade social studies, which all fifth-graders could be expected to master.

The pupil in a nongraded school is encouraged to progress in the various aspects of his development at rates appropriate to his own unique traits. As Goodlad and Anderson say:

The job of elementary education is not to convert the low horsepower child into a high horsepower machine, nor is it to promote senseless races between the two. The real job is to keep both tuned and operating at top level efficiency and then to clear the road blocks so that each may proceed at his unique and appropriate pace.[14]

Another argument against the grade-level system is the fear of failure that it generates. At the end of each year in the traditional system, the teacher must decide whether to promote each student to the next grade. Students who are not promoted bear the stigma of failure in the eyes of parents, peers, teachers, and, more importantly, themselves. Children who experience such failure feel degraded or inferior—they are made to believe there is something wrong with them. In fact, they may be unable to keep up with the pace set for the rest of

[13] John I. Goodlad and Robert H. Anderson, *The Nongraded Elementary School* (New York: Harcourt, Brace & World, 1963), p. 21.
[14] Goodlad and Anderson, pp. 28–29.

class, but perfectly capable of learning all the material if allowed to work at their own pace. In a nongraded school, the question of promotion or failure never comes up. Instead, each student moves through the curriculum as rapidly as he is able, with each member of the class likely to be at a different point at any given time.

Goodlad and Anderson's comparison of graded and nongraded structures will help highlight some of the differences between the two systems.[15]

Graded Structure

A year of progress in subject matter is roughly comparable with a child's year in school.

Each successive year of progress is comparable to each past year or each year to come.

A child's progress is unified: advancing in rather regular fashion in all areas of development; probably working close to grade level in most subject areas.

Specific bodies of content are appropriate for successive grade levels and so labeled; subject matter packaged grade by grade.

Adequacy of progress determined by comparing child's attainment to coverage deemed appropriate to the grade.

Inadequate progress made up by repeating the work of a given grade: grade failure the ultimate penalty for slow progress.

Rapid progress provided for through enrichment: encouragement of horizontal expansion rather than vertical advancement in work; attempt to avoid moving to domain of teacher above.

Rather inflexible grade-to-grade movement of pupils, usually at end of year.

Nongraded Structure

A year of school life may mean much more or much less than a year of progress in subject matter.

Progress is irregular; a child may progress much more rapidly in one year and quite slowly in another.

A child's progress is not unified. He spurts ahead in one area of progress and lags behind in others; may be working at three or four levels in as many subjects.

Bodies of content are appropriate over a wide span of years. Learning viewed vertically or longitudinally rather than horizontally.

Adequacy of progress determined by comparing child's attainment to his ability and both to long-term view of ultimate accomplishment desired.

Slow progress provided for by permitting longer time to do given blocks of work; no repetitions but recognition of basic differences in learning rate.

Rapid progress provided for both vertically and horizontally: bright children encouraged to move ahead regardless of the grade label of the work; no fear of encroaching on work of next teacher.

Flexible pupil movement; pupil may shift to another class at almost any time: some trend toward controlling shifts on a quarter or semester basis.

[15] Goodlad and Anderson, pp. 58–59.

Kevin   *As far as I'm concerned, the nongraded approach to school organization is definitely superior to a graded approach.*

Jim   *I feel the same way, but I'd be interested in your reasons.*

Kevin   *I think we let time influence the curriculum far more than it should. If we're really interested in helping students acquire new knowledge, skills, and attitudes, we should organize our curriculum so they can achieve mastery rather than automatically promoting them to a higher grade level that assumes prior knowledge and skills which they may or may not have actually acquired.*

Jim   *In other words, you think that if we arranged the curriculum so students could spend as long as they need to master basic skills and knowledge, we wouldn't have so many high-school students who can barely read or perform simple arithmetic.*

Kevin   *Right. But nongradedness by itself won't do the job. We'd need new curricular materials that allow students to work at their own pace; teachers would have to change their style from teaching to groups to working more with individuals, and generally, a new philosophical approach to learning and instruction would have to be adopted by many teachers.*

How successful are nongraded schools? Are they really working? Do students learn better in a nongraded system than in a graded one? Because individual nongraded schools are so different in aim and organization it is extremely difficult to generalize about nongrading as a whole. Furthermore, it is very difficult to prove that there is a direct relationship between broad organizational changes and changes in pupil achievement. However, in an extensive review of the research on nongraded schools one investigator concluded: 1) comparisons of graded and nongraded schools using standardized achievement tests favor nongrading, 2) measures of student self-concept and attitudes toward school tend to favor nongraded schools, and 3) a nongraded environment is beneficial for blacks, boys, and underachievers.[16] This same investigator notes that nongradedness and open education are born of the same philosophy—each having the underlying belief that every individual is unique and needs different experiences to reach his maximum growth potential.

School systems currently experimenting with nongraded schools are finding curricular reform and teacher education activities necessary. The existing curriculum was developed for incremental grade levels, not for longitudinal organization spanning several years. Goodlad and Anderson confront this problem by visualizing a nongraded curriculum that allows for continuous pupil progress from kindergarten through college, with each learner proceeding at a different rate of speed along various curriculum threads running the entire length of the school's program.

[16] Barbara Nelson Pavan, "Good News: Research on the Nongraded Elementary School," *The Elementary School Journal* 73 (March 1973): 333–334.

Competitive education and accountability

Teachers are commonly held responsible for what their students learn, principals are judged in part by the performance of students in their school, and superintendents are accountable to school boards for the progress of their districts. But the public is increasingly demanding that the public schools as a whole be held accountable for producing demonstrable learning in children. The poor, minority groups, disillusioned students, and education critics cite the frequency with which schools fail to achieve their goals, and as consumers they are demanding alternatives to the public-school system. Critics charge that for the poor there are few feasible alternatives to the public schools, and yet the schools are not really held responsible for children's learning. Statistics indicate that the children of the poor receive an education inferior to that of middle class children. When large groups of children fail—even if there is strong evidence that the responsibility lies primarily with the school—the poor lack the alternative of moving to another district or sending their children to expensive private schools. They must continue sending their children to the same school to warm seats for another semester.

However, the urban poor are becoming increasingly vocal about the quality of public education, and "storefront schools" have been created in a number of urban communities to meet the needs of students that the public school isn't filling. And the poor are not the only group decrying the quality of public education. Throughout the country, "para-schools" have been established in churches and communes by people who find the public educational system too stifling and homogeneous.

Psychologist Kenneth Clark believes that the public educational system needs more competition. He argues that competitive education would make schools accountable for their performances, and cause them to take pride in their work. If we accept, and even take pride in, competition and free enterprise as the basis of our economic system, he continues to say, there is no reason to fear it in our educational system.

Christopher Jencks of Harvard University says that private schools can and should be made an alternative to the public schools for the poor. People should, he declares, be free to send their children to the schools that best suit their needs, whether student-centered schools patterned after A. S. Neill's Summerhill or Montessori schools with their special approaches to teaching young children. Since there aren't at present enough private schools to handle large numbers of transfers from the public schools, Jencks proposes two ways of encouraging private initiative in educating the poor.[17] The first is to provide tuition grants equal to the cost of public education to students who opt out of publicly controlled schools. One of these grants, or vouchers, could be taken to any "participating" school—public, parochial, or private—in which a child had enrolled, and

[17] Christopher Jencks, "Is the Public School Obsolete?" *Public Interest* (Winter 1966): 18–27.

What's new in education?

the local government would reimburse the school for the amount of the voucher. In effect, the "voucher plan" would allow competing publicly financed schools to coexist. Jencks also proposes that a university, a local business group, or a group of teachers might contract to manage a school. Existing school districts would rent facilities to these various groups, with contracts subject to renewal each year.

Jencks's two proposals are aimed at radical decentralization of both power and responsibility. The private schools he envisions would not be subject to the central school administration, but would be directly accountable to the parents who send their children there. If the parents are dissatisfied with the education their children are receiving, they are free to transfer them to another school.

Controversy surrounds the idea of the voucher system. The major objections seem to be that it could encourage the creation of all-black or all-white schools. Opponents point out that this is, in effect, the case today in areas where federally enforced integration has been subverted by the creation of state-supported white private schools. It would also lead to direct public support of church-related schools. The parent's lack of knowledge about each school's qualifications could lead, critics claim, to a spate of fly-by-night schools. But the most serious objection to the voucher system is that it diverts attention and energy from the real task: improving the public school system, rather than seeking alternatives to it.

At any rate, in the fall of 1971 the U.S. Office of Economic Opportunity began testing the viability of Jencks's proposal in several demonstration communities, the most notable of which is the Alum Rock Union School District in San Jose, California. In this "regulated" voucher plan, the program is limited to six Alum Rock public schools. Within these six schools, however, exist over twenty alternative minischools from which the students and their parents may choose. For each child the parents receive a voucher equal to the average amount of money the district spends for each child. Each minischool administrator then has available to finance his program the amount of money equal to the sum of the vouchers he receives from parents who elect to enroll their children in his program.

The programs range from traditional curricula to School 2000, a future-oriented curriculum, where students are taught to be aware of change and how to deal with it. This school is nongraded, with first- and fifth-graders often working on the same lesson. From all reports, the parents, administrators, teachers, and students are enthusiastic about how the voucher plan is working at Alum Rock.

There seem to be many reasons to try the voucher plan on an experimental basis. If it works, the voucher plan may do more to shake up the public schools than any other method of reform. The competitive school approach won't divert attention from the task of public-school improvement; instead, it will force public-school educators to respond to new societal demands.

Middle schools

The middle school is an alternative to the junior high school; it generally encompasses grades 5–8 or 6–8, while junior high schools ordinarily comprise grades 7–9. During the last decade there has been a remarkable increase in the number of middle schools in the United States; by 1970 it was estimated that there were 2,300, most built since 1960.

The middle school movement represents a return to the basic rationale that was originally used to promote junior high schools; that is, the necessity to provide an educational program that uniquely meets the needs of early adolescents. While junior high schools were originally founded for this purpose, many educators believe they have become smaller reflections of the senior high schools.

Middle school advocates believe there are a number of significant advantages to the concept of a middle school. First of all, it offers a better environment for early adolescents than does the junior high school. Critics of the traditional junior high charge that it has been too imitative of the high school, with its graduation ceremonies, cheerleaders, and dances. This kind of atmosphere is not appropriate for early adolescents. Why should they be subjected to the pressures of a high-school milieu? The middle school offers a unique environment where eleven-to fourteen-year-olds are free to grow up at their own rates, and where attention is focused on the needs of this age group rather than on competition at a "junior" level.

Middle schools also offer a major opportunity for curricular experimentation. Core curricular experiences and electives could be designed to focus on the identity and maturation problems of the early adolescent, thus providing learning experiences best suited to the child's needs. A variety of instructional procedures could be adopted to match the varied learning styles of students of this age. A core curriculum based on different learning rates and the abolition of grade levels would lead naturally to the implementation of nongraded experiences and classrooms. By giving the ninth grade—which is still considered the first year in the college entrance sequence—to the high school, middle schools would be free to try new programs and new approaches without having to make them specifically applicable to college preparation.

In addition, middle schools are uniquely suited to perform an enlarged guidance function for children. Because of the earlier onset of puberty in today's children, sixth-graders may be better served in a school designed for early adolescents in grades 6, 7, and 8 than in an elementary school. This grouping of children who are just becoming conscious of their potential roles as high-school students and as adults offers an opportunity to provide meaningful guidance when children need it most. Often the high-school student finds himself assigned to a "track" or grouping of classes which, according to Talcott Parsons and reported in Chapter Six, in large part determines his future role in life; guidance and counseling at or before this crucial juncture are ordinarily scanty or nonexistent. Theodore Moss, a leading advocate of the middle school, considers teachers the key element in the middle school, and urges that guidance-oriented teachers be specifically recruited to teach ten- to fourteen-year-olds.[18]

Middle schools have as yet not taken advantage of these opportunities; a unique program for early adolescents is more a dream than a reality. Clearly defined purposes have not yet been developed to serve as guidelines for middle schools. If the rationale of the emergent middle school is not clearly distinguished from that of the junior high movement earlier in the century, the results will be no different. Merely subtracting the ninth grade and adding the sixth won't change much.

[18] Theodore Moss, *Middle School* (Boston: Houghton Mifflin, 1969).

What's new in education?

Secondly, though the middle-school movement may challenge junior highs to change their approaches or at least adopt some new concepts and techniques, there is still too great a disparity between the theory and the reality of what is occurring in existing middle schools. A 1967–68 survey indicates that relatively few of the middle schools operating at that time had curricula that differed significantly from those of the junior high schools they were designed to replace.[19] Few had adopted team teaching, few varied the types of instructional procedures used, and only about 10 percent had abandoned the traditional marking system.

While the overall picture of middle schools does not show much improvement over the junior high schools they were designed to replace, there are signs that more middle schools are becoming diverse and innovative in their programs. (See the description of the Beloit-Turner Middle School in Chapter Six.) There is an increase each year in the percentage of schools reporting the following innovative practices: interdisciplinary team teaching; exploratory programs; nongraded and individualized instruction; flexible scheduling; open classrooms; innovative plans for reading instruction; personalized guidance services.[20]

If these positive trends continue, then the middle school may begin to fulfill the promise and expectations that originally led to its development.

Year-round schools Have you ever given any thought as to why most public schools start each year around September and end by early June? What is the educational rationale for giving the students three months of vacation? Why are most of the school buildings permitted to sit idle for one-quarter of the year? The basic rationale for this calendar pattern of schooling stems from two causes—an agrarian society and the climate. At a time when the United States was primarily an agrarian society children were needed to help harvest crops in the late spring and the summer. Furthermore, when summer temperatures were high classwork became difficult. The present school calendar was designed to accommodate both of these situations.

Because we are no longer an agrarian society, and because air conditioning is possible, serious consideration is being given to new ways of organizing the school calendar. There are two basic motivating factors for rearranging the school calendar. With construction costs so high and with school bond issues being defeated at a record rate, extending the school year to include summer classes could save a great deal of money in construction costs.

The second major factor is an educational concern that during the long summer students actually regress in their retention of concepts and skills learned the previous year. This concern is evident each September when one looks at the great amount of time spent by teachers, particularly at the elementary level, reviewing skills and concepts from the year before.

How would the year-round schools work? Actually there are a number of different plans being tried across the country at this time. Two of the most popular ones

---

[19] W. Alexander and R. Kealy, "From Junior High School To Middle School," *High School Journal* 53 (December 1969): 154–155.
[20] Thomas E. Gatewood, "What Research Says About the Middle School," *Educational Leadership* 31 (December 1973): 223.

are the 45–15 plan and the staggered quarter plan. In the 45–15 plan each student attends school for 45 days (or 9 weeks) and is on vacation for 15 school days (3 weeks). At any given time, one-quarter of the students are on vacation. Besides the elimination of the summer "forgetting" time and the greater use of the physical plant, other advantages of this plan include the frequent breaks in the routine of schooling; the fact that shorter, more innovative courses can be developed; and the possibility that family vacations can be spread out over the year. Disadvantages include the possible inconvenience to families if various schools fail to coordinate schedules; in severe winter climates, some families might not want the children home for three weeks; interscholastic sports may be disrupted; vacations longer than three weeks would not be possible without interrupting the child's schooling; and maintenance of physical plants will be more difficult without long vacations. For some of these, and other reasons, the 45–15 plan has been applied more to elementary than to secondary schools.

The four quarter plan is being tried in a number of elementary- and secondary-school districts, including those in Atlanta, Georgia. In the Atlanta plan, at the secondary level, after attending four consecutive quarters students can attend any three of the following four, all four, or part-time in each of the four as long as their total attendance is equal to that of three quarters. Each quarter, the students can schedule the courses in which they wish to enroll.

Atlanta's main motivation for this calendar rescheduling was educational, not financial. School officials wanted to offer courses that were easily digestable and interesting. It appears that they have succeeded; one school administrator links a drop of 41 percent in the failure rate to the introduction of the quarter system. The chairperson of the English department in an Atlanta high school commented:

Boredom is a natural disease, and students reflect this problem. But with shorter courses there is innovation, excitement, creativity, and relevance—and a sense of closure. Bright students take in more. Strugglers can review material without going back over a whole year or even a semester.[21]

Teacher contracts are, of course, affected by the year-round plans. One Illinois school district now offers 52 different contracts to its teachers, depending on the portion of the whole year they wish to teach.

Many different kinds of year-round schedules are being experimented with across the country. They will be given serious consideration. Whether year-round schools become the rule rather than the exception has yet to be decided. Parental, teacher, and student attitudes toward the actual operation of year-round schools will ultimately decide their fate.

School design

The need for a fresh approach to school design is clear if we ask why, in any community in this country, a school building is instantly recognizable as such to a stranger. A school built in 1968 usually has more characteristics in common with a school built in 1898 than it does differences. Even schools that have received awards for their design seem to offer only slightly different ways of distributing space and people.

---

[21] N. S. Rifkin, "A Round-Up on Year-Round Schools," *Today's Education* 63 (November-December 1973): 60.

Educators are beginning to ask why school buildings are being designed to be isolated from the rest of the community and the natural environment. The answer is that education, like all institutions, has developed organized structures for the achievement of pre-established goals, and tends to permit and encourage only those experiences that contribute to the attainment of those goals. The public schools limit contacts and educational experiences in an attempt to preserve for themselves the transmission of the accumulated knowledge and values of the society.

The schools' attempt to circumscribe experience is reflected in the architectural nature of school buildings, which are almost invariably characterized by closed organizational structures and monumental architectural forms. Schools tend to be "eggcrates," or large groupings of small boxes of equal size and shape. Despite differences in appearance, the organizational structure of a school building is based on the principle of authority and characterized by a hierarchy of spaces, absence of osmosis between the different parts, and interruption and control in internal and external communications. As the noted architect and urban designer Giancarlo DeCarlo has explained, organizational structures in architecture are defined as authoritarian when the articulation of the spaces does not stimulate the community (in this case, the school) to exchange communications at any time at a level of complete equality.[22] By this definition, virtually all public-school buildings must be termed authoritarian.

Schools without walls

School buildings built especially to house educational activity can house, therefore, only that part of this activity which is in the interest of the institutions which construct the school buildings. The rest of education—the richest and most active part—goes on elsewhere and has no need of buildings; or perhaps it has not yet found the appropriate spaces in which it would take place as a whole, becoming a part of a sphere of total experiences.[23]

In this paragraph, DeCarlo expresses one of the most dramatic and imaginative views currently being advocated by some educators and school designers: that the city and its streets provide a richer and more diversified experience than that offered by the school system, and that the school as an established and codified institution may no longer have any reason for being.

Before you dismiss this idea as too extreme or idealistic, remember our discussion in Chapter Six of Chicago's Metro High School, which utilizes the entire city of Chicago and its resources as a campus. Although there are designated meeting-places where students and teachers gather on a regular basis, this is only one aspect of the educational program of Metro. The rest of the program is designed by the students and teachers to take advantage of the resources of the city itself, so the program is not confined to a single building.

Any building, no matter how "flexible" it is designed to be, has definite limitations. It can house only a certain number of people, some meaningful learning

[22] Giancarlo DeCarlo, "Why/How to Build School Buildings," *Harvard Educational Review* 39 (1969): 18.
[23] DeCarlo, p. 19.

activities cannot occur within its walls, and, as the interests of the children change and grow, the school building imposes definite limits on their expression. Educators who espouse the "school without walls" concept argue that the school cannot be a closed structure, but must encompass a network of social activities and be capable of continual variations. The entire environment must be the school if the school is to be relevant to society. Isolating the school from the rest of society is the best way possible to ensure irrelevance.

In a sense, then, one of the new types of school design is no design at all, but a plan to utilize the existing community as an "open laboratory." In the next decade or two many more "schools without walls" will appear, particularly in large metropolitan areas where the community offers myriad resources. Teachers and students will continue to meet in buildings for certain purposes, but those buildings will not be considered the school. It is likely, however, that "schools without walls" will continue to be the exception rather than the rule. For one thing, smaller towns and cities do not have sufficient resources to support such a program. But the "schools without walls" concept will definitely affect the education that occurs within traditional school buildings by legitimizing the idea that all formal schooling need not take place within four walls.

What's new in education?

Kevin	*If I were to rank man's achievements in order of their impact on the world, I'd put media and communications very high on my list.*
Jim	*So what? This is a book about education, not media.*
Kevin	*The point I'd make is that despite the availability of films, television, satellite communication, and videotape, the formal educational process makes very little use of media.*
Jim	*That's undeniably true, but you have to remember that informal education depends heavily on these media.*
Kevin	*That's exactly my point. Elementary- and secondary-school students grow up in a culture that uses the world's most advanced technology to sell them commercial products and to show them historic events the very days they happen, and the students interact intellectually and emotionally with the medium. But our schools don't begin to compete in the degree of sophistication they use to communicate with students.*
Jim	*What effect do you think this has?*
Kevin	*The major effect, I think, is that the schools bore young people used to learning from television. I think programs like* Sesame Street *have shown that they can be educational and entertaining at the same time. But so many schools still rely on lecturing, textbooks, and dull drills to teach students.*
Jim	*Kevin, if that's so, how come we wrote this textbook?*
Kevin	*Because we're hoping NBC will buy the rights and do a weekly series based on it.*

Individualized learning and school facilities

The traditional school is designed for the instruction of children in groups; the class, the primary unit of instruction, takes place in a classroom containing twenty-five to thirty desks, all facing the teacher. When the teacher serves as the dispenser of information, the traffic controller, and the focal point of the classroom, this physical arrangement is probably appropriate. But as students begin to assume more self-direction and self-pacing responsibilities, a new physical arrangement is necessary to facilitate independent study and small-group discussion.

The major obstacle to be overcome in designing such facilities is the rigidity of spaces. It is difficult to adapt to a new purpose rooms which were designed for another. Consequently, either separate rooms must be designed for each specific purpose, or spaces must be available for adaptation to a variety of uses. Some designers believe that a space designed exclusively for one purpose suppresses the individual by dictating to him exactly how it should be used. Instead, they believe, spaces should be created that each individual can make relevant to his own needs. They advocate the use of large open spaces that are adaptable to many purposes.

School designers are attempting to individualize instruction by providing a variety of facilities. Learning laboratories which include several "how to" areas are being designed for a variety of student groupings — individual, tutorial, team discussion, small groups, and large groups. A learning laboratory might include an art area where students working on particular projects could go any time they were free, a stand-up work area, scientific laboratories, and the like.

Instructional materials centers would house instructional materials and tools for independent student or small group use. Individual student carrels would be available, perhaps with audiovisual tools such as cassettes and portable video-tape playback units for special instruction. The recently developed television cassette is a type of video phonograph which converts any television set into a movie projector and screen. Video cartridges make a variety of programs, ranging from Shakespearean plays to carefully controlled science experiments, available to students at any time. In the future, schools will be able to develop video cartridge libraries similar to libraries that house books, enormously enhancing the teacher's ability to individualize instruction for his students. More importantly, such a center could provide all the materials necessary to the truly self-educating person.

An electronic information center would house modern equipment for assistance in seeking information. Students could engage in computer-based independent study and store their own computer programs in the center. This equipment possibly could be made available to students at home via television, so that learning could become a continuous process.

Many new schools are including teacher studios, where teachers can collect and store materials and information, and can prepare lessons or counsel individual students. Some schools have built student recreational facilities where students can listen to records, dance, play games, and buy food and beverages. Students need to unwind, too, and this kind of facility can be extremely beneficial.

The school designed to individualize instruction will contain many of these facilities. Square pegs will not fit into round holes — new schools must be developed to facilitate new approaches.

Perhaps we should ask ourselves, when we discuss the future of innovations in education, who is going to pay for it. The property-tax dollar which supports local schools will stretch only so far; most school districts can't afford to implement nationally acclaimed innovations in education or experiment on their own without outside financial support. In large part, the future of educational innovation depends on government support, particularly at the federal level. Without such support, there might not be Head Start, day care centers, open classroom implementation, bilingual education, career education, or studies of the effectiveness of the voucher plan. Government funds are also needed by university research centers, where innovations such as IPI and IGE are developed. In addition, financial support from private foundations must continue; without private aid, research on variations in class size and scheduling would not have been undertaken, and new approaches in teacher education, urban education, and educational television such as *Sesame Street* would not have been developed.

If educators seek outside help for the development and implementation of new ideas in education, they must inevitably respond to outside influence and direction. Yet, without this aid, education would be hopelessly stuck in its pre-space-age rut. One of the crucial questions of the seventies will be how educators handle the issue of influence through financial assistance for innovation.

391   What's new in education?

Discussion Questions

1 Are you more in sympathy with the principles of the open classroom or with those of systems such as IPI and IGE?

2 Do you feel you could have benefited from the implementation of a career education program while you were in elementary and secondary school? Why or why not?

3 What place do you believe moral education has in our schools?

4 Do you agree with the U.S. Supreme Court's ruling that children should be taught in their native language until they learn English?

5 Will you welcome or resist the changes in teacher roles that will be brought about by the widespread use of computers in schools?

6 What problems might be anticipated by a school making a transition from graded to nongraded organization? What does the cartoon on page 379 imply about such a transition? Try to remember yourself at, say, eight years old — do you think you would have been capable of taking major responsibility for your own learning? Why or why not?

7 Do you believe voucher plans offer hope as a way to reform the public schools, or are they a threat to destroy them?

8 Would you like to have attended a year-round school? Do you think you would prefer the 45-15 or the quarter plan?

9 Does it make sense to you that the style of a school's architecture can be authoritarian? Did your high-school building have an authoritarian effect on students? Can you think of ways other than those we described to counteract this effect? Can you think of any inexpensive ways to do so?

10 Do you plan to become a teacher? Why or why not?

For further reading

- Anderson, Robert H. "How Organization Can Make the School More Humanistic." *National Elementary Principal* 49 (January 1970): 6–13. A good article discussing essential components of school organization, including the absence of gradedness, abandonment of the self-contained classroom, and the need for a more open, larger, and more heterogeneous pupil family.

- *Educational Leadership* 31 (December 1973). This issue contains fourteen articles on middle schools.

- Goodlad, John, and Anderson, Robert H. *The Nongraded Elementary School*, rev. ed. New York: Harcourt, Brace & World, 1963. A strong argument for the nongraded elementary school.

- Gross, Beatrice, and Gross, Ronald. "A Little Bit of Chaos." *Saturday Review* (May 16, 1970): 71–73, 84–85. An easy-to-read article describing the British infant school.

- *Harvard Educational Review* 39 (1969), "Architecture and Education." The whole issue is devoted to exploring the relationship of architectural values to significant human experience and, in particular, to basic educational goals.

- Hedges, William D. "Computer-Assisted Instruction and the Schools." *Educational Leadership* 30 (January 1973): 361–365. A brief review of research on CAI and its capabilities for instruction.

- Hertzberg, Alvin, and Stone, Edward. *Schools Are For Children: An American Approach to the Open Classroom.* New York: Schocken Books, 1971. A practical book for teachers who wish to open up their classrooms.

- Hull, Ronald E. "Selecting An Approach to Individualized Education." *Phi Delta Kappan* 55 (November 1973): 169–173. Article compares IPI, IGE, Project PLAN, and open education attempts to individualize instruction.

The real world

- Jencks, Christopher. "Is the Public School Obsolete?" *Public Interest* (Winter 1966): 18–27. A strong argument for alternative school systems to compete with the public schools.
- *The Journal of Teacher Education* 24 (Summer 1973). This issue carries six articles on career education.
- Joyce, Bruce. *The Teacher and His Staff: Man, Media and Machines.* Washington, D.C.: National Commission of Standards and Center for the Study of Instruction, NEA, 1967. In this booklet the author outlines a team approach to instruction and the kinds of media necessary to carry it out.
- McLain, John D. *Year-Round Education: Economic, Educational, and Sociological Factors.* Berkeley: McCutchan Publishing Corporation, 1973. A book that covers the major considerations for year-round schools.
- Nachtigal, Paul. *A Foundation Goes to School.* New York: Ford Foundation, 1972. A follow-up report on the innovative projects in which the Ford Foundation invested over $30 million during the years 1960–1970. The major finding is that little change has occurred as a result.
- Perrone, Vito. *Open Education: Promise and Problems.* Bloomington, Ind.: Phi Delta Kappa Educational Foundation, 1972. An excellent summary of what open education is all about by a leader in the area.

Films

- *The A, B, C's of Behavioral Education* (Hallmark, color, 20 min., 1969). This film describes the behavioral modification program at the Anne Arundel County Learning Center, home for students between ages twelve and seventeen who have been ejected from other county schools. Success is sought by placing an emphasis on individualized instruction using a curriculum broken down into surmountable academic tasks. When students are free to leave a work area at any time, the film argues, they are motivated to remain, and when they receive positive reinforcement, they have the will to complete their work.
- *Breaking the Lockstep* (Educational Coordinates, color, 29 min., 1970). Shot on location in five elementary schools around the country, this film illustrates flexible modular scheduling in action. Students, teachers, and principals discuss the opportunities and pitfalls contained in this approach to school management. In all cases, the accent is on how flexible scheduling transfers emphasis from "teaching" to "learning" and from "teacher" to "student."
- *The Child of the Future: How He Might Learn* (Contemporary/McGraw-Hill, 16mm, b&w, 58:06 min., 1965). Jerome Bruner of Harvard University and Marshall McLuhan draw conclusions about the effects of new mechanical and electronic teaching aids on the learning process.
- *Children as People* (Polymorph, b&w, 35 min., 1969). A documentary film about the Fayerweather Street School in Cambridge, Mass. A well-made film which involves the audience directly in the work and freedom of an alternative school, with commentary by John Holt. Says Holt, "No film conveys better the feeling of what children in such a place are like, how they look and talk, how they relate to the adults in the school, above all, the vivacity, enthusiasm, and good sense with which they manage their lives and learning."
- *Choosing to Learn* (EDC, color, 26 min., 1970). This film was made at the World of Inquiry School in Rochester, New York. Children from a variety of racial and economic backgrounds are free to decide what and when they will learn. The film shows children making their own learning decisions and working closely and informally with teachers and with one another.

What's new in education?

- *Deeps and Highs* (Negative Entropy/Allegra May, 16mm, b&w, 35 min.). This film uses Trout Fishing in America, formerly a free school in Cambridge, Massachusetts, as a vehicle to depict children's hopes for a different way of being. Focuses on kids who are alienated from everything, even "radical society," and who begin to find a sense of comfort and community at Trout Fishing.
- *Education Under a Thatched Roof* (Indiana University Audio-Visual Center, 16mm, b&w, 19 min.). The preparation and implementation of a unit team-teaching approach at a secondary school in Bangkok, Thailand, are illustrated in this film. Innovative resources such as media, team teaching, field trips, and student-made materials are used to teach a unit on food sanitation.
- *English Primary Education Series*. Three films available from EDC on the English primary-school movement and its relationship to the open classroom concept. *Battling Brook Primary School* (b&w, 23 min., 1969) records a large but happy classroom of children aged seven to eleven in a Leicestershire school during the first few days of the term. Lillian Weber filmed *Infants School* (b&w, 32 min., 1967) in Gordonbrock, an old school with several large classrooms located in a racially mixed London neighborhood. *Medbourne Primary School* (b&w, 12 min., 1968) is a rural three-room school in Leicestershire, where many different children's activities are allowed to proceed simultaneously, including painting, printing a booklet, and cooking a chicken.
- *Four Years Old and Ready to Grow* (Center for Urban Education, 16mm, color, 27 min.). Documents some of the main features of a new approach to the teaching of young inner-city children. The goal of this program is continuous skill development in such language areas as vocabulary, syntax, listening, speaking, writing, and reading.
- *Future Shock* (Contemporary/McGraw-Hill, color, 42 min., 1973). Based on the bestseller by Alvin Toffler, this rapidly paced film provides an overview of some of the more alarming scientific advances in the replication of the human mind and body. Although it does not address itself to schooling for the future, its key message is that today's children will be victims unless we and they prepare to make decisions about the directions and applications of technology.
- *High School Team Teaching* (Bailey, color, 26 min., 1966). An explanation of the theory of team teaching, this film uses the example of the planning and experimentation conducted at the Ferris High School in Spokane, Washington. This school also used flexible modular scheduling in its teaching innovations. A student and a teacher are each followed through their schedules, which include large group instruction, seminars, labs, and resource centers.
- *I Am Here Today* (EDC, b&w, 43 min., 1971). This film shows the integrated-day approach in a classroom of five-, six-, and seven-year-olds at Shady Hill School in Cambridge, Mass. The children are shown taking charge of their own learning and helping one another. A log kept by the teacher, Betsye Sargent, is available to document how this style of classroom management can be accomplished.
- *Knowing to Learn* (Contemporary/McGraw-Hill, b&w, 58 min., 1969). An overview of new technology in North American classrooms, made by the National Film Board of Canada with help from many United States institutions. Among other tools and approaches, the focus is on the computer, tape recorder, and television in their impact on the learning process. This film is a good example of the projections that even a very wise educational filmmaking group succumbed to during the first period of heightened interest in the instructional uses of technology.

- *Learning How to Learn—The Open Classroom in America* (IDEA, color, 22 min., 1970). The development of an environment carefully designed to meet the needs of its child population is the subject of this film. Different curriculum areas and different student-teacher groupings can all be accommodated within the open classroom setting, where one of the most noticeable features is the variety of simultaneous activity. The film is most helpful when used in conjunction with films on the open classroom developments in England.
- *Open Classroom* (Sherwin Rubin, b&w, 13 min., 1971). Shot in actual public-school classrooms in Southern California, this film shows open classroom students designing their own learning environments. Each student uses a planning diary to schedule himself for basic skills and for special creative opportunities in the learning center. Parents, community members, and older student volunteers aid the teacher, who becomes a combined resource person, diagnostician, facilitator, and encourager. At the end of the film the teacher checks with each child to determine how his activities for the day compare with his diary entries.
- *Play Mountain Place* (Cinema Kiva, color, 28 min., 1973). Created 25 years ago as an alternative to public education, Play Mountain Place has remained a noncoercive learning environment. Children seen in the film relate to teachers as equals and to one another without competition. Music is performed by the students, who also operate the sound equipment. Their role serves as a symbol of the independence and self-confidence that the school tries to impart.
- *The Remarkable Schoolhouse* (Contemporary/McGraw-Hill, 16mm, color, 25 min., 1967). Originally produced for CBS television, this film examines the educational problems that have led to the introduction of technological innovations in elementary and junior high instruction. In addition, it defines the role of "new hardware," such as computers, television, and educational games, in the educational system.
- *Sign On/Sign Off* (University of California, color, 24 min., 1967). Basic methods of computer-assisted instruction (CAI) are presented in nontechnical terms to introduce the importance and effectiveness of computers as a principal teaching source for individual students. The film shows sequences of students at a terminal being aided and advised as well as corrected by a computer. Short descriptions of the tutorial and inquiry methods of CAI are presented, emphasizing the flexibility, accuracy, speed, and individuality of the computer when accessed by a single student.
- *Teach Me How I Can Do It Myself* (International Film Bureau, color, 29 min., 1973). Photographed at a Montessori Kindergarten and a Public Elementary Montessori School in the Netherlands, this film documents the philosophy and practices of the Montessori method of elementary education. It illustrates how to combine the arousal of curiosity and a spontaneous desire for learning with ordered activity in a prepared environment. Children are shown working together and by themselves, with the assistance of trained adults when requested.
- *Teaching Machines and Programmed Learning* (Pennsylvania State University, b&w, 29 min., 1960). This film takes viewers back fifteen years to the first stirrings of behaviorism and teaching machines in American education. B. F. Skinner explains the theory of programmed learning, A. Lumsdaine describes a variety of teaching machines and programmed materials, and R. Glaser discusses the implications of such machines and materials for education.
- *Team Teaching in the Elementary School* (IDEA, color, 22 min., 1969). This training film is narrated by the principal of an innovative elementary school. It

focuses on the increased planning activities and collective instructional efforts of a team of teachers working with young children.

- *The Way It Is* (Indiana University Audio-Visual Center, 16mm, b&w, 60 min., 1967). Depicts the chaos of the New York City schools, focusing on what is being done in one school in the Bedford-Stuyvesant section of Brooklyn to improve the situation. Participants in a New York University special learning project are shown visiting with parents, teachers and students.
- *What Did You Learn in School Today?* (NET, b&w, 48 min., 1973). New York newswoman Joan Murray narrates this examination of the open classroom method being used in England and in some areas in the United States. After an interview with Lady Bridget Plowden, whose report on education is largely responsible for many changes in England, the film moves to North Dakota to trace the implementation of the open classroom in that state. Also visited are the Grape School in Watts and a teacher-training workshop in Connecticut. One segment of the film treats the idea of satellite high schools in suburban areas.

Audiotapes

- *Alternatives in Education* (Big Sur, 2 hours 45 min., 1970). John Holt and George Dennison participate in a discussion on the problems and possibilities of the New School Movement. This tape was recorded at a conference on experimental education attended by representatives of free schools and communes, progressive teachers from traditional schools, and administrators from city and state public-school systems.
- *The Curriculum* (National Education Association, 3.75 ips, reel or cassette, 56:30 min.). This hour-long audiotape is divided into seven short sections, each intended to serve as the basis for a complete discussion session. Three of the sections discuss the Parkway Program, in which the entire Philadelphia community has become the school campus. Another section describes a one-week Experiment in Free Form Education at a suburban high school and other programs in "affective education."
- *Gestalt Training Tapes* (Big Sur, 3.75 ips, reel, mono or stereo). Tape recordings of Frederick S. Perls discussing his approach to Gestalt Therapy: *Dream Theory and Demonstration*—a concise one-hour Gestalt Awareness presentation. *Lecture Demonstrations*—a full series of confrontations and self-encounter demonstrations (6 hours). *The Perls Encounter*—A complete weekend seminar of demonstrations of Gestalt Awareness with a wide variety of participants (9 hours).
- *Individualizing Teaching and Learning Series* (Listener, one hour each, 1973). This series of six tapes details a step-by-step progression for opening the primary classroom to personalized teaching and learning based on British successes with open education. Dr. Virgil Howes and Dr. Robert Keuscher present principles of open education, beginning steps, pupil choice, record keeping, and advice to the teacher, which they have tested in many American schools. Each cassette title has a fairly detailed external index, and the set of six comes in an album with reference materials.
- *The Person of Tomorrow* (Big Sur, 3.75 ips, reel or cassette, mono or stereo, 90 min., 1970). Carl Rogers presents his views on rock music, violence on campus, and the encounter group movement, and in so doing discusses some changes necessary in education.
- *Predictions for Education in the Future* (Big Sur, one hour, 1966). George Leonard theorizes on the state of education in the year 2000. He emphasizes that the

majority of the curriculum will deal with subjects that today do not have names, and that most teaching will be done by electronic programming of data and skills. Every member of the community, he predicts, will be a member of the learning society. This tape is especially interesting if it is used together with *USA 2000* (Big Sur, one hour, 1968), which features Carl Rogers and Alan Watts in conflict over the likely directions of human self-fulfillment.

Videotapes

- *Alternative 70's* (People's Video Theatre, $\frac{1}{2}$″, Sony, Old Generation). A survey on videotape of people in culture, science, politics, education, media, and government service about their views of the coming decade.
- *California Experimental High School* (Videofreex, $\frac{1}{2}$″, Sony, 1969). A videotape made at an experimental high school in California.
- *Clinton Project* (Raindance, $\frac{1}{2}$″, Sony, 1 hour). One hour of edited tapes made by junior high-school students, tracing their video class from the first session to the last.
- *System of Teaching Reading by Coloring Coding Words* (Electric Eye, $\frac{1}{2}$″, several hours). This tape, produced by a group whose motto is "tell a vision, not sell a vision," presents the work of Dr. Caleb Gattegno at San Jose State.

Multimedia

- *Individualized Instruction Kit* (National Education Association, 1970). A set of six filmstrips with audiotapes, case study booklets, and a group leader's manual, to facilitate study of individualized instruction. The filmstrips and tapes deal with the procedures, objectives, problems, and effects of individualized instruction, as well as providing sample materials and making recommendations for the implementation of the system.
- *Living and Learning Schools* (Living and Learning Schools, 140 frs., record, 15 min., automatic synchronization when used on a Dukane filmstrip projector). A document on the "open classroom" program at the Living and Learning Day Care Center in Braintree, Massachusetts. The sounds and images are intended to show that a community-oriented, privately owned day care center can be "an educational program and not just custodial care."
- *The Building of a School as a Learning Experience* (Harvard Graduate School of Education Library, films, slides, cassettes, tapes). This illustrated paper by William Coperthwaite explains the building of a school in New Hampshire by twelve students and two teachers who found that a more conventional institution did not serve their needs. They built the school from a design based on the shelter of nomadic Mongol tribes. Constructed of wood, these round structures, called "yurts," provide "classrooms without corners."

Refer to Appendix for addresses of distributors.

Appendix
Addresses of distributors

Note: Many of these distributors maintain regional offices. In these cases the address of the national office is given. The agencies listed below are generally rental distributors. Requests for purchase of film prints should be directed to the original producer.

ABC Media Concepts
1330 Avenue of the Americas
New York, New York 10019

AFL-CIO
Film Division, Department of Education
815 Sixteenth Street, N.W.
Washington, D.C. 20006

American Association of Colleges for Teacher Education
One Dupont Circle
Washington, D.C. 20036

American Association of School Administrators
1801 North Moore Street
Arlington, Virginia 22209

American Educational Films
331 North Maple Drive
Beverly Hills, California 90210

Anti-Defamation League of B'nai B'rith
315 Lexington Avenue
New York, New York 10016

Bailey Films, Inc.
11559 Santa Monica Boulevard
Los Angeles, California 90025

Behavioral Sciences Media Laboratory
Department of Psychiatry and Behavioral Sciences
University of Oklahoma Medical Center
Oklahoma City, Oklahoma 73104

BFA Educational Media
2211 Michigan Avenue
Santa Monica, California 90404

Big Sur Recordings
117 Mitchell Boulevard
San Rafael, California 94903

Canadian Broadcasting Corporation Learning Systems
Box 500, Station "A"
Toronto, 116, Ontario, Canada

Carleton College Video Tape Project
Northfield, Minnesota 55057

Carousel Films, Inc.
1501 Broadway, Suite 1503
New York, New York 10036

Center for Curriculum Design
823 Foster Street
Evanston, Illinois 60204

Center for the Study of Democratic Institutions
P. O. Box 4446
Santa Barbara, California 93103

Center for Urban Education
105 Madison Avenue
New York, New York 10016

Cinema Kiva
314 Marguerita Avenue
Santa Monica, California 90402

Contemporary/McGraw-Hill Films
1221 Avenue of the Americas
New York, New York 10020

CRM Productions
1104 Camino del Mar
Del Mar, California 92014

EDC: Education Development Center, Inc.
55 Chapel Street
Newton, Massachusetts 02160

Educational Coordinates
Box 348
Bedford, Massachusetts 01730

Educational Film Library Association
17 West 60th Street
New York, New York 10023

Educational Service Bureau
1835 K Street, N.W.
Washington, D.C. 20006

The Film Bureau
267 West 25th Street
New York, New York 10001

Films Incorporated
1144 Wilmette Avenue
Wilmette, Illinois 60091

General Programmed Teaching
Quail Hill
San Rafael, California 94903

Great Plains National ITV Library
Box 80669
Lincoln, Nebraska 68501

Hallmark Films, Inc.
1511 East North Avenue
Baltimore, Maryland 21213

Holt, Rinehart, and Winston, Inc.
383 Madison Avenue
New York, New York 10017

IDEA: Institute for Development of Educational Activities, Inc.
Information and Services Division
P. O. Box 446
Melbourne, Florida 32901

Indiana University Audio-Visual Center
Bloomington, Indiana 47401

Infomatics
8531 Schaefer
Detroit, Michigan 48228

International Film Bureau, Inc.
332 South Michigan Avenue
Chicago, Illinois 60604

Lawren Productions
P. O. Box 1542
Burlingame, California 94010

Listener Corporation
6777 Hollywood Boulevard
Hollywood, California 90028

Macmillan/Macmillan Audio Brandon Films
34 MacQuesten Parkway, South
Mount Vernon, New York 10550

McGraw-Hill Films
See Contemporary/McGraw-Hill

Media Five
1011 North Cole Avenue
Hollywood, California 90038

National Education Association
1201 Sixteenth Street, N.W.
Washington, D.C. 20036

National Film Board of Canada
1251 Avenue of the Americas, 16th Floor
New York, New York 10020

NBC Educational Enterprises
30 Rockefeller Plaza
New York, New York 10020

NET: National Educational Television Film Service
Indiana University Audio-Visual Center
Bloomington, Indiana 47401

Newsreel Features
28 West 31st Street
New York, New York 10001

Oakland Community College
2480 Opdyke Road
Bloomfield Hills, Michigan 48013

Judith Pacht
10218 Chrysanthemum Lane
Los Angeles, California 90024

Pacifica Tape Library
2217 Shattuck Avenue
Berkeley, California 94704

Pennsylvania State University Audio-Visual Services
7 Willard Building
University Park, Pennsylvania 16802

Time-Life Films, Inc.
43 West 16th Street
New York, New York 10011

Addresses of distributors

UNIPUB, Inc. [UNESCO]
Box 433, Murray Hill Station
New York, New York 10016

United Artists Corporation
729 Seventh Avenue
New York, New York 10019

University-at-Large
70 West 40th Street
New York, New York 10018

University of California Extension Media Center
Berkeley, California 94720

Western Behavioral Sciences Institute
Film Library
1150 Silverado
La Jolla, California 92037

Zipporah Films
54 Lewis Wharf
Boston, Massachusetts 02110

An invitation to respond

In the first edition of *Those who can, teach*, we included a form with which the students evaluated the book and provided us with feedback. Many of the changes made in this edition were based on these student evaluations. Please help us respond to the interest and needs of future readers by completing the questionnaire below and returning it to us.

Kevin and Jim

Please tell us your overall impression of the text.

		Excellent	Good	Adequate	Poor	Very poor
1	Was it written in a clear and understandable style?	_____	_____	_____	_____	_____
2	Were difficult concepts well explained?	_____	_____	_____	_____	_____
3	How would you rate the cartoons and illustrations?	_____	_____	_____	_____	_____
4	How does this text compare with texts you are using in other education courses?	_____	_____	_____	_____	_____
5	Did the book's informality help your reading?	_____	_____	_____	_____	_____

Can you cite examples that illustrate any of your above ratings?

_____

_____

_____

Were there any chapters or features that you particularly liked or disliked? If so, why?

_____

_____

_____

Were there any topics that were not covered that you believe *should have* been covered?

_____

_____

_____

Do you think this book has influenced your career choice? Which way? And how?

_____

_____

_____

Which chapters did you read because they were required by your instructor?

_____

Which chapters did you read on your own?

_____

We would appreciate any other comments or reactions you are willing to share with us:

_____

_____

_____

Index

Photo credits

vii   **Peter Travers**
2, 3   **Anna Kaufman Moon**
19   **Peter Travers**
29   **Anna Kaufman Moon**
34   **Paul Conklin**
43   **Julie Green/Stock,Boston**
46   **Nicholas Sapieha/Stock,Boston,** left
    E. Trina Lipton/Stock,Boston, top right
    Cary S. Wolinsky/Stock,Boston, bottom right
47   **Norman Hurst/Stock,Boston,** top
    courtesy SDC Magazine, bottom left
48   **Peter Travers,** top left
    Cary S. Wolinsky/Stock,Boston, bottom
49   **Anna Kaufman Moon/Stock,Boston,** top
    Anna Kaufman Moon, center left and right
    Anna Kaufman Moon/Stock,Boston, bottom
64   **John Running/Stock,Boston**
71   **Peter Travers**
82   **Frank Siteman**
87   **Peter Travers**
99   **Ruth Silverman/Stock,Boston**
103   **Anna Kaufman Moon/Stock,Boston**
113   **Paul Conklin**
125   **Peter Travers**
136   **Elizabeth Hamlin/Stock,Boston**
156   **Peter Travers**
163   **Jerry Schrader/Stock,Boston**
170, 171   **Peter Travers**
186   **Donald Dietz, Dietz/Hamlin**
194   **Elizabeth Hamlin, Dietz/Hamlin,** top left
    Frank Siteman, top right
    Clif Garboden/Stock,Boston, bottom
195   **Clif Garboden/Stock,Boston,** top
    Peter Travers, bottom
196   **Frank Siteman,** top
    Anna Kaufman Moon, bottom left
    Frank Siteman, bottom right
197   **Peter Travers,** top
    William B. Finch/Stock,Boston, bottom
198   **Clif Garboden/Stock,Boston,** top
    Peter Travers, bottom left
199   **Marjorie Pickens,** left
    Anna Kaufman Moon, right
205, 207, 209   **Elizabeth Hamlin, Dietz/Hamlin**
221   **Peter Travers**
243   **Patricia Hollander Gross/Stock,Boston**
249   **Peter Vandermark/Stock,Boston**
268, 269   **Anna Kaufman Moon**
284   **Peter Travers**
289   **Jerry Berndt/Stock,Boston**
317   **Peter Travers**
333   **Donald Dietz, Dietz/Hamlin**
336   **E. Trina Lipton/Stock,Boston**
340   **Donald Wright Patterson/Stock,Boston**
346   **Anna Kaufman Moon**
352   **John Running/Stock,Boston**
360   **Frank Siteman**
361   **Donald Dietz, Dietz/Hamlin,** top
    courtesy SDC Magazine, bottom
363   **Elizabeth Hamlin, Dietz/Hamlin**
369   **Anna Kaufman Moon**
375   **Owen Franken/Stock,Boston**
389   **Patricia Hollander Gross/Stock,Boston**

Cover design by Alice Webber